*Children Helping Children*

WILEY SERIES IN
DEVELOPMENTAL PSYCHOLOGY
AND ITS APPLICATIONS

*Series Editor*
**Professor Kevin Connolly**

**Morality in the Making: Thought, Action and the Social Context**
*edited by Helen Weinreich-Haste and Don Locke*

**Children's Single-Word Speech**
*edited by Martyn Barrett*

**The Psychology of Gifted Children: Perspectives on Development and Education**
*edited by Joan Freeman*

**Teaching and Talking with Deaf Children**
*David Wood, Heather Wood, Amanda Griffiths and Ian Howard*

**Culture and the Development of Children's Action: A Cultural-Historical Theory of Developmental Psychology**
*Jaan Valsiner*

**Computers, Cognition and Development**
*edited by Julie Rutkowska and Charles Crook*

**Psychological Bases for Early Education**
*edited by A. D. Pellegrini*

**The Child in the Physical Environment: The Development of Spatial Knowledge and Cognition**
*Christopher Spencer, Mark Blades and Kim Morsley*

**Children Helping Children**
*edited by Hugh C. Foot, Michelle J. Morgan and Rosalyn H. Shute*

# *Children Helping Children*

*Edited by*
**Hugh C. Foot,**
**Michelle J. Morgan**
and
**Rosalyn H. Shute**
*University of Wales College of Cardiff*



JOHN WILEY & SONS
Chichester · New York · Brisbane · Toronto · Singapore

*Other Wiley Editorial Offices*

John Wiley & Sons, Inc., 605 Third Avenue,
New York, NY 10158-0012, USA

Jacaranda Wiley Ltd, G.P.O. Box 859, Brisbane,
Queensland 4001, Australia

John Wiley & Sons (Canada) Ltd, 22 Worcester Road,
Rexdale, Ontario M9W 1L1, Canada

John Wiley & Sons (SEA) Pte Ltd, 37 Jalan Pemimpin #05-04.
Block B, Union Industrial Building, Singapore 2057

***Library of Congress Cataloging-in-Publication Data:***

Children helping children / edited by Hugh C. Foot, Michelle J.
Morgan, Rosalyn H. Shute.
p. cm. — (Wiley series in developmental psychology and its applications)
Includes bibliographical references.
ISBN 0-471-92292-7
1. Peer-group tutoring of students. 2. Team learning approach in education. 3. Interpersonal relations in children. 4. Group work in education. 5. Child psychotherapy. I. Foot, Hugh C. II. Morgan, Michelle J. III. Shute. Rosalyn H. IV. Series.
LB1031.5.C47 1990
371.3′94—dc20 89-27163
CIP

***British Library Cataloguing in Publication Data:***
Children helping children. — (Wiley series in developmental psychology and its applications)
1. Children. Interpersonal relationships with children
I. Foot, Hugh C. (Hugh Corrie) II. Morgan, Michelle J.
III. Shute, Rosalyn
305.2′3

ISBN 0-471-92292-7

Phototypeset by Dobbie Typesetting Limited, Plymouth, Devon
Printed by Courier International Ltd, Tiptree, Colchester, Essex

# Dedication

To all the children who have helped
in the preparation of this book

# Contributors

ADRIAN F. ASHMAN, *University of Queensland.*

ANNE-MARIE BARRON, *University of Wales College of Cardiff.*

AGNÈS BLAYE, *Université de Provence.*

JUDITH J. CARTA, *University of Kansas.*

SUSAN COLMAR, *Birmingham Education Authority.*

CATHERINE R. COOPER, *University of California.*

HELEN COWIE, *University of Sheffield.*

WILLEM DOISE, *Université de Genève.*

J. RICHARD EISER, *University of Exeter.*

JOHN ELKINS, *University of Queensland.*

DAVID FONTANA, *University of Wales College of Cardiff.*

HUGH C. FOOT, *University of Wales College of Cardiff.*

CHARLES R. GREENWOOD, *University of Kansas.*

MICHAEL J. GURALNICK, *University of Washington.*

ANDRE J. IMICH, *Essex Educational Psychology Service.*

DEBRA KAMPS, *University of Kansas.*

PAUL LIGHT, *The Open University, Milton Keynes.*

MICHELLE J. MORGAN, *University of Wales College of Cardiff.*

RICHARD PATES, *South Glamorgan Health Authority, Cardiff.*

DOUGLAS PATON, *University of St Andrews.*

JEAN RUDDUCK, *University of Sheffield.*

LINDA ST. JOHN, *University of California.*

SHLOMO SHARAN, *Tel-Aviv University.*

ROSALYN H. SHUTE, *University of Wales College of Cardiff.*

LILYA WAGNER, *Union College, Lincoln, Nebraska.*

KEVIN WHELDALL, *University of Birmingham.*

# Contents

# Foreword

Most parents are soon aware of the powerful influence that other children can exert on their own offspring. Often enough this awareness arises first in the context of worries about whether another child, or group of children, may be a bad influence on their child. The preoccupation which parents frequently have with negative effects is reflected in the interest shown by many psychologists in aggressive or hostile behaviour. However, despite anxiety about bad influences, most parents quickly come to appreciate the importance of peer relationships and the positive effects these have for the development of their children. Psychologists too have become increasingly concerned with peer interaction and prosocial behaviour, that is with what can loosely be called helping behaviour.

Helping behaviour is not easy to define or describe partly because it covers a great range of different situations and behaviours. Some helping behaviour takes place in formal professional settings, such as doctors treating patients or therapists guiding clients, but most occurs in informal settings and is probably spontaneous and unsolicited. In the case of children almost all their help-giving is informal and impromptu but in an educational context it can be engineered by adults. The model of the adult transferring knowledge to the child in an almost passive manner has given way to a view of knowledge as a negotiated commodity and the importance of the interpersonal dimension in tutoring is widely recognized. We see learning as a communal activity in which a culture is shared and transmitted, and much of this learning is informal. A child makes knowledge his or her own in the context of a community and, of course, other children are extremely important components of the community.

The editors have brought together a wide range of contributions in which the state of our knowledge of children helping children is reviewed. The bulk of the material comes from formal educational settings which is not surprising since this is where work has largely centred over the past two decades. However, there are also studies from outside the classroom context including: sibling relations in the family, the social competence of handicapped children and how this is affected by their contact with other children, and the help which children can give in supporting the adjustment of chronically sick peers. All of this serves to underline the importance of the help given by children to other children and how this supports their coping and their development. This conclusion may not be surprising but its wider significance, both theoretically and practically, is only just becoming apparent. The editors have done a valuable service to developmental psychologists and others interested in children by bringing together and critically reviewing this material for it will surely stimulate more research and discussion.

KEVIN CONNOLLY

# Preface

One of the exciting features of compiling this edited volume has been the ever-growing feeling of pioneering a new field—of being in at the forefront of new advances and applications within the disciplines of social and developmental psychology. This claim may appear somewhat bold but we do not believe it is an overstatement of the potentiality of children as sources of help and benefit for other children.

There has, of course, been a recognition for a very long time of the potential value of children as helpers of other children in educational settings, and over the past two decades there has been a steady growth in the development of structured same-age and cross-age peer tutoring programmes. However, many such programmes have been developed for highly specific educational purposes (for example, to teach children with reading disabilities or other particular deficits) and their application is still by no means widespread.

Outside the classroom, however, peer-helping relationships have received minimal attention. Yet there clearly are other vitally important contexts for studying the impact of peer relations. What is the quality of helping relationships between siblings in the home, for example? What of the plight of children with crippling or terminal illnesses? How might those with similar conditions be useful sources of information and social support for them? What about children with behavioural and emotional disorders? From whom can they best draw emotional support to understand and help them with their problems? What of young adolescents with addiction problems? How might the peer group help them overcome rather than reinforce their addictions? Extraordinarily little research exists on the applications of children's helping relationships to these familial, medical, therapeutic and health education contexts.

Because this is essentially a review book, however, it inevitably reflects the state of research at the present time, and the bulk of the chapters indicate a clear bias towards educational applications. The aim of the book is, therefore, to bring together in a single volume some of the most influential thinking and research in these various fields. Ideas and insights are truly international:

contributors have been selected from the USA, the United Kingdom, Australia, France, Switzerland, and Israel to represent a broad array of theoretical and practical perspectives on the issues surrounding children's helping relationships. Our best hope for this book is that it spurs on future research in these areas and helps lay down the foundations for realizing an 'untapped potential'.

*July 1989*

HUGH C. FOOT
MICHELLE J. MORGAN
ROSALYN H. SHUTE

# An Introductory Perspective

CHAPTER 1

# Children's Helping Relationships: an Overview

HUGH C. FOOT*, MICHELLE J. MORGAN* and ROSALYN H. SHUTE†

**School of Psychology, University of Wales College of Cardiff, PO Box 901, Cardiff CF1 3YG, UK*

*†Department of Optometry, University of Wales College of Cardiff, PO Box 905, Cardiff CF1 3YJ, UK*

## RESEARCH ON HELPING

The origins of research into particular psychological phenomena are usually relatively blurred and fuzzy. Just occasionally one can point to a seminal paper, dramatic insight, a crucial piece of new evidence which *by itself* launched a whole new arena for research. The more usual pattern, at least so it seems to those working on the outside, is a gradual dawning or awareness that a new research field has 'taken off' and that various pieces of interconnected research produced by different research groups over a period of months, if not years, have come together to steer a new course or open up a new field.

If one looks at the emerging psychological literature on prosocial behaviours in the mid-1960s, one might be forgiven for thinking that the impetus for research in this field was indeed driven by one particular event which 'caught the imagination of a nation', although not quite in the sense that this expression conveys. Textbooks in social psychology written in the late 1960s and 1970s preface the surge of new interest in social responsibility, altruism and helping behaviours with the very unsavoury account of a young girl who was stalked

Children Helping Children
Edited by H. C. Foot, M. J. Morgan and R. H. Shute

and savagely stabbed over a period of at least 30 minutes before she died in the respectable Kew Gardens of New York City under the gaze of 38 witnesses (e.g. Mann, 1969; Elms, 1972; Freedman, Sears and Carlsmith, 1970). What struck the nation's imagination about this event was how so many apparently respectable law-abiding citizens could witness such an unambiguously murderous attack perpetrated over such a long period of time without intervening or calling the emergency services.

The point we are making is that it was the public outcry over this single event about the reasons for bystander apathy which drove social psychologists into their laboratories and into the field to study people's reactions to victim plight and distress in emergencies. Inevitably, therefore, research on the circumstances influencing people's *non-intervention* in emergency situations also spilled over into research on the reasons for *intervention* in situations where others are in need of help. While the reasons and circumstances for non-intervention are now relatively well understood and hardly researched any further, the motivation for and circumstances surrounding helping are much more complex and this has remained a much more enduring field of research.

Throughout the 1970s the fostering of helping behaviour was regarded as wholly desirable. This may well be because, as we have just seen, the roots of psychologists' interests in prosocial behaviours lay in the reasons for apathy and non-intervention and the consequential focus upon the attributed intentions and social responsibility of the helper, with little consideration for the needs of the victim or recipient of help. More recently, however, researchers and practitioners working in applied fields have come to recognize that the reaction of the recipient to help is also important, and that the impact of the help can have undesirable as well as desirable consequences upon the recipient (Brammer, 1985; DePaulo, Nadler and Fisher, 1983; Fisher, Nadler and Whitcher-Alagna, 1982). Many instances of misguided or undesirable help come from the field of counselling where those seeking advice often expect to receive practical solutions to their problems and possibly become dependent upon their counsellors for guiding them through their problems. Present day philosophy enshrined in most definitions of counselling assumes the role of counsellors is to help clients to help themselves rather than simply to provide a crutch (cf. Brammer, 1985). Nelson-Jones (1987, p. 2), for example, defines counselling as 'a process whose aim is to help clients to help themselves by making better choices and by becoming better choosers'. In other words, the emphasis of counselling, as with other helping services, is to enable clients to engage in self-help and to provide them with learning and problem-solving skills necessary for seeking out their own resources and support for assisting them through their difficulties.

The helping actions of others can also have negative consequences for the recipient's self-esteem and feelings of autonomy and self-worth. Help offered or help given can, under certain circumstances, 'highlight the recipient's relative inferiority and lead to negative affect and unfavorable recipient self-evaluations' (Nadler and Mayseless, 1983). Even if the donor's intentions are entirely altruistic and non-exploitative, the recipient is likely to experience a sense of guilt or obligation which may endure until a reciprocal favour can be discharged.

**Children as potential helpers**

So far we have focused upon helping relationships in a very broad sense, and the helping contexts described (e.g. counselling) are clearly more appropriate to help seeking and help giving amongst adults than amongst children. Helping relationships amongst children have been less researched although sporadic reviews of the development of helping behaviours in children have appeared over the past 20 years and there is a substantial developmental literature which has examined the ways that helping behaviour maps on to patterns of social, cognitive and moral growth (e.g. Bryan and London, 1970; Bar-Tal, 1976; Rushton, 1976; Staub, 1978; Cialdini, Baumann and Kenrick, 1981; Eisenberg, 1983).

In retrospect, what is striking is that helping behaviour has, by and large, been seen purely as another vehicle by which to study the developing social awareness of young children, along with conformity behaviour, aggression, sex-role stereotyping, racial prejudice and a host of other emergent social and anti-social behaviours. While such a theoretical interest is perfectly laudable, scant attention has been paid to the practical potential for 'harnessing' children as sources of expertise and support in their interaction with their peers. As Damon (1984, p. 331) has pointed out, 'psychological and educational research has established beyond doubt that children can have a powerful influence upon one anothers' intellectual development', and yet formal educational programmes with their emphasis upon competition, one-way transmission of information from teacher to pupil, and private study, seem to spurn any hint of cooperative learning. It is small wonder that Damon refers to peer-based learning as an 'untapped potential'.

Of course, many pressures in society have strengthened the myth that children should only be treated as *recipients* of help and instruction. The whole conception of the family in the Western world is one based upon the assumption that healthy, capable and mature adult members shield and provide for the needs of the weaker, less capable and immature members—the dependants in moral, legal and social role terms. Educational systems across the globe operate on a similar assumption that adults have a monopoly of knowledge and wisdom for coping with the demands of everyday life and that these commodities have to be imparted to children as novice and inexperienced members of society. We propose no challenge to this philosophy: the whole fabric of our culture is woven around it. We would make the point, however, that such culturization may blinker us to the very real contributions that children could make as care-takers and help givers, if provided with more opportunities and more responsibility.

In this context it is interesting to note how educationalists and researchers in developmental psychology have come to recognize in quite recent years that children are in fact capable of much more sophisticated thinking than they had hitherto been given credit for throughout much of this century. Studies of metacognition, for example, have revealed that quite young children are capable of planning, organizing, selecting strategies and executing a variety of other subtle and implicit cognitive processes which traditional observational and experimental inquiry had failed to reveal (Flavell and Wellman, 1977; Kail, 1979). Perhaps, then, the emergence of our realization of children's potentialities as sources of practical help and guidance is also at a very primitive level and we are only just beginning to appreciate the richness of ways in which children might be capable of providing sources of practical assistance and emotional support as well as exerting powerful influences upon each others' cognitive and social development.

**Ethical issues**

It must be recognized that behind these objectives lie various kinds of ethical concerns which should be briefly addressed. Overriding our thoughts in the preparation of this volume has been the awareness of the potential 'exploitation' of children. Much of the language used to define children in helping relationships is borrowed from the applications of behaviour technology which talks of children as 'resources' as 'behaviour change agents' and as 'managers of peer relationships', and so on. Yet rarely can these terms be seen as defining the characteristics of spontaneously occurring events or outcomes in children's peer relationships. Most of the helping situations considered in this book and in the general field of behavioural technology are structured programmes engineered by adults who regulate both the physical and social contexts in which the children operate. Perhaps, as Cowie and Rudduck (Chapter 11) suggest, children should have a choice about opting out of cooperative learning situations. Perhaps they should have a say in whether they wish to 'help' or 'be helped' by their peers. After all, differences in adults' study habits are well recognized by teachers in the higher education sector: some students like complete solitude for working; others like the stimulation of a busy library environment. Why should we assume that all children are the same, and all are going to benefit from our manipulations of them in the same way?

Even this level of discussion makes a further presumption that while we might contemplate children opting in or out of child–child learning situations, there can never be any question of challenging the assumption that children cannot opt out of adult–child learning situations. Clearly this is dictated by the times and culture in which we live (see Wagner, Chapter 2). Children formally remain a disenfranchised group and do not have the political means of securing their own rights (Shore, 1979). As Katz (1972) has pointed out, children fall within the rubric of uncomprehending subjects as do adults who are intellectually or psychologically problematic with respect to their ability to make enlightened decisions about their own welfare.

Nevertheless, it is interesting to note that many researchers and practitioners in the cooperative learning field make the point that peer-based learning techniques should not be seen to substitute for traditional teaching methods, but merely to complement or augment them (e.g. Ehly and Larsen, 1980; Gerber and Kauffman, 1981; Topping, 1988). We have no reasons for disputing this point, but we wonder whether the impetus for seeing peer-based methods in this way is out of political exigency rather than on strictly pedagogic grounds. As Cowie and Rudduck (Chapter 11) point out, many teachers are still very suspicious of the wisdom of any peer-based teaching technique, and are not likely to be easily convinced to adopt a method which they believe might undermine their own position or profession (see also Foot and Chapman, 1982).

An excellent discussion of specific ethical issues in relation to children or peer groups acting in the role of behaviour-change agent is provided by Greenwood (1981), who reviews problems of risks and benefits and issues relating to informed consent, peer-manager competency, accountability and the need for adequate monitoring systems.

## TERMS AND DEFINITIONS

As Brammer (1985) has argued, *helping* is a difficult process to describe because it has such individualized meanings. Also, the context of helping extends from formalized, professional help settings, such as counselling, careers advice or marriage guidance, to informal, spontaneous and unsolicited instances of help-giving as in response to a distraught neighbour or relative calling round to unburden his or her woes.

Although children may be recipients of help in either formal or informal helping contexts, their role as help-givers and interventionists is almost entirely confined to informal and impromptu helping relationships outside those engineered for them by adults, such as peer tutoring. It is also likely that what adults may define as a helping relationship between two children may not actually be recognized by the participants as such, although there is virtually no research comparing children's and adults' cognitions about what constitutes a helping relationship.

It may well be that this uncertainty about the designations which children themselves attach to certain aspects of their peer interactions has led to a reluctance amongst researchers and practitioners to talk about helping relationships between children, with the notable exception of recent classroom research by Nelson-Le Gall and associates (Nelson-Le Gall and Glor-Scheib, 1985; Nelson-Le Gall and Gumerman, 1984). Also significant is the point that, since children's helping relationships have hardly been explored outside educational and social contexts, it has been conventional to talk about peer cooperation as a more generic term for children in helping relationships (see also Hertz-Lazarowitz, 1989, for a very recent analysis linking the cooperative learning and prosocial/helping traditions).

It is not our intention to provide a detailed taxonomy of the terms and concepts used in this book, and inevitably different contributors define their key concepts in slightly different ways. For present purposes we shall confine ourselves to a very broad classification.

As a starting point helping relationships between children are more usually defined as 'peer cooperation' and we are taking this as our umbrella label, to subsume all the particular forms of prosocial peer interactions that are described in this book. Another term frequently used in this volume is 'peer-based learning' which we have taken to be more or less synonymous with peer cooperation. A distinction, however, should be made in that peer-based learning clearly applies to all those situations in which learning and cognitive growth are judged as the eventual or desired outcome. This might not, therefore, be so readily applicable to cooperation in social, therapeutic and emotionally supporting settings. The use of 'peer-based learning' is slightly more restricted for our present purposes and is confined to educational settings.

One particular advantage of the term 'cooperation' is that it contrasts with 'competition' and therefore draws attention to the essentially shared nature of the joint activity or experience between interacting peers. As a theoretical construct cooperation stems from a long tradition of social psychological theories of cooperation (Deutsch, 1949) which sees cooperation and competition as two mutually exclusive dimensions of interaction governed by the interdependence or independence of goals. Much has been written on the relative role of cooperation and competition in society and in particular in education. Given that schools are among the institutions in our society that are least characterized by cooperative activity (Slavin, 1981), it is not surprising that the educational system in western society has been at the forefront of attempts towards reform in this respect.

Peer cooperation between children is represented in this book by three main approaches which seem to embrace most of the research and practice, at least in the educational, cognitive and social fields (see Figure 1.1). These approaches are *peer tutoring, peer collaboration* and *cooperative learning*, which Damon and Phelps (1987) also identify as the three main types of peer-based instruction in use in the educational world today. Damon and Phelps differentiate these approaches on the basis of two main dimensions of interaction: 'equality' and 'mutuality of engagement'. Equality is an unquestionable marker of a peer relationship, marking both equivalence of age and stage of cognitive development and equivalence of knowledge or skill in the task or problem to be solved. Mutuality of engagement refers to the extent to which the children are 'connected', or 'in tune' with each other or working synchronously on the same aspect of the same problem.

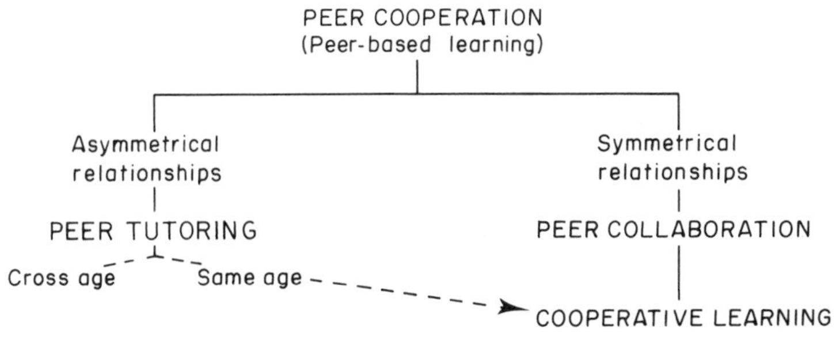


FIGURE 1.1. Broad classification of helping/cooperative relationships

As Damon and Phelps argue, the three types of peer learning reflect these dimensions quite differently. 'Peer tutoring is relatively low on equality and high on mutuality; cooperative learning is high on equality and low on mutuality; and peer collaboration is high on both' (Damon and Phelps, 1987, pp. 8–9).

This distinction serves our own purposes well, although we have preferred to use the terms 'symmetrical' and 'asymmetrical' to signify equality or lack of equality. We do not see the three approaches as quite as mutually exclusive as the distinction above may imply, and Figure 1.1 indicates how we see their interrelationships. In particular, cooperative learning methods in our scheme are characterized as a subgroup of peer collaboration techniques which involve largely symmetrical relationships and a varying amount of mutuality of engagement, but some cooperative learning methods may also involve tutoring (e.g. a technique called Jigsaw—see Chapter 8). Because the theoretical bases of these approaches are taken up in more detail in individual chapters, we shall only briefly describe them here.

### Peer tutoring

At its most basic level peer tutoring involves children teaching other children usually on a one-to-one basis (Ehly and Larsen, 1980). Peer tutoring describes those situations in which a person provides instructional assistance and guidance to another person (Cohen, Kirk and Dickson, 1972). The term 'peer' is used somewhat loosely for two reasons. First, we are following the practice of other researchers and practitioners in using peer tutoring to describe both cross-age and same-age tutoring relationships (e.g. Ehly and Larsen, 1980). Many research studies and tutoring programmes use tutors who are marginally if not significantly older than their tutees. Secondly, whatever the relative ages of the tutor and tutee may be, there is a necessary and inevitable asymmetry in the knowledge or skill between them, at least as far as the tutoring task is concerned. The tutor is the 'expert', the tutee is the 'novice' and the relationship between them, therefore, is one which demands that the expert instructs, guides and manages the efforts of the other in mastering the task. This asymmetrical relationship is advocated by Vygotsky (1978) as the basis of cognitive growth. The more capable or knowledgeable children push the less capable or knowledgeable to the leading edge of their intellectual potentiality. Vygotsky's views are described in more detail by Foot, Shute, Morgan and Barron in Chapter 4.

### Peer collaboration

A second approach is that of peer collaboration which refers to children of roughly equal abilities (at least equally novice or inexperienced at the task in hand) actively exchanging ideas about a problem rather than having one child passively learning from the other (Damon, 1984). Collaborative learning experiences are ones in which participants discover solutions and create knowledge together by sharing, discussing and challenging their own partial and incomplete perspectives on a problem. Such discovery learning implies a relatively symmetrical relationship between the children in an atmosphere of mutual respect and trust and where there is no authority relation between them. Collaborative relationships of this kind may extend to a group of children rather than purely to a dyad. Underlying this form of peer-based learning is Piaget's theory of cognitive growth (Piaget, 1928, 1932, 1950, 1970) with its emphasis upon peer interaction as providing children with uniquely constructive feedback on which real cognitive development depends. The essence of this view, which has been considerably elaborated by Doise and his co-workers (Doise and Mugny, 1979; Doise, Mugny and Perrett-Clermont, 1976), is that children are introduced to new perspectives on problems by engaging in conversation with peers, having their own ideas challenged, and being forced to 'decentre' in order to take account of these new perspectives. When children disagree with one another, and when they have to come to terms with other perspectives, they experience both social and cognitive conflicts which act as the catalyst by which a clearer understanding of the problem emerges. These views are discussed in more detail in this volume by Doise (Chapter 3), and by Foot, Shute, Morgan, and Barron (Chapter 4).

### Cooperative learning

The third approach, cooperative (or small group) learning, is also based upon an essentially symmetrical relationship between the interacting children within a classroom. We see it as an extension or development of peer collaboration rather than as a distinctly different technique. As Ashman and Elkins define it in Chapter 10, 'cooperative learning involves the organization of the classroom activities and structure so that cooperation is necessary to attain mutually attractive objectives'. Students typically work on learning activities in small groups (perhaps four or five in a group) and receive rewards or recognition based upon their group's performance (Slavin, 1980). Cooperative learning is relatively structured in the sense that curriculum problems are often segmented into different components and the children take specified and complementary roles in working towards a solution. So, in practice, each student may either be given or required to find a unique piece of information which then has to be pooled with the information provided by the other group members.

This is not always the case: in some cooperative learning methods all students work together to accomplish a common product. Another common ingredient of cooperative learning methods is their use of group reward structures, whereby students are rewarded on the basis of a single group product or on the basis of the sum of the individual learning performances within the group (which can lead to some intra-group competition). Rewards may take the form of praise, extra grades, certificates, earning privileges or other forms of public recognition. Generally speaking, rewards are contingent upon the performance of the group as a whole, not on the performance of individual members. As Slavin (1980) points out, the reward delivered to the group is not the only one present in a cooperative work situation, nor indeed may it be the most important one:

> When individuals in a cooperative contingency want to be rewarded, they have two primary means of increasing their chances. First, they can work hard themselves. But, second, they can try to influence or help their groupmates to do their best. That is, a cooperative contingency sets up a situation in which group members administer a highly contingent reward structure with their groupmates; if they do what helps the group to be rewarded, they receive praise; if they do not, they receive blame. Even if praise and blame are not directly delivered, a cooperative reward structure can create a general group norm favoring performance. (Slavin, 1980, p. 317)

Many of the cooperative learning methods (e.g. Teams-Games-Tournament, Student Teams-Achievement Divisions, Learning Together, Jigsaw and the Group Investigation Method) are described in some detail in other chapters of this book, in particular by Ashman and Elkins (Chapter 10), Greenwood, Carta and Kamps (Chapter 9) and Sharan (Chapter 8).

We have said that cooperative learning is an extension or development of peer collaboration and at times the distinction between them is somewhat blurred. Slavin (1987, p. 31) has indicated, for example, that the simplest form of cooperative learning methods is one in which students 'sit together to discuss or help one another with classroom texts'. Similarly he has suggested that group rewards are an optional element of cooperative learning. Since the peer collaboration paradigm that we have described imposes neither a role nor a reward structure on its group members, then it could be taken as a minimalist condition for cooperative learning and be placed at the bottom end of a continuum which is characterized by increasing degrees of task, role and reward structure.

Our preference for maintaining a distinction between peer collaboration and cooperative learning methods is twofold. First, by far the majority of what are commonly referred to as cooperative learning methods are relatively highly structured in terms of task, role, reward and authority structure (Slavin, 1980). Second, cooperative learning methods refer to a behavioural approach to classroom teaching which has to be imposed and sanctioned from above, i.e. by the teacher. In this sense any outcomes of learning for the students can be said to have been achieved by a formal and deliberate educational intervention. By contrast, peer collaboration may occur informally on frequent occasions within the classroom every time one child turns to another to seek help with a particular difficulty; and equally, peer collaboration may occur on countless occasions outside the classroom when children are at home or at play.

## STRUCTURE AND CONTENT

The chapters in this book are sectioned with two main criteria in mind: first and foremost, the context within which the helping or peer cooperation occurs; and second, the classification of peer interactions outlined in the previous section of this chapter.

It has not, however, been possible to keep these criteria entirely separated. Many of the chapters cross boundaries from one type of peer cooperation to another: for example, several contributors talk about both cooperative learning and peer tutoring. Only two chapters (Willem Doise, Chapter 3; Paul Light and Agnès Blaye, Chapter 7) focus on peer collaboration, as we have defined it. Whereas they might have been grouped along with the chapters on cooperative learning in Part II, we have chosen to include them with studies on peer tutoring in Part I, because material in Doise's chapter, in particular, is of general historical and theoretical interest and is better placed in the first section of the book. Division of the material, is therefore, somewhat arbitrary in some cases, and our selection of chapters to group together has been as much shaped by convenience as by any objective criteria.

Part I relates, then, to peer tutoring and collaborative learning in largely educational contexts. This section comes first because, as we have said in the Preface to this book, the tradition of peer tutoring is longer than for any other form of peer cooperation and it is here that the roots of children's helping relationships lie. Lilya Wagner (Chapter 2) sets the scene for modern day tutoring programmes by tracing the historical origins of peer tutoring in Western civilization and by relating changes in peer teaching to prevalent social, economic and political influences. Willem Doise's chapter (Chapter 3) is also partly historical in nature as he maps out a general theoretical framework on the links between social interaction and individual cognitive development. Three mechanisms are described through which social interaction (collaboration) intervenes in cognitive development: the coordination of interdependent actions, socio-cognitive conflict and social marking. Doise concludes by proposing the outline of a more comprehensive constructivist theory of communicative interaction.

The editors' joint chapter (Chapter 4), in conjunction with another member of their research team (Anne-Marie Barron), draws together what they see as the strongest theoretical traditions in the peer tutoring and peer collaboration movements. They also devote attention to some aspects of the mismatch between theory and practice in the peer tutoring literature. Drawing partially upon their own research they map out three main areas where they believe future research should be focused: children's perceptions of tutoring roles, children's teaching strategies and tutors' sensitivity to the needs of learners.

The next two chapters review specific uses for peer tutoring. Andre Imich (Chapter 5) examines the development of locus of control orientation and the particular contribution of pupil tutoring programmes to the promotion of internality in children, which is associated with a wide range of positive educational, psychological and social attributes. He also demonstrates that pupil tutoring can be an effective strategy for improving school attendance. Kevin Wheldall and Susan Colmar (Chapter 6) address the use of peer tutoring in the field of reading, specifically in relation to low-progress or slow readers with whom much of their own work has been involved. They review research using the 'Pause, Prompt and Praise' (PPP) method, outline a series of studies in their own programme of research, and evaluate the effectiveness of PPP methods.

The final chapter in Part I by Paul Light and Agnès Blaye (Chapter 7), investigates the computer as an effective motivator for group work within the classroom. Far from encouraging isolation and withdrawal in children, computer-based work supplies the context for genuine collaborative discussion between children. Very little research has yet been conducted on whether child–child interaction facilitates the learning of programming concepts and skills but what little evidence there is points strongly toward the importance of the social dimension.

Part II continues a review of peer-based learning methods in educational contexts. Chapters in this part, however, deal predominantly (although by no means exclusively) with methods which come into the category of cooperative learning, as defined earlier in this chapter.

Shlomo Sharan (Chapter 8) introduces the philosophy behind cooperative learning and outlines four major cooperative learning techniques. He then reviews research studies which have evaluated the effects of cooperative learning experiences on pupils' helping behaviour in multi-ethnic classrooms, concluding that cooperative learning has considerable impact in promoting positive relationships and prosocial behaviours in ethnically desegrated classrooms. Charles Greenwood, Judith Carta and Debra Kamps (Chapter 9) take up the theme of peer-mediated classroom instruction by stressing the ways in which such peer-assisted instruction can favourably affect pupil–teacher ratios and best serve the individualized goals of pupils. Various effective instructional processes and practices are reviewed including both cooperative learning methods and peer tutoring. The advantages and disadvantages of teacher- versus peer-mediation are carefully weighed up and the teacher's change of role from directly imparting information to that of supervising students' responding during peer-mediated instruction is considered. Ashman and Elkins (Chapter 10) explore the potentiality of cooperative learning methods amongst children with learning difficulties and mild intellectual disabilities. They review various peer-based learning methods, including peer tutoring, which contribute to the classroom teacher's store of successful instructional strategies in the special education domain but caution against the uncritical application of any specific strategy. Helen Cowie and Jean Rudduck (Chapter 11) pursue the question of caution in the application of cooperative learning strategies by emphasizing the challenge they pose to traditional educational values. Despite the lip-service paid to cooperative techniques and their well-documented effectiveness in many teaching situations, they are viewed with distrust by teachers and pupils alike, at least in the United Kingdom. Considerable attitudinal barriers need to be broken down if the enormous potential children have for learning from one another is to be realized.

Part III of the book takes as its underlying theme peer cooperation in social and clinical contexts. The chapters here present a wide variety of processes and settings and what most cements them together is that they concern helping relationships strictly outside the classroom context. Catherine Cooper and Linda St John (Chapter 12) review the whole field of sibling helping relationships, adopting the view that helping must be understood in terms of its 'relational perspective' or the dynamics of the relationship in which it occurs, rather than as a skill or behaviour of the individual. Developmental patterns in sibling helping are plotted through early and middle childhood and into adolescence.

Michael Guralnick (Chapter 13) focuses upon preschool age handicapped children and examines the limitations imposed on the growth of their peer relations due to their associated behaviour problems. A particular focus of this chapter is the importance of the characteristics of their companions and the extent to which non-handicapped peers are able and willing to adapt and accommodate their social and communicative behaviours to interact effectively with children of lower developmental status. Comprehensive intervention programmes are advocated to promote the peer-related social competence of handicapped children.

Michelle Morgan and Dick Eiser (Chapter 14) resume the theme of peer influence, but within the context of smoking education amongst children and adolescents. The peer group is traditionally seen as a potentially bad influence but could equally be viewed as a force for good. Health education programmes are generally aimed at rescuing the individual *as an individual* from his or her folly and pay scant regard to social identity, social categorization processes and peer group influences. Various peer group techniques such as the use of peer models and cross- and same-age peer tutors are reviewed and their potential for fostering understanding of health education issues is advocated.

Adopting a social-cognitive developmental framework, Rosalyn Shute and Douglas Paton (Chapter 15) identify the potential of peers for promoting good adjustment in the chronically sick child. They map out how chronic illness may influence development and review peer-based interventions within the contexts of the family, the school and medical care settings. Many of the ideas are as yet untested, but the authors express a hope that their integration of previously disparate literatures will be a spur to new developments in both research and practice. The clinical theme is continued in Rosalyn Shute's chapter with Richard Pates (Chapter 16) which reviews the field of group therapy with children and adolescents experiencing peer relationship difficulties and emotional problems. They note the general lack of adequate theoretical bases for such interventions and the paucity of evaluative studies, but also outline some promising recent developments.

The final overview chapter by David Fontana (Chapter 17) presents a personal perspective on peer cooperation methods through the eyes of an educationalist. We invited such a chapter in view of the general emphasis on peer cooperation in educational contexts. Inevitably, then, the focus is very much on education and in particular peer tutoring, but more general issues and questions relating to the direction of future research in the applications of children helping other children are posed in the concluding pages.

## REFERENCES


Bar-Tal, D. (1976). *Prosocial Behaviour: Theory and Research.* New York, Wiley.

Brammer, L. M. (1985). *The Helping Relationship.* (3rd edn) Englewood Cliffs, New Jersey: Prentice-Hall.

Bryan, J. H., and London, P. (1970). Altruistic behaviour in children, *Psychological Bulletin*, **73**, 200–211.

Cialdini, R. B., Baumann, D. J., and Kenrick, D. T. (1981). Insights from sadness: a three step model of the development of altruism as hedonism, Developmental Review, **1**, 207–223.

Cohen, A. D., Kirk, J. C., and Dickson, W. P. (1972). Guidebook for Tutors with an Emphasis on Tutoring Minority Children. Stanford: Stanford University Committee on Linguistics (ERIC Document Reproduction No. ED 084–326).

Damon, W. (1984) Peer education: the untapped potential, *Journal of Applied Developmental Psychology*, **5**, 331–343.

Damon, W., and Phelps, E. (1987). Peer collaboration as a context for cognitive growth. Paper presented at the Tel Aviv University School of education Annual Symposium on human development and instruction (June).

DePaulo, B. M., Nadler, A., and Fisher, J. D. (eds) (1983). *New Directions in Helping (Vol. 2): Help Seeking.* New York: Academic Press.

Deutsch, M. (1949). A theory of cooperation and competition, *Human Relations*, **2**, 129–152.

Doise, W., and Mugny, G. (1979) Individual and collective conflicts of centrations in cognitive development, *European Journal of Social Psychology*, **9**, 105–108.

Doise, W., Mugny, G., and Perret-Clermont, A. (1976). Social interaction and cognitive development: further evidence, *European Journal of Social Psychology*, **6**, 245–247.

Ehly, S. W., and Larsen, S. C. (1980). *Peer Tutoring for Individualized Instruction*. Boston: Allyn and Bacon.

Eisenberg, N. (1983). Developmental aspects of reactors to aid. In J. D. Fisher, A. Nadler and B. M. DePaulo (eds), *New Directions in Helping Vol. 1: Recipient Reactions to Help*. New York: Academic Press.

Elms, A. (1972). *Social Psychology and Social Relevance*. Boston: Little, Brown.

Fisher, J. D., Nadler, A., and Whitcher-Alagna, S. (1982). Recipient reaction to aid: a conceptual review, *Psychological Bulletin*, **91**, 27–54.

Flavell, J. H., and Wellman, H. M. (1977). Metamemory. In R. V. Kail and J. W. Hagen, (eds), *Perspectives on the Development of Memory and Cognition*. New Jersey: Erlbaum.

Foot, H. C., and Chapman, A. J. (1982). A case of child tutors? *British Psychological Society: Education Section Review*, **6**, 44–46.

Freedman, J. L., Sears, D. O., and Carlsmith, J. M. (1970). *Social Psychology*. Englewood Cliffs, New Jersey: Prentice-Hall.

Gerber, M., and Kauffman, J. M. (1981). Peer tutoring in academic settings. In P. S. Strain (ed.), *The Utilization of Classroom Peers as Behavior Change Agents*. New York: Academic Press.

Greenwood, C. R. (1981). Peer-oriented behavioral technology and ethical issues. In P. S. Strain (ed.), *The Utilization of Classroom Peers as Behavior Change Agents*. New York: Academic Press.

Hertz-Lazarowitz, R. (1989). Cooperation and helping in the classroom: a contextual approach, *International Journal of Research in Education*, **13**, 113–119.

Kail, R. (1979). *The Development of Memory in Children*. San Francisco: Freeman.

Katz, J. (1972). *Experimentation with Human Beings: The Authority of the Investigator, Subject, Professions and State in the Human Experimentation Process*. New York: Sage.

Mann, L. (1969). *Social Psychology*. Sydney: Wiley.

Nadler, A., and Mayseless, O. (1983). Recipient self-esteem and reactions to help. In J. D. Fisher, A. Nadler and B. M. DePaulo (eds), *New Directions in Helping Vol. 2: Recipient Reactions to Help*. New York: Academic Press.

Nelson-Jones, R. (1987). DOSIE: a five stage model for problem management counselling and helping, *Counselling*, **61**, 2–10.

Nelson-Le Gall, S., and Glor-Scheib, S. (1985). Help-seeking in elementary classrooms: an observational study, *Contemporary Educational Psychology*, **10**, 58–71.

Nelson-Le Gall, S. A., and Gumerman, R. A. (1984). Children's perception of helpers and helper motivation, *Journal of Applied Developmental Psychology*, **5**, 1–12.

Piaget, J. (1928). *Judgement and Reasoning in the Child*. New York: Harcourt, Brace.

Piaget, J. (1932). *The Moral Judgement of the Child*. London: Routledge & Kegan Paul.

Piaget, J. (1950). *The Psychology of Intelligence*. London: Routledge & Kegan Paul.

Piaget, J. (1970). Piaget's theory. In P. Mussen (ed.), *Carmichael's Manual of Child Psychology*. Vol. 1. New York: Wiley.

Rushton, J. P. (1976). Socialization and altruistic behavior of children, *Psychological Bulletin*, **83**, 898–913.

Shore, M. F. (1979). Legislation, advocacy and the rights of children and youth, *American Psychologist*, **34**, 1017–1019.

Slavin, R. E. (1980). Cooperative learning, *Review of Educational Research*, **50**, 315–342.

Slavin, R. E. (1981). Synthesis of research on cooperative learning, *Educational Leadership*, May, 655–660.

Slavin, R. E. (1987). Cooperative learning: where behavioral and humanistic approaches to classroom motivation meet, *Elementary School Journal*, **88**, 29–37.

Staub, E. (1978). *Positive Social Behavior and Morality: Vol 1 Social and Personal Influence*. New York: Academic Press.
Topping, K. (1988). *The Peer Tutoring Handbook: Promoting Co-operative Learning*. London: Croom Helm.
Vygotsky, L. S. (1978). *Mind in Society*. Cambridge, Massachusetts: Harvard University Press.

PART I

# Peer Tutoring and Collaboration

CHAPTER 2

# Social and Historical Perspectives on Peer Teaching in Education

LILYA WAGNER

*Union College, 3800 South 48th Street, Lincoln, Nebraska 68506, USA*

## INTRODUCTION

Helping relationships between students in formal and planned learning situations have been utilized by teachers as early as the first century AD. Since that time, the practice of peer teaching has seen intermittent use. History can create a perspective through which a knowledgeable educator wishing to use the technique of peer teaching can judge the merits and assess the possible problems of that practice. This chapter presents accounts of peer teaching in the historical context in which they occurred. When gaps occur in tracing the practice of peer teaching, it is because of the scarcity of written records in certain eras (such as medieval times), or because of economic and political influences on education which impinged on the practice of this technique.

Peer teaching refers to the practice of students teaching other students in a setting directed and planned by the teacher. Informal learning from peers outside of the educational environment is not included in that definition. This chapter excludes a world view of peer teaching; only countries in the Western Hemisphere are included.

## EARLY ORIGINS

The city-states of Greece were the first known political entities to plan for schooling for the young, with the intention of training a select few for state

Children Helping Children
Edited by H. C. Foot, M. J. Morgan and R. H. Shute

leadership. Aristotle is reported to have used peer teaching. Student leaders or archons apparently handled many details for the celebrated teacher. Given the popularity of Aristotle, student helpers may indeed have been a necessity (Wise, 1964).

Greek influence was evident during the latter days of the Roman Republic, and considerable during the days of the Empire. Greek slaves were employed as teachers, and Roman education was bilingual. In this educational setting, older students assisted the younger ones. Also, boys tested each other by taking dictation and then reciting the information (Wise, 1964; Bonner, 1977). This practice of peer teaching took place in the schools of rhetoric, since oratory was considered the most important skill necessary for success in the Roman life.

The first noteworthy name connected with the practice of peer teaching is that of Quintilian, for more than twenty years the head of a leading school of oratory in Rome. In his *Institutio Oratoria*, which appeared in AD 93, he pointed out how much younger children could learn from the older ones in the same class. He maintained that the new learner was the best teacher, and he was a leading proponent of making education more humane, moral, practical, and profound (Kennedy, 1969; Gill, 1889).

During the Middle Ages, education as a preparation for service to the state largely ceased, and the church became the leading educator of Western Europe. Education was limited to the privileged classes and focused on spiritual matters. Not until the fourteenth century did classical learning once again become prominent. Religious reforms during the Renaissance and Reformation restricted the authority of the church, and under this influence new aims and methods of education developed.

Educational leaders of this new era espoused intellectual freedom for all—wealthy or poor, male or female (although females benefited little from this idea as put into practice), commoners or nobility. The methods utilized by Protestant reformers, the Jesuits, and grammar school teachers in England included the practice of peer teaching.

The development of the Gymnasium, the German classical school, came about through the educational influence of Melanchthon. The most successful of these schools, and one which became a model, was the institution at Strasbourg established by Johann Sturm, who was born in 1507. His stated aim was to train pious, learned and eloquent men for service in both church and state. Of great importance to him was that education should be suited to the age and level of achievement of each pupil, and teaching should be clear and definite ('Life and Educational System of John Sturm', 1857a,b; Williams, 1892).

Sturm published his education plan in 1538 under the title of *De litteratum ludis recte apriendis (The Right Mode of Instituting Schools)*. This plan included the use of decurions: one student was assigned to ten others and he performed specific duties in the classroom ('Monitorial System', 1861).

Valentine Trotzendorf, born in 1490, directed a well known and widely respected school in Silesia. While the subjects taught differed little from other contemporary schools, his school utilized a unique method of instruction. He instructed older scholars who in turn taught the lower classes. His system even extended to the use of older students in administrative roles. In time his 'teachers' were in demand throughout Europe ('Valentine Friedland Trotzendorf', 1858).

During the Reformation, the grammar schools of England came under scrutiny by the Anglican church. Those which met the high standards as being preparatory schools for institutions such as Oxford continued to exist. One of these, Winchester College, utilized advanced scholars to superintend the activities, both learning and behavioural, of their fellow students (Seaborne, 1971). Eton College, closely modelled after Winchester, also introduced peer teaching during the period of educational reform (Barnard, 1949).

Another English school, St Paul's in London, was directed by John Colet, a leading exponent of the humanist ideas of the Renaissance. In his system, a 'head boy' or captain had some authority over the learning activities of a designated number of his peers (Seaborne, 1971). Colet was probably following the example set by Winchester and Eton, where the 'head boy' had some authority over the others, and he in turn answered to the master (Orme, 1973). Other English schools using peer teaching were Manchester Grammar School and the Westminster School.

During the Counter-Reformation, the number of Jesuits in Italy, Spain, Portugal, much of France, and southern Belgium increased rapidly and their educational influence was remarkable. A manual, *Ratio Studiorum*, published in 1599, evidenced the practical nature of Jesuit education (Quick, 1896). Classes were divided into groups of ten (*decuriae*), and each had a captain in charge (*decurio*). These captains monitored student academic progress as well as behaviour (Farrell, 1938). The Jesuit schools were well organized and highly respected during the sixteenth and seventeenth centuries. By 1764 the influence of Jesuit education had largely declined.

## THE SEVENTEENTH CENTURY

The seventeenth century witnessed a stress on practical education, including mathematics, sciences and modern languages. Realism in education predominated, focusing on concrete knowledge and practical skills. The use of the vernacular in education was a concept popular in the classical schools, the predominant institutions of the seventeenth century. To a large extent, however, schools remained largely similar to those which evolved in the Renaissance, the Reformation and the Counter-Reformation. However, the writers who propounded the ideas of Realism were not teachers and had little influence over schools. Consequently their ideas did not have much impact until decades later.

In spite of this, educational progress and reform occurred during the seventeenth century. Conditions in the schools were addressed by some individuals, particularly the harsh discipline, the meaningless of much of the education available, and inefficient teaching.

Participants in this reform were John Brinsley and Charles Hoole. Brinsley's two books, *Ludus Literarius* published in 1612 and *A Consolation for Our Grammar Schooles*, which appeared in 1622, promoted the use of the vernacular in the school and decried excessive punishment of children (Brinsley, 1612, 1943). His reforms included larger classes than were commonly found in schools, and in each of these he had helpers. These monitors were elected by the boys themselves. Brinsley's second book became vital in the establishment of education in colonial Virginia.

In 1660 Charles Hoole published a treatise similar to those of Brinsley entitled *A New Discovery of the Old Art of Teaching Schools; in Four Small Treatises* (Hoole, 1913). In it he mentions that those who were more able should help themselves by assisting their weaker fellow students.

Jan Amos Komenský, better known as Comenius, was born in Moravia in 1592. During his career as a student and teacher, he formulated a complete system of principles of education in the renowned volume, *Didactica Magna* (Keatinge, 1921, 1923), which he wrote while an exile in the Polish town of Leszna. He believed education should be a well-rounded training and should be available to all. He advocated the use of peer teaching. In *Didactica Magna* he wrote, 'The saying "He who teaches others, teaches himself," is very true, not only because constant repetition impresses a fact indelibly on the mind, but because the process of teaching in itself gives a deeper insight into any subject taught' (Keatinge, 1923). Comenius's reforms were not adopted during his time and his influence was not felt until the nineteenth century.

The seventeenth century also witnessed educational reform in France. The Oratorians established a school system that was very modern in outlook. The curriculum emphasized the vernacular, history, mathematics and science. Originally intended for candidates for the priesthood, the schools of the Oratorians extended secondary education for other classes of boys and young men.

Although antagonism existed between the Jesuits, whose system was based on memorization, and Oratorians, both orders used peer teaching. Each class had a monitor who collected the work of the students and, within limits, heard lessons (Barnard, 1922).

A major movement promoting popular education in France was undertaken by Jean Baptiste de la Salle, born in 1651. He became active with a free school at Rheims, one designated for the poor. Eventually the Institute of Christian Brothers was established through his influence. Their purpose was to make good Catholics of the children of the poorer classes. He instituted what became known as the simultaneous methods, which divided students into classes rather than instructing each student individually. In addition, these schools used monitors to teach younger pupils (Good, 1947; Adamson, 1905). La Salle's pedagogical work, *Conduite des 'Ecoles*, was published in 1720, a year after his death.

Toward the end of the seventeenth century, new efforts at reform were made in France. One of the leaders in this movement was Charles Rollin, born in 1661. Rollin instituted major reforms in the curriculum, such as use of the vernacular in place of Latin. Educational historians maintain that Rollin advocated the use of peer teaching, although there is scarce mention of it in his *Traité des Etudes*, a four-volume work on French education (Rollin, 1810).

Little evidence is to be found of educational innovation in American colonies during the seventeenth century. However, the Reverend John Barnard, born in 1681 in Massachusetts, wrote of an unnamed school mistress who appointed him to teach other children, both older and younger than he. He later commented that this unnamed school mistress used the monitorial system long before it became immensely popular in the nineteenth century, both in England and the United States (Barnard, 1836).

## THE EIGHTEENTH CENTURY AND EDUCATIONAL TRANSITION TO THE NINETEENTH CENTURY

The eighteenth-century concepts of the natural rights of the individual, of life, liberty, and the pursuit of happiness, arose in direct opposition to autocratic conditions effected by both church and state. These attitudes eventually led to the revolutions that changed the face of governments, particularly in France and America. New theories of education surfaced; schools were to be maintained by civilians, not churchmen, and they were to promote societal interests. Educators advanced new concepts of health and physical education, the need for students to think for themselves, the value of practical arts. These new concepts and theories were not well received and only a few schools, directed by innovators, adopted the enlightened viewpoints. During this era, peer teaching was used only in France and England.

Educational efforts in eighteenth-century England were carried out by individuals and occasionally assisted by church support or voluntary organizations. Charity schools for the poor became prevalent, and these provided a basic education. Unfortunately these schools reached only a small proportion of the poor. Sunday schools were later added with the aim of reaching those children who worked during the week or lived in the streets daily. They were the first attempt to establish mass education that could adjust to the needs of a changing society. These schools, however, did not utilize peer teaching until the nineteenth century. Peer teaching was evidenced only in isolated incidents.

Eighteenth-century English educators David Williams and David Manson used innovative educational ideas in their schools. These were populated by the well-to-do, and because high tuition fees were charged, Williams and Manson could experiment with educational reforms (Stewart and McCann, 1967). One of the unorthodox methods Williams tried was the use of 'reciprocal assistances'. This experiment began as a means to aid a physically disabled student, but Williams was interested to see how quickly the boy learned. Williams' school only functioned for two years and there is little evidence that he influenced English education to any great degree.

David Manson started an evening school in Belfast in 1762. His daily school routine combined amusement with lessons and he established a system of self-government for his students. In addition, children recited their lessons under the supervision of monitors (Stewart and McCann, 1967). His school continued until he died in 1792. Neither Williams nor Manson brought about any kind of reform during their time, nor did they influence educational thought to any extent.

The Ackworth School, established by the Friends Society in 1779, employed an apprenticeship system whereby boys in their teens taught many of the elementary subjects (Stewart, 1953). Apprentices in the Quaker schools were widespread until the middle of the nineteenth century.

In France, several individual teachers used peer teaching, such as a Madame de Maintenon, the second wife of Louis XIV. She established a school for poor girls and introduced a monitorial system. A Frenchman named Herbault and a knight named Paulet are also named in educational history as practitioners of peer teaching. Neither, however, influenced his contemporaries any more than did the English educators of that time.

There is no record of peer teaching taking place in North America at this time. Only in the first half of the nineteenth century did peer teaching see widespread use in that part of the Western Hemisphere.

Rather than being an era of significant educational innovation, the eighteenth century served as a transition to educational reform in the nineteenth century. In England there existed much social and political unrest. Due to this condition, education remained highly undeveloped and riddled with controversy. The onset of the Industrial Revolution caused an influx of peasants to the cities and eventually created a wage-earning class. However, the conditions of the poor in England were appalling. Those in the higher social classes feared that educating the poor meant upsetting the social structure and therefore resisted the idea. Education was the right of the well-to-do, while the working-class children were limited to a bare minimum of schooling. Charity schools continued to grow. By 1802 the state intervened by dictating that factory owners were to provide basic instruction and ensure religious teaching for an hour every Sunday. Private schools flourished, as did the grammar schools in which the classics remained the basic curriculum. The monitorial concept had little acceptance in these schools, which were the domain of the privileged class. A shortage of teachers and lack of funds in the elementary educational system for the working class led to a widespread adoption of peer teaching.

In the United States little interest in education existed before 1820. Mostly church and private schools, together with a few educational efforts on behalf of the poor existed at that time. Here, as in England, education of the masses was considered dangerous. In time, however, the idea that education was in the best interests of the nation prevailed and caused a movement in which the average person exercised more control over educational efforts and ideas. However, the social-class structure continued to influence education even into the nineteenth century. The elementary school, where lessons were taught in the vernacular, served the lower classes while the Latin secondary school was for the upper classes. As the influence of democracy and nationalism increased, arguments for widespread schooling that would prevent poverty, diminish crime and become the natural right of each individual, became prevalent. Peer teaching was adopted as an economical means of expanding the educational system of the nineteenth century.

Of all the countries on the European continent, France showed the most interest in peer teaching during the eighteenth century. The French Revolution precipitated a rise in education for the masses—in universal education—although reforms were delayed due to the chaotic post-Revolution condition. Only during the Restoration were monitorial schools established for the education of the public.

During the first half of the nineteenth century, great efforts to promote education among the lower classes took place in England. The French Revolution had caused much alarm, and the nobility felt the vulnerability of their position. The upper classes wished to educate the lower classes in order to promote intelligence and reverence for status in the social classes.

In France, however, many saw education of the poor as a distinct danger, believing that the aim of education should be to influence proper behaviour without raising individuals' aspirations beyond their appropriate level in society.

Two opposing views surfaced at this time. One view was that education should be given as required for religious purposes. Traditional social values would be safeguarded if the children of the poor had a godly and religious upbringing. On the other hand, utilitarianism, a dominant, influential philosophical view, maintained that education was to be free of religious teaching and should be conducted for social and political ends. As a result of these influences, education of the masses became a popular cause. Problems beset efforts to educate the vast numbers of poor children, and due to the influence of the industrial era, a type of peer teaching became the most effective way to solve the problems of insufficient funds and lack of interest on the part of the state.

## LANCASTER AND BELL: THE MONITORIAL SYSTEM

The most visible educator of that era was born in England in 1778. Joseph Lancaster began a school for poor children in 1798 but soon outgrew his quarters. He had many excellent qualities of a great teacher, such as enthusiasm and ingenuity (Salmon, 1932). Because he was too indigent himself to pay for assistants, the idea occurred to him that the boys who knew a little could teach those who knew less. He published his ideas in a volume called *Improvements*: by the third edition of this book (Lancaster, 1973), he had evolved a new type of teaching and school management. This novel educational plan attracted much attention, and his fame grew, even to the point of attracting the attention of King George III.

At the heart of Lancaster's system was the monitor. The school was actually conducted by the pupils. The older students were instructed by the master, and they in turn drilled the younger or less-learned pupils. The school was arranged in classes with a monitor appointed to each class who was responsible for cleanliness, order and improvement of each student's learning. A visitor to one of Lancaster's schools would witness an orderly spectacle accompanied by the noise of work emanating from several hundred students in one large room. However, one of Lancaster's educational techniques was discipline, and the students could be called to order by a mere command. Lancaster abhorred corporal punishment, so popular in schools at that time, and he had an elaborate system of fitting punishments that suited the crime, coupled with a reward system for commendable behaviours.

Although Lancaster was a respected teacher and innovator in educational methods, he lacked in financial management skills. Friends and proponents of his educational system frequently had to come to his aid and bail him out of financial difficulties. In time, a society was formed by Joseph Fox, a surgeon-dentist, and William Corston, a Moravian hat maker. They were joined by others and this group became the trustees of the Royal Lancasterian Institution for Promoting the Education of the Children of the Poor. In 1813 the name was changed to the British and Foreign School Society, partly as a reaction to Lancaster's excesses both in his actions in calling attention to himself and his lack of responsibility in handling finances. The Society dissociated itself from Lancaster but continued to establish schools under the monitorial system. By 1839 the Society declared that it was not bound by Lancaster's methods and eventually abandoned them altogether.

Andrew Bell was another leading British educator. Born in 1753 in Scotland, he decided to try to make a name for himself in India, then a British colony. He became superintendent of the Military Male Asylum at Madras, a charity school and asylum for children of British soldiers and native wives. He experimented with novel teaching techniques but was met by opposition from his four teachers. Since they would not adopt his methods, he selected an eight-year-old, John Frisken, who accomplished his tasks to the satisfaction of Dr Bell. Later Bell dismissed the teachers and relied on boy instructors, thereby adding peer teaching to his system of education at the Military Male Asylum at Madras. The system became popular and the government approved of it as an economical way to teach in other schools.

Bell returned to England in 1794 and wrote *An Experiment in Education, made at the Male Asylum, Madras; suggesting a System by which a School or Family may Teach itself under the Superintendence of the Master or Parent* ('Bell and Lancaster's System of Education,' 1811). The book went through four editions, each increased in length, and discussed Bell's system of tutors and pupils, with one teacher in charge. Ushers and sub-ushers were in charge of the organization of the school. His system rested on the basic principle of scholars teaching each other and, therefore, themselves. He stressed the economy of his system as well as its effectiveness in teaching large numbers of students at one time.

In 1804 Lancaster wrote to Bell to invite discussion of their educational views. At first their exchanges were cordial, and would have remained so had it not been for a Mrs Sarah Trimmer. She was an active promoter of Sunday schools, editor of the magazine, *The Guardian of Education*, and author of several children's books. The fact that Lancaster had expressed his wish that every poor child should read the Bible, but that he did not teach any particular creed, alarmed Mrs Trimmer. The ensuing controversy, precipitated by Mrs Trimmer, actually represented a struggle between the Church of England and the Nonconformists to control the educational system of England (Jarman, 1952). Lancaster was a Quaker, while Bell was an ordained Anglican minister. Mrs Trimmer approved of the fact that Lancaster's system could be applied to religious education, but criticized the fact that he required his students to attend church only on Sunday. She felt religious education should be prevalent in the charity schools.

Mrs Trimmer began to correspond with Bell, stating that he should declare himself founder of the monitorial system, arguing that he would be unfaithful to his church if he did not do so. Subsequently both men claimed to have invented the monitorial system. This issue became one of public interest due to Mrs Trimmer's efforts, particularly when she published *A Comparative View of the New Plan of Education* in 1805 (Trimmer, 1805) in which she discussed the merits of both plans but expressing strong views in favour of Bell's system.

The controversy grew, and eventually involved the Anglican church and political parties in England at that time. At the height of the dispute, Mrs Trimmer died, but the controversy had grown to such proportions that her death had no impact on it. A Cambridge professor, Dr Herbert Marsh, began a movement to establish a society which would oppose the work of Lancaster, particularly his unsectarianism. The National Society was formed and was successful in increasing educational opportunities for poor children.

The basic concepts of the monitorial system were adopted in many parts of the British Isles. Jeremy Bentham, a utilitarian philosoper born in 1748, wrote a volume call *Chrestomathia* (Bentham, 1962) in which he lauded the new instructional system of Lancaster and Bell. His ideas of management of the school reflected those of the industrial revolution—economy and efficiency.

Another individual who admired the monitorial system was Robert Owen, Head of the New Lanark Mills in Scotland. He praised the system and saw it as a way to increase public acceptance of his own educational theories, which included limiting working days and not employing children under the age of ten. Eventually he abandoned the monitorial system, calling it a mockery of learning (Stewart and McCann, 1967). Why this change in his thinking took place is not clear, but it is conjectured that he had become acquainted with the ideas of the Swiss educator Pestalozzi. His action coincided with a time when the defects of the monitorial system were beginning to be noticed.

Schools for children of the poor were not the only ones which used peer teaching in the early nineteenth century. Hazelwood School, attended by middle-class sons of successful industrialists, used students as instructors. Although the principles of Lancaster and Bell had some influence, these were used with caution. The educators at Hazelwood, however, did not attempt to gain a group of followers for their system, which appeared to have combined some of the monitorial principles with innovations of their own regarding peer teaching. The latter included discipline administered by students themselves and required monitors not to teach but merely to 'hear' lessons. Although Hazelwood School was probably one of the finest systems of the time, no one emulated it (Stewart and McCann, 1967).

The use of the monitorial system spread throughout the British Isles. In places the principles were adhered to entirely, and seen as the panacea for educating the poor, whilst elsewhere the principles were modified. Naturally, a system as popular and widespread as the monitorial system received much study and criticism, but it cannot be denied that it influenced educational efforts for the poor and made significant inroads against illiteracy.

In 1839 the first Committee of the Privy Council for Education was established for the purpose of studying all education available to the people. The first secretary of this committee was Dr James Kay-Shuttleworth, who conducted an extensive study of schools in England as well as on the continent. He decried the use of the monitorial system because of the poor standards of educational achievement under this method. He put into practice some reforms which he advocated including a pupil–teacher system patterned after educational practice in Holland. He selected monitors carefully and apprenticed them to schoolmasters; through this means these student teachers would be trained in a systematic way and would avoid the rote-learning methods of the monitorial system (Stewart and McCann, 1967). These students were older, ranging from ages 14 to 30. Kay-Shuttleworth established his own training school, Battersea Training College, in 1840. The pupil–teacher system was a temporary method designed to bridge the gap between the monitorial method and the training of adult teachers (Barnard, 1949).

Toward the middle of the century, the defects of the system had become more obvious to educators of the time. In an analysis of Lancaster's and Bell's methods and the criticism they received during this period, Evans stated that little worthwhile education was taking place, denominational rivalry was increasing, and low standards were being set for elementary education, as reflected by the large classes and narrow educational ideas (Evans, 1975).

By the late nineteenth century the monitorial system had been largely abandoned because the working class, as it achieved rights such as the privilege of voting, became dissatisfied with the shallowness of the education provided by the system. In the final analysis, however, the monitorial system made schooling available to the poor at a time when they would have had none, and thereby contributed to the idea that education is a fundamental right.

During the nineteenth century the state gradually began to assume control over education, which became a means for promoting literacy and citizenship. In addition, nationalism gained strength and education was increasingly employed for the promotion of patriotism. It came to be considered the foundation on which the welfare of the common people would be developed.

## DEVELOPMENTS ON THE CONTINENT IN THE NINETEENTH CENTURY

In European countries on the continent the demand for education was satisfied largely by the monitorial system. By 1831 the monitorial system was in use in Belgium, Denmark, Sweden, Norway, Russia and parts of Italy, and the system was later adopted in Spain as well. Much of this spread of the system can be attributed to the efforts of the British and Foreign School Society, the reports of which mention schools in Haiti, Jamaica, Egypt, Malta, Ceylon, India, Australia, the Bahamas, and Africa.

Parts of Europe, however, could claim the use of peer teaching prior to the advent of the monitorial system. Switzerland had used peer teaching before the turn of the century and in Holland the use of pupil-teachers later influenced similar educational methods adopted in England.

Peer teaching had been used in France prior to the Lancasterian influence, which reached that country in the second decade of the nineteenth century. In 1792 'moniteurs' were advocated in public instruction, and this enabled one teacher to teach four classes simultaneously. By 1814 major efforts were made in France on behalf of the adoption of mutual instruction. Because the state had spent its funds on war, none was left for education, yet the training of the child became a prominent issue. Four members of the Society for the Encouragement of National Industry were sent to England to investigate the monitorial system. Upon their return, they resolved to begin a new society which would advance the education of the lower classes. In June of 1815 a new school opened under the direction of the Reverend Francis Martin. The method thrived and by the following year there were 80 monitorial schools in France (Karaczan, 1819).

Not long after, however, the same type of controversy as had occurred in England over monitorial instruction began in France over what was called 'mutual instruction'. The change in terminology was an effort to dissociate it with the monitorial system which was seen as a foreign element. The clergy opposed the method, perhaps because of the prevalence of Protestant teachers. These teachers were dismissed and the method of simultaneous instruction used by the Christian Brothers, a Catholic order, was adopted. Both methods of instruction were used, and mutual instruction had much influence in the establishment of mass education in France (Salmon, 1910).

In the last decade of the eighteenth century, Switzerland was a land ruled and occupied by France. Several of the Swiss cantons fought the French armies, resulting in much slaughter and devastation among the Swiss people. Many children were orphaned, and Johann Heinrich Pestalozzi was sent by the French government to establish a school for these children. He had no assistant, yet had 80 children under his care, so he trained child-helpers: children taught children, he reported in *How Gertrude Teaches Her Children* (Pestalozzi, 1915). He differed from Lancaster and Bell, however, in that he awakened in children an awareness of their own capabilities and mental powers, and shunned the drill methods used by the monitorial system. Pestalozzi's school lasted less than a year and there is no further evidence that he used peer teaching.

Another Swiss, Jean-Baptiste Girard, proposed a plan for national education, and sought to begin by establishing a primary school for vagrant children made homeless by the war. He was later called the founder of mutual instruction in Switzerland, and did not hear of Bell or Lancaster until 1815; subsequently his educational methods were an adaptation of the monitorial system combined with practices of Pestalozzi (Pollard, 1957).

Actual monitorial schools were established in Switzerland as late as 1854, when an American visitor, Henry Barnard, reported that monitors were chosen from the advanced pupils when teachers were not available (Barnard, 1949).

The Scandinavian countries were decidedly influenced by the French Revolution and its ideals of the rights of the average citizen. In particular there was an awakening of interest in education.

In Denmark a committee was appointed to reorganize the school system. By 1816 the monitorial system had aroused an interest and a young officer, Captain Josef Nicolai Abrahamson, who had become acquainted with the method of mutual instruction while serving in France, received permission to establish a model school in Copenhagen (Barnard, 1872). The monitorial system spread until 2814 schools were established by 1823, and it was used until the middle of the century.

Educational reform took place in Sweden after 1800 and was largely the result of the introduction of the monitorial system into Denmark (Cubberley, 1920). It was officially recognized by royal decree in 1824, and by 1841 approximately five hundred schools used the method. After 1842, when a law made support of schools obligatory by local municipalities, education became a national concern and the use of monitors declined.

In Norway the monitorial system also enjoyed a certain amount of popularity; it was recognized as an inexpensive way to educate children of the poor (Pollard, 1957).

The monitorial system had been tried and rejected in Holland, where educators thought the system was deficient in application to moral and intelligent beings (Cousin, 1838). Instead, Holland utilized a pupil-teacher system, which England eventually copied. Students served as apprentices, receiving instruction for an hour each evening, and they in turn taught the other students. However, these pupil-teachers were carefully supervised and were paid as well.

The German states established an educational system based on the ideas of Pestalozzi. The monitorial system was experimented with but did not take hold (Horner, 1838); nevertheless, reports exist that monitors or helpers were used as assistants to the teacher (Seeley, 1896).

The monitorial system became popular in Russia because of the interest Alexander I showed in the method: he commissioned Joseph Hamel to report on the monitorial system in England. Subsequently, four young men were sent to England for training. The Lancasterian method served as a catalyst for opposing views on education in Russia. Some felt that educating the masses was dangerous while others believed it was a means of achieving social and economic progress. At the death of Alexander I, Nicholas I became Emperor of Russia and under him educational efforts increased, using the monitorial system. By the 1820s, however, monitorial schools declined, not because of disenchantment with the system but because of political reasons and activities (Zacek, 1967).

Reports of the use of the monitorial system in Greece, Spain, and Italy can also be found, but these were not significant in the development of educational opportunities in these countries.

## PEER TEACHING IN NORTH AMERICA IN THE NINETEENTH CENTURY

In the United States, a growth of communication and transportation resulted in a desire among the working class for better social conditions. Labourers began to unite in demanding more rights for the working class, and education was often seen as a remedy for social evils and inequality. The great majority of children received virtually no schooling at the beginning of the nineteenth century. Not until the second half of the nineteenth century did public support, free universal education, government control and support, and the training of teachers take place.

The Lancasterian system of education was introduced into the United States mostly through humanitarian agencies such as free-school societies. Enthusiam for the monitorial system was engendered by anxieties about changing social conditions. While economic factors favoured the Lancasterian system, its effectiveness was also attractive. Because humanitarians were mainly interested in providing an education for the poor, the schools were considered pauper schools. Financial support came from societies established by humanitarians as well as state and city appropriations, and in this way, control could be achieved over the kind and amount of education given to the lower classes.

The Lancasterian system came to the attention of Americans through visits by philanthropists to England, representatives from the British and Foreign School Society, publications from England, trained teachers migrating to the United States, and by Lancaster's own presence. There was no question about which monitorial system to adopt. In a country where freedom in religion reigned, Dr Bell and the National Society were not favoured. Features of the plan were similar to those used in English schools, although some adaptation to American conditions took place, such as the use of books rather than cards from which children read.

By the time Lancaster came to the United States in 1818, he found that his methods had preceded him. At first he was received with great honour and he lectured widely, but he soon discovered that he was not indispensable to the Lancasterian movement. He settled in Baltimore and established the Lancasterian Institute, wanting it to be a perfect model for the system of education. He travelled quite widely from there, promoting his system and searching for the recognition that seemed to elude him. In 1838 he died in New York, having been run over by a horse and carriage. His direct influence was not significant in the United States, but the adoption of his methods, with modifications, led to the eventual establishment of free public education for all.

In 1805, New York was the largest city in the United States, yet the state of education was dismal, with only five charity schools for children of specific religious denominations. New York was not unique, because at the beginning of the nineteenth century educational opportunities were universally inadequate.

The earliest school society was organized in 1805, the New York Free School Society (Eggertsen, 1939). A school was established the following year and due to limited funds, the society introduced the monitorial system. The system also appealed to the society because many of the founders were Quakers, therefore, the methods of a fellow Quaker in London (Lancaster) favourably impressed them; in addition, the trustees of the society felt the system was specially adapted to the necessities of the masses of society. Mayor DeWitt Clinton, speaking at the opening of a new building of the free school, said, 'The system operates with the same efficacy in education as labour-saving machinery does in the useful arts' (Palmer, 1905).

In 1826 the Free School Society changed its name to the Public School Society of New York, which became the basis for free public education in the city. The monitorial system was used in these schools until about 1850, when the New York

City Board of Education was created. At that point the monitorial system was designated a failure because of the lack of practical results in terms of learning and because there was no foundation of sound, tested theory. However, the organization and discipline of the system were lauded.

John Griscom, a prominent New Yorker, visited Europe in 1818–1819 and returned to write a two-volume work called *A Year in Europe*. In it he discussed the various types of schools, including the monitorial methods. He determined to establish a school patterned after the High School of Edinburgh, which had impressed him in the use of the monitorial system. In 1825 he opened the New York High School, and the following year a school for girls was also established. Although a strong advocate of the monitorial system, he used it with discretion. The New York High School was considered eminently successful in its day.

The monitorial school system was adopted in Pennsylvania as well. The reasons stated were the economy, orderliness and flexibility of the Lancasterian methods (McCadden, 1969). The School Law of 1818 prescribed the use of the monitorial system. Although its use waned by the middle of the century, it had played a vital role in popularizing public education.

The Philadelphia Association of Friends for the Instruction of Poor Children, incorporated in 1807 in Philadelphia, established the first school in Pennsylvania, the Adelphi School, which adopted the monitorial system. Other schools opened which were based on that system and flourished until the 1820s. After 1826, when an act was passed which established free public instruction through Pennsylvania, the Lancasterian method declined in popularity and use.

Private teachers introduced the system in Baltimore, Maryland, one of the first being Robert Ould, a monitor under Lancaster. Lancaster himself came to that city in 1820 and established a Lancasterian Institute which continued to function until 1824. The monitorial system was not widespread in Maryland and its use was largely confined to Baltimore.

The Lancasterian method never saw much success in Boston or the rest of New England. Lancaster visited Boston and ran foul of the school leadership by criticizing their system. He had one major proponent of his system, however. William Bentley Fowle tried to convince the Boston school committee to set up Lancasterian Schools.

In 1821 Fowle was elected to the Primary School Committee, which worked to establish schools for children too ignorant for the grammar schools. Because of lack of funds, the monitorial system was adopted. The school admitted girls for the entire year, instead of just part of the school term, as had been the generally accepted practice, and in 1823 Fowle established the Female Monitorial School, which was greatly successful. He defended the use of the monitorial system, stating that children were not required to teach anything of which they were ignorant, and that the master reviewed the students often enough to ensure that the monitors were teaching successfully. He said that monitors were assistants, not substitutes for teachers (Fowle, 1847; William Bentley Fowle, 1861).

Discussion of the merits of the monitorial system and whether or not it should be used in the public schools of Boston continued throughout the late 1820s and into the 1830s, in the newspapers and in public debate. In 1831 the school committee voted to conduct all Boston schools according to the monitorial system, but by the end of two years it was declared a failure. Fowle's Female Monitorial School continued until 1840, when he resigned because of ill health. He continued to be a proponent of the system, and published a collection of his lectures. *The Teacher's Institute* (Fowle, 1847). He extolled the advantages of the system, but the concept never caught on in the rest of New England with the exception of two monitorial schools in New Haven and Hartford, Connecticut, which were established by disciples of Lancaster.

By the time Lancaster arrived in the United States in 1818, there were more than 150 monitorial schools located as far west as Cincinnati, Detroit and New Orleans. Educators and proponents of public education listed the advantages as: every child usefully occupied at every moment, rapid learning, lessening of distinctions in societal class, and economical to operate.

Among the southern states, Virginia was the most prominent in the use of the system, perhaps because Lancaster lectured widely in that area. By the 1830s, other parts of the South had established monitorial schools, including Tennessee, Kentucky, Mississippi, and Georgia.

A popular educational concept such as the monitorial system inevitably received much coverage in the contemporary journals and newspapers. The system was both lauded and decried, and a review of the contemporary literature exemplifies the extent to which both sides verbalized their opinions. What cannot be denied is that the monitorial method was significant in paving the way for a universal public-school system in the United States, even though the methods themselves were discarded. The reasons for abandoning the system were a growing emphasis on professional teacher training, the extension of suffrage and the idea that all citizens had the right to serve in public office (and if people were to rule, they should rule well), and demands from the working class that they should receive equal treatment in the educational system.

The monitorial movement in England did not escape notice in Canada. As early as 1810, Lancasterian schools were established in Quebec and Nova Scotia. Lancaster arrived in Canada in 1829, wishing to establish a school there and make a name for himself. He was successful, and planned to stay in Montreal for some time. However, due to political reasons he left in 1833. By the late 1830s the monitorial system had fallen into disuse.

## PEER TEACHING IN LATIN AMERICA IN THE NINETEENTH CENTURY

The early nineteenth century in Latin America was a time of wars and independence. Common people began to have a voice in government and as a result demands for better education increased. The Lancasterian movement was promoted in Latin America by the British and Foreign School Society, who dispatched James Thompson as its representative. His progress throughout South America is recorded in *Letters on the Moral and Religious State of South America* (Thompson, 1827). He arrived in Buenos Aires, Argentina, in 1818 and established eight schools for boys, all conducted on the monitorial system. Before he left there in 1821, he also established a school for girls.

Thompson then moved on to Chile on the invitation of the government and established monitorial schools in Santiago. From there, individuals were sent to others parts of Chile to establish monitorial schools. From Chile Thompson went to Peru and successfully instituted the system, but political unrest hindered his progress. He journeyed through Columbia and Ecuador, establishing schools. At the end of his Latin American efforts, Thompson wrote that his principal intention had been to circulate the Holy Bible in the places where he worked and visited. After he left South America, Church intervention and a lack of trained monitors caused the decline of the system.

Lancaster visited Caracas in 1825, at the invitation of Bolivar. He established an institute there, but his influence and efforts appear to have accomplished little and he left disenchanted, claiming that Bolivar had not lived up to his side of the financial aspects of the invitation.

## TWENTIETH-CENTURY DEVELOPMENTS IN THEORY AND PRACTICE OF PEER TEACHING

From the latter part of the nineteenth century until the 1960s, no major figures or proponents of the technique appeared, and peer teaching received little notice, with one exception. Numerous writers mention the use of peer teaching in the rural schools of the United States. The one-room school depended heavily on older students teaching younger ones since the teacher could not manage all the educational experiences for the grades represented in any particular school.

In 1917 a handbook, *Teaching in Rural Schools*, discussed the use of older pupils as teachers' assistants (Woofter, 1917). Peer teaching in the rural schools began to receive attention in educational literature after the 1930s. Tyler (1975) indicated that the one-room school depended heavily upon cross-age teaching since one teacher could not manage all the learning levels alone. Thelen (1969) stated that learning in the one-room school took place consistently, even if only by students eavesdropping on each other's recitations. Martin (1972) wrote that children learned to lead, direct, follow and ask in relationships that were natural to them.

An experiment with student tutors took place in Ohio, when Horst used students to give their peers help in various school subjects. He felt that tutoring allowed students to develop a sense of responsibility (Horst, 1931). A few years later, David (1938) wrote about another student-tutoring program in a Cleveland,

Ohio high school; She maintained that 77.4% of pupils raised their grade or kept it from being lowered. While teaching, she claimed, students also learn for themselves.

In 1956 Wayne wrote of a program at Fresno State College for future business teachers. He said that the best way to learn something is to teach it, and listed four groups who benefited from tutoring: those doing the tutoring, those receiving it, the school, and the institution which would eventually hire the tutors (Wayne, 1956).

After 1960 peer teaching received more attention; the theory and rationale of peer teaching became the focus of many studies and scholarly articles.

Wright (1960) noted that peer teaching not only aided children's learning but promised to alleviate a shortage of trained teachers. However, the latter did not become a major issue as more educators saw the utility and feasibility of peer teaching.

Lippitt (1975) reported on cross-age tutoring programmes and made suggestions for implementing a similar programme. She also discussed possible pitfalls of cross-tutoring and reviewed other types of peer teaching programmes. Lippitt and Lohman (1965) reported on pilot projects carried out at the University of Michigan and they listed five aspects of the programme: (1) providing opportunities for cross-age interaction; (2) collaboration between teachers and students; (3) the fostering of peer-group attitudes which promote the value of cooperation; (4) training for the helper role; and (5) providing immediate help with learning. Lippitt and Lippitt (1968) wrote an update on cross-age teaching in which they noted the favourable results that younger students made gains in achievement because they were helped by older students, while older students provided the younger ones with a listener and companion. In addition, older students increased academic achievement as well and developed social skills.

Gartner, Kohler and Riessman wrote one of the first books on peer teaching in 1971. They reviewed programmes that had been used and outlined the mechanics of peer teaching. They stated that children learn more from teaching other children than they do in a traditional classroom setting with a teacher providing all the instruction. They also indicated that individualized instruction is a benefit of peer teaching.

Johnson and Johnson (1974) have written extensively on competition versus cooperation and have pointed to the benefits of cooperation as it is used in support of mutual learning. It develops respect for individual differences, teaches the ability to communicate, develops empathy, and minimizes failure. In particular, they have argued, peer tutors can sometimes communicate with children who do not respond well to adults and be more effective than teachers in transmitting knowledge.

Tyler (1975) found that the failure to use peer teaching was a major source of waste in schools. Children learning from each other contributed significantly to their intellectual achievement. Bloom (1976) stated that self-esteem was enhanced by favourable interaction with one's peers, and that this personal growth could be accomplished through peer teaching.

Allen (1976) wrote that peer teaching can contribute to the socialization of children and aid in the development of social skills. Melaragno (1976) listed five conclusions on the effectiveness of peer teaching: (1) many content areas can utilize peer teaching; (2) the more structured the peer teaching relations, the more favourable results are possible; (3) both participants in a peer teaching relationship show cognitive gains; (4) positive affective changes are noticeable; and (5) a tutoring programme can be established without great cost or difficulty.

In 1969 Thelen wrote that no other innovation has been so consistently successful, and stated that the tutor can develop his or her own academic skills or knowledge while teaching others. In addition, a better character and more positive attitudes can be formed.

Buckholdt and Wodarski summarized several studies on peer teaching and they concluded that through development of helping behaviours, student performance is increased. Peer teaching can reduce anxiety in pupil/teacher relationship, allow for more individualized instruction, cause a tutor to increase his own understanding as well as self-esteem and self-confidence, provide more motivation for learning, and reinforce previous learning (Buckholdt and Wodarski, 1978).

Good and Brophy (1978) wrote *Looking in Classrooms* and included a section on peer teaching. They established guidelines for the use of this method of teaching, stating that the teacher should be ultimately in charge by creating the appropriate mental set and by working out the details of the interaction.

## CONCLUSION

After studying educational history one can readily agree with an old German proverb, 'What is new is seldom true; what is true is seldom new.' Sometimes 'new' ideas in education are actually 'old' ideas in new guises, and this is indeed so in the practice of peer teaching. Some of its advantages, as claimed by past educators, are being supported by recent academic research, as witnessed by other chapters in this book. There may be academic benefits for tutors and tutees, as well as positive changes in learning-related attitudes and behaviours. Research can also highlight problems in implementing cooperative learning methods, and point the way to interventions aimed at ensuring success.

This historical review has highlighted the fact that the utilization of peer teaching methods is driven by a mixture of idealistic and pragmatic forces. For example, at a time when many researchers and practitioners are advocating its use because of the benefits which can accrue to the individual child, Jamaica today provides an instance of its use as a crisis-management technique to cope with teacher/pupil ratios of 1 : 60 (Shute, personal communication). It is also interesting to note how peer teaching methods introduced for practical reasons can have unexpected advantages, as in the case of Williams' disabled student in the eighteenth century (a historical precursor of the use of peer education methods for disadvantaged students today). Within an historical context, the importance of society at large also becomes apparent: peer methods have come and gone not only because they have succeeded or failed within particular narrow educational contexts, but because they have served, or failed to serve, the prevailing political forces of the day.

## REFERENCES

Adamson, J. W. (1905). *Pioneers of Modern Education, 1600–1700*. London: Cambridge University Press.

Allen, V. L. (ed.) (1976). *Children as Teachers: Theory and Research on Tutoring*. New York: Academic Press.

Barnard, H. (1854). *National Education in Europe*. 2nd edn. New York: Charles B. Norton.

Barnard, H. (1872). *National Education: Systems, Institutions, and Statistics of Public Instruction in Different Countries*. 2 vols. New York: E. Steiger.

Barnard, H. C. (1922). *The French Tradition in Education*. London: Cambridge University Press.

Barnard, H. C. (1949). *A Short History of English Education from 1760–1944*. London: University of London Press.

Barnard, J. (1836). *Autobiography of the Rev. John Barnard*. Collections of the Massachusetts Historical Society, 3rd Series, Vol. 5. Boston: John E. Eastburn.

Bell's and Lancaster's System of Education (1811). *Quarterly Review*, **6**, 264–304.

Bell, A. (1808). *The Madras School*. London: T. Bensley.

Bentham, J. (1962). 'Chrestomathia.' *Works of Jeremy Bentham*. Edited by J. Bowring, vol. 8. New York: Russell & Russell.

Bloom, B. S. (1976). *Human Characteristics and School Learning*. New York: McGraw-Hill.

Bonner, S. (1977). *Education in Ancient Rome*. London: Methuen.

Brinsley, J. (1612). *Ludus Literarius*. London: Thomas Man.

Brinsley, J. (1943). *A Consolation of our Grammar Schooles*. New York: Scholar's Facsimiles and Reprints.

Buckholdt, D. R., and Wodarski, J. S. (1978). The effects of different reinforcement systems on cooperative behaviors exhibited by children in classroom contexts, *Journal of Research and Development in Education*, **12**, 50–68.

Cousin, V. (1838). *On the State of Education in Holland*. Translated by L. Horner. London: John Murray.

Cubberley, E. P. (1920). *The History of Education*. Boston: Houghton Mifflin.

David, A. I. (1938). Student tutoring: a success at Collinwood High School, *Clearing House*, **12**, 288–89.

Eggertsen, C. A. (1939). The monitorial system of instruction in the United States, Doctoral dissertation, University of Minnesota.

Evans, K. (1975). *The Development and Structure of the English Educational System*. London: University of London Press.

Farrell, A. P. (1938). *The Jesuit Code of Liberal Education: Development and Scope of the Ratio Studiorium*. Milwaukee: Bruce Publishing.

Fowle, W. B. (1847). *The Teacher's Institute*. 2nd edn. Boston: William B. Fowle.
Gartner, A., Kohler, M. C., and Riessman, F. (1971). *Children Teach Children: Learning by Teaching*. New York: Harper & Row.
Gill, J. (1889). *Systems of Education*. Boston: D. C. Heath.
Good, H. G. (1947). *A History of Western Education*. New York: Macmillan.
Good, T. L., and Brophy, J. E. (1978) *Looking in Classrooms*. New York: Harper & Row.
Hoole, C. (1913). *A New Discovery of the Old Art of Teaching Schools; in Four Small Treatises*. Liverpool: The University Press.
Horner, L. (1838). Preliminary observations. Introduction to *On the State of Education in Holland*, by Victor Cousin. London: John Murray.
Horst, H. M. (1931). History of student tutoring at West High School, Akron, Ohio, *Clearing House*, **6**, 245–249.
Jarman, T. L. (1952). *Landmarks in the History of Education*. New York: Philosophical Library.
Johnson, D. W., and Johnson, R. T. (1974). Instructional goal structure: cooperative, competitive, or individualistic, *Review of Educational Research*, **44**, 213–240.
Karaczan, F. F. (1819) *Der Wechselseitige Unterricht nach der Bell-Lancasterschen Methode*. Kaschau, Germany: Otto Wigand, Buchhandler.
Keatinge, M. W. (1921). *The Great Didactic of John Amos Comenius*, part 1. London: A. & C. Black.
Keatinge, M. W. (1923). *The Great Didactic of John Amos Comenius*, part 2. London: A. & C. Black.
Kennedy, G. (1969). *Quintilian*. New York: Twayne Publishers.
Lancaster, J. (1973). *Improvements in Education as it Respects in Industrious Classes of the Community*. 3rd edn. Clifton: Augustus M. Kelley.
Life and Educational System of John Sturm (1857a). *American Journal of Education*, **4**, 167–182.
Life and Educational System of John Sturm (1857b). *American Journal of Education*, **4**, 400–415.
Lippitt, P. (1975). *Students Teach Students*. Bloomington, Inc.: Phi Delta Kappa Educational Foundation.
Lippitt, P., and Lippitt, R. (1968). Cross-age Helpers, *NEA Journal*, **57**, 24–26.
Lippitt, P., and Lohman, J. E. (1965). Cross-age relationships—an educational resource, *Children*, **12**, 113–117.
Martin, J. H. (1972). The grade school came from Prussia, *Educational Horizons*, **51**, 28–33.
McCadden, J. J. (1969). *Education in Pennsylvania, 1801–1835*. New York: Arno Press and The New York Times.
Melaragno, R. J. (1976). *Tutoring with Students*. Englewood Cliffs: N.J.: Educational Technology Publications.
Monitorial System (1831). *American Annals of Education*, **1**, 135–140.
Monitorial System (1861). *American Journal of Education*, **10**, 461–466.
Orme, N. (1973). *English Schools in the Middle Ages*. London: Methuen.
Palmer, A. E. (1905). *The New York Public School*. New York: Macmillan.
Pestalozzi, J. H. (1915). *How Gertrude Teachers Her Children*. Translated by L. E. Holland and F. C. Turner. London: George Allen & Unwin.
Pollard, H. M. (1957). *Pioneers of Popular Education, 1760–1850*. Cambridge, Mass.: Harvard University Press.
Quick, R. H. (1896). *Essays on Educational Reformers*. New York: D. Appleton.
Rollin, C. (1810). *The Method of Teaching and Studying the Belles Lettres*. London: W. Otridge and Son.
Salmon, D. (1904). *Joseph Lancaster*. London: Longmans, Green.

Salmon, D. (1910). The monitorial system in France, *Educational Review*, **40**, 30–47.
Salmon, D. (1932). *The Practical Parts of Lancaster's Improvements and Bell's Experiment*. London: Cambridge University Press.
Seaborne, M. (1971). *The English School: Its Architecture and Organization, 1370–1870*. Toronto: University of Toronto Press.
Seeley, L. (1896). *The Common-school System of Germany and Its Lessons to America*. New York: E. L. Kellogg.
Stewart, W. A. C. (1953). *Quakers and Education*. London: Epworth Press.
Stewart, W. A. C., and McCann, W. P. (1967). *The Educational Innovators, 1750–1880*. New York: St Martin's Press.
Thelen, H. A. (1969). Tutoring by students, *The School Review*, **77**, 229–243.
Thompson, J. (1827). *Letters on the Moral and Religious State of South America, Written During a Residence of Nearly Seven Years in Buenos Aires, Chile, Peru, and Colombia*. London: James Nisbet.
Trimmer, S. (1805). *A Comparative View of the New Plan of Education*. London: T. Bensley.
Tyler, R. (1975). Wasting time and resources in schools, *Viewpoints*, **52**, 59–73.
Valentine Friedland Trotzendorf (1858). *American Journal of Education*, **5**, 107–113.
Wayne, W. C. (1956). Tutoring service: a project for future business teachers, *The Journal of Business Teachers*, **31**, 330.
William Bentley Fowle (1861). *American Journal Education*, **10**, 597–610.
Williams, S. G. (1892). *The History of Modern Education*. Syracuse, NY: C. W. Bardeen.
Wise, J. (1964). *The History of Education*. New York: Sheed & Ward.
Woofter, T. J. (1917). *Teaching in Rural Schools*. Boston: Houghton Mifflin, 1917.
Wright, B. (1960). Should children teach? *The Elementary School Journal*, **60**, 353–369.
Zacek, J. C. (1967). The Lancasterian school movement in Russia, *The Slavonic and East European Review*, **45**, 343–367.

CHAPTER 3

# The Development of Individual Competencies Through Social Interaction

WILLEM DOISE

*Faculté de Psychologie et des Sciences de l'Education, Université de Genève, Case Postale 26, 1211 Genève, Switzerland*

## INTRODUCTION

As is well known, Durkheim (1902) describes two prototypes of society. One—the mechanical—is essentially characterized by its homogeneity, with individual states of consciousness being common to all members of a social segment, so that there can be no question of individual and collective consciousness coming into conflict. This is said to hold for societies which are highly fragmented into isolated segments with few interdependent links between them. Within the different segments, uniform beliefs and norms imposed by oppressive laws are the rule. By contrast, the society with organic solidarity is characterized by its variety, with different individuals having their own separate consciousness. Here, social organization is not highly fragmented and the various parts are strongly interdependent. Legal sanctions tend more to restitution than to punishment. Collective consciousness loses importance and morality becomes more rational and open to discussion, and is not seen to be transcendent since it is ultimately founded on the rights of the individual.

These ideas have operated in the manner of a grand theory, that is, they have highlighted general areas of research and have encouraged other investigators

Children Helping Children
Edited by H. C. Foot, M. J. Morgan and R. H. Shute

to describe more specific processes. A quotation from Piaget's (1932) book on *The Moral Judgment of the Child* demonstrates the persistent influence of Durkheim's famous dichotomy:

> As Durkheim himself has pointed out, one cannot explain the passage from the forced conformity of 'segmented' societies to the organic solidarity of differentiated societies without invoking the diminished supervision of the group over the individual as a fundamental psychological factor. The 'denser' the community, the sooner will the adolescent escape from the direct constraint of his relations and, coming under a number of fresh influences, acquire his spiritual independence by comparing them with one another. The more complex the society, the more autonomous is the personality and the more important are the relations of cooperation between equal individuals. (Piaget, 1932, p. 336).

In his book the Genevan psychologist places much emphasis on the difference between relations of constraint and relations of cooperation. I consider the distinction drawn by Piaget between constraint and cooperation to be a social-psychological version of Durkheim's theory. Relations of constraint hinder cognitive development. To quote Piaget again, from a paper first published in 1928 in a philosophical review, but re-published with his permission in 1976:

> In a society where the generations thus heavily weigh upon each other, none of the conditions required to eliminate childish mentality can be met. There is no discussion, no exchange of views. (Piaget, 1976a, p. 76).

Thus only social relations based on cooperation can lead to a liberation of rational thought:

> Cooperation opposes both autism and constraint. It progressively reduces autistic or egocentric processes of thought . . . . Discussion generates inner reflection. Mutual control generates the need for proof and objectivity. The exchange of thought implies adopting the principles of contradiction and identity as discourse regulators. As regards constraint, cooperation destroys it whenever differentiation and free discussion between individuals develop. (Piaget, 1976a, p. 77).

The present concern is not with finding out whether Piagetian 'primitive societies' really exist, nor with judging if there really are such important differences between 'primitive' and 'modern' societies. Rather, the purpose is to consider whether there really exist important causal links between patterns of social relations and the development of moral or cognitive competencies in the individual.

According to contemporary sociologists and psychologists such links do exist. Bernstein's (1973) distinction between elaborated and restricted speech styles implies differences in cognitive functioning—which does not mean differences in competencies—and these differences in functioning are related to differences in social relationships. The more the actors in a situation have characteristics in common, the more they share, in Durkheim's terms, mechanical solidarity, and the more they share meanings which need not be made explicit on every occasion. This results in a special 'restricted' discourse, one which cannot be understood outside the situation. Other kinds of situations may be characterized by differences between the actors: in these situations of more organic solidarity meanings must be made more explicit. The code in this case will be more 'universalist' or 'elaborated' so as to permit expression of the special experience of each individual.

Bernstein's theory is, in my view, a socio-psychological theory which acknowledges the coexistence in our society of patterns of mechanical and organic solidarity. His distinction between 'positional families' and 'person-oriented families' relates also to the more typological opposition of patterns but one can again conceive that both patterns co-exist to some extent in the same family. It is my opinion that such typological differences are only useful insofar as they clarify complex concrete situations in which the two types of relationships are in fact intimately intermingled.

The French psychologist Lautrey (1980) has also elaborated a typology of family environments, in this case based on a Piagetian cognitive concept:

> In contrast with both nativist and empiricist theories, interaction between individual and external environment is here conceived of as a confrontation between two organized structures. The individual integrates or 'assimiliates' the organisation of the environments into her/his own, which means that the structures ('schemata') available to her/him are thereby modified or 'accommodated'. The process of equilibration, the keystone of the theory, regulates the relationship between assimilation and accommodation. The existence of regularities in the environment is one of the elements of the interaction between individual and environment—and therefore of the process of equilibration. It is perhaps the most fundamental of the 'critical ingredients' for cognitive development which the environment can provide. (Lautrey, 1980, p. 62).

The nature of the regularities characteristic of a given social environment is a factor in the activation of the processes of accommodation and assimilation. Three kinds of regularity are distinguished by Lautrey, based on a questionnaire completed by parents. They relate to the structuring of rules which govern family life, and more especially the relations between parents and child in different domains. A weak structure is characterized by lack of stable, predictable rules such that the child cannot know, for example, whether watching TV is allowed or when it is bedtime. A flexible structure implies the existence of stable rules which may nevertheless be modified in a predictable way, as for example, when the child knows she/he must go to bed early because there is school next day but may go to bed later when the following day is a holiday. In families with a rigid structure, immutable rules control the child's behaviour. Lautrey found, in support of his hypotheses, that children in a family environment with flexible rules are ahead of children from the two other environments on a Piagetian cognitive test. However, one should note that the results also show greater effects as a function of the values the parents claimed to hold: children of parents who said they encouraged a critical attitude or curiosity achieved on average far better scores than children of parents who attached relatively more importance to politeness or obedience.

Though Lautrey (1980) does not refer directly to Durkheim, his research paradigm certainly deals with the causal effects of social organization on cognitive functioning. However, the present writer feels that there is too great a distance between what could be said to be his independent variable—the structure of social rules in the family—and performance on a particular cognitive task. There is no doubt that several other variables could intervene to account for these performances. Lautrey himself isolated a very important one when he studied the values subscribed to by the parents. Work by my research team has, therefore, tried to study the intervention of social marking, which will be presented in a later section of this chapter.

In conclusion let me reiterate that Durkheim's ideas have operated in the manner of a grand theory, that is, they have pointed to general areas of research which have allowed other investigators to describe more specific mechanisms. In order to explain cognitive development one needs to bring in the prior structuring of the social environment, which means the norms, representations, rules, or, to use more up-to-date concepts, the scenarios or scripts (Abelson, 1981; Nelson, 1981) which govern the social interactions in which children may participate. These are the kind of social regulations which guide the individual in the organization of her/his own actions on external reality. Peer interactions are also subject to such regulations often enforced through direct interventions of adults. This will certainly be the case in the experimental settings described below, but it is more generally true for most natural settings in which interactions between children are at least partially prestructured by adults and societal norms.

## SOCIAL REGULATIONS IN COGNITIVE OPERATIONS: GENERAL FRAMEWORK

The theoretical framework of the research to be summarized in this chapter is constructivist: it is while acting in and upon the environment that the individual develops. But further than that it is socioconstructivist: it is above all through interacting with others, coordinating his/her approaches to reality with those of others, that the individual masters new approaches. In line with authors as diverse as Bourdieu (1979, 1980), Piaget (1975), Staats (1976) and Trevarthen (1982), the individual is seen in this model as mastering schemas, regulations of actions, behavioural repertoires and motives which enable him or her to participate in social interactions. In the course of these interactions, individual principles of organization are integrated within complex social regulations which, under certain conditions, produce in these individuals capacities for more complex coordination. These new competencies then allow the individual to benefit from more complex social regulations and so on. Certainly, different authors invoke different processes, such as equilibration (Piaget), attitudinal and directional reinforcement (Staats), internalization (Bourdieu), cooperative understanding (Trevarthen), to account for these growing structures. The aim of this model is to integrate the descriptions of these processes within a more general socio-psychological conception of development.

This conception is based on the notion of a spiral of causality: a given state of the individual makes possible participation in certain social interactions which give rise to new individual states. Of course, at a certain level of generality it is arbitrary to begin the process with an individual state or a social interaction, since there is a continuous interaction between the two.

General as these ideas may be, they are not compatible with each and every specific proposition. Thus with respect to cognitive development they do not allow one to assume a positive effect of any social interaction at any point in individual development. Only those interactions which give rise to the union of clearly determined individual approaches will result in new regulations; individuals who have not mastered certain minimal schemas or organizations will not be able to profit from social interaction in the same manner as those who have such initial schemas at their disposal. This does not necessarily mean that an individual's progress will be manifested during the interaction itself as individual restructuring may extend far beyond the particular interaction.

By definition, this conception is concerned only with development: not all interaction is necessarily constructive and there may be destructive interactions. The heuristic value of the general conception sketched here can of course be tested only through its use in theoretical and empirical enquiry. Some of these empirical researches will now be briefly presented to illustrate three notions: *coordination of interdependent actions; socio-cognitive conflict; social marking.*

## COORDINATION OF INTERDEPENDENT ACTIONS

The general thesis is that cognitive operations are not just individual coordinations of actions, which are 'internalized, reversible . . . and coordinated into general structures' (Piaget, 1976b, p. 187) but that these coordinations are, to an important extent, social in nature. It is through the very coordination of these actions with those of others that the individual acquires mastery of systems of coordination which are subsequently individualized and internalized. One of the tasks my research team has used in order to illustrate this idea is basically a motor coordination task requiring that a central target connected by strings to a number of pulleys (one for each player) be moved along a predetermined route which has been divided into a number of segments. Scores are obtained by summing the number of segments in which the target remains correctly on the track and subtracting the number of segments where the target leaves the route. By manipulating the pulleys, each player can make one direct action (winding his/her string in moving the pulley towards him/her), and two indirect actions (keeping the string steady which prevents any forward or backward movement, and letting the string out, which allows the target to be moved away by pressure from another pulley). The game was developed especially for the investigation of interindividual coordination of these three actions on several pulleys, and it has the particular advantage that the problem posed by the task (i.e. moving the target along the prescribed track) can only be resolved when actions are intercoordinated on the various pulleys. As this coordination can be executed by one player operating more than one pulley at once as well as by several players each operating a single pulley, the game provides a suitable means of comparing collective performances with those of the individual participants before and after interaction.

In the first experiment using the game, Doise and Mugny (1975) compared the individual performances of younger children (7–8 years) and older children (9–10 years) with the collective performance of pairs in which each member handled only one pulley. As predicted, more advanced performances occurred in the interindividual interactions than with individuals performing the same task alone. The younger subjects performed significantly better in the collective situation than when alone, but this was not the case for the older subjects.

Using this paradigm, four experiments (Doise and Mugny, 1984, chapter 3) showed that developmentally more advanced responses appear in collective situations before individuals are capable of them. Superiority of group performance, however, occurs only with subjects who are just beginning to develop the particular skill being investigated here (i.e. coordination of the three actions). Later, at an age at which the skills first produced in the collective situation have been internalized by each individual, the interactive situation no longer produces superior performance (see Table 3.1).

Certain cognitive prerequisites are necessary for a given interaction to benefit the individual participants. In order that a given interaction can successfully integrate the activities of the interactants, some less advanced level of regulation must, of course, already exist. However, for individuals at a given state of development not all interactions lead to progress and we will see that socio-cognitive conflict and social marking are important conditions for generating individual progress through social interaction. But, more generally, some

TABLE 3.1. Individual and group progress (+) in relation to specific skills

| | Individual work | Group work |
|---|---|---|
| Prior to elaboration | ○ | ○ |
| During initial elaboration | ○ | + |
| After initial elaboration | + | + |

characteristics of social interactions can hinder such progress: for example, too great an asymmetry between the contributions of two partners, or a search for agreement through mere compliance. It is, therefore, not unexpected that some authors (for instance, Russell, 1982; Taal, 1985) have observed social interactions which do not result in significantly more progress than individual working sessions. Often, interventions by adults to enable children to share their decision making are necessary. An experiment by Glachan and Light (1982) illustrates the effects of such an intervention. Their experimental task used the Tower of Hanoi problem. The material consists of a baseboard with three vertical pegs and a number of square tiles with a hole in the centre. The tiles vary regularly in size and at the beginning of the session are placed on one of the pegs in seriated order, the largest at the bottom. The problem is to move all the tiles to another specified peg while using the spare peg and under the constraints that only one tile may be moved at a time, and that a larger tile may never be placed on top of a smaller one. The effects of different conditions with two children working together were compared; one of these conditions was a *structured interaction* condition in the sense that subjects were required to jointly move the tiles through the use of two handles. In an *unstructured* condition such a requirement of joint action was not made. Results show that subjects in the *structured* condition used more efficient strategies at an individual post-test and that they were able more often than subjects in the other condition to demonstrate transfer of their learning to other related problems.

In an as yet unpublished experiment with Hanselmann, Doise has recently compared the effects of two interaction conditions in the acquisition of conservation of volume (see Piaget, Inhelder and Szeminska, 1948, chapter 14). Basically children of about nine-and-a-half years had to construct a tower made from small cubes so that the volume of cubes would be kept the same as in a tower already constructed on a different surface. In order to succeed they had to compensate for differences in length and width by differences in height. In a *control* condition each child worked alone; in a *spontaneous* interaction condition two children interacted freely, and in a *directed* interaction condition two children were instructed to take turns in placing a cube in order to construct the new tower. The main experimental prediction was that the difference between the *directed* condition and the *control* condition would be bigger than the difference between the *spontaneous* and the *control* condition. Results reported in Table 3.2 show that the predicted order between the three conditions is significant.

## STRUCTURING EFFECTS OF SOCIO-CONFLICT

A recurring theme in Durkheim and Piaget is the necessity for confrontation between different points of view for promoting cognitive development on the societal as well as on the individual level. The research on socio-cognitive

TABLE 3.2. Frequencies of progress in conservation of volume after different experimental sessions (percentages between brackets)

| | Directed interaction | Spontaneous interaction | Control condition |
|---|---|---|---|
| Progress | 29(50) | 21(39) | 7(24) |
| No progress | 29(50) | 33(61) | 22(76) |

Jonckheere test, z: 2.179, $p$: <0.015, unilateral hypothesis.

conflict tries to study this effect experimentally. Socio-cognitive conflict is said to exist when, in one and the same situation, different cognitive approaches to the same problem are socially produced. Given appropriate conditions, the confrontation of these different approaches may result in their being coordinated into a new approach, more complex and better adapted to solving the problem in hand than any one of the previous approaches alone.

An example of this can be drawn from the classical studies on the conservation of equal lengths (Inhelder, Sinclair and Bovet, 1974). Five- to six-year-old children rightly think that two identical rods placed parallel to each other so that their extremities coincide perceptually are of equal lengths. But if this perceived equality is disturbed by sliding one of the rods a few centimetres along the other, the same children will declare that one of the rods is longer because, in evaluating the respective lengths, they centre their attention on only one projecting end of a road without taking into account that it is compensated by the projecting end of the other rod on the opposite side. In several experiments, Doise and Mugny (1984, chapter 5) have placed children who were non-conservers during an experimental phase in a situation of socio-cognitive conflict by contradicting them: when a child said that one of the rods was longer because it stuck out at one end, the experimenter or another child answered that the other rod was longer because it stuck out at the other end. This incorrect and opposed response was often sufficient to make children progress. Presented here is a summary of the main conclusions of these experiments.

First, many children who are confronted with an incorrect centration proposed by an adult or by another child adopt what is called a 'relational' solution to this conflict by saying that they agree with their contradictor. In this case, compliant responses prevail over innovating cognitive work; the children seem as unconcerned about the contradictory responses of others as they are about their own contradictions when one rod and then the other are shifted successively. Therefore, it was ensured that in situations of conflicting centrations both responses were kept in mind by having an associate experimenter remind the child of his/her initial answer whenever the child gave in to the experimenter. Under such an intensification of the socio-cognitive conflict, progress was consistently more often achieved than in another situation where the child was led to give a succession of incorrect and contradictory answers alone.

Furthermore, upon considering the results of a generalization test (using a test of conservation of unequal lengths), the condition of socio-cognitive conflict proved to be as efficient in generating progress as a 'modelling' condition in which the experimenter gave the correct answer and justified it by pointing to the compensations at the two opposite ends. Theoretically, the results obtained in the condition of socio-cognitive conflict cannot be explained by a modelling effect as the child is never provided with the correct answer; on the other hand, the modelling situation may be reduced to a situation of socio-cognitive conflict. Indeed, in giving the correct answer, the experimenter emphasizes the existence of the two opposite projections. The correct answer, therefore, does imply a socially activated conflict of centration.

The main conclusion that can be drawn from this experiment is as follows: having to keep one's own point of view in mind while being obliged to take into account another incompatible perspective can lead to progress. This is also true when the conflict occurs in a more spontaneous manner between two children.

In another series of experiments (Doise and Mugny, 1984, chapter 6) a paradigm of spatial transformation was re-used. A model-village of several houses arranged on a cardboard base by the experimenter had to be reproduced by the subjects on an identical base but with a different orientation. However, the children involved were not yet capable of the spatial transformations required to conserve the intrafigural relations (left/right and front/back) and, therefore, produced an 'egocentric' copy of the village.

Having found in a first experiment that a pair of children accomplished the correct transformations more easily than a child alone, a further series of about twenty experiments (see also De Paolis, Doise and Mugny, 1987) was carried out to elucidate the superiority of collective performances over individual ones. And, again the socially created obligation to consider another point of view, different from one's own, was revealed as an important source of progress.

Consider such an experiment in more detail. Figure 3.1 shows the layout of a situation used during the experimental phase. The subject in the difficult position must transform front/back and right/left spatial relations despite having been selected especially for inability to do so at a pre-test task. By contrast, the subject in the easy position has simply to rotate his/her visual plane by 90 degrees, something that most of the children in this age category are able to do.

If the subject in the easy position does not experience any difficulty, then it might seem likely that s/he will not make any progress at all. But progress should be made when confronted with another child who, being on the opposite side, is faced with a more complex cognitive problem, provided, however, that the child in the difficult position proposes incorrect solutions. Any misplacement of a village house should create a problem for the child in the easy position for whom the correct solution is quite obvious. Such a conflict may oblige that subject to take another point of view into account, to coordinate their differing

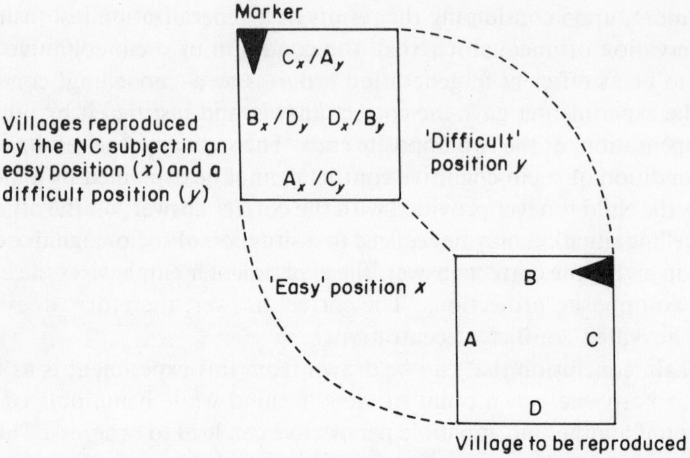


FIGURE 3.1. Positions of houses as placed by two equally non-conserving subjects, one working from a 'difficult' position, and the other from an 'easy' position

points of view and eventually to grasp the error committed by the other subject, and even to go as far as to convince the subject in the difficult position (who originated this socio-cognitive conflict) what the correct answer is. It is highly probable that the subject in the easy position will achieve cognitive progress from having dealt with this conflict.

This is the basic principle, but things do not always run as smoothly in practice. Experiments have given us further insight into the complex social dynamics which may take place between children and thwart the beneficial effects of socio-cognitive conflict. One major difficulty is due to the asymmetry generated by a dynamic of compliance, especially when one of the interacting members is overtly sure of his or her answers.

It had already been observed in an experiment with the same material (Doise and Mugny, 1984, chapter 6, experiment 2) that a highly asymmetric interaction between a subject who unhesitatingly adopted the correct solution and another who was not yet able to find it, very rarely ended in progress for the latter. The more advanced subject, being more confident, simply imposed his solution without even considering the solution offered by the other, and there was no real confrontation of views.

Such an asymmetric situation also exists in the 'easy/difficult' version of the paradigm: there is an obvious solution for the 'easy' subject, not for the 'difficult' subject. To overcome this problem, the 'difficult' subject must be given a chance to defend his or her point of view. This can be done by bringing a social support into the situation.

In the experimental situation presumed to be the most propitious for the emergence of a socio-cognitive conflict, one 'easy' subject is confronted with two 'difficult' subjects, hoping that the latter will lend each other support in maintaining their initial centrations. In another experimental condition, only one 'difficult' subject will be opposed by one 'easy' subject.

The results confirmed the expected differences between the two situations: in the case where the 'easy' subjects were opposed more flagrantly to an incorrect solution (i.e. by two 'difficult' subjects), their progress on a post-test which placed them in a difficult position was definitely more marked.

These results were confirmed with other experiments. Their purpose was to show that someone who already knows the correct answer can nevertheless learn from someone who, seeing the problem from a different angle, offers incorrect answers. In order to control these responses even further and to stress their impact, an adult collaborator was placed in the difficult position with the instruction systematically to offer incorrect solutions; or, in another experiment, the child who had not yet mastered the transformations required in this difficult position had to execute the task before the child in the easy position was allowed to step in. In every instance, approximately half of the children progressed after having been confronted with such a clear-cut opposition to their own centration. More discriminating analyses again revealed the presence of two types of interaction: one, dominated by compliance, where the child simply applies the solution the other person proposes and so does not progress; the other, over which socio-cognitive conflict prevails, where the child progresses through having insisted on defending his/her own solution while having had to consider the other erroneous solution at the same time.

The same distinction between regulation through compliance and regulation through cognitive work has been confirmed by other experiments, including those of Lévy (1981). Several of these experiments share the procedure of confronting a child in the difficult position with different kinds of responses from an adult. The only types of answers that were not conducive to progress were those which were obviously arbitrary, while incorrect answers which were not haphazard but structured according to a logical plan did contribute to the child's progress. Similar effects were observed when the adult refrained from offering a solution but merely challenged each and every position that the child proposed for a house. However, as shown in yet another experiment, progress diminished if the credibility of the adult giving incorrect answers was questioned. This indicates once more that the child's cognitive work is activated primarily through his or her being seriously confronted with a challenging point of view.

Other experimenters (Ames and Murray, 1982; Glachan and Light, 1982; Silbereisen, 1982) have also shown that socio-cognitive conflict can lead to progress provided that the cognitive work remains free of interfering compliance regulations. A form of socio-cognitive conflict that is very efficient and that can be easily introduced in educational settings is systematic questioning as used by Lévy (1981, see Doise and Mugny, 1984, chapter 6, experiment 6). Deutsch and Pechmann (1982) report results of a cross-sectional study using subjects aged 3, 6, and 9, compared with adults, in which they analysed the interaction between speaker and addressee in a referential communication task. They showed that all the referential ambiguities in the 6- and 9-year-olds and in the adults disappeared when the addressee was not satisfied with incomplete descriptions but repeated them in question format. If not totally successful for 3-year-olds such questioning did lead to a very high percentage of resolutions of ambiguities even in this age group. In this context it should be recalled that Robinson and Robinson (1984) found that only questions drawing explicit attention to non-understanding during early family life, such as 'What do you mean?', predicted better referential communication years later in a sample of children studied by Wells (1981). In a different cultural context Ng (1983) found in Hong Kong that inducing conflict through systematic questioning also improved his subjects' understanding of social institutions, such as shop profit (at the age of 8 to 10), and the functioning of a bank (at the age of 10 to 13).

## SOCIAL MARKING IN COGNITIVE OPERATIONS

The notion of social marking refers to the kind of correspondence which may exist between, on the one hand, the social relations which are part of the interaction between protagonists actually or symbolically present in a given situation, and, on the other, the cognitive operations on particular properties of objects which mediate these social relations. Such a correspondence exists when, for instance, two individuals have equal rights according to a norm of equality or equity and when they have to master conservation of equality in the Piagetian sense in order to comply with this norm when dividing a given quantity between them.

The specificity of social relationships in a given situation depends on a system of norms and representations which exists prior to the experimental situation. Of course these norms and representations may be modified in a particular situation. These changes do not occur in an arbitrary way: a certain necessity characterizes the principles and schemata which govern the development of a social interaction. On the other hand, at the level of cognitive organization, necessity is also invoked, notably that which characterizes the operational structures described by the developmental psychologists of the Genevan school. The notion of social marking should allow us to study the links between principles of social regulation and principles of logic by showing how the regulatory effects of the former intervene in the cognitive rules used with physical objects.

A first experiment on social marking was intended to show that hierarchical social relations too can induce cognitive progress (Doise, Dionnet and Mugny, 1978). Therefore, a correspondence was experimentally aroused between asymmetry in adult–child relations and asymmetric relations in a cognitive task.

The experiment dealt with conservation of equal and unequal lengths. Based on pre-test, subjects (around 6 years) were used who gave non-conserving

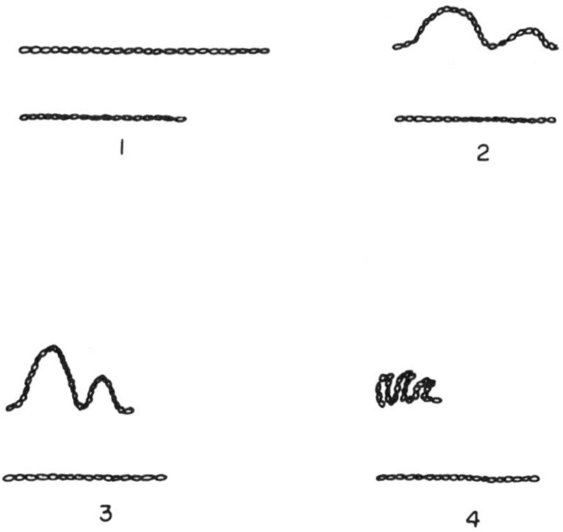


FIGURE 3.2. Arrangements of unequal lengths in the experimental phase of the 'bracelet' experiment

replies to the test and who, therefore, did not recognize the equality (or difference) of two bars (or two bracelets) objectively equal (or different) when the figurative arrangement was made perceptually 'deceptive' (for details see Doise and Mugny, 1984, chapter 5, experiment 4).

For the experimental phase, only the conservation of unequal lengths was retained, using the four configurations shown in Figure 3.2. In each case, the subject was asked to judge relative lengths of the bracelets (and to explain the judgement), and then to choose either which bracelet would fit the experimenter and which would fit the child her/himself (experimental condition) or which of the bracelets would best fit each of two cylinders of diameters proportional to wrists of adult and child (control condition). The bracelets were then tried. The experimental condition implies social marking because the child is required to make an unequal selection within a social context in which the adult needs a larger object than the child. In the control condition, the difference of diameters is there but it is only functional.

For each item (except the last), two kinds of counter-suggestions were made. If the child made a wrong choice, the adult asked: 'Why doesn't it fit?'. If the child chose the correct bracelets in spite of an earlier mistaken judgement, the experimenter asked the child to explain the discrepancy between judgement and choice. In other words, the experimenter centred the cognitive activity of the child on her/his own contradiction, but without ever suggesting any particular solution.

At the post-tests where all the subjects were tested again with the non-socially marked material, more than half of the subjects in the marked condition progressed against about only one-fifth of those in the unmarked condition.

Many more studies were carried out by the research team at Geneva (see De Paolis, Doise and Mugny, 1987) and also elsewhere on the effects of social marking. A good number of them have adapted the spatial transformation task in which the village task was replaced by the classroom situation: the houses being replaced by pupils sitting at their desks and the lake as a reference point now being the teacher's desk. The important characteristic of this adaptation is that it is possible to introduce a conflict between the usual cognitive strategies children adopt and the social norms implying, for instance, that the teacher should be facing the pupils. Social marking in many experiments has been shown to lead the child to an awareness that her/his approach to a cognitive problem is inappropriate as it violates social norms and regulations. At the same time these rules provide the means of reorganizing the child's cognitive approach. We are, therefore, dealing with processes which take account of the fact that social rules may actively intervene in cognitive development.

The following experiments, for instance, illustrate how it is possible to create social marking outside the actual interaction of the protagonists by appealing to symbolic norms in the experimental material itself. In these experiments, a test of conservation of spatial relations was used: this involved copying a model arrangement of objects onto a base presented in a different orientation (Figure 3.1). In the non-marked condition (in most cases a village), some houses were arranged in relation to a swimming pool: no intrinsic norm governed the left/right or in-front/behind relationship between houses and a pool. In the marked condition (usually a classroom), pupils' desks were arranged relative to a teacher's desk: in this condition the social relationship teacher–pupil was incorporated into the arrangements of the objects, and marked the spatial relations between objects.

In the pre- and post-test phases, subjects were presented with a model village made up of three or more Lego houses of different colours, arranged on a square base, with a swimming pool as reference point for orientation of the base. An identical base with swimming pool is set at an angle of 90 degrees to the model: subjects were given an identical set of houses and were asked to copy the model. The copy base always remained stationary, with the reference point in the left-hand far corner from the subjects: the model village could be rotated so that the positions of the reference point changed (90 degrees for a first practice item, 270 degrees for all test items). Subjects were required to copy the model so that the village 'is just the same, so that a man coming out of the swimming pool (on the copy) would find all the houses in just the same place as on this one (model)'. In the experimental phase, the same instruction was given to subjects in the unmarked condition (village), while in the marked condition subjects were instructed to 'copy the classroom so that this class (copy) is just the same as this (model) one, so that the teacher would see all her pupils in just the same place as in this one (model)'.

A three-level classification system, developed by Mugny and Doise (1978) was used to evaluate subjects' performance. Subjects who are not able to compensate for the difference in orientation between model and copy base, and who merely make 90 degree rotations of the material, or simply copy the whole village as they can see it, are deemed to be non-compensating (NC level). At an intermediate level, subjects are aware of the different orientation but can carry out the correct transformation on only one dimension. They compensate for the in-front/behind relationship of the houses or for the left/right relationship, but are unable to coordinate the two (PC level). Subjects who can coordinate the two dimensions and who offer the correct solution are called totally compensating (TC level). In all phases (pre-test, experimental and post-test) subjects are classified on the basis of their best performance.

In a first experiment (Doise and Mugny, 1984, pp. 151–153), four conditions were compared in which subjects worked with either the marked material (classroom) or the unmarked (village), and either alone or in pairs. All subjects were unable to conserve spatial relations on individual pre-test with unmarked materials. For the pairs condition, an interactional situation was used which usually does not lead to much cognitive progress as children at the same cognitive level approach the task from the same point of view, which does not give rise to any interpersonal conflict of perspective (Mugny and Doise, 1978). Improvement in performance following this kind of interaction with the marked material would, therefore, depend on the conflict between the children's incorrect cognitive solutions to the problem and the social norms structuring the classroom situation.

The results of the experimental phase clearly show better performance for subjects who worked with the classroom rather than the village. Subjects in the two marked conditions placed on average 72% of the desks correctly compared with subjects in the two unmarked conditions who placed only 21% of houses correctly. The impact of the socially marked material on post-test performances is particularly strong in the pairs condition (13 subjects out of 16 progress). However, the clearly improved performances of subjects in the individual marked condition (7 subjects out of 9) show that social marking enhances performance even when the child attempts to solve the problems alone. In the latter condition, a conflict was produced between the child's usual way of dealing with the task and the solution necessary to respect social conventions embedded in the classroom material. It should also be reported that in both marked conditions together more than half of the subjects (13 for a total of 25) reached the conservation level at the post-test against less than one-fifth (3 on 17 subjects) in the unmarked conditions.

The effects of social marking on conservation of spatial relationships have been further confirmed by an experiment which put a child in conflict with an adult (De Paolis *et al.*, 1981). It was possible to demonstrate the role played by marking not only as a condition which is favourable to cognitive development, but also as an essential instrument for the child in the conflictual situation of being systematically confronted with an incorrect solution proposed by an adult confederate of the experimenter. In each condition, one socially marked (classroom) and one not (village), children were confronted with an incorrect solution suggested by the adult, when they were in a position permitting them to find the correct solution (see Figure 3.1).

What will the child do when faced with an incorrect solution suggested by an adult? We know that this kind of situation can lead to compliance by the child (Carugati, De Paolis and Mugny, 1980–81; Mugny, De Paolis and Carugati, 1984). However, such responses should be rarer when social marking helps the child to maintain her/his correct response in opposition to the adult. Moreover, such a socio-cognitive conflict should lead to better understanding of spatial relationships and a generalization to post-test performance.

Results show that in the interaction with an adult phase, children in the 'village' condition were less likely to maintain their own solution in the face of the incorrect one proposed by the adult. In fact, out of 16 houses to be placed, they only averaged 6.5 correctly positioned, and reproduced the incorrect adult solution on more than six occasions. By contrast, introduction of the socially marked classroom material permitted the child to resist the adult's incorrect suggestions since on average 14.6 of the 16 pupils' desks were correctly placed, and only an average of 0.6 desks were misplaced out of compliance with the adult.

At post-test, results for 'village' subjects were significantly less good than those for 'classroom' subjects. Thus we can see that social marking of the material used for the interaction effectively led to higher cognitive levels at post-test on unmarked (village) material. Indeed, 6 of the 14 subjects in the 'classroom' condition were able to offer systematically correct responses for all post-test problems (which included a particularly difficult test item with 5 houses), whereas none of the 10 subjects in the 'village' condition did so (Fisher's test, $p \leqslant 0.025$).

The progress by children in the 'classroom' condition arose from their ability to deal with the conflict with the adult during the interaction: they usually stood out against the adult, replying that it was necessary to maintain certain spatial relationships between teachers and pupils. This awareness of the social norm symbolized in the task helped them escape the 'social weight' of their adult partner. They took part in a socio-cognitive conflict with the adult and very rarely showed compliance. The social marking produced a correspondence between the correct response and the social norm which required that certain spatial relationships be maintained in a hierarchical social relation: this correspondence allowed a cognitive regulation of the conflict with the adult which led to restructuring of the abilities required to carry out the task.

The norm of equal sharing has also proved to be very efficient in furthering conservation of liquids (Doise *et al.*, 1981). When such conservation upholds the social right to a fair recompense non-conserving children resist the usual perceptual transformation on other related conservation tasks. Zhou (1987) also studied the effects of equal sharing on the acquisition of conservation of quantity, but this time discrete quantities were involved. He varied conditions under which children had to judge the equivalence of the number of sweets in identical or different glasses. The condition leading to the best performance was one in which the children shared between themselves sweets awarded to them on the basis of the equality norm as a fair recompense. It is especially interesting to note that in some conditions, for instance when non-transparent glasses were used, children used an adequate cognitive strategy to solve the problem of equality by putting alternatively one sweet in each glass. But only in conditions with social marking does such an objectively correct strategy lead to conservation.

Furthermore, social marking intervenes equally in more advanced reasoning. Roux and Gilly (1984) have illustrated such an intervention in the context of rules of greeting involving two criteria: gender and age, the latter being more important than the former. Girotto (1987, see also Girotto, Light and Colbourn, 1988) showed, on the one hand, that specific forms of conditional reasoning do not manifest themselves even in adults using socially meaningless materials, but that, on the other hand, children are skilful in solving the same logical problems when they are embedded in socially significant material. One task he used with his subjects involves a hive with toy-bees of which some are 'buzzers' and others are 'non-buzzers'. Subjects are instructed to check in one condition if the rule of the Queen Bee is obeyed: 'All buzzing bees must stay inside in the evenings in order not to be gobbled up by a bee-eater bird' and in another condition to check the statement of a naturalist according to whom buzzing bees stay inside. Results show that most children and adults in the latter condition do not answer correctly when asked which sets (inside-bees, outside-bees or both) they have to check in order to know if the naturalist is wrong. They correctly answer that they would check the outside-bees in the former condition where they have to check if the Queen is disobeyed. These and other results reported by Girotto not only extend the social marking research into a new area but they also draw attention to the possible cognitive structuring effects of fairy-tales, old pedagogical stratagems which still can be useful.

To conclude this section, it is of course true that all social rules are not inevitably in all circumstances a source of cognitive development. Often relational processes (particularly compliance) interfere with cognitive work. According to Piaget (see above) a social relationship based on authority would necessarily play an inhibiting role in cognitive development. Converging results obtained in four different laboratories (Aix-en-Provence, Bologna, Geneva and Padua, see De Paolis, Doise and Mugny, 1987) now show, however, that such a view is too restrictive and that an asymmetrical social relationship may equally well give rise to a structuring effect in cognitive development, on condition that subjects can freely confront divergences between their own point of view and the one induced by social marking. At this point, it is particularly important to emphasize that, in most of the experiments described, the improvement found is not only in the cognitive coordinations using the material directly implicated in social rules, but that it extends equally to post-test material in which social rules are not directly implicated. This is clear evidence that cognitive structures produced socially are not contingent and arbitrary, but permit the individual to expand her/his new cognitive competence to other areas, and even to resist incorrect suggestions made by an adult.

## TOWARDS A MORE COMPREHENSIVE CONSTRUCTIVIST THEORY OF COMMUNICATIVE INTERACTION

If we badly need a socio-constructivist theory of cognitive development we need even more urgently a comprehensive socio-constructivist theory of communicative behaviour and of ethics. Social psychology has invested much energy in studying how various social factors distort cognitive and moral functioning: how, for instance, self-interest or prejudice intervene in reasoning and attribution processes or how submission to authority makes an individual abandon firm ethical principles. But in studying such distortions social psychologists too often have forgotten to study the socio-constructive processes at the origin of advanced cognitive functioning and moral reasoning.

This situation is now changing in the field of cognitive development but even more rapidly in the field of interpersonal understanding and of social moral judgement, thanks especially to the work of authors such as Kohlberg (1981, 1983), Selman (1980) and Youniss (1980). Fundamentally, this research and its European offspring (see Eckensberger and Silbereisen, 1980; Edelstein and Keller, 1982; Oser, 1986) revitalize the early Durkheimian and Piagetian thesis that forms of communicative interaction encourage the development of social perspective taking and moral awareness. Oser (1986, p. 922) describes in the following way the main characteristics of interactional situations which should promote and stimulate moral judgement development in educational settings, through socio-cognitive conflict:

> 1. presentation of the subjective truth completely and exhaustively (competence) as conceived by the participants in the conflict; 2. absence of an authority presenting an outside or observer's point of view of the 'right' answer; 3. creation of a disequilibrium by presenting different arguments and different opinions to stimulate development of moral judgment on increasingly complex grounds; 4. interaction among students (discussants) coordinated in such a way that everyone reacts openly and fairly to one another's point of view (positive climate and transactional discourse); 5. linking of the principles of discourse to the principles of justice.

These characteristics are homologous to the ones I have described in the previous sections and which are important for furthering cognitive development: confrontation and coordination of viewpoints, avoidance of compliance, socio-cognitive conflict, articulation of organizing social principles with more abstract cognitive principles (for the social construction of the intellect) or with fundamental justice principles (for social construction of ethics). And interestingly enough, these conditions are also homologous to some of those that, according to Janis (1982) should prevent 'groupthink' from exerting its often disastrous effects in political collective decision making.

After all, once modern man has dismissed supernatural and imposed authorities the only way for him to reach truth and justice is to construct them through social interaction. This, of course, cannot be done without acknowledging clearly normative or axiological intentions. And here experimental social psychology has a contribution to make. If Piaget in his work on moral judgement stressed the role of peer interaction, he did not study the effects of such interactions. It remains to be shown how social interaction furthers growth of moral judgement, how the interactional characteristics described by Oser (1986) are effective.

In order to promote ethical behaviour social representations of ideal relationships have to govern interaction patterns. Normative meta-systems such as the democratic conception of freedom and equality are necessary to further moral development in the Piagetian and Kohlbergian sense. Emler, Renwick and Malone (1983) report results on the intervention of meta-systems in so-called moral reasoning: students who define themselves as radicals achieve significantly higher scores on principled moral reasoning than other students. However, right-wing and moderate students also significantly increase their scores when they are invited to respond as radicals. Moral reasoning should be considered as an actuation of social representations bearing on idealized relation patterns. The much debated stage 6 of Kohlberg is such an ideal representation:

> In our theoretical conception, a sixth stage is based on a process of ideal role-taking or 'moral musical chairs' in which each person imaginatively changes place with every other in the dilemma before stating his claims as rightful. (Kohlberg, Levine, and Hewer, 1983, p. 87).

As citizen it is not possible for modern man to act without models of idealized interaction situations. Piaget's and Kohlberg's work shows that such normative models are also necessary to do research in the area of social and cognitive development. One of the tasks for social and developmental psychologists is to search for situations which promote advanced cognitive and moral behaviour. Experimental research constructs prototypes of such situations or at least studies processes which supposedly intervene in such situations.

## CONCLUSION

The general conception of intelligence which has inspired most of the research reported in this chapter postulates that cognitive coordinations are also social coordinations. Of course, such a conception is too general to be studied experimentally; its function is to guide researchers when they elaborate more specific proposals, which can be studied experimentally. The following proposals have been illustrated in research reported in this chapter:

1. It is through coordinating their own actions with others that children are led to construct new cognitive coordinations they are not capable of individually.
2. Children who have participated in various social coordinations often become capable of executing these coordinations alone.
3. Cognitive operations accomplished with respect to one set of materials and in a specific social situation none the less assume characteristics of stability and generality, being to some degree transposable to other situations and materials.
4. Social interaction becomes a source of cognitive progress by virtue of the socio-cognitive conflict it engenders; it is the simultaneous confrontation of different individual perspectives or centrations that gives rise to their integration within a new structure.
5. Initial competencies are necessary for individuals to benefit from a specific interaction situation.
6. Social regulations governing a given interaction constitute important factors in the establishment of new cognitive coordinations when a correspondence (social marking) exists between the former and the latter.

## REFERENCES

Abelson, R. P. (1981). The psychological status of the script concept, *American Psychologist*, **36**, 715–729.

Ames, G. J., and Murray, F. B. (1982). When two wrongs make a right: promoting cognitive change by social conflict, *Developmental Psychology*, **18**, 694–729.

Bernstein, B. (1973). *Class, Codes and Control*. St Albans: Paladin.

Bourdieu, P. (1979). *La Distinction, Critique Sociale du Jugement*. Paris: Editions de Minuit.

Bourdieu, P. (1980). *Le Sens Pratique*. Paris: Editions de Minuit.

Carugati F., De Paolis P., and Mugny G. (1980–81). Conflit de centrations et progrès cognitifs III: régulations cognitives et relationnelles du conflit socio-cognitif, *Bulletin de Psychologie*, **34**, 843–852.

De Paolis P., Carugati F., Erba M., and Mugny G. (1981). Connotazione sociale e sviluppo cognitivo, *Giornale Italiano di Psicologia*, **8**, 149–165.

De Paolis, P., Doise, W., and Mugny, G. (1987). Social marking in cognitive operations. In W. Doise and S. Moscovici (eds), *Current Issues in European Social Psychology, Volume II*. Cambridge: Cambridge University Press.

Deutsch, W., and Pechmann, T. (1982). Social interaction and the development of definite descriptions, *Cognition*, **11**, 159–184.

Doise, W., Dionnet, S., and Mugny, G. (1978). Conflit sociocognitif, marquage social et développement cognitif, *Cahiers de Psychologie*, **21**, 231–243.

Doise, W., and Mugny, G. (1975). Recherches sociogénétiques sur la coordination d'actions interdépendentes, *Revue Suisse de Psychologie Pure et Appliquée*, **34**, 160–174.

Doise, W., and Mugny, G. (1984). *The Social Development of the Intellect*. Oxford: Pergamon Press.

Doise, W., Rijsman, J. B., Van Meel, J., Bressers, I., and Pinxten, L. (1981). Sociale markering en cognitieve ontwikkeling, *Pedagogische Studiën*, **58**, 241–248.

Durkheim, E. (1902). *De la Division du Travail Social*. Paris: Alcan, 2nd edition.

Eckensberger, L. H., and Silbereisen R. K. (1980). *Entwicklung sozialer Kognitionen*. Stuttgart: Klett-Cotta.

Edelstein, W., and Keller, M. (1982). *Perspektivität und Interpretation*. Frankfurt am Main: Suhrhamp.

Emler, N., Renwick, S., and Malone, B. (1983). The relationship between moral reasoning and political orientation, *Journal of Personality and Social Psychology*, **45**, 1073–1080.

Girotto, V. (1987). *Conoscenze Pragmatiche e Ragionamento Deduttivo nei Bambini*. Bologna, Università, Dipartimento di Scienze dell'Educazione, Dottorato di Ricerca in Psicologia.

Girotto, V., Light, P., and Colbourn, C. (1988). Pragmatic schemas and conditional reasoning in children, *The Quarterly Journal of Experimental Psychology*, **40A**(3), 469–482.

Glachan, M., and Light, P. (1982). Peer interaction and learning: can two wrongs make a right? In G. Butterworth and P. Light (eds), *Social Cognition: Studies of the Development of Understanding*. Chicago: University of Chicago Press.

Inhelder, B., Sinclair, H., and Bovet, M. (1974). *Apprentissage et Structures de la Connaissance*. Paris: Presses Universitaires de France.

Janis, I. L. (1982) *Victims of Groupthink*. Boston: Houghton Mifflin.

Kohlberg, L. (1981). *Essays in Moral Development. Vol I: The Philosophy of Moral Development*. New York: Harper & Row.

Kohlberg, L. (1983). *Essays in Moral Development. Vol II: The Psychology of Moral Development*. New York: Harper & Row.

Kohlberg, L., Levine, C., and Hewer, A. (1983). *Moral Stages: A Current Formulation and a Response to Critics*. Basel: Karger.

Lautrey, J. (1980). *Classe Sociale, Milieu Familial, Intelligence*. Paris: Presses Universitaires de France.

Lévy, M. (1981). *La Nécessité Sociale de Dépasser une Situation Conflictuelle*. Genève, Thèse de Doctorat présentée à la Faculté de Psychologie et des Sciences de l'Education.

Mugny, G., De Paolis, P., and Carugati, F. (1984). Social regulations in cognitive development. In W. Doise and A. Palmonari (eds), *Social Interaction in Individual Development*. Cambridge: Cambridge University Press.

Mugny, G., and Doise, W. (1978). Socio-cognitive conflict and structuration of individual and collective performances, *European Journal of Social Psychology*, **8**, 181–192.

Ng, S. H. (1983). Children's ideas about the bank and shop profit: developmental stages and the influence of cognitive contrasts and conflict, *Journal of Economic Psychology*, **4**, 209–221.

Nelson, K. (1981). Social cognition in a script framework. In G. H. Flavell and L. R. Ross (eds), *Social Cognitive Development*. Cambridge: Cambridge University Press.

Oser, F. K. (1986). Moral education and values education: the moral discourse perspective. In M. C. Wittrock (ed.), *Handbook of Research on Teaching, Third Edition*. New York: Macmillan.

Piaget, J. (1932). *The Moral Judgment of the Child*. London: Kegan Paul.

Piaget, J. (1975). *L'Equilibration des Structures Cognitives*. Paris: Presses Universitaires de France.

Piaget, J. (1976a). Logique génétique et sociologie. In G. Busino (ed.), *Les sciences sociales avec et après Jean Piaget*. Genève: Librairie Droz.

Piaget, J. (1976b). Problèmes de la psycho-sociologie de l'enfance. In G. Busino (ed.), *Les Sciences Sociales avec et après Jean Piaget*. Genève: Librairie Droz.

Piaget, J., Inhelder, B., and Szeminska, A. (1948). *La Géométrie Spontanée de l'Enfant*. Paris: Presses Universitaires de France.

Robinson, E. J., and Robinson, P. W. (1984). Coming to understand that referential communication can be ambiguous. In W. Doise & A. Palmonari (eds), *Social Interaction in Individual Development*, Cambridge: Cambridge University Press, 107–123.

Roux, J. P., and Gilly, M. (1984). Aide apportée par le marquage social dans une procédure de résolution chez des enfants de 12–13 ans: données et réflexions sur les mécanismes, *Bulletin de Psychologie*, **38**, 145–155.

Russell, J. (1982). Cognitive conflict, transmission and justification: conservation attainment through dyadic interaction, *Journal of Genetic Psychology*, **140**, 283–297.

Selman, R. L. (1980). *The Growth of Interpersonal Understanding*. New York: Academic Press.

Staats, A. W. (1976). *Social Behaviorism*. Homewood: Dorsey Press.

Silbereisen, R. K. (1982). Untersuchungen zur Frage sozialkognitiv anregender Interaktionsbedingungen. In D. Geulen (ed.), *Perspektivenübernahme und soziales Handeln*. Frankfurt-am-Main: Suhrkamp.

Taal, M. (1985). De ontwikkeling van het compensatiebegrip: samen of ieder afzonderlijk? In P. Vedder and M. Bloemkolk (eds), *Samenwerken en Probleemoplossen*, Lisse, Zwets en Zeitlinger, 7–17.

Trevarthen, C. (1982). The primary motives for cooperative understanding. In G. Butterworth and P. Light (eds): *Social Cognition*. Chicago: University of Chicago Press.

Wells, C. G. (1981). *Learning through Interaction: the Study of Language Development*. Cambridge: Cambridge University Press.

Youniss, J. (1980). *Parents and Peers in Social Development: a Sullivan-Piaget Perspective*. Chicago: University of Chicago Press.

Zhou, R. M. (1987). *Marquage Social. Conduites de Partage et Construction de la Notion de Conservation chez des Enfants de 5–6 ans*. Aix-en-Provence, Université, Thèse de Doctorat.

CHAPTER 4

# Theoretical Issues in Peer Tutoring

Hugh C. Foot*, Rosalyn H. Shute†, Michelle J. Morgan* and Anne-Marie Barron*

**School of Psychology, University of Wales College of Cardiff, PO Box 901, Cardiff CF1 3YG, UK*

*†Department of Optometry, University of Wales College of Cardiff, PO Box 905, Cardiff CF1 3YJ, UK*

## INTRODUCTION

Children's interactions with other children are qualitatively different from their interactions with adults. Children are highly sensitive to age and competency differences between themselves and adults which cast them into a status position that is subordinate by definition (Hatch, 1987). In contrast, children's interactions with children offer special opportunities for practising social skills and for developing a wide range of interactive competencies with relative equals. In peer interaction, therefore, status is renegotiated at each encounter (Hatch, 1984).

Peer tutoring, however, presents an unusual kind of social relationship in which children of relatively equal standing are given formal roles (by adults) in which their status is differentiated, possibly artificially or arbitrarily, for a specific purpose. Frequently, this purpose is concerned with promoting the academic achievement of the participants, but changes of a social nature, such

Children Helping Children
Edited by H. C. Foot, M. J. Morgan and R. H. Shute

as improving social competencies or changing attitudes towards classmates, may also be desired. Even when the primary aims are academic, social considerations lie at the heart of tutoring processes. Process variables have been given relatively scant attention in comparison with outcome variables (cf. Morgan and Foot, 1985), although the latter must depend, ultimately, on the former. This chapter is aimed at elucidating some of the theoretical issues which are likely to be important for promoting understanding of tutoring processes.

In practice, children acting as tutors may be the same age as their tutees, or somewhat older and more competent than those whom they tutor—a two–three year age gap is sometimes quoted as optimal (e.g. Damon, 1984; Topping, 1988)—but little systematic evidence has been obtained relating differences in tutoring process and outcome to differences in age between tutor and tutee.

Focusing upon the peer interaction literature, several observations concerning age differences of the interactants can be made which are relevant to a consideration of the tutor–tutee relationship. It is generally true that children not only devote the bulk of their childhood interactions to others of a similar age to themselves (siblings excepted), but also tend to choose their best friends from amongst those close to their own chronological age (Hartup, 1978). Nevertheless, as Lewis and Rosenblum (1975) suggest, the relative levels of behavioural complexity of interacting children are probably of more salience than chronological age *per se*. Similarity may be particularly important when children working together confront a problem that is near the boundary of their cognitive capacities.

Cross-age social relationships may differ qualitatively as well as quantitatively from same-age interactions (Hartup, 1978). Social adaptation requires the development of a diversity of social competencies, and cross-age interactions are likely to expand the repertoire of social skills available to the child. For example, nurturant and caretaking roles are more likely to occur in interaction with younger children, while dependency and modelling are more likely to occur in interaction with older children (Thelen and Kirland, 1976). Cross-age social contacts may, therefore, serve children in ways that same-age contacts do not.

Cross-age relationships also assist in the development of accommodative behaviours (e.g. Gormly *et al.*, 1980). Children are sensitive to age and competency differences between themselves and other children and make appropriate behavioural adjustments to compensate for these differences (Lougee, Grueneich and Hartup, 1977). Shatz and Gelman (1973), for example, found evidence of downward speech accommodation amongst four-year-olds when interacting with two-year-olds (i.e. they used simpler and shorter words and sentences). Graziano *et al.* (1976) found that older children put more effort into group problem-solving tasks when with younger children than when with same-age children.

It is this equilibrium, or lack of it, in relationships with other children and adults that lies at the root of some of the major theories of children's cognitive development, and attention will be given to these first. Following a summary of these theoretical positions, peer tutoring will be considered more specifically, examining some of the processes in tutoring which seem particularly worthy of attention.

## THEORETICAL UNDERPINNINGS

### Symmetrical relationships

The importance of peer relationships within Piaget's notions concerning cognitive development is that they are essentially symmetrical relationships (Piaget, 1928, 1932, 1950, 1970). Only in the presence of collaborating peers is the ideal social setting created for producing cognitive conflict and conflict resolution both of which are seen as essential ingredients of cognitive development. As children coordinate their plans and perspectives through play and problem-solving tasks, they learn about their own and each others' cognitive activities (Forbes and Lubin, 1979; Gearhart, 1979; Gearhart and Newman, 1980), and they seriously come to question their own and others' perspectives and centrations. According to Piaget (1932), 'criticism is born of discussion, and discussion is only possible among equals'. Peers speak the same language—a theme pursued by Bruner (1985) and by Allen (1976) in their role theory approach to peer tutoring—and find it easier, therefore, to challenge each others' views and to take seriously feedback from other children in reconciling the differing viewpoints being presented. It is clear that confrontations with their peers force children to recognize that other perspectives exist, to reconsider their own, and to explain, justify and defend them. By contrast, in interactions with adults, children rarely have an opportunity to argue their case; even when they do, they normally have the adult's perspective imposed upon them, so they may have little motivation to think through a defence of their own position. Furthermore, adult questioning may be seen as monitoring the child's understanding of the adult viewpoint rather than as a joint search for a solution to a problem (Wood, 1988).

In the peer collaboration situation (see Introductory chapter) children are involved in both social and cognitive conflict, and benefits may accrue from both. The social benefits are improved communication skills (e.g. defending a point of view) and increased awareness of the perspectives of others. The cognitive benefits are the increased ability to reexamine one's own ideas, modify them and provide feedback to others on their ideas. The interaction between peers is the trigger for change, although the change itself is achieved by the child alone.

The social context of cognitive conflicts has been pursued by Doise and his collaborators at Geneva, who took the view that the confrontation of different perspectives to the same problem 'may result in their being coordinated into a new approach more complex and better adapted to solve the problem than any one of the previous approaches alone' (Doise, 1985). Using a variety of Piagetian tasks Doise and his colleagues found that the performance of children working in pairs may often be superior to that of children working alone, and that this superiority cannot simply be explained by children imitating their more able partners (Doise, Mugny and Perret-Clermont, 1975, 1976; Mugny and Doise, 1978). The superiority of paired performances carries over into individual performance on post-test. Mugny, Perret-Clermont and Doise (1981) are of the view that even if a child is confronted with a conflicting solution that is incorrect, it may provide him or her with 'some relevant dimensions for a progressive elaboration of a cognitive mechanism new to him (or her)'. The improvement on the post-test emanates from the child's reappraisal of his or her own solution. Further discussion of this is provided in the chapters by Doise, and Light and Blaye.

Various other considerations have entered the debate about socio-cognitive conflicts. Bearison, Magzamen and Filardo (1984) have drawn attention to the level of conflict involved. They found that large degrees of conflict in peer dyads were counterproductive and inversely related to change; only moderate conflict was associated with change in a constructive direction. Similarly, in an earlier study, Damon and Killen (1982) found that children who most disagreed with one another were least likely to progress, whereas children who accepted one another's views and worked positively with them were the most likely to change. Emler and Valiant (1982), however, conducted a study in which inter-individual conflict was trained and in which measures of disagreement were obtained. There was a significantly greater pre- to post-test gain in the high disagreement category than in the low disagreement category, suggesting that greater conflict is conducive to greater cognitive gains. So there are various contradictions in this research. A second line of inquiry has challenged the view that it is the conflict in centrations *per se* which has produced the cognitive gains, but rather the opportunity to collaborate and 'co-construct' a new solution from incomplete, but not necessarily conflicting, part-perspectives. Damon and Phelps (1987) reinterpreted some of Doise's findings in a spatial coordination task (cf. Doise, Mugny and Perret-Clermont 1976) and suggested that the results may well be attributable to the collaboration of the two children involved rather than socio-cognitive conflict. In their own study of peer collaboration in maths and science learning exercises, Damon and Phelps (1987) found that a high proportion of the groups they observed were positive and amicable in quality rather than negative and conflictual, and that they were no less constructive in achieving gains.

A third approach has examined the source of the conflict in terms of its social status. If conflict is the catalyst for cognitive growth, then does it matter if the conflict is generated by other peers or by conflicting perspectives? Doise and Mugny's (1979) finding that paired training resulted in greater subsequent progress than solitary practice was replicated by Emler and Valiant (1982) using a similar model village reconstruction task. However, these latter authors found that paired training was no more effective than training designed to induce intra-individual conflict (i.e. to perceive different perspectives oneself). This result confirms the importance of cognitive conflict for developmental change but suggests that the circumstances under which such conflict arises are not particularly relevant. Emler and Valiant (1982) proposed that cross-cultural differences may explain the variations in findings. Inter-individual conflict may be more effective in cultures emphasizing cooperation, like Doise and Mugny's Spanish Catholic children and Mackie's (1980) Samoan and Cook Island Maoris, whereas intra-individual conflict may be more effective in cultures with a more individualistic orientation to learning, like Mackie's New Zealand sample and Emler and Valiant's British sample.

Other criticisms of the cognitive conflict perspective have come from studies which have examined the nature of the interactions between collaborating children at a more micro-level. Working with children aged 4–8 years, Russell (1981a, 1981b) found no advantage for dyadic performance over solitary performance and argued that correct dyadic solutions to reasoning and spatial tasks were frequently based upon the incorrect child's compliance with the correct partner's judgement. Light and his colleagues (cf. Glachan and Light, 1982, Light and Glachan, 1985; Light *et al.*, 1987) confirmed Russell's findings for unstructured collaborative tasks where the bulk of the decision making and moves were typically made by one child (the dominant one of the pair), while collaboration only worked to the children's advantage where the collaboration was structured or where children showed some evidence of a strategic approach to the task at pre-test (Glachan and Light, 1982). Other extensions of the cognitive conflict debate are taken up by Doise in Chapter 3.

Before leaving this discussion of the importance of symmetrical relationships for cognitive development, the work of Sullivan (1953) and Youniss (1980) should also be acknowledged. They placed particular emphasis upon the shared co-construction of reality between peers who respect each other because they are matched closely in knowledge and ability, and between whom, therefore, there is no authority relationship. Their perspective, however, is not one based upon cognitive gains stemming from conflict but rather that development comes from mutual collaboration in which the interactants share ideas, seek agreement, compromise willingly with each other and generally pool their resources to achieve a solution to a problem. This equality of effort encourages interactants to engage in discovery learning and to explore new ideas which are fundamental to the grasping of basic concepts.

### Asymmetrical relationships

Despite their adherence to experimental paradigms using 'novice' children, Doise and Mugny (1984) pointed out that it is too simplistic to view relations between peers as a source of development just because of the social equality involved. It is the nature of the social interaction which is crucial to development, and interaction with adults, although qualitatively different from interaction with peers, may be just as effective. This theme echoes the views of Vygotsky (1962, 1978) in relation to children's interaction with others, be they children or adults. Damon (1984) summarizes succinctly Vygotsky's views about how children come to benefit from other interactants by internalizing the cognitive processes implicit in their interactions and communications.

> children are introduced to new patterns of thought when they engage in dialogues with peers. This is because peer dialogue is by nature a cooperative [illegible]ge of ideas between equals and therefore emulates several critical features o[illegible] thinking. In particular, the verification of ideas, the planning of strate[illegible]vance, and the symbolic representation of intellectual acts are en[illegible]rough peer communication. Eventually, after repeated exposure to coop[illegible]eer exchange, the child's own thinking becomes influenced. That is, the child [illegible]r 'internalizes' the very communicative procedures that the child experienc[illegible]nteracting with a peer. In this manner, the child's intellectual abilities are [illegible]tly modified for the better. (Damon, 1984, pp. 333–34)

It is not, however, just peer encounters that can bring a[illegible]ut this improvement in learning or problem-solving capacities. Vygotsky stressed the need for communication or instruction from more capable peers or adults. A child's developmental growth is thus facilitated by others stretching his or her comprehension to its leading edge. Vygotsky developed his notion of the 'zone of proximal development' to explain the discrepancy between solitary and social problem-solving. He defined the zone as 'the distance between actual developmental level as determined by independent problem solving and the level of potential development through problem solving under adult guidance or in collaboration with more capable peers' (Vygotsky, 1978, p. 86).

The potential level of development is percei[illegible]d as important, if not more important, than the actual level of developme[illegible]earning is the outcome of joint cognitive activity being internalized a[illegible]ning the structure of the child's independent cognitive functioning. So [illegible]teractional processes are internalized and development proceeds whe[illegible]ychological regulation is transformed into intrapsychological regulati[illegible] Vygotsky postulated that children would be better able to solve probl[illegible] assistance from an expert peer or adult than in isolation, but instructi[illegible] effective when it proceeds ahead of development in the sense that it [illegible]nto activity a whole set of functions which are at the stage of maturing [illegible] which lie within the zone of proximal development.

The process by which interpsychological processes transform into intrapsychological processes is rather vague in Vygotsky's own writings. Working with mothers and preschool children, Wertsch (1979) described a four-stage developmental process based upon the differing 'situation definitions' which they bring to a particular situation. The notion of situation definition refers to the way that objects, people and events are represented or defined. Sharing the same physical world does not lead to similar representations because each individual defines his or her surroundings in terms of his or her own past experiences and cultural history.

At the first stage communication between mother and child is very difficult: their situation definitions are so disparate; at the second stage the child shares some of the mother's basic understanding in relation to objects in their settings; at the third stage the child responds appropriately to 'other regulation' (i.e. strategic control by the mother) and shows some signs that intrapsychological functioning is beginning to account for much of the child's performance. Finally, the child takes over complete responsibility for carrying out the task. In relation to task performance amongst older children in, say, a tutoring relationship, the perspectives of the interactants probably go through at least the latter stages of this process to translate interpsychological into intrapsychological functioning.

## Social interaction and cognitive growth

There are two major points to be extracted from this brief summary of these theoretical positions. The first concerns the focus upon social interaction as the seed-corn for cognitive growth. The theories are not just arguing that interaction is important or desirable for cognitive development; they are saying that interaction is a necessary condition for cognitive development. Children's understanding of the world, as aspirant members of a culture, was summed up by Bruner (1985) when he said:

> That world is a symbolic world in the sense that it consists of conceptually organized, rule-bound belief systems about what exists, about how to get to goals, about what is to be valued. There is no way, none, in which a human being could possibly master that world without the aid and assistance of others for, in fact, that world *is* others. (Bruner, 1985, p. 32)

The second point is that it is Vygotsky's approach, emphasizing cooperation with more capable peers and enabling children to enter into new areas of potential that is the more appropriate model for peer tutoring. By definition peer tutoring implies that one child (the tutor) starts out with superior knowledge to the other (the tutee) and both are conscious of their roles as expert and novice and that the objective is for the expert to impart his or her knowledge to the novice.

In the remainder of this chapter we shall outline some of the crucial processes involved in a one-to-one tutoring situation, drawing on some of our own experimental findings.

## OVERVIEW OF PEER TUTORING RESEARCH

It is not intended to offer here a comprehensive review of the peer tutoring literature. Both research findings and the development of tutoring programmes have been extensively reviewed in a number of other sources, in particular: Gartner, Kohler and Riessman (1971); Allen (1976); Devin-Sheehan, Feldman and Allen (1976); Goodlad (1979); Sharpley and Sharpley (1981); Topping (1988), Goodlad and Hirst (1989).

The particular emphasis here is upon certain specific processes which have been neglected by those concerned with research and practice in peer tutoring and which deserve closer attention. These processes are:

(i) The child's perception of his or her role in the tutoring relationship and the conception the child has of being a teacher.
(ii) The teaching strategies employed by children and in particular the way children distribute their attention amongst the different components of the task.
(iii) The child tutor's sensitivity to the needs of the tutee with special emphasis upon the tutor's awareness of and response to lack of understanding on the part of the tutee.

Before embarking on an examination of these processes, however, a brief statement about research and practice needs to be made to provide an appropriate context for the subsequent discussion. This statement will focus upon the role of the tutor because it is tutoring processes with which we are most concerned. Additionally, it is often claimed that tutoring programmes are designed more to benefit the tutor than the tutee and, whether this is true or not, it frequently is the tutor who derives most benefit. These benefits are claimed to operate at four main levels of functioning: cognitive, affective, evaluative and behavioural. At a cognitive level tutors may gain a deeper understanding of the material learned, by virtue of having to teach it, and 'learning how to learn' strategies may spill over into learning contexts other than the immediate learning task (e.g. Gartner *et al.* 1971). At the affective or socio-emotional level tutoring may increase maturity, sense of responsibility, sensitivity, concern and empathy for others (e.g. Lippitt and Lohman, 1965). At an evaluative level tutoring may enhance self-esteem, self-confidence and levels of aspiration, and it may inculcate more positive attitudes not only towards learning but also towards teachers and others in authority (e.g. Haggarty, 1971). Finally, at the behavioural level it may promote prosocial behaviours and better social skills all round (e.g. Robertson, 1972).

According to role theory, the success of tutoring in these various respects will depend upon the effectiveness of the role enactment: the more convincing the performance and the more the tutor perceives him or herself to have enacted in a way which is consistent with role expectations (and this in turn will be influenced by tutee reaction), the more likely it is that the enactment will confer positive effects (Sarbin and Allen, 1968).

As Allen (1983) pointed out, however, these glowing reports from practitioners and participants about the strong impact of tutoring on the tutor stand in 'sharp contrast' to the conclusions drawn from *research* aimed at evaluating the effects of tutoring programmes on the participants. Data from both long- and short-term programmes confirm the view that research evidence is nowhere near as consistent as practitioners claim. Several reasons have been suggested for this, based mainly upon shortcomings of the research paradigms and their generality. In summary:

(1) Research instruments, procedures and designs may be in some way defective or not sufficiently sensitive.
(2) Too limited a range of dependent variables is measured, so crucial components are either being missed or are not included in the design.
(3) Tutoring experiences may simply be too weak, too diluted or too brief to produce a measurable impact on the tutor.
(4) Any positive influence of tutoring may be confined to the specific tutoring situation *per se* and may not generalize into a measurable overall effect.

Allen (1983) proposed ways of overcoming role-specificity in tutoring by increasing the range and variety of situations in which individuals engage in role enactment and in increasing 'role penetration' by expanding the tutor role so that it impinges upon other roles in relation to other activities in school or at home.

## THE CHILD'S PERCEPTION OF TUTORING ROLES

There is substantial behavioural evidence that children understand implicitly what taking on the role of a teacher means. Role theory approaches, as already mentioned, emphasize the notion that donning a particular role drives the behavioural and cognitive changes ensuing from the enactment of that role. According to Allen (1983) 'It is a basic tenet of role theory that enactment of a role produces changes in behaviour, cognition and affect in a direction consistent with the expectations associated with the role' (p. 373). While this is not in dispute, it needs to be pointed out that a child cannot successfully enact a role unless he or she already has a relatively clear representational understanding of the repertoire of behaviours which are appropriate for that role. So, if the tutor role involves being a friend as well as a teacher (Sarbin, 1976), if it involves accommodative verbal and non-verbal behaviours towards a younger tutee (Hartup, 1976), if it promotes caretaking, empathy and prosocial behaviours (Lippitt and Lohman, 1965), and so on, then successful enactment of these behaviours has to be the outcome of a considerable implicit knowledge-base on the part of the child. Of course, this is of considerable theoretical interest because it could be argued that if a child already 'knows' what behaviours are associated with a particular role, why is it necessary for him or her to have to enact that role in order for demonstrable cognitive, affective, evaluative and behavioural changes to occur? One might adopt a cognitive dissonance explanation here and argue that the behaviour has to be acted out first in order to render the appropriate attitudes and cognitions sufficiently salient for change. Alternatively, one might argue that changes in attitudes and cognitions consequential upon role enactment are a more subtle outcome of the social impact that the role behaviours have upon others. If tutors receive positive feedback from their tutees about the success with which they are performing their role, then they are going to be reinforced in the cognitions and attitudes associated with the role. Support for this view comes from evidence that unsuccessful tutoring may result in a negative self-concept, reduced sense of competence and more adverse attitudes towards teachers (Allen, 1983).

Be that as it may, what evidence is there that children have any clear conception of what the role of teacher involves? In an informal (unpublished) study we have asked children between eight and eleven years of age about their perceptions of teaching and of teachers. Specifically the children were invited to respond to a set of questions concerning what they believe adult teachers typically do when they teach, and a parallel set of questions concerning what they themselves would do if they were teaching. Other questions were aimed at assessing the appeal of teaching to children and whom they would most like to teach.

Results of this small-scale study were quite interesting. Children consistently offered the altruistic view that teaching is about *helping* children, recognizing their perception of learning as equipping children with necessary knowledge and skills for coping with later life. More selfishly children found the role of being in charge and having control over others as appealing and even exciting. There was less consensus, however, about the negative aspects of teaching and children listed a variety of reasons for not wanting to teach: dealing with awkward questions, not being liked by pupils, too much work, coping with badly behaved children and being bored. On questions concerning explanations of work to children and knowing if a child does not understand, children had much greater difficulty taking the teacher's perspective relative to their own. Children seemed to draw upon their own experience in demonstrating, exemplifying and simplifying when describing how they would explain a lesson to another child, but applied no more than very general 'helping' principles when describing teacher explanations. Children were equally vague in their descriptions of how a teacher knows when a child does not understand, and suggested that teachers would know only because their pupils would tell them or because their pupils would 'get their answers wrong'. However, they attributed somewhat more active recognition of non-understanding to themselves as teachers: for example, they would ask their tutees whether they understood and continue to ask; they would recognize puzzled facial expressions; they would see tutees not working or copying others' work.

Finally, on questions concerning to whom children would turn in class when they were confused by their work, many stated they would seek help from a friend before they would turn to the teacher. Children seemed to assume that their misunderstanding would be judged by the teacher as stemming from lack of attention and, therefore, would run the risk of incurring the teacher's anger.

What this study appears to show generally is that children have quite a clear conception of the necessary skills and functions involved in teaching and have no difficulty applying their own informal experiences of helping others in or out of school to their own models of teaching. However, they show less certainty about applying these models to adult teachers. Why this should be is not at all clear. Perhaps children believe that adult teachers have some other fund of more sophisticated knowledge or expertise about how to teach, to which they are not privy. This might explain why they are more reticent to offer opinions about what adult teachers do and why they couch their descriptions in more general and vague terms.

## The child's implicit theory of teaching

A long-standing research approach in the area of children's perception of teaching has been the use of essays or questionnaires as a means of eliciting children's own constructs about teachers (e.g. Blishen, 1969, 1973; Makins, 1969; Taylor, 1962). Examining the characteristics of teaching produced by such studies, it is not difficult to generate a list of positive and negative teaching qualities. For example, to give a representative sample of the factors mentioned in the above studies, teachers should: explain clearly, encourage, keep order, show interest, let you talk, be willing to accept points made against them, provide variety, help slow learners catch up with others, have a sense of humour, be a good listener, be capable of informality, be understanding, patient, humble, kind, pleasant, friendly, helpful, interesting and fair. Teachers should not: shout, ignore pupils, give monotonous work, give unclear instructions or explanations, be unhelpful, lazy and unsympathetic. What is of interest here is that the majority of these kinds of descriptors reflect on the children's perceptions of teachers rather than on their perception of teaching *per se*. In practice, then, children write or talk much more about the qualities of the good and bad teacher than they spontaneously mention good teaching practice (although obviously the two overlap to some extent). Taking a Piagetian perspective, this may reflect their use of concrete operational rather than abstract thought.

While children may be explicitly aware of certain characteristics of the good teacher, it is reasonable to assume that they may also be susceptible to other factors or governed by other assumptions in the teaching situation of which they are largely unaware and which they certainly could not easily articulate.

Amongst these factors are children's accommodative behaviours mentioned in the opening pages of this chapter which refer largely to shifts in verbal communication as a function of the age or competence differences between interacting children. Ludeke and Hartup (1983), working with 11- and 9-year-old tutors teaching a board game to same-age or younger tutees, found that children varied the content of their communications according to the age difference between themselves and their tutees. When tutoring younger children tutors repeated the rules more frequently, gave more 'strategic advice', checked up on progress more frequently, gave more direct assistance and praise than they did when tutoring same-age tutees. Ludeke and Hartup proposed that these findings are entirely consistent with the view that children possess a theory of teaching involving two developmental assumptions:

> (a) that younger children compared to children of one's own age are cognitively limited and therefore require extra consideration in delivering information; and (b) that younger children, compared to same-age children, require more frequent support, confirmation and praise in acquiring information. (Ludeke and Hartup, 1983, p. 913)

Where the child's implicit theory of teaching comes from is unclear, as Ludeke and Hartup admit. Since tutor behaviour was not correlated with tutee behaviour and could not be attributed to any differences in instruction, it seems very plausible that the children came to the experimental situation with a pre-formed developmental theory rather than constructing it in the course of their interaction with the tutees.

Our own research with 9- and 11-year-olds extends these points and suggests further that, although child tutors may operate on the basis of assumptions already established, there is flexibility in the application of some of these assumptions, which is dependent upon the course of the interaction. The tutoring task used in our research involved learning how to classify animals into five categories: mammals, fish, reptiles, amphibians and birds. For each animal, tutors were provided with four 'clue cards', each giving information about one of four attributes appertaining to that animal. The four clues were related to: type of skin; breathing (air or water); body temperature (warm or cold blood); and feeding young (milk or no milk). The tutor's task was to instruct the tutee how to use these clue cards with a chart which related the attributes to the five animal categories. Adult, 11- and 9-year-old tutors received training on a series of animals and, after being tested, taught the task to their tutees (all 9-year-olds) using both the set of animals that they had been trained on themselves and a new set of animals which they had not seen before. The training and testing procedures for both tutors and tutees are described in more detail by Foot and Morgan (1988).

While there were several interesting findings relating to children's teaching strategies (which will be mentioned later) two particular findings emerged from this study which are relevant to a discussion of children's implicit theories of teaching. The first of these concerns the control of task materials exercised by tutors during the course of tutoring—specifically decision-making in relation to consultation of the clue cards and chart-usage. Whereas adults progressively relinquished control of these materials to their tutees as tutees' competence at the task increased, the 11-year-old tutors maintained high degrees of control throughout the tutoring period. This strongly suggests that these children perceived the role of teacher as being 'in control' to the extent that the task materials were to be manipulated primarily by the teacher and only dispensed sparingly to the tutee. Coupled with this control of the materials was the finding that child tutors covered fewer task elements in explaining the task to their tutees and gave less encouragement. It may be that the children's implicit theory of teaching involves viewing the teacher–pupil relationship in terms of an active–passive dichotomy, at least when tutoring a younger child. The 9-year-old tutors did not show the same level of control as the 11-year-olds at any stage during tutoring and this suggests that active–passive roles are less marked when the tutor is younger. Same-age children may indeed work more collaboratively, so that tutor and tutee function on more equal terms, and this has been shown to be beneficial for concept acquisition (Glachan and Light, 1982). It is worth noting that 9-year-old tutors performed as well as 11-year-olds on a post-training test, so it does not appear that their reduced control resulted from an inadequate grasp of the task.

The second finding relates to Ludeke and Hartup's assumption that children recognize that younger children require extra consideration as recipients of information by virtue of their cognitive limitations. It may well be that children bring such an assumption to the laboratory with them. Our results with tutors and tutees drawn from different classes have suggested further that child tutors may, from cues picked up during tutoring, be relatively sensitive to the ability of the children they are tutoring, irrespective of tutee-age. Factor-analysis of tutee and tutor behaviours and test scores revealed that tutor test score and amount of tutor information and encouragement were positively related to tutee chart use and negatively to tutee academic performance (as measured by school examinations). The interpretation of this is in two parts: firstly, that the higher scoring (possibly more able) tutors were better equipped to give more task-relevant information, enabling the tutee to make more use of the chart, for which encouragement was then given. Secondly, this information and encouragement was given to the academically less able tutees who were poorer at the task (school examination performance and experimental test performance were correlated). Taken together these findings suggest that tutors were gauging the amount of information they gave according to the needs of the tutee. Tutors somehow perceived early on in learning which tutees were in greater need of instruction and encouragement. The findings of Allen and Feldman (1974), that strong primacy effects operate in children's attributions of ability, are relevant here: it is the initial learning success by the tutee which determines the tutor's attributions about the tutee's ability, even if subsequent performance changes markedly.

The main thrust of the argument, however, is that not only may children bring certain assumptions with them into a teaching context (as Ludeke and Hartup suggested) but also that they may be sensitive to the pupils they teach and accommodate their own behaviours according to the perceived ability of the tutees. This suggests that a more dynamic interpretation of children's conceptions of teaching is needed which can take account of varying tutee needs.

A final caveat to this discussion of children's perceptions of tutoring is that, however children may seek to model adult teachers, child tutoring roles have an essentially game-like quality. As Allen (1983) warns, the child tutor is not really a teacher 'in the sense of legitimately occupying this position in the macrosocial structure'; tutoring is not entirely authentic, not really part of adult reality, and tutors' enjoyment of tutoring may derive at least in part from its being construed as play rather than as work.

## CHILDREN'S TEACHING STRATEGIES

There is relative agreement amongst researchers that children' teaching techniques generally resemble those employed by adults (Ludeke and Hartup, 1983). Cooper, Ayers-Lopez and Marquis (1982), in an observational study of spontaneous peer instruction, found that the most common techniques used by the children were: describing the task, issuing directives and making evaluative comments. Demonstrating, pointing, labelling, questioning and giving criticism and praise also featured in the children's interactions, indicating that children are quite capable of using cognitive structuring in their teaching as well as discriminative feedback. Some practitioners have argued that children are natural teachers and tutor best when they are given minimal training (cf. Ehly and Larsen, 1980). Others have argued for extensive training with clearly articulated training goals. Deterline (1970), for example, has enumerated ten goals for tutor training, which are clearly prescriptive of the kinds of teaching strategies which children are expected to learn:

(1) putting the tutee at ease;
(2) clarifying the prescribed task;
(3) showing the tutee how to verify his or her answer;
(4) directing the tutee to read each problem aloud;
(5) having the tutee respond overtly before the tutor provides feedback;
(6) having the tutee verify each response;
(7) avoiding any form of punishment;
(8) providing verbal praise when appropriate;
(9) providing a tangible reward when appropriate;
(10) evaluating elements of mastery.

Although such goals are fairly specific, they are also wide-ranging in scope and for many situations it may just not be feasible to train students in such a broad array of skills, without considerable investment of time if the training is to have any impact. 'On-the-job' training of specific skills may be a more desirable feature for many tutoring situations. Probably much depends upon the initial organization and structure of the material to be tutored and the responses expected from the tutees. It may well be easier to train specific teaching strategies to be adopted where the material is already organized in a programmed format or in some other clear hierarchical and sequential arrangement which the tutor can easily follow (Gerber and Kauffman, 1981). In many such cases, though, the types of responses required from tutees are relatively simple and unambiguous, such as writing the solution to an arithmetic problem, reading or spelling a word, articulating a sound (e.g. Collins and Calevro, 1974; Ehly and Larsen, 1977; Epstein, 1978). This type of structure clearly assists the tutors in delivering appropriate reinforcement or correction. An excellent example of training tutors to use highly-structured, predetermined strategies for a specific task is the use of Pause, Prompt and Praise in tutoring remedial readers (Wheldall and Colmar, this volume).

Returning, however, to children's spontaneous teaching strategies the main point to be made is that while children and adults may employ similar types of technique, both the quantity and quality of these techniques may differ. One of the main areas for these differences is, not surprisingly, in the amount of verbal information supplied. Children rely more heavily upon non-verbal instruction, like demonstration and modelling of tasks, whereas adults typically give more complex chains of verbal instructions providing details about the rationale, purpose, principles and procedures involved in the task (Ellis and Rogoff, 1982; Mehan, 1977). Child tutors also elicit less tutee participation in the task as evidenced both by Ellis and Rogoff (1982) and by our own work (Foot and Morgan, 1988).

Quantity and quality of instruction is also, of course, reflected by developmental changes and by children's accommodative behaviours. Ludeke and Hartup (1983) found that 11- and 9-year-olds repeated the rules of a board game more frequently when teaching younger children than same-age children. They also found that strategic advice, involving the application of rules, was more forthcoming when tutors were with younger tutees, as was praise and tutor questioning.

Despite some evidence that children are in some respects superior teachers to adults (e.g. child tutors are more direct and businesslike with their tutees and less willing to resort to coaxing and games, Thomas, 1970), the overwhelming body of research points to adults being more effective teachers than children. Ellis and Rogoff (1986) suggested that the problems children have in providing effective instruction seem to be largely due to difficulties in coordinating the numerous demands involved in managing the instructional task.

This poses some interesting questions about the priorities that child tutors give to different aspects of the tutoring task and it is to this issue that the remainder of this section is addressed.

**Task management**

For Ellis and Rogoff (1986) the child tutor's management of instruction is itself a problem-solving task, and children's relative ineffectiveness in tutoring may be the outcome of a failure to distribute their limited cognitive resources adequately between the various components of the task (Shatz, 1978). Ellis and Rogoff used two classification tasks not unlike the animal classification task used in our own research. Their tasks involved realistic concept learning similar to activities in the home and at school. The 'home' task consisted of placing 18 grocery items on six shelves corresponding to six food items (e.g. fruits, baking goods, snacks). The 'school' task involved sorting 18 colour photographs into six compartments corresponding to machines, cutting tools, table settings and three other kinds of utensils. Adult and child tutors (aged 8–9) were familiarized with the organization of these items and were required to teach child learners (aged 6–7) how to classify them. After instruction the learners sorted eight of the original items and 12 new items which were introduced to test generalization of the category structure.

These tasks like many other problem-solving or concept learning tasks have three main components:

(1) physical-active component: sorting or manipulating the task materials;
(2) information component: understanding the rationale, principles, rules and procedures necessary for integrating and organizing the materials;
(3) social management component: maintaining good relations between tutor and tutee.

The management of these components is primarily the responsibility of the tutor and Ellis and Rogoff found that child tutors dealt with the complexity of the tasks by focusing on two of the components at the expense of the third. Specifically the tutors were relatively successful in physically sorting the items and most managed the interpersonal aspects, but they fell down most in providing category information or other information which ensured that the tutees understood the basis for grouping the items. Ellis and Rogoff interpreted their findings in terms of the children focusing upon the immediate demands of the task—item placement and managing the social interaction—while neglecting the longer term demands—assisting the tutees in understanding the classification system and thereby preparing them for the memory test. The researchers drew upon the transcripts of their tutoring sessions to support this view, suggesting a number of reasons why the information component might be the component most liable to neglect. To summarize their actual findings from the transcripts, they noted that child tutors generally failed:

(1) to provide any orientation to the nature of the classification task (i.e. did not provide any introductory statement prior to the placement of items):
(2) to prepare learners for the impending memory test which they were aware learners had to take;
(3) to provide any explanation of the rationale for organizing items as they placed objects into categories;
(4) to involve learners at a 'comfortable yet challenging' level in seeking the solution to the task (i.e. satisfactory participation level in decision-making regarding category membership or rehearsing for the test).

The reasons for these various failures may reside in the tutors' preoccupation with working out the problem for themselves and the other immediate physical and social demands of the task, such that they may have been relatively insensitive to their tutees' current state of understanding or have had difficulty in assessing learner needs. Other reasons for the failures may be that the tutors had difficulty in establishing effective means of communication to serve both immediate and long-term goals, and difficulty in determining the appropriate level at which to provide support for the learner to engage profitably in the task. In Vygotskian terms, it appears that a child tutor is likely to have difficulty in operating appropriately within the tutee's zone of proximal development.

One way of exploring the balance between the task components is to alter or modify the demands of one or more of the components. Some of our research has focused upon manipulating the demands of the social component by varying the relationship between tutor and tutee. In particular we have focused upon friendship, on the assumption that a tutor would need to expend less time and effort in managing an already established relationship with a friend than in managing a new relationship with an unknown tutee. Support for this assumption comes from Sharabany and Hertz-Lazarowitz (1981) who found that non-friends have to invest more time and display more verbal and non-verbal communicative behaviours with each other than friends in order to establish a certain level of closeness and coordination in the performance of their joint task activity. If there are fewer demands in 'managing' a friend, then it is plausible that the tutor will have more time to devote to other aspects of the task, such as managing the instructions and explanation of the task.

In a series of recent, as yet unpublished, studies Barron and Foot have investigated the tutoring styles of friends and non-friends. In practice mixed results emerged and it is becoming clear that the nature of the task itself is crucial to any shifts in the balance of task demands. For example, the first study used a food-sort task modelled closely on the 'home' task employed by Ellis and Rogoff in that it required the sorting of items into six categories with memory and generalization tests after tutoring. However, differences between friend and non-friend tutors on social interactional measures like encouragement and looking were non-existent and the few differences which emerged on the instructional component sometimes favoured friends (e.g. non-verbal directions, task duration). There were no overall differences in amount and types of explanations of the task or on tutees' performance levels.

Our overall impression was that the focus on the physical manipulation of cards in this task was so strong that there was a general paucity of any social interactional cues, and hence little opportunity for any kind of social management. We have since used other tasks which were designed to provide tutors with rather more opportunities for social interaction. One was a less complex constructional task (copying a model built out of Lego pieces) which again produced few differences in social interactional measures or in tutoring styles. The other involved tutoring in the Country Code, a set of rules for respecting the countryside. This was also less complex than the food-sort task, but avoided some of the practical constraints of the construction task which might have inhibited social interaction, such as the screen transposed between the tutee and the tutor's pre-assembled model. The Country Code task was considerably more promising in separating out qualitative differences between friends and non-friends in coping with task demands. There was clear evidence that tutors who were friends with their tutees gave significantly more instruction and addressed significantly more questions to their tutees than did those who were non-friends. Friend tutors also responded more to questions from their tutees than did non-friend tutors. So, in this study at least, there was evidence of an increase in focus amongst friends on the information component of the task, as we predicted.

Another way in which we have attempted to manipulate the balance of the task components is in connection with the tutor's degree of participation in the active, physical component of the task. In an animal classification task similar to that mentioned earlier, Foot, Shute and Morgan (1988) examined tutee memory for specific items of information and for learned principles to be applied to new material. Tutors were specifically trained to take either an 'active' or 'passive' role in relation to the sorting of four items of information about each of six pictured animals into a $2 \times 2$ grid. In the active role they were instructed to demonstrate the sorting of the cards to their tutees; in the passive role they were to instruct but leave their tutees to handle the cards. In practice several tutors failed to follow their instructions (in nearly all cases choosing to be more rather than less participative in the passive condition) and had to be reallocated to active or passive conditions on the basis of their actual participation. In fact, from data as yet unpublished from this study, those who took a more active role asked *more* questions and gave the *same* amount of instruction as more passive tutors, but gave considerably *less* encouragement. It may well be that if children are preoccupied with being in control of task materials when enacting the role of tutor, they may never do justice to the social management aspect of the task. Ellis and Rogoff (1986) observed that their children had difficulty determining the optimal amount of assistance to provide. Typically child tutors either provided too much assistance by carrying out the task themselves or by 'involving the learners in completing concrete steps without understanding the overall goal' (p. 324). Alternatively, as McLane (1981) has shown, child tutors may provide too little assistance, expecting young learners to carry out the task almost without guidance.

## TUTORS' SENSITIVITY TO THE NEEDS OF LEARNERS

The role theory approach of Vernon Allen (1976) has focused upon the closeness in age and competence between tutor and tutee as affording a much more similar match in perspectives than can be achieved with adult teachers. According to this view the child tutor can more easily adopt the role of learner and recognize when he or she is experiencing learning difficulties. In a teaching situation, as Allen and Feldman (1976) have argued, it is often necessary for the teacher to rely heavily upon non-verbal cues to determine how much the learner understands about the lesson being taught. There is, however, very little evidence about the accuracy of an observer's estimate of the level of understanding by another person on the basis of non-verbal cues alone. Only comparatively recently has children's decoding ability been explored in the context of children's accuracy in discriminating facial expression (Camras and Allison, 1985; Edwards, Manstead and McDonald, 1984; Zabel, 1979).

Allen and Feldman (1976) proposed two alternative hypotheses concerning children's ability to decode non-verbal behaviour depending upon whether the encoding of non-verbal behaviour is assumed to be qualitatively different for children and adults. If the process of encoding is different, then children should be superior to adults on the basis of their cognitive closeness; if the process of encoding is similar, then adults should be more accurate than children on the basis of their greater experience in interacting with people in general. Watching 30-second silent film clips of 20 stimulus children listening to either an easy or difficult arithmetic lesson, 96 children of third and sixth grades and 36 adults rated how much they estimated each stimulus child to have understood of the lesson. The main finding of a significant interaction between age of observer and type of lesson (easy or difficult) revealed that both third- and sixth-graders were more accurate in their ratings than adults. Indeed only the children significantly perceived differences in the degree of understanding of the stimulus children as a function of level of difficulty of the lesson. Adults appeared to overestimate degree of understanding in the difficult lesson considerably more than the children did. Allen and Feldman concluded that children are better able than adults to decode the non-verbal cues signalling lack of understanding emitted by other children and that either children's non-verbal encoding is different from that of adults or else adults may believe it to be so.

Research in this area is extremely sparse and we have found no corroborating evidence. Even if Allen and Feldman are correct about the decoding of non-verbal behaviours, there is no evidence that children have any clearer conception of what others are having difficulty in understanding. It must be emphasized that, in the Allen and Feldman study, it was purely observers' sensitivity to non-verbal information that was gauged in the absence of any verbal or task-related information. There were no findings relating to children's appreciation of the nature of the difficulties which other children experience in grasping difficult concepts or procedures. Indeed, given other findings that both younger and older children are poorer than adults in recognizing when a communication is ambiguous (Ironsmith and Whitehurst, 1978; Robinson and Robinson, 1983), it would not be surprising if any advantage for children in decoding the meaning of non-verbal behaviours would be more than offset by their failure to comprehend the reasons for any misunderstanding or lack of understanding to have occurred.

Our ideas and concepts about how children cope with non-understanding on the part of other children are still at a very primitive level and there is virtually no research to review on this point. It seems to us, however, that there is a fundamentally important reason for further research on this issue, especially in relation to tutee benefits. Reviewers of peer-based learning programmes (e.g. Damon, 1984) have pointed out that, as a technique of pupil-assisted learning, tutoring achieves most of its success when applied to tasks which are essentially rule-governed and focused upon the exchange of skills and information. This stands in contrast to tasks involving the acquisition of basic reasoning skills for which a collaborative relationship is preferable (Sharan, 1984). It may well be that the learning contexts for peer tutoring are limited by child tutors' cognitive incapacity to cope with non- or misunderstandings by their tutees other than those arising purely from the infringement of a rule or misapplication of a principle. If successful tutoring is to be extended to a wider range of more sophisticated learning tasks involving reasoning and problem-solving, then this may only be brought about by our being able to render assistance to tutors in recognizing the nature of and reasons for tutee non-understanding. This may not be an easy task but we can briefly point to one or two areas where future research might be fruitfully directed.

## Tutors' sensitivity to the signalling of non-understanding

An obvious distinction should be made between a lack of understanding (non-understanding) and misunderstanding. The former refers to situations described in the preceding pages where children lack the knowledge or ability to comprehend the lesson or instruction wholly or in part. The latter refers to situations where children think they understand the lesson or misconstrue it wholly or in part. The processes whereby lessons or instructions are misunderstood by children appear to be completely unresearched and it is, therefore, strictly non-understanding that is considered here.

There are relatively few ways in which children (tutees) can signal to their partners (tutors) that they do not understand an instruction or message, or that they are stumped by the problem in hand. Close examination of the transcripts of tutoring sessions in our animal classification study (Foot and Morgan, 1988) revealed three main types of signal (not reported in the published work). These types can be classified as task-related cues, verbal cues or non-verbal cues. Task-related cues are 'incorrect responses' or 'overlong response latencies', where, for example, the child stares at the task materials without doing anything, or plays aimlessly with an item. Verbal cues either take the form of 'specific questions' designed to clarify a point or procedure, or they consist of a 'general declaration of non-understanding' (e.g. 'I don't understand', or 'what do you mean?'). Non-verbal cues consist of 'puzzled looks' or perhaps a vague state of detachment.

Tutor reactions are also relatively limited in type and consist of the following typical kinds of responses: ignoring the signal from the tutee or failing to correct an error; seeking more information about the tutee's problem; repeating an instruction or information about the task, reformulating the instruction or information; supplying the answer or carrying out their own instruction.

Lack of tutor reaction may, of course, mean that the non-understanding is not resolved, that the tutee's errors are not corrected and that learning is ineffectual or incomplete. Peterson (1972) reported that young children, while recognizing that help may be needed in response to an 'I don't understand' request for help, lack the skill of knowing precisely what forms of help are necessary or how to ascertain exactly what the problem is. Responses by tutors to signals of non-understanding by tutees may serve to resolve the non-understanding, but they may not do so, and merely set up another cycle of non- or misunderstanding. We do not have any thoroughly worked through results here, and our data-base of signalled non-understandings was relatively small, but a few suggestive results emerged from our analyses. Non-understandings (all types) related inversely to tutor information-giving and tutee chart use (i.e. use of the information chart relating animal characteristics to the classification system) and these are all measures taken to indicate tutee-sensitive behaviours by the tutors. Consequently those tutors (especially adults) engaging in more tutee-sensitive behaviours generated fewer non-understandings. When non-understandings did occur, girls were more likely to resolve them than were boys (same-sex tutoring dyads). Other results indicated that failure to correct an incorrect response and ignoring the tutee's signals of non-understanding fell entirely within the province of child tutors; adult tutors never failed to respond. We have recently carried out some further work on children's ability to deal with verbal and non-verbal indicators of lack of understanding and this will be reported in due course (Shute, Foot and Morgan, in preparation).

**Tutor initiatives in gauging tutee understanding**

Not all non-understandings or learning difficulties are signalled by the tutee. Most teachers concerned with monitoring their tutees' progress carry out regular checks on understanding without waiting for explicit signals of non-understanding to occur. Adults in particular ask frequent 'sensitive questions' (of the type: 'do you understand?') rather than merely task-related questions, and although in our study inter-observer reliability for 'sensitive questions' was not very high ($r=0.61$, $p=0.05$), there was some indication that this type of teacher-initiated sensitivity is linked to absence of non-understanding, encouragement, looking and other tutee-sensitive behaviours.

A wider issue generally for tutor initiatives relates to the teacher's immediate realization of the level of competency of the child whom he or she is tutoring. Reference was made earlier to the ability of children to accommodate their conversation or instruction to match the cognitive capabilities of those with whom they are interacting. While this general phenomenon has been well documented even in very young children (e.g. Shatz and Gelman, 1973), no research has been directed at linking individual differences in accommodative verbal behaviours to other measures of tutee-sensitivity like monitoring tutees' progress or resolving non-understanding. Research of this kind would establish important general links in children's capacities for displaying sensitivity behaviour which might have payoffs both for guiding judgements on the suitability of particular children to serve as tutors and for the training of sensitivity skills. The mere fact that adults were generally more sensitive than children to their tutees suggests that sensitivity is learned through experience and can therefore be taught.

Finally, in discussing tutors' sensitivity to the needs of their tutees, it is interesting, as we have seen, that tutee academic performance (as indicated by English examination result) was related inversely to tutee-sensitive measures. The implication exists that tutors are gauging the amount of information they give to tutee needs. Thus, children whom they recognize as being of lower ability are given more information, more encouragement, and are asked more sensitive questions. Quite when or how tutors gauge this need is unclear, but it must happen during the early stages of tutoring and it may be consequential upon the tutors picking up cues either from the tutees' linguistic or paralinguistic behaviours or possibly from their total lack of verbal behaviour.

## CONCLUSION

In this chapter we have attempted to draw together some of the main theoretical issues which relate to peer tutoring amongst children and to stress the importance of social interaction as a necessary condition for cognitive growth. After reviewing the cognitive-developmental perspectives of the Piagetian and Vygotskian traditions we embarked upon a discussion of three major processes which, for theoretical reasons, seem to us particularly crucial for an adequate understanding of tutoring relationships. Children's perception of their tutoring roles is important because it helps to provide an understanding of children's awareness of the processes involved in learning and their implicit assumptions about the requirements for teaching. Consideration of children's teaching strategies is important because it focuses attention on children's management skills and their distribution of resources between different components of the learning task. It also focuses attention upon task typologies which may be useful for developing appropriate tutoring strategies. Finally, emphasis upon children's sensitivity to the needs of others in a learning context is also of great theoretical interest because it throws light upon children's developing awareness of and tolerance for the lack of understanding by others and the need for effective communication.

These issues are not only of theoretical interest but also of considerable practical concern both for tutor training and for the design of tutoring programmes. A knowledge of what assumptions and perspectives children bring to a teaching context means that we can seek to identify and, if necessary, correct tutors' misapprehensions about tutee skills and tutee needs for instruction and guidance. A knowledge of how children deploy their resources across the task components and the conditions under which such deployment may change is essential to the appropriate construction of tutor–tutee dyads. The varying demands of tutoring tasks in terms of their physical, social, and informational components may well help determine what the nature of the relationship between the tutor and tutee should optimally be: whether they should or should not be friends; whether the tutor should take an active or passive role, and so on. An understanding of the components of a task which child tutors have particular difficulty handling, such as the informational component or explaining the rationale of the task, can guide tutor training programmes to help offset the children's limitation in these areas. Equally it can assist in constructing tutoring tasks in such a way as to minimize the demands of those aspects of tutoring with which tutors typically have the greatest difficulty.

Sensitivity to the needs of the learner is an obvious area for tutor training and more research needs to be focused both upon developing tutor awareness of cues to lack of understanding on the part of the tutee, and upon providing tutors with appropriate skills for monitoring and evaluating tutee progress and performance.

The mismatch between practitioners' experience of the usefulness of peer tutoring programmes and researchers' evaluations of such programmes may hopefully be eroded if practitioners and researchers alike pay more attention to these fundamental processes.

## ACKNOWLEDGEMENT

The authors' work cited in this chapter was conducted as part of a programme of research on children's understanding of misunderstanding sponsored by the ESRC (Grant Ref: C00232235) 1986–1987.

## REFERENCES

Allen V. L. (1976). *Children as Teachers: Theory and Research on Tutoring*. New York: Academic Press.

Allen, V. L. (1983). Impact of the role of tutor on behavior and self-perceptions. In J. M. Levine and M. C. Wang (eds), *Teacher and Student Perceptions: Implications for Learning*. Hillsdale, New Jersey: Erlbaum.

Allen, V. L., and Feldman, R. S. (1974). Tutor attribution and attitude as a function of tutee performance, *Journal of Applied Social Psychology*, **4**, 311–320.

Allen, V. L., and Feldman, R. S. (1976). Studies on the role of tutor. In V. L. Allen (ed.), *Children as Teachers: Theory and Research on Tutoring*. New York: Academic Press.

Bearison, D., Magzamen, S., and Filardo, E. (1984). Socio-cognitive conflict and cognitive growth in young children. Paper presented at the Jean Piaget Society Annual Symposium, Philadelphia.

Blishen, E. (1969). *The School that I'd Like*. Harmondsworth: Penguin.

Blishen, E. (1973). Why some secondary teachers are disliked? *Where* (Nov) 330–334.

Bruner, J. (1985). Vygotsky: a historical and conceptual perspective. In J. V. Wertsch (ed.), *Culture, Communication and Cognition: Vygotskian Perspectives*. Cambridge: Cambridge University Press.

Camras, L. A., and Allison, K. (1985). Children's understanding of emotional facial expression and verbal labels, *Journal of Nonverbal Behaviour*, **9**, 84–94.

Collins, J. F., and Calevro, M. J. (1974). Mainstreaming special education using a peer tutoring system and minimum objective curriculum for nine eighth-grade students. ERIC Document Reproduction No 102-788 (May).

Cooper, C. R., Ayers-Lopez, S., and Marquis, A. (1982). Children's discourse during peer learning in experimental and naturalistic situations, *Discourse Processes*, **5**, 177–191.

Damon, W. (1984). Peer education: the untapped potential, *Journal of Applied Developmental Psychology*, **5**, 331–343.

Damon, W., and Killen, M. (1982). Peer interaction and the process of change in children's moral reasoning, *Merrill-Palmer Quarterly*, **28**, 347–367.

Damon, W., and Phelps, E. (1987). Peer collaboration as a context for cognitive growth. Paper presented at the Tel Aviv University School of Education Annual Symposium on human development and instruction (June).

Deterline, W. C. (1970). Training and management of student-tutors. Final Report. Palo Alto, California: General Programmed Teaching. ERIC Document Reproduction No ED 048-133.

Devin-Sheehan, L., Feldman, R. S., and Allen, V. L. (1976). Research on children tutoring children: a critical review, *Review of Educational Research*, **46**, 355–385.

Doise, W. (1985). Social regulations in cognitive development. In R. A. Hinde, A. N. Perret-Clermont and J. Stevenson-Hinde (eds), *Social Relationships and Cognitive Development*. Oxford: Oxford University Press.

Doise, W., and Mugny, G. (1979). Individual and collective conflicts of centrations in cognitive development, *European Journal of Social Psychology*, **9**, 105–108.

Doise, W., and Mugny, G. (1984). *The Social Development of the Intellect*. Oxford: Pergamon.

Doise, W., Mugny, G., and Perret-Clermont, A. (1975) Social interaction and the development of cognitive operations, *European Journal of Social Psychology*, **5**, 367–383.

Doise, W., Mugny, G., and Perret-Clermont, A. (1976). Social interaction and cognitive development: further evidence, *European Journal of Social Psychology*, **6**, 245–247.

Edwards, R., Manstead, A. S. R., and McDonald, C. J. (1984). The relationship between children's sociometric status and ability to recognize facial expression of emotion, *European Journal of Social Psychology*, **14**, 235–238.

Ehly, S. W., and Larsen, S. C. (1977). Sex, status, and liking of tutor and learner as predictors of tutorial outcomes, *Perceptual and Motor Skills*, **45**, 335–336.

Ehly, S. W., and Larsen, S. C. (1980). *Peer Tutoring for Individualized Instruction*. Boston: Allyn and Bacon.

Ellis, S., and Rogoff, B. (1982). The strategies and efficacy of child versus adult teachers, *Child Development*, **53**, 730–735.

Ellis, S., and Rogoff, B. (1986). Problem solving in children's management of instruction. In E. C. Mueller and G. R. Cooper (eds), *Process and Outcome in Peer Relationships*. New York: Academic Press.

Emler, N., and Valiant, G. L. (1982). Social interaction and cognitive conflict in the development of spatial coordination skills, *British Journal of Psychology*, **73**, 295–303.

Epstein, L. (1978). The effects of intraclass peer tutoring on the vocabulary development of learning disabled children, *Journal of Learning Disabilities*, **11**, 518–521.

Foot, H. C., and Morgan, M. J. (1988). Process variables in peer tutoring: children's understanding of misunderstanding. ESRC End of Award Report (C00232235). University of Wales College of Cardiff. 1–17.

Foot, H. C., Shute, R. H., and Morgan, M. J. (1988). Peer tutoring and children's memory. In M. M. Gruneberg, P. E. Morris, and R. N. Sykes (eds), *Practical Aspects of Memory: Current Research and Issues*. Vol 2: *Clinical and Educational Implications*. Chichester: Wiley.

Forbes, D., and Lubage.in, D. (1979). Reasoning and behavior in children's friendly interactions. Paper presented at the meeting of the American Psychological Association, New York (September).

Gartner, A., Kohler, M. C., and Riessman, F. (1971). *Children Teach Children: Learning by Teaching*. New York: Harper & Row.

Gearhart, M. (1979). Social planning: role play in a novel situation. Paper presented at meeting of the Society for Research in Child Development, San Francisco (March).

Gearhart, M., and Newman, D. (1980). Learning to draw a picture: the social context of individual activity, *Discourse Processes*, **3**, 169–184.

Gerber, M., and Kauffman, J. M. (1981). Peer tutoring in academic settings. In P. S. Strain (ed.), *The Utilization of Classroom Peers as Behavior Change Agents*. New York: Plenum Press.

Glachan, M., and Light, P. (1982). Peer interaction and learning: can two wrongs make a right? In G. Butterworth and P. Light (eds), *Social Cognition: Studies of the Development of Understanding*. Chicago: University of Chicago Press.

Goodlad, S. (1979). *Learning by Teaching*. London: Community Service Volunteers.

Goodlad, S., and Hirst, B. (1989). *Peer Tutoring: A Guide to Learning by Teaching*. London: Kogan Page.
Gormly, C. M. R., Chapman, A. J., Foot, H. C., and Sweeney, C. A. (1980). Accommodation in children's mixed-age social interactions. In H. Giles, W. P. Robinson, and P. M. Smith (eds), *Language: Social Psychological Perspectives*. Oxford: Pergamon.
Graziano, W., French, D., Brownell, G. A., and Hartup, W. W. (1976). Peer interaction in same- and mixed-age triads in relation to chronological age and incentive condition, *Child Development*, **47**, 707–714.
Haggarty, M. (1971). The effects of being a tutor and being a counselee in a group on self-concept and achievement level of underachieving adolescent males, *Dissertation Abstracts International*, **31** (9-A), 4460.
Hartup, W. W. (1976). Peer interaction and the behavioral development of the individual child. In E. Schopler, and R. J. Reichler (eds), *Psychopathology and Child Development*, New York: Plenum.
Hartup, W. W. (1978). Children and their friends. In H. McGurk (ed.), *Child Social Development*. London: Methuen.
Hatch, J. A. (1984). The social goals of children: a naturalistic study of child-to-child interaction in a kindergarten. Unpublished doctoral dissertation, University of Florida, College of Education.
Hatch, J. A. (1987). Peer interaction and the development of social competence. *Child Study Journal*, **17**, 169–183.
Ironsmith, M., and Whitehurst, G. J. (1978). The development of listener abilities in communication: how children deal with ambiguous information, *Child Development*, **49**, 348–352.
Lewis, M., and Rosenblum, L. A. (1975). *Friendship and Peer Relations*. New York: Wiley.
Light, P., Foot, T., Colburn, C., and McLelland, I. (1987). Collaborative interactions at the microcomputer keyboard, *Educational Psychology*, **7**, 13–21.
Light, P., and Glachan, M. (1985). Facilitation of individual problem-solving through peer interaction, *Educational Psychology*, **5**, 217–225.
Lippitt, P., and Lohman, J. E. (1965). Cross-age relationship—an educational resource, *Children*, **12**, 113–117.
Lougee, M. D., Grueneich, R., and Hartup, W. W. (1977). Social interaction in same- and mixed-age dyads of preschool children, *Child Development*, **48**, 1353–1361.
Ludeke, R. J., and Hartup, W. W. (1983). Teaching behaviors of 9- and 11-year-old girls in mixed-age and same-age dyads, *Journal of Educational Psychology*, **73**, 908–914.
Mackie, D. (1980). A cross-cultural study of intra- and inter-individual conflicts of centrations, *European Journal of Social Psychology*, **10**, 313–318.
Makins, V. (1969). Child's eye view of teacher, *Times Educational Supplement* (19 September), 21–22.
McLane, J. B. (1981). Dyadic problem solving: a campaign of child–child and mother–child interaction. Unpublished doctoral dissertation. Northwestern University.
Mehan, H. (1977). Students formulating practices and instructional strategies, *Annals of the New York Academy of Sciences*, **285**, 451–475.
Morgan, M. J., and Foot, H. C. (1985). The understanding of learning difficulties: implications for peer-tutoring, *Education Section Review*, **9**, 7–11.
Mugny, G., and Doise, W. (1978). Socio-cognitive conflict and the structure of individual and collective performances, *European Journal of Social Psychology*, **8**, 181–192.
Mugny, G., Perret-Clermont, A.-N., and Doise, W. (1981). Interpersonal coordinations and sociological differences in the construction of the intellect. In G. M. Stephenson and J. M. Davis (eds), *Progress in Applied Social Psychology*, Vol. 1. Chichester: Wiley.

Peterson, C. L., Danner, F. W., and Flavell, J. H. (1972). Developmental changes in children's response to three indications of communicative failure, *Child Development*, **43**, 1463–1468.
Piaget, J. (1928). *Judgement and Reasoning in the Child*. New York: Harcourt, Brace.
Piaget, J. (1932). *The Moral Judgement of the Child*. London: Routledge & Kegan Paul.
Piaget, J. (1970). Piaget's theory. In P. Mussen (ed.), *Carmichael's Manual of Child Psychology*. Vol 1. New York: Wiley.
Robertson, D. J. (1972). Intergrade teaching: children learn from children. In S. L. Sebesta and C. J. Wallen (eds), *The First R: Readings on Teaching Reading*. Chicago: Scientific Research Association.
Robinson, E. J., and Robinson, W. P. (1983). Children's uncertainty about the interpretation of ambiguous messages, *Journal of Experimental Child Psychology*, **36**, 81–96.
Russell, J. (1981a). Dyadic interaction in a logical reasoning problem requiring inclusion ability, *Child Development*, **52**, 1322–1325.
Russell, J. (1981b). Children's memory for the premises in a transitive measurement task assessed by elicited and spontaneous justifications, *Journal of Experimental Child Psychology*, **31**, 300–309.
Sarbin, T. (1976). Cross-age tutoring and social identity. In V. Allen (ed.), *Children as Teachers: Theory and Research on Tutoring*. New York: Academic Press.
Sarbin, T. R., and Allen, V. L. (1968). Role theory. In G. Lindzey and E. Aronson (eds), *The Handbook of Social Psychology*, Vol. 2. Reading, Massachusetts: Addison-Wesley, 488–567.
Sharan, S. (1984). *Cooperative Learning*. Hillside, New Jersey: Erlbaum.
Sharabany, R., and Hertz-Lazarowitz, R. (1981). Do friends share and communicate more than non-friends? *International Journal of Behavioral Development*, **4**, 45–59.
Sharpley, A. M., and Sharpley, C. F. (1981). Peer tutoring: a review of the literature. *Collected Original Resources in Education* (CORE), **5**, 3, 7-C11 (fiche 7 and 8), Abingdon, Oxon: Carfax.
Shatz, M. (1978). The relationship between cognitive processes and the development of communication skills. In C. B. Keasey (ed.), *Nebraska Symposium on Motivation*, Vol 26. Lincoln: University of Nebraska Press.
Shatz, M., and Gelman, R. (1973). The development of communication skills: modification in the speech of young children as a function of listener, *Monographs of the Society for Research in Child Development*, **38**, No 152.
Sullivan, H. S. (1953). *The Interpersonal Theory of Psychiatry*. New York: Plenum.
Taylor, P. H. (1962). Children's evaluations of the characteristics of the good teacher, *British Journal of Educational Psychology*, **32**, 258–266.
Thelen, M. H., and Kirkland, K. D. (1976). On status and being imitated: effects on reciprocal imitation and attraction, *Journal of Personality and Social Psychology*, **33**, 691–697.
Thomas, J. L. (1970). Tutoring strategies and effectiveness: a comparison of elementary age tutors and college age tutors. Unpublished doctoral dissertation, University of Texas, Austin.
Topping, K. (1988). *The Peer Tutoring Handbook: Promoting Co-operative Learning*. London: Croom Helm.
Vygotsky, L. S. (1962). *Thought and Language*. Cambridge, Massachusetts: MIT Press.
Vygotsky, L. S. (1978). *Mind in Society*. Cambridge, Massachusetts: Harvard University Press.
Wertsch, J. V. (1979). The regulation of human action and the given-new organization of private speech. In G. Zivin (ed.), *The Development of Self-regulation through Private Speech*. New York: Wiley.

Wood, D. (1988). *How Children Think and Learn*. Oxford: Blackwell.
Youniss, J. (1980). *Parents and Peers in Child Development*. Chicago, Illinois: University of Chicago Press.
Zabel, R. H. (1979). Recognition of emotions in facial expressions by emotionally disturbed children and non-disturbed children, *Psychology in the School*, **16**, 119–126.

CHAPTER 5

# Pupil Tutoring: the Development of Internality and Improved School Attendance

ANDRE J. IMICH

*Educational Psychologist, Essex Educational Psychology Service, 20 The Avenue, Hadleigh, Benfleet, Essex SS7 2DL, UK*

## INTRODUCTION

Although the educational benefits of pupil tutoring were initially highlighted by accounts of the Bell-Lancaster monitorial system in the early nineteenth century, controlled experimental investigation into outcomes for tutors and tutees has only emerged in the past 25 years. During this relatively brief period, there has mushroomed a huge volume of research material, the vast majority of which supports the view that pupil tutoring is a valuable activity for all participants. The earlier studies into effectiveness of pupil tutoring tended to focus on the attainment gains of tutees (especially in reading). As it became established that tutees invariably made significant gains in performance, attention turned to the effects of tutoring upon the child acting as the tutor. A review of the earlier research was carried out by Devin-Sheehan, Feldman and Allen (1976) indicating that, in academic terms, tutors made gains at least as great as those of the pupils they were teaching. This was confirmed in a later review by Goodlad (1979). However, the evidence for social or personality benefits was more variable and was often based on methodologically weak research; as Topping (1988) points out, the generalized improvements accruing to the tutor in behaviour and in self-concept have proven more difficult to

Children Helping Children
Edited by H. C. Foot, M. J. Morgan and R. H. Shute

demonstrate and to reproduce. The present chapter aims to present an account of research into the effects of pupil tutoring on the development of locus of control orientation and on the school attendance of tutors. Both are areas which to date have received little empirical attention but which, if positive effects can be demonstrated, would lend further support for the effectiveness of pupil tutoring and justify its inclusion as a valuable experience offered by schools.

When carrying out a review of the research into pupil tutoring studies, one needs to be aware of the debate about the value of the different forms of evaluation that can be made. Paolitto (1976) emphasized the need for rigorous quantitative research into pupil tutoring, but added that there is an important role for the more descriptive and clinical approaches to evaluation, primarily because they can throw light onto the adolescent's viewpoint about the tutoring experience. Goodlad's (1979) review of British pupil tutoring studies proposed a gentler style of evaluation. In his view, anecdotal evidence (or 'positive testimony') has shown that improvements in the attitudes of tutors is enormous, despite the lack of support from more quantitative research. Clearly, there is a need for both forms of evaluation. Generally speaking, pupil tutoring studies have involved small numbers of subjects, which reduces the probability of evaluation revealing statistically significant outcomes. In these cases, authors have tended to support their hypotheses with observations reported by the adults or children involved in such studies and to have included other anecdotal evidence. Such methodology serves a valid function in advancing our knowledge of the potential effects of pupil tutoring and our understanding of the processes involved, although it should be regarded primarily as a source of further hypotheses for investigation.

## CHARACTERISTICS RELATED TO LOCUS OF CONTROL

The locus of control construct stems from the social learning theory of Rotter (1966). It is a dimension of personality concerned with the attribution of reinforcement: when a reinforcement is perceived by a subject as following some action of his or her own but not being entirely contingent upon that action, then it is typically perceived as the result of luck, chance, fate, as under the control of powerful others, or as unpredictable because of the great complexity of the surrounding forces. If an individual interprets an event in this way, he or she is deemed to have a belief in *external* control. Perception of the event as contingent upon one's own behaviour or own personal characteristics is said to indicate a belief in *internal* control. That individuals can be distinguished in terms of locus of control orientation has been the subject of much research (e.g. Nowicki and Barnes, 1973; Lefcourt, 1976; Phares, 1976) and is now a well-established feature of theories of personality development.

There is much evidence to suggest that internals show higher levels of adaptive functioning within their environment than do externals. Phares (1962) demonstrated that, when required to learn nonsense syllables, those subjects who felt they were in control of the learning situation performed more efficiently than those who felt they were not in control. Other experiments (James and Rotter, 1958; Rotter and Mulry, 1965; Hiroto, 1974) also showed that when people feel they control a situation, they are more likely to behave in ways which enable them to cope successfully with potentially threatening situations than are subjects who feel that chance or other uncontrollable forces determine whether their behaviour will be successful.

In 1966, the Coleman Report underlined the relationship between belief in personal control over academic rewards and academic achievement. This report stressed the crucial role of locus of control beliefs in understanding the academic achievement of children. The authors concluded that 'a pupil attitude factor, which appears to have a stronger relationship to achievement than do all the "school" factors together, is the extent to which an individual feels that he has some control over his own destiny' (Coleman *et al.*, 1966, p. 23). This conclusion led educational researchers to examine the strength of the relationship between locus of control and achievement.

Crandall, Katkovsky, and Preston (1962) found that internal scores were highly related to the amount of time boys chose to spend in intellectual activities during free play and the intensity with which they were striving in these activities. Chance (1965; cited in Phares, 1976) found that locus of control orientation correlated with several achievement indices, including reading skills, arithmetic performance, spelling and even intelligence, with internals performing better on all these measures. Crandall, Katkovsky, and Crandall (1965) showed internals to be superior to externals in reading, mathematics, language, and total achievement test scores from the Iowa Tests of Basic Skills. There was also a correlation between report card grades for effort and behaviour and locus of control scores. Further studies have continued to provide evidence that a greater belief in personal control is linked to higher levels of school achievement (e.g. Bar-Tal *et al.*, 1980; Chandler, 1980; Duke and Nowicki, 1974; Gozali *et al.*, 1973; Kanoy, Johnson and Kanoy, 1980; Julian and Katz, 1968; Lefcourt, 1966; Lefcourt, Lewis and Silverman, 1968; Messer, 1972; Nowicki and Barnes, 1973; Swanson, 1981). As Williams (1980, p. 15) points out 'it is very probable that locus of control plays a mediating role in determining whether a person becomes involved in the pursuit of achievement'.

Further characteristics related to internals have been firmly identified. James, Woodruff, and Werner (1965) found that internals were less likely to be smokers. Getter (1966), Ritchie and Phares (1969) and Strickland (1970) demonstrated that externals were more amenable and susceptible to outside influences, whilst internals tended to follow their own inclinations and to be discriminating about what influences they would accept. Bar-Tal *et al.* (1980) showed that internals are less anxious and have higher levels of aspiration. Externals have a lower self-concept than internals (Kanoy, Johnson and Kanoy, 1980). Children who exhibit behaviour problems at school are more externally orientated (Annesley, 1974; Allie, 1979). Internals are more popular amongst their peers (Nowicki and Rountree, 1971; Nowicki and Strickland, 1973).

La Place (1976) found that locus of control was useful in helping to explain attendance behaviour. There was a statistically significant linear relationship between the attendance behaviour of students and their measured locus of control. Ollendick (1979) found that absenteeism for boys from two-parent families was significantly and positively correlated with a higher level of external control. Imich (1984) showed that a group of secondary school male truants was significantly more external in its locus of control orientation than a group of good attenders. However, whilst such evidence is indicative of a relationship between the two factors, it is not sufficient for an inference of causality. As Imich points out 'it is far more likely that lack of belief in personal control and unjustified absence from school are merely two of several symptoms of a major under-lying problem' (p. 44).

It can, therefore, be seen that there is a wealth of evidence that the perception of causality makes a considerable difference to the ways that pupils will meet the demands of their schools. Internals have greater academic success and achievement; they use time more efficiently; they use information more productively; they depend more upon their own judgements; they react more appropriately to threatening situations; they are less easily influenced and they have better school attendance. For these reasons Lawrence and Winschel (1974) state that 'the development of internality appears fundamental to education in a free society . . . .' Internality 'suggests responsibility and self reliance—the individual as an effective agent of his own destiny' (p. 484). The promotion of internality would, therefore, appear to be a valid aim of schools.

## DEVELOPMENT OF INTERNALITY

Despite the abundance of studies into the locus of control construct, there is a disappointing lack of research into training programmes specifically designed to shift locus of control beliefs. Most researchers who have studied the antecedents of locus of control orientation have assumed that they are learned through children's continuous experiences with their parents. Findings from Katkovsky, Crandall, and Good (1967), Liftschitz (1973), and Halpin, Halpin, and Whiddon (1980) would lead one to predict that schools which are warm, praising, and supportive, have an effective pastoral care system, have little or no corporal punishment, give reinforcement for autonomous behaviour, allow freedom of self-organization, and give pupils responsibility to organize their own affairs, contain more internals than schools that do not stress these characteristics.

Nowicki and Barnes (1973) predicted that a structured camp experience which made clearer the connection between a child's behaviour and the resultant reinforcement should have the effect of making the children perceive themselves to be more in control of events and thus more internal. Children attending a summer camp were divided into three groups for one week, with an aim of working together within the group to accomplish shared goals. Each group had its own two counsellors, who helped the children see how their own efforts could bring about results. Social reinforcement was provided at every opportunity. On the basis of pre- and post-tests of locus of control, Nowicki and Barnes found that the camping experience brought about a significant shift towards internality for these children. However, there was only an interval of one week between the pre- and post-test measures of locus of control, and the study contained no control groups. Martin and Shepel (1974) found that student nurses who received training in personal counselling skills moved towards internality. Again, however, there was no control group, and the change was recorded only 48 hours after training had ceased.

De Charms (1972) examined personal causation, a construct very similar to locus of control. A group of teachers was shown how to develop 'origin' behaviours in school. 'Origin' behaviour is the deliberate initiation by an individual of actions aimed at producing a change in his or her environment. De Charms found that personal causation training did increase origin-related behaviour in children, and that it significantly affected the academic achievement of the children. He also found that, during spelling games, children became more moderate in their risk taking, which he attributed to an increase in realistic goal-setting. Gaa (1979) found that goal-setting conferences enhanced students' perceptions of their ability to control reinforcements in the classroom. Johnson and Croft (1975) found that participation in a personalized system of instruction course, in which expectations are stated very closely so that a student recognizes the consequences of his or her performance, led to a movement towards internality.

In a wider examination of the effects of tutoring on psychological growth, Strodtbeck, Ronchi and Hansell (1976) looked at ego development and individual efficacy. The authors were carrying out an investigation into the Neighbourhood Youth Corps (NYC) programmes in which poor achievers could earn money for carrying out tasks in school, of which pupil tutoring was one option. One hypothesis was that the experience of being involved in such programmes and being rewarded would make the greatest contributions to the sense of efficacy if the student felt that his or her own efforts had brought about the involvement in the rewarding activity. Comparisons were made between NYC students who acted as tutors and those who did not. It was found that, on a measure of locus of control, neither the tutors nor the non-tutors showed a significant shift towards internality—the measure of increased efficacy. The failure of tutors to develop internality may, however, be accounted for by a methodological problem with the design of the NYC programme—success on the scheme was likely to disqualify students from further participation and the opportunity to earn. It was shown that placement in tutoring had a positive effect on grammar scores, self-esteem, and attendance. The study suggested that tutoring could be stressful for the pupils with the very lowest ego-development in ways that other roles at school are not, and Strodtbeck, Ronchi, and Hansell concluded that 'a certain maturity level was necessary for tutoring to set in motion the positive growth potential measured by the sense of efficacy score' (p. 215).

## PUPIL TUTORING AND THE DEVELOPMENT OF INTERNALITY

That pupil tutoring may be seen as a positive event and, therefore, an effective means for altering locus of control orientations has been directly investigated in only two studies. In the first of these, Chandler (1980) selected 13 junior high students who were high in externality, low in academic achievement, and judged by school staff to have negative views towards school, and trained them to be tutors. They were assigned to tutees in the second and third grade levels and matched as closely as possible on temperament, type of school-related problem, and level of academic achievement. Each tutor worked with a tutee at the tutee's school for 45 minutes a day over a six-week period.

At the conclusion of the study, the tutors were again given the same test of locus of control orientation. Analysis of the data indicated that the training group changed significantly towards internality after training. This suggested that tutors who were high in externality prior to involvement in pupil tutoring moved significantly towards internality after working as tutors. Of the 13 tutors, ten of them moved significantly from an external locus of control orientation toward an internal locus of control orientation. As Chandler put it, the tutors learned 'that they could have an effective control over another child. What they did to another child could have a positive effect on that child' (p. 717).

Unfortunately, however, Chandler did not employ a control group, and therefore no definitive conclusions could be reached from his study, particularly as the results could be accounted for by the Hawthorne effect. Nevertheless, there is evidence that locus of control orientations do not shift significantly over a three-month period (Nowicki and Strickland, 1973), and that test–retest reliability is quite high. One could therefore suggest that there would have been no significant change in a control group over the same period.

The second investigation into the effects of pupil tutoring on locus of control orientations was carried out by Imich (1984). Ten male truants in the third year of a secondary school were assigned into either an intervention group, who were to act as tutors, or a control group, who received no intervention. The two groups were matched for sex, age, school class, and attendance records. Administration of the Nowicki–Strickland Locus of Control Scale for Children (CNSIE) revealed that there was no difference between the two groups in their locus of control orientation.

The tutor group tutored poor readers in a primary school for one hourly session per week for an eleven-week period. On completion of the programme, the CNSIE was again administered to both groups. Results showed that, for the tutors, there was a median shift of three locus of control points towards internality, whereas the corresponding median shift for the non-tutors was only one point over the same period. However, an analysis of covariance indicated that these differences were not statistically significant. This was, in part, accounted for by the small sample size of five in each group. Analysis of individuals' scores indicated that all those truants who acted as tutors showed a movement towards internality, with two of these shifts being of six points. This contrasted with the group of non-tutoring truants who either remained constant, or showed a minimal shift in either direction. It was also pointed out that there was a lack of objective feedback during the programme about the progress that the tutees were making as a result of the tutors' input. In the study by Nowicki and Barnes (1973) children were directly taught the connections between their behaviours and the consequences or outcomes, and they argued it was this learning coupled with successful experiences that led to increased internality. It would seem, therefore, that for pupil tutoring programmes to effect change in an individual's locus of control orientation there is a need for a structured record-keeping system, sensitive to small improvements in the area being taught, if tutors are to have objective evidence that they are making a difference and therefore to develop the belief that they can have control over events.

This account of the locus of control construct has suggested that an internal locus of control is associated with a wide range of positive educational, psychological, and social attributes, and can justifiably be included as a valid aim in education. Ways of changing an individual's locus of control orientation have been less well examined in research, but two studies in particular have suggested that involvement in pupil tutoring can help individuals move towards internality. Clearly, further evidence is required, particularly studies involving larger numbers of subjects over a longer period of time, and providing tutors with frequent feedback about tutees' progress.

## SCHOOL NON-ATTENDANCE

Studies into absenteeism from school have historically focused on two seemingly distinct groups: truants and school phobics. In simple terms, the difference between the two populations is that truancy can be viewed as a social problem whereas school phobia is more of a clinical concern. More recently, however, researchers have queried the validity of this distinction. The term school phobia has been favoured in Britain by Chazan (1962), Berg, Nichols and Pritchard (1969), and Blagg (1981). Khan (1974) prefers the umbrella term 'school refusal' to the distinction between truancy and school phobia. However, this term has added to the confusion, since many researchers use it to refer simply to school phobia (e.g. Tyrer and Tyrer, 1974; Waller and Eisenberg, 1980). Doubts as to the utility of the dichotomy have also arisen as a result of research findings. Cooper (1966), for example, has found that, while differing in several aspects, truants and school phobics had the following characteristics in common: poor physique, timidity, fantasy, inability to enjoy success, and withdrawal. In addition, both groups had less contact with their teachers and their peers than other children. Galloway (1976) suggests that of all chronic absentees, only between 1.2% and 4.2% can be called school phobics, supporting Chazan's (1962) low estimate of 1%. Rutter, Tizard and Whitmore (1970) found no cases of school phobia. Reynolds and Murgatroyd (1977), in a series of studies into school attendance in comprehensive schools in South Wales, argued that, for the basis of their research, all pupils absent from school without good reason were truants. Carroll (1977) chose to employ the term 'absenteeism', on the grounds that it encompassed all forms of poor attendance, and did not have the usual connotations associated with labelling. Galloway (1985) used a similar term in his research, arguing that, generally, labels tend to relate to family or child variables, thereby making questionable assumptions about the nature of persistent absenteeism.

Galloway's view reflects the development of studies into those pupils with poor attendance. Initially, research focused on their characteristics such as sex differences, intelligence, achievement, family background, friendship patterns, self-concept, rates of delinquency, and other psychosocial factors. However, the abundant findings in these areas did not lead either to greater prediction about those who were potential absentees or more effective methods for dealing with them. As a result, attention turned to the characteristics of the schools themselves.

Studies by Reynolds, Jones and St Leger (1976), Reynolds and Murgatroyd (1977) and Reynolds *et al.* (1980) in nine Welsh comprehensive schools, and by Rutter *et al.* (1979) in 12 London comprehensives have suggested that differences in pupil behaviour stemmed from 'their differing experiences during the secondary school years'. The Rutter study strongly substantiated suggestions that the main source of variations between schools could be found in the school's functioning as a social organization, and as a setting for teaching and learning. Similarly, Reynolds *et al.* (1980) concluded that there were great differences between schools in terms of attendance, delinquency, and attainment. High rates of attendance were associated with enforcement of uniform in lower school, operating a prefect system, and minimal use of corporal punishment. Fogelman, Tibbenham and Lambert (1980) found from the National Child Development Study data that high attendance was associated with compulsory uniform, low teacher turnover, and frequent parent–teacher meetings. Emmerson, Carter and Lasalle (1981) found that most children were in favour of school rules, but only if they were applied impartially and consistently. Reynolds and Murgatroyd

(1977) found that schools that have diminished pastoral care have poorer rates of attendance than schools with sufficient pastoral care. Kavanagh and Carroll (1977) hypothesized that 'the school itself, e.g. its organization and the attitudes of the teachers towards the pupils and one another, has an important part to play in reducing both attendance problems and the possible effects of poor attendance' (p. 59), but did not test this hypothesis. Moos and Moos (1978) found that classes seen as high in competition and teacher control and low in teacher support had high absenteeism rates. Galloway (1982) noted that poor attenders were high on a 'fear-of teacher' rating. Few studies have explored the direct effects of the daily curriculum on attendance, but one can sympathize with Galloway's view (1985) that the curriculum can either encourage or discourage attendance. The growing suspicion that the new General Certificate of Secondary Education (GCSE) curriculum introduced into British schools in 1986 may be perpetuating the failure of previous examination systems in failing to provide for the educational needs of a significant percentage of the school population, suggests that, far from increasing enthusiasm from school, pupils may become disillusioned at an earlier age and attendance rates for 15- and 16-year-olds may deteriorate. As Galloway (1985) points out, pupils need to feel that attendance at school rather than absence can result in greater personal and social benefits.

## PUPIL TUTORING AND SCHOOL ATTENDANCE

The possibility that involvement in a pupil tutoring scheme could constitute an attractive element of a school curriculum and result in increased attendance for tutors, has received scant attention. A literature search revealed a number of studies which support this possibility, although it must be noted that only a handful specifically investigate the effects on pupils identified as poor attenders. The majority examine the effects on pupils who may already have had acceptable levels of attendance.

The first indication of changes in school attendance was found in a long-term evaluation of a pupil tutoring programme carried out by Lippitt and Lippitt (1968). In this programme, seventh and eighth grade students tutored low achieving fourth, fifth, and sixth grade students in reading, arithmetic, and language, three times a week for approximately half-hourly sessions. Amongst the results was the finding that tutors developed a more positive sociometric profile, as measured by a social acceptability scale. When one considers the evidence that truants tend to have poor peer group relationships (Croft and Grygier, 1956; Tyerman, 1968; Seabrook, 1974; Galloway, 1982), one could hypothesize that, should truants improve their social status through pupil tutoring, there may also be a related improvement in their school attendance. Lippitt and Lippitt also found that, compared with controls, the pupil tutoring programme resulted in higher school attendance rates for both tutors and tutees.

The finding that the attendance of tutees was enhanced when receiving pupil tutoring has not been reproduced (nor, indeed, investigated since this study) but is an area that is worthy of follow-up.

A younger group of tutors, aged twelve years, was employed in a pupil tutoring project by Frager and Stern (1970). The 48 tutors were divided into groups of high and low achievers on the basis of their reading scores, and the two groups tutored remedial kindergarten children. In overall terms, Frager and Stern reported that amongst the tutors, there was high morale, good attendance, and general satisfactory adjustment to the school setting. Looking at differences between the two groups, they found that the low achieving group experienced significant improvements in their school morale, attitudes, feelings about themselves, and school attendance. Since there is evidence (e.g. Tyerman, 1968; Fogelman and Richardson, 1974; Kavanagh and Carroll, 1977; Baum, 1978) that truants are generally inferior to good attenders in their basic school attainments, one may suggest on the basis of the Frager and Stern study that pupil tutoring can justifiably be employed with low-achievers since it results in improved attendance, and may therefore be a factor in preventing later truancy.

Wing (1972) investigated the effects of a tutoring programme which involved high school students who were identified as having high potential for dropping out of school. This study is one of the largest reported investigations into pupil tutoring, with 74 high school pupils tutoring 75 elementary school pupils over a period of one year. Data for the number of days missed during the project year were compared with the attendance record for the previous year. The difference was found to be highly significant, with the average number of days missed by the pupil tutors being significantly less than for the comparison year. Wing concluded that involvement in the programme had a significant and positive effect on school attendance. Wing also compared the dropout rate of the tutors during the semester following the pupil tutoring programme with that of peers who did not participate in the programme. No significant differences were found in this comparison, although Wing reports that the tutor group had a lower dropout rate. Other findings in this study showed that tutors gained in self-confidence and developed more positive attitudes towards school.

Strodtbeck, Ronchi and Hansell (1976) investigated a similar population of students when carrying out an evaluation of the Neighbourhood Youth Corps (NYC), which was part of a Department of Labour sponsored programme. The NYC enrolled inner-city youths who were at least two years below grade level in reading and were from impoverished homes. These youngsters could earn money for carrying out certain tasks around the school, in the expectation that this might discourage dropping out of school. One option available was to participate in a Youth Tutoring Youth (YTY) programme, either in their own school or at nearby elementary schools. No detailed analysis is given about the length of time that NYC students tutored nor whether they were seen as having attendance problems. However, positive results were found with regard to school attendance: compared with the previous school year, tutors increased their average days in attendance by 8.26 days, in contrast with an increase of 1.70 days for non-tutors on the NYC programme, a significant difference. It was felt that since excessive absence is frequently a precursor of dropping out, the decrease in absences was in line with the stated objectives of the NYC programme. Whether there actually was a decrease in the rate of dropping out for those who acted as tutors was unfortunately not followed up. Nevertheless, this study does again support the effectiveness of pupil tutoring in bringing about improved attendance.

A smaller and briefer study was carried out by Saunders in 1977. The aim of the study was to determine whether pupils who were involved as tutors in a cross-age tutoring programme would show an attitude change in self-concept, in reading, and toward school, as measured by attendance, when compared with student non-tutors. The tutors were selected from a ninth-grade class in a junior high school and from an eleventh and twelfth grade class in a senior high school. They each tutored an elementary school child once a week for a period of eight weeks. Measures of school attendance were recorded for the tutors and the non-tutors during the semester in which the programme was carried out. Results from the study indicated that the pupil tutors from both the senior and junior high school did not show any significant changes in attitude towards self. However, Saunders did find that the junior high school tutors had significantly better school attendance rates when compared with non-tutors. This finding did not hold for the senior high school tutors. Saunders concluded that involvement in a cross-age tutoring programme has a positive effect on the school attendance of ninth-grade pupils. It should be noted, however, that the tutors selected were not identified initially as having poor attendance records, and no evidence is presented as to whether their attendance improved *during* the programme compared with their previous attendance records or whether there was any lasting effect on attendance following cessation of the programme. It may be that pupil tutoring is an attractive supplement to the usual school curriculum which leads to improved attendance whilst it is being offered, but which has no long-lasting effect once it is withdrawn. Nevertheless, the finding that involvement in a cross-age tutoring experience brought about better attendance rates for 14-year-olds in comparison with non-tutoring peers than it did for 16-year-olds has implications for the planning of future programmes. It may be that for those pupils in their final year of schooling, attitudes towards school and poor attendance patterns are too deep-rooted to be significantly altered by a pupil tutoring programme. Such a programme may be more effective at an earlier stage of intervention and in the prevention of long-term attendance problems.

Ratti (1980), faced with the all-too-common problem of motivating a class of slow-learning 16-year-old pupils, organized a highly structured tutoring programme with slow-learning primary school pupils over a two-term period. The tutors were all seen as having a poor self-image, disenchanted with a normal school curriculum which served only to reinforce the fact that they were educational failures, and starting to compensate through antisocial acts and poor school behaviour. Most were seen as latecomers to lessons, and many as persistent truants. Evaluation of the programme suggested that the self-image of the tutors was enhanced, because for the first time in their school careers, they felt important in an educational setting. Of the ten tutors involved, eight attended for 90% or more of the tutoring sessions. There is no empirical evidence of generalization to their attendance when not involved in pupil tutoring sessions, although there is an anecdotal comment provided by the tutors' headmaster about their 'sudden (but lasting) improvement in attendance, punctuality, and dress' (Ratti, 1980, p. 22).

In 1982, Maher examined the effects of cross-age tutoring on a group of behaviour-problem adolescents. In this study, 18 high school students, classified as emotionally disturbed, were randomly assigned to one of three intervention groups. In the first group, each subject served as a cross-age tutor to an elementary school-aged child who was classified as educably mentally retarded. The second group of subjects received peer-tutoring from a non-handicapped student in the high school as part of the school's peer tutoring programme. The final group was provided with group counselling by a highly experienced school psychologist. Intervention for all three groups was provided twice a week for one-half hour per session, and lasted for ten weeks. Evaluation examined the effects of each intervention on academic scholastic performance, number of disciplinary referrals, and the percentage of days in school attendance, taking into account a baseline period of 20 weeks before intervention, the ten-week intervention period, and a follow-up period of ten weeks.

Results were found that suggested the potential usefulness of having behaviour problem adolescents act as cross-age tutors. For example, when compared with the groups who received either peer tutoring from older high school students, or group counselling from a school counsellor, those students who had acted as cross-age tutors were found to have improved significantly in their language, arts, and social science performance. These results were maintained during the follow-up period. Similar findings were noted for the numbers of students referred by their teachers for disciplinary problems. The cross-age tutors showed a decline in their number of disciplinary referrals during the intervention and follow-up periods. However, the number of referrals for the group counselling and same-age tutoring groups increased during the follow-up period and continued to increase during the remainder of the school year. With respect to school attendance, similar findings were reported, with significant differences occurring between the three groups. Students who acted as cross-age tutors had significantly fewer absences than those who received same-age tutoring or group counselling during both the intervention and the follow-up periods. The rate of absenteeism of the cross-age tutors was reduced significantly during the course of the year, whereas the rate for the same-age tutoring and group counselling groups increased significantly during the academic year.

Maher concluded that the use of cross-age tutoring with behaviour problem adolescents 'may not only be a potentially effective behavioral intervention procedure to remediate extant behavioral problems, but may also be a potentially effective preventive approach' (p. 364). A further study by Maher (1984) described in clear detail the organization and evaluation of a programme in which emotionally disturbed high-school pupils tutored elementary-aged educable mentally retarded pupils in arithmetic, reading and language twice a week for ten weeks. Results were again impressive, showing that the tutors raised the completion rates of their own work assignments, and improved their performances on tests and quizzes. As in his previous study, Maher also showed a significant decline in the disciplinary referrals of tutors during intervention which remained stable during the ten-week follow-up period. However, unlike the 1982 study, there were no comparison groups, and in neither study did Maher employ a control group which was not subject to some form of intervention technique. The 1984 study did not attempt to reproduce the earlier encouraging findings of the effects of cross-age tutoring on school attendance.

These results can be interpreted as further evidence that involvement in a cross-age tutoring programme will lead to improved school attendance. However, it should be noted that Maher's population of students was not identified on the grounds of attendance problems alone, but through the more encompassing label of conduct problems, of which attending school may or may not have been a secondary problem. One conclusion that may be accepted, however, is that in bringing about improved attendance, involvement in cross-age tutoring was significantly more effective than same-age tutoring; in fact, those students involved in same-age tutoring showed a gradual deterioration in school attendance. This latter finding needs to be considered when planning pupil-tutoring projects. More detailed accounts of the advantages and disadvantages of cross-age versus same-age tutoring are presented by Lippitt (1976) and Gredler (1985).

## PUPIL TUTORING AND POOR ATTENDERS

A study by Bond (1982) was the first to examine the effects of acting as pupil tutors on a group of poor attenders. Six pupils attending a Truancy Centre were selected on the basis of their individual needs for participation in a pupil tutoring scheme. They tutored 12 infants in reading and maths over an eight-week period, for one two-and-a-half hour session per week. Outcomes of the programme were examined primarily on the basis of subjective observation by teachers and self-reports by the tutors. A number of positive outcomes were indicated, including improved literacy and numeracy skills of tutors and tutees, improved tutor's attitudes to school and teachers, and enhanced self-concept of pupil-tutors.

Bond suggested that for this group of pupils, pupil-tutoring had given them insight into the source of their own problems, softened their attitudes to school and teachers and offered them an opportunity to practise their basic skills in a safe environment. Most importantly, it had provided them with feelings of self-worth not previously held.

In terms of the effects on attendance, Bond presented data which suggest that none of the six tutors played truant from any of the tutoring sessions. Three achieved 100% attendance, two missed only one session, and one missed half the sessions. However, whenever sessions were missed, valid excuses were put forward, such as illness or holiday. Nevertheless, such excuses need to be carefully considered, since there is evidence in the case of poor attenders that often their absence is condoned by parents. It is encouraging to note such high attendance at tutoring sessions amongst a group of poor attenders, but it would be difficult to justify its use for such subjects if there was no evidence of carry-over effects in general school attendance. Such evidence is not provided in Bond's study, nor was there a control group.

The study by Imich (1984) previously referred to in examining the effects of pupil-tutoring on the development of internality also attempted to investigate the intervention and long-term effects on the attendance patterns of truants. A group of third-year secondary school pupils were identified as truants on the basis of form teacher ratings, head of year ratings, and an attendance record of less than 85%. They were randomly divided into two groups of five pupils, one group receiving no intervention—the control group and the second participating in a cross-age tutoring programme. In addition, a third group was employed to measure the normal attendance pattern over the academic year, this group being the class-mates of the poor attenders.

The intervention group acted as tutors to seven-year-old pupils in a primary school who were experiencing difficulties in their reading. Sessions lasted an hour, with one session each week over an 11-week period. Attendance at the tutoring sessions was generally high, with two of the group achieving maximum attendance. However, one pupil-tutor attended for only half the sessions. This pattern of attendance mirrors that shown in Bond's (1982) programme. It may, therefore, be the case that, for the majority of participants, pupil-tutoring is an attractive activity, but that it is inevitably subject to individual differences in taste, as with any part of the school curriculum. The evidence presented here and by Bond strongly suggests, however, that pupil-tutoring is a more popular activity than most other school activities, judging by its ability to attract a higher rate of attendance amongst a group of reluctant attenders. More global measures of the potential effects on actual school attendance were investigated using the attendance figures for a baseline period of 13 weeks, the intervention period of 11 weeks, and a follow-up period of eight weeks. Results suggested that involvement in the pupil-tutoring programme brought about an improvement in the attendance pattern of a group of truants during the programme, with continuing improvement after cessation. During the follow-up period of eight weeks, the pupil-tutors recorded an average attendance level of 80%. In real terms, the figures indicated that truants who acted as tutors attended for the equivalent of 11 more school days than the control group of truants. However, none of these results was found to be statistically significant, possibly on account of the small number of subjects involved, and no definitive conclusions could, therefore, be reached about the outcome of this pupil tutoring programme on the attendance pattern of poor attenders.

In conclusion, studies into the effects of pupil-tutoring on the attendance behaviour of tutors have all shown evidence of improved attendance, at least during the period of the tutoring programme. None has indicated a deleterious effect. However, the quality and utility of findings is variable. Some studies have merely presented the attendance figures of tutors at tutoring sessions which, although always encouraging, would on their own be unlikely to convince curriculum planners, or those dealing with the problems of non-attendance, that students (or regular absentees) should be offered the opportunity to participate in tutoring programmes. Evidence of generalization to the rest of school attendance during a programme, and maintenance after the cessation of the programme has also been presented which, while suggesting improved attendance, has tended not to be significant, possibly due to the few subjects involved. Nevertheless anecdotal evidence adds to the view that pupil-tutoring does lead to longer-term improved attendance.

There have been few studies specifically examining the effects on a homogeneous group of poor attenders. The majority of these have tended to examine changes in attendance as one of several variables, and it has not necessarily been the case that subjects had poor attendance records. Researchers may have been deterred by the difficulty in organizing any school-based programmes for known poor attenders, but the evidence of the studies by Ratti (1980), Bond (1982), and Imich (1984) show that such pupils do put in good attendance, at least for the tutoring sessions. Pupil tutoring would appear to have a higher probability of improving the attendance of younger students, namely those not in their final year or two at school with well-formed patterns of behaviour, and may serve to prevent long-term behaviour and attendance problems. One study has shown clear evidence that cross-age tutoring is more likely to improve attendance than same-age tutoring. Finally, one early study showed that receiving tutoring can also bring about better school attendance, and it is proposed that this would be a fruitful area for further research.

## THE EFFECTIVENESS OF PUPIL TUTORING: CONCLUSIONS AND IMPLICATIONS

This review has presented evidence which suggests that pupil tutoring may be an effective technique for promoting internality, and does bring about improved attendance, although it is not yet clear how effective it is with homogeneous groups of poor attenders. It is suggested that these are two further positive outcomes which lend support to the introduction of cross-age tutoring programmes into the school curriculum. However, in addition to hard-core evidence, there needs to be an understanding of the reasons why pupil tutoring is effective, and a justification for including such programmes in an already very wide curriculum.

The tutoring schemes carried out by Allen (1976) adopted a role-theory framework for the conceptual analysis of tutoring. The basic tenet of role theory is that enactment of a role produces changes in behaviour, attitudes and self-perceptions consistent with expectations associated with the role. 'In the case of the child who enacts the role of teacher for another child, the role represents prestige, authority, and feelings of competence; it would seem reasonable to expect that enacting the role of teacher would increase self-esteem and produce a more positive attitude toward school and teachers' (Allen and Feldman, 1976, p. 115). McWhorter and Levy (1971) also favour the role theory explanation. That role play situations can increase the feelings of competence of the actor has been well demonstrated by role theorists; that acting as a tutor can increase the belief that one has control over outcomes has been partially demonstrated in this chapter.

The social relationship between tutor and tutee is another source of possible benefit. The older children learn to be nurturant and to take responsibility for another person, which fosters more socially mature behaviour in general. Being emulated and respected by a younger child enhances the tutors' self-esteem, and promotes positive social behaviour. Being a role model for a younger child constrains one's behaviour along socially desirable directions.

Allen and Feldman (1976) felt that the most central characteristic is 'helping another person' which clarifies self-identify and feelings of increased personal competence. Ehly and Larsen (1980) propound a similar view in concluding that most of the effectiveness of their tutoring scheme lay in the personal nature of the tutor–tutee interaction. Thelen (1969) noted that co-operative learning was a more promising alternative to competitive learning implicitly advocated by most school curricula, and felt that the acquisition of knowledge and skills was being promoted as a way of engaging in personally significant interaction with others. Hargreaves (1983) argued that a major shortcoming of British comprehensive schools lies in their failure to give pupils worthwhile social experiences; it would seem that pupil tutoring can go some way towards remedying this situation.

Socio-linguistic theory stresses the effect of social up-bringing on patterns of speech and therefore of self-perception. Goodlad (1979) notes that tutoring offers pupils practice in speech codes with which they may be unfamiliar. Ratti (1980) points out that, conversely, gains are made because pupil-teachers speak the same language as their charges. Thus there is no breakdown in communication due to conflicting language codes, as discussed by Bernstein (1971), and as experienced by a large proportion of pupils in school.

This may go part of the way towards accounting for the improvements made by tutees who have spent relatively little time in school and have not fully appreciated the difference in language codes between home and school. However, it is difficult to imagine that a small weekly amount of pupil tutoring can compensate for many years of education where there may have been a breakdown in communication. In fact, one could hypothesize that pupil-tutoring may serve to reinforce and strengthen the feeling in pupils that schools do offer them a different socio-linguistic experience, thereby increasing their alienation from the situation.

Paolitto (1976) argued that planners of pupil tutoring programmes ought to consider the psychological development of the child, and that there ought to be an understanding of what it means for the tutor to act as a teacher. Greenspan (1976) has elaborated an integrated theoretical model to account for the efficacy of cross-age tutoring. She lists four crucial aspects of developmental theory as a rationale for adolescents to engage in pupil tutoring:

(1) By assuming adult roles, adolescents are helped to link transformations in thought from the previous stages of concrete operations to formal operational thinking.
(2) Opportunities for social participation and role-taking stimulate movement from conventional to post-conventional moral thinking.
(3) Role-taking, in combination with experiences related to childhood, assists in adolescent identity formation.
(4) The adolescents' need for intimacy will facilitate interpersonal development.

The influences of Piaget, Kohlberg and Erickson can be found in the strands of this model. However, despite the careful conceptualization of this model, and a highly structured programme designed to incorporate each aspect, Greenspan failed to demonstrate any significant effects of cross-age tutoring on the ego development of adolescent tutors. As Paolitto (1976) points out, such development takes time and a one-semester involvement in pupil tutoring may not be sufficient time for such complex processes to develop. This explanation can also be advanced to account for the variable findings on the effectiveness of pupil tutoring in promoting social, personality or behavioural changes.

A further explanation for the effectiveness of tutoring stems from behaviourist theory, which asserts that learning will be efficient if correct responses by a pupil are rewarded, the reward acting as a stimulus to make another step in learning. This explanation is favoured by Sharpley and Sharpley (1981), Carlson (1973), and by Cloward (1976) who concluded that an important factor in the successful outcome of his pupil tutoring programme was that the tutors had received social rewards for academic activities. Strodtbeck, Ronchi and Hansell (1976) felt that the experience of tutoring coupled with financial reward would make the greatest contribution to feelings of personal effectiveness if the tutors believed that their own efforts had actually brought about their involvement in the rewarding activity. This would again suggest that tutoring may lead to an increased belief by the individual that he or she has control over outcomes. Some support for a behavioural explanation of improved attendance can be derived from findings of high levels of attendance at tutoring sessions, suggesting that the experience was a rewarding one, and from some evidence that the improved attendance generalized to everyday school attendance and was maintained after pupil tutoring ceased.

It may, however, be more constructive to examine pupil tutoring within the wider context of the school curriculum. The aims of education are currently under greater scrutiny than ever in Britain, and schools and teachers are under increasing pressure to justify their activities to government, educationalists, and parents. As Galloway (1985) pointed out, because of the difficult unemployment situation in the early 1980s, teachers have had to persuade their students that the curriculum they are being presented with is useful and worthwhile for what it offers in the here and now, not for what it may offer in the future. Innovations in British schools such as the Technical and Vocational Education Initiative (TVEI) have had limited influence to date on curricular opportunities for fourth and fifth year pupils. The recently introduced General Certificate of Secondary Education (GCSE) structure, which requires continuous assessment of students over a two-year period and, therefore, considerable long-term motivation towards academic achievement, may serve only to reinforce the failure of a large proportion of pupils. It is primarily through the school curriculum that schools can promote or undermine pupils' views of themselves and their self-esteem. Evidence was presented earlier which indicated that an internal locus of control is significantly associated with a wide range of positive personal attributes, and it is therefore proposed that the promotion of internality should be an aim of all schools. In a study of non-attendance, Jones (1980) argued that schools do not give pupils the opportunity to learn that they can exercise control over events. In her view, schools do not demand enough of their pupils, who are typically over-organized, overruled and not allowed to make mistakes and learn from them. She found that, when a scheme was introduced into her own school which involved greater pupil-participation and responsibility in the everyday organization of the school, there was a dramatic increase in attendance. Waller and Eisenberg (1980) also felt that many pupils were denied the opportunity to master situations on their own and, therefore, found it more difficult to cope with the challenges of school. Galloway (1985) writes that 'it is intrinsically desirable that children and adolescents should learn at school that they have something worthwhile to contribute to others in the community' (p. 143). It is the contention of this chapter that pupil tutoring is an activity that facilitates the acquisition of such learning by promoting increased belief in one's ability to effect outcomes. Evidence has also been presented which demonstrates not only that pupils who are poor attenders actually put in good attendance at tutoring sessions, but also that there is an element of generalization to attendance throughout the school curriculum. What can be deduced is that, within the curriculum, pupil tutoring can offer an attractive supplement which will be embraced by many pupils who are otherwise failing to benefit from their schooling.

## REFERENCES


Allen, V. L. (1976). *Children as Teachers*. New York: Academic Press.

Allen, V. L., and Feldman, R. S. (1976). Studies in the role of tutor. In V. L. Allen (ed.), *Children as Teachers*. New York: Academic Press.

Allie, S. M. (1979). The normative and structural properties of the children's Norwicki–Strickland scale of Internal–External Control: children with adjustment problems, *Psychology in the Schools*, **16**, 32–37.

Annesley, F. R. (1974). A study of the relationship between normal and behaviour problem children on reading achievement, intelligence, self concept, and locus of control, *The Slow Learning Child*, **21**, 185–196.

Bar-Tal, D., Kfir, D., Bar-Zohar, Y., and Chen, M. (1980). The relationship between locus of control and academic achievement, anxiety and level of aspiration, *British Journal of Educational Psychology*, **50**, 53–60.

Baum, T. (1978). Surveys of absenteeism. *Educational Research*, **20**, 226–230.

Berg, I., Nichols, K., and Pritchard, C. (1969). School phobia—its classification and relationship to dependency, *Journal of Child Psychology and Psychiatry*, **10**, 123–141.

Berstein, N. (1971). *Class, Codes and Control, Volume 1. Theoretical Studies towards a Sociology of Language*. London, Routledge & Kegan Paul.

Blagg, N. R. (1981). A behavioural approach to school refusal. Behaviour modification in education, *Perspectives*, **5**, School of Education, University of Exeter.

Bond, J. (1982). Pupil tutoring; the educational conjuring trick, *Educational Review*, **34**, 241–252.

Carlson, R. T. (1973). An investigation into the effect student tutoring has on self-concept and arithmetic computation achievement of tutors and tutees, *Dissertation Abstracts International*, **34**, 2265A.

Carroll, H. C. M. (1977). *Absenteeism in South Wales: Studies of Pupils, their Homes and their Secondary Schools*. Faculty of Education, University College of Swansea.

Chance, J. E. (1965). Internal control of reinforcements and the school learning process. Unpublished paper presented at Society for Research in Child Development Convention, Minneapolis, cited in *Locus of Control in Personality* (ed. E. J. Phares, 1976), New Jersey, General Learning.

Chandler, T. A. (1980). Reversal peer tutoring effects on powerlessness in adolescents, *Adolescence*, **15**, 715–722.

Chazan M. (1962). School phobia, *British Journal of Educational Psychology*, **32**, 209–217.

Cloward, R. D. (1976). Teenagers as tutors of low achieving children. In V. L. Allen (ed.), *Children as Teachers*. New York: Academic Press.

Coleman, J. S., Campbell, E. Q., Hobson, C. J., McPartland, J., Mood, A. M., Weinfeld, F. D., and York, R. L. (1966), *Equality of Educational Opportunity*. Superintendent of Documents Catalogue No. FS 5.238: 38001, US Government Printing Office, Washington DC.

Cooper, M. G. (1966). School refusal: an inquiry into the part played by school and home, *Educational Research*, **8**, 223–229.

Crandall, V., Katkovsky, W., and Preston, A. (1962). Motivational and ability determinants of young children's intellectual achievement behaviors, *Child Development*, **33**, 643–661.

Crandall, V. C., Katkovsky, W., and Crandall, V. J. (1965). Children's belief in their own control of reinforcements in intellectual academic-achievement situations, *Child Development*, **36**, 90–109.

Croft, I. J., and Grygier, T. G. (1956). Social relationships of truants and juvenile delinquents, *Human Relations*, **9**, 434–466.

De Charms, R. D. (1972). Personal causation training in schools, *Journal of Applied Social Psychology*, **2**, 95–113.

Devin-Sheehan, L., Feldman, R. S., and Allen, V. L. (1976). Research on children tutoring children: a critical review, *Review of Educational Research*, **46**, 355–385.

Duke, M. P., and Nowicki, S. (1974). Locus of control and achievement—the confirmation of a theoretical expectation, *Journal of Psychology*, **87**, 263–267.

Ehly, S. W., and Larsen, S. C. (1980). *Peer Tutoring for Individualised Instruction*. Boston: Allyn and Bacon.

Emmerson, P., Carter, A., and Lasalle, J. (1981). Talking about schools, *Journal of Association of Educational Psychologists,* **5**, 48–57.

Fogelman, K., and Richardson, K. (1974). School attendance from the National Child Development Study. In *Truancy* (ed. B. Turner), London, Lock.

Fogelman, K., Tibbenham, A., and Lambert, L. (1980). Absence from school: findings from the National Child Development Study. In L. Hersov and I. Berg (eds), *Out of School.* Chichester, Wiley.

Frager, S., and Stern C. (1970). Learning by Teaching, *The Reading Teacher*, **23**, 403–405, 417.

Gaa J. P. (1979). The effect of individual goal setting conferences on academic achievement and modification of locus of control orientation, *Psychology in the Schools*, **16**, 591–597.

Galloway, D. (1976). Size of school, socio-economic hardship, suspension rates, and persistent unjustified absence from schools, *British Journal of Educational Psychology*, **46**, 40–47.

Galloway, D. (1982). A study of persistent absentees and their families, *British Journal of Educational Psychology*, **52**, 317–330.

Galloway, D. (1985). *Schools and Persistent Absentees*. Oxford: Pergamon Press.

Getter, H. (1966). A personal determinant of verbal conditioning, *Journal of Personality*, **34**, 397–405.

Goodlad, S. (1979). *Learning by Teaching: an Introduction to Tutoring*. London: Community Service Volunteers.

Gozali, H., Cleary, T. A., Walster, G. W., and Gozali, J. (1973). Relationship between the I–E control construct and achievement, *Journal of Educational Psychology*, **64**, 9–14.

Gredler, E. G. (1985). An assessment of cross-age tutoring, *Techniques*, **1**, 226–232.

Greenspan, B. M. (1976). Facilitating Psychological Growth in Adolescents through a Child Development Curriculum. Unpublished doctoral dissertation, Harvard University Graduate School of Education.

Halpin, G., Halpin, G., and Whiddon, T. (1980). The relationship of perceived parental behaviors to locus of control and self-esteem among American Indian and white children, *Journal of Social Psychology*, **111**, 189–195.
Hargreaves, D. (1983). *The Challenge of the Comprehensive School: Culture, Curriculum and Community*. London: Routledge & Kegan Paul.
Hiroto, D. S. (1974). Locus of control and learned helplessness, *Journal of Experimental Psychology*, **102**, 187-193.
Imich, A. J. (1984). The Development of a Pupil-Tutoring Scheme as a Method of Improving School Attendance and Developing Internality. Unpublished Master of Education Dissertation, University College of Swansea.
James, W. H., and Rotter, J. B. (1958). Partial and 100% reinforcement under chance skill and conditions, *Journal of Experimental Psychology*, **55**, 397–403.
James, W. H., Woodruff, A. B., and Werner, W. (1965). Effect of internal–external control upon changes in smoking behaviour, *Journal of Consulting Psychology*, **29**, 184–186.
Johnson, W. G., and Croft, R. G. F. (1975). Locus of control and participation in a personalised system of instruction course, *Journal of Educational Psychology*, **67**, 416–421.
Jones, A. (1980). The school's view of non-attendance. In L. Hersov and I. Berg (eds), *Out of School*. Chichester: Wiley.
Julian, J. W., and Katz, S. B. (1968). Internal control and the value of reinforcement, *Journal of Personality and Social Psychology*, **8**, 89–94.
Kahn, J. (1974). School phobia or school refusal. In B. Turner (ed.), *Truancy*. London: Lock.
Kanoy, R. C. Johnson, B. W., and Kanoy, K. W. (1980). Locus of control and self-concept in achieving and underachieving bright elementary children, *Psychology in the Schools*, **17**, 395–399.
Katkovsky, W., Crandall, V. C., and Good, S. (1967). Parental antecedents of children's beliefs in internal–external control of reinforcements in intellectual achievement situations, *Child Development*, **38**, 766–776.
Kavanagh, A., and Carroll, H. C. M. (1977). Pupil attendance in three comprehensive schools; a study of the pupils and their families. In H. C. M. Carroll (ed.), *Absenteeism in South Wales: Studies of Pupils, their Homes and their Secondary Schools*. Faculty of Education, University College of Swansea.
La Place, M. J. (1976). The relationship of locus of control, demographic and personal variables to school attendance, *Dissertation Abstracts International*, **37**, 6A, 3310–3311.
Lawrence, E. A., and Winschel, J. F. (1974). Locus of control: implications for special education, *Exceptional Children*, **41**, 483–491.
Lefcourt, H. M. (1966). Internal versus external control of reinforcement, *Psychological Bulletin*, **65**, 206–220.
Lefcourt, H. M. (1976). *Locus of Control: Current Trends in Theory and Research*. New Jersey: Erlbaum.
Lefcourt, H. M., Lewis, L., and Silverman, I. W. (1968). Internal versus external control of reinforcement and attention in decision-making tasks, *Journal of Personality*, **36**, 663–682.
Liftschitz, M. (1973). Internal–external locus of control as a function of age and socialisation, *Child Development*, **44**, 538–548.
Lippitt, P. (1976). Learning through cross-age helping: why and how. In V. L. Allen (ed.), *Children as Teachers*. New York: Academic Press.
Lippitt, R., and Lippitt, P. (1968). Cross-age helpers, *Today's Education*, **57**, 24–26.
Maher, C. A. (1982). Behavioural effects of using conduct problem adolescents as cross-age tutors, *Psychology in the Schools*, **19**, 360–364.

Maher, C. A. (1984). Handicapped adolescents as cross-age tutors: program description and evaluation, *Exceptional Children*, **51**, 56–63.

Martin, R. P., and Shepel, L. F. (1974). Locus of control and discrimination ability with lay counsellors, *Journal of Consulting and Clinical Psychology*, **42**, 741.

McWhorter, K. T., and Levy, J. (1971). Influences of a tutorial programme upon tutors, *Journal of Reading*, **14**, 221–225.

Messer, S. B. (1972). The relation of internal–external control to academic performance, *Child Development*, **43**, 1456–1462.

Moos, R. H., and Moos, B. S. (1978). Classroom social climate and student absences and grades, *Journal of Educational Psychology*, **70**, 263–269.

Nowicki, S., and Barnes, J. (1973). Effects of a structured camp experience on locus of control orientation, *Journal of Genetic Psychology*, **122**, 247–252.

Nowicki, S., and Rountree, J. (1971). Correlates of locus of control in a secondary school population, *Developmental Psychology*, **4**, 477–478.

Nowicki, S., and Strickland, B. R. (1973). A locus of control scale for children, *Journal of Consulting and Clinical Psychology*, **40**, 148–154.

Ollendick, D. G. (1979). Some characteristics of absentee students in Grade 4, *Psychological Reports*, **44**, 294.

Paolitto, D. P. (1976). The effect of cross-age tutoring on adolescence: an inquiry into theoretical assumptions, *Review of Educational Research*, **46**, 215–237.

Phares, E. J. (1962). Perceptual threshold decrements as function of skill and chance expectancies, *Journal of Psychology*, **53**, 399–407.

Phares, E. J. (1976). *Locus of Control in Personality*. New Jersey: General Learning Press.

Ratti, M. C. (1980). Comrades in distress, *Links*, **5**, 19–22.

Reynolds, D., Jones, D., and St. Leger, S. (1976). Schools do make a difference, *New Society*, **37**, 223–225.

Reynolds, D., and Murgatroyd, S. (1977). The sociology of schooling and the absent pupil: the school as a factor in the generation of truancy. In H. C. M. Carroll (ed.), *Absenteeism in South Wales: Studies of Pupils, their Homes and their Secondary Schools*. Faculty of Education, University College of Swansea.

Reynolds, D., Jones, D., St. Leger, S., and Murgatroyd, S. (1980). School factors and truancy. In L. Hersov and I. Berg (eds), *Out of School*. Chichester: Wiley.

Ritchie, R., and Phares, E. J. (1969). Attitude change as a function of internal–external control and communicator status, *Journal of Personality*, **37**, 429–443.

Rotter, J. B. (1966). Generalized expectancies for internal versus external control of reinforcement, *Psychological Monographs*, **80**, 1–28.

Rotter, J. B., and Mulry, R. C. (1965). Internal versus external control of reinforcement and decision time, *Journal of Personality and Social Psychology*, **2**, 598–604.

Rutter, M., Tizard, J., and Whitmore, K. (1970). *Education, Health and Behaviour*. London: Longman.

Rutter, M., Maughan, B., Mortimore, P., and Ouston, J. (1979). *Fifteen Thousand Hours*. London: Open Books.

Saunders, L. (1977). An analysis of attitude changes towards school, school attendance, self-concept, and reading of secondary school students involved in a cross-age tutoring experience, *Dissertation Abstracts International*, **38**, 3A, 1323.

Seabrook, J. (1974). Talking to truants. In B. Turner (eds.), *Truancy*. London: Lock.

Sharpley, A. M., and Sharpley, C. F. (1981). Peer tutoring: a review of the literature, *CORE*, **5**, 3.

Strickland, B. (1970). Individual differences in verbal conditioning, extinction and awareness, *Journal of Personality*, **38**, 364–378.

Strodtbeck, F. L., Ronchi, D., and Hansell, S. (1976). Tutoring and psychological growth. In V. Allen (ed.), *Children as Teachers*. New York: Academic Press.
Swanson, L. (1981). Locus of control and academic achievement in learning-disabled children, *Journal of Social Psychology*, **113**, 141–142.
Thelen, H. A. (1969). Tutoring by students, *The School Review*, **77**, 229–244.
Topping, K. (1988). *The Peer Tutoring Handbook*. London: Croom Helm.
Tyerman, M. J. (1968). *Truancy*. London: University of London Press.
Tyrer, P., and Tyrer, S. (1974). School refusal, truancy, and adult neurotic illness, *Psychological Medicine*, **4**, 416–421.
Waller, D., and Eisenberg, L. (1980). School refusal in childhood—a psychiatric–paediatric perspective. In L. Hersov and I. Berg (eds), *Out of School*. Chichester: Wiley.
Williams, D. G. (1980). *Developing Internality in Secondary School Pupils*. Unpublished Master of Education Dissertation, University College of Swansea.
Wing, C. J. (1972). The effect of a youth tutoring youth program on potential dropout, *Dissertation Abstracts International* **33**, 1452A.

CHAPTER 6

# Peer Tutoring for Low-progress Readers Using 'Pause, Prompt and Praise'

KEVIN WHELDALL* and SUSAN COLMAR†

**Centre for Child Study, School of Education, University of Birmingham, PO Box 363, Birmingham B15 2TT, UK*

*†Central Psychological Service, Birmingham Education Authority, 74 Balden Road, Harborne, Birmingham, B32 2EH, UK*

## INTRODUCTION

Numerous studies, completed all over the world, have demonstrated the effectiveness of peer tutoring and many of these have been concerned with the tutoring of reading. This is not surprising, as problems associated with literacy are perennial. The extent of illiteracy in the United Kingdom is difficult to determine, not least because the term illiterate is itself difficult to define in a meaningful way. Mary Hamilton (1987) explores this issue in her report of research conducted as a follow up to the National Child Development Study. At age 23 years, 13% of those participating in the study reported that they had experienced difficulties with literacy and numeracy after leaving school. (Hamilton estimates that this means around six million adults in Britain are in a similar position.) Men are apparently twice as likely to report such problems. What is of particular concern is the fact that very few of these young adults had been picked up by their teachers at 16 as being in need of help in this area, i.e. before they leave school. Of those

Children Helping Children
Edited by H. C. Foot, M. J. Morgan and R. H. Shute

reporting difficulties, around 30% report difficulties specifically concerned with reading.

If children have not mastered the basics of reading by age seven or eight years, their educational prospects are bleak. Their opportunities to read will become increasingly restricted as remedial help often focuses on sub-skill teaching (usually phonics), sometimes out of the classroom context. They will spend less time in the one-to-one interactions which have been shown to be helpful for progress in reading. The use of peer-tutors can help to redress this imbalance, by ensuring that frequent appropriate oral reading interactions will occur.

## PEER-TUTORING OF READING

In recent years we have witnessed a renewal of interest in peer-tutoring in educational circles. Peer-tutoring has its origins within school settings in the Lancaster-Bell monitorial system pioneered in the nineteenth century, re-emerging as a subject for educational research in the United States in the 1960s. A review of this work is provided by Wagner in this book. As we said earlier, many of the studies carried out on peer-tutoring have involved the tutoring of reading. Topping (1987a), for example, provides an account of twelve action research studies in which peer-tutors used the 'paired reading' procedures of Morgan and Lyon (1979). Research has shown that peer-tutors, given thorough training in reading tutoring, can be employed to very good effect, bringing about major reading gains in their tutees.

Peer-tutoring is particularly beneficial for the pupil who is having difficulties in learning to read. Children with limited reading skills are clearly disadvantaged and this disadvantage will continue and may increase throughout their school careers unless some intervention is applied which allows them to improve, and to improve quickly. Much of the curriculum will become increasingly unavailable to pupils who are unable to read effectively. They clearly need programmes which will enable them to achieve accelerated progress in order to catch up with their peer group in reading skills. Given their previous histories of failure in reading, in our view they need a fresh start with more appropriate reading material and a skilled reading tutor, employing a powerful set of tutoring skills of proven effectiveness, to hear them read frequently.

This is difficult to achieve in most schools without cutting into the teacher's broader curricular remit, not to mention time. The only other possibilities (apart from classroom assistants) are parents (not necessarily of the low progress readers) and peers (other pupils with more advanced reading skills). Research has clearly shown that parents can be employed to very good effect, bringing about major gains in the reading skills of their children (Glynn, 1987). Without wishing to minimize the importance of the role of parents in the education of their children, we would like to argue the case for the increased utilization of peers for reading tutoring, for the following reasons:

(1) Parents may not always be available, willing or even suitable since they may be too involved emotionally with their own child's difficulties to tutor effectively.

It is a sad fact to be faced that not all parents are interested in their child's education. Most, of course, care deeply but then not all of these feel that they have the time or the necessary skills. Some parents are themselves barely literate while others are so anxious about their child's lack of progress that they can do more harm than good. One mother told us of nightly reading sessions with her child lasting up to two hours, often ending with both of them in tears. Many parents can help their children learn to read, but some cannot.

(2) Peer tutors are plentiful, available for training and can be readily monitored and organized.

If we include peer-tutoring within schools as part of our educational philosophy, then at least some of the problems of class size are eased. Instead of one teacher to a class of 30 pupils, we have the potential for regular one-to-one teaching. The ready and, in our experience, willing volunteer tutors are available for regular, daily tutoring within the recognized educative environment. Their training and the careful monitoring of their tutoring performance can be readily achieved by teachers.

(3) Low progress readers respond readily to peer tutors.

In common with other researchers and practitioners in the field of peer tutoring, we have found that children enjoy being tutored by other pupils. Given that the tutors have been trained to use positive, non-punitive tutoring styles, the reading context becomes more relaxed for low-progress readers and less threatening. We believe that, as a result, tutees will be more likely to risk making errors which, as we shall argue, are an important part of the process of learning to read.

(4) Tutoring has also been shown to be beneficial to the peer tutors and can be an important aspect of a pastoral curriculum.

From time to time teachers and parents question the ethics of employing pupils as peer tutors, arguing that their education may suffer as a result. This is not the case; substantial benefits have been shown to be gained by the tutors as well as the tutees. Teachers frequently refer to improvements in the self-esteem of pupils and research has demonstrated that tutors can make academic gains as a result of their tutoring. For example, Limbrick, McNaughton and Glynn (1985) demonstrated that the reading skills of their tutors improved as well as that of their tutees. Our own research has produced similar supporting evidence. But there is an equally important pastoral dimension to this argument: peer-tutoring promotes caring and concern for others, in contrast with the overly competitive edge evident in much contemporary schooling. Peer-tutoring also provides a means for learning valuable parenting skills.

In this chapter we will discuss peer-tutoring of low-progress readers, employing a form of remedial reading tutoring known as 'Pause, Prompt and Praise' (McNaughton, Glynn and Robinson, 1981; 1987). This method is dependent upon peer tutors learning a carefully defined set of skills and procedures and hence our concern will not be restricted to outcome or product measures of tutees' reading performance. We will pay equal attention to measures of the process of tutoring by which low-progress readers can be helped to become better, and more independent, readers.

It is important to emphasize that the tutoring methodology we are referring to in this chapter was designed specifically for use with low-progress readers and is not to be confused with the several other more general reading tutoring strategies which have been proposed. These tutoring methods vary from the highly informal and unstructured tutoring of what is sometimes known as 'relaxed reading', where tutors receive little instruction beyond being generally kind and supportive to their tutee, to the more specific strategies of 'paired reading'. Topping (1988) provides a review of these procedures in the context of peer-tutoring.

Paired reading (Morgan and Lyon, 1979), in essence, requires the tutor to read aloud in time with the tutee, stopping when the tutee signals the tutor to do so and resuming when the tutee hesitates or makes an error. A key feature is that the tutees have a free choice of what book they will read. Very large claims have been made for the effectiveness of paired reading but there is still uncertainty as to whether the specifics of paired reading *per se* are necessarily the cause of the reading gains claimed.

Topping (1987b) has claimed that it is 'now the best researched technique of its kind'. This may be true of the quantity of research reported but the quality of this work is less certain. There are very few carefully controlled experimental studies of paired reading in which the method is compared with an alternative form of tutoring. However, Lindsay, Evans and Jones (1985) found no significant differences in their experimental study between the reading gains of pupils experiencing paired reading and those receiving relaxed reading. Even fewer studies are reported which examine the processes of paired reading tutoring as against the proliferation of simple one shot pre/post product measure studies. Winter's (1988) paper on paired reading, 'a study of process and outcome', concluded that many tutors do not adhere to the advocated procedures of paired reading and that there is no evidence for any relationship between adherence to the procedures and reading gains. This neglect of process in much of the paired reading research, which Pumphrey (1987) has also criticized, is accompanied by a disregard for theory. It is almost a case of 'that's all very well in practice, but how does it work in theory?', except that we are not sure that in practice it really is any more effective than, say, relaxed reading or any other simple listening procedure. There appears to be little theoretical or empirical backing to suggest why it works, if it works. As Bennett (1988) (in the context of peer-tutoring generally) puts it, 'No self-respecting teacher educator would urge teachers to implement an innovation which was theory-free; practice without theory is blind'.

We have elaborated this point in order to emphasize the competing claims of Pause, Prompt and Praise. As we shall see, the research supporting this methodology includes empirical process and product studies which demonstrate that this form of tutoring yields superior gains for low-progress readers than other listening procedures, and that these gains are clearly attributable to specific tutoring behaviours. Moreover, the reading tutoring methodology is securely anchored within both a cognitive/developmental theory of reading (Clay, 1979; McNaughton, 1988) and a 'behavioural interactionist' theory of tutoring (Wheldall and Glynn, 1988; 1989).

## 'PAUSE, PROMPT AND PRAISE'

The set of remedial reading procedures known as 'Pause, Prompt and Praise' (PPP) is predicated upon the assumption that children learn to read by reading, not by learning a large number of separate words, letters or sub-skills. The tutoring procedures were developed from reading research carried out by its authors: Ted Glynn, Stuart McNaughton and Viviane Robinson (McNaughton, Glynn and Robinson, 1981; 1987), and are based, in part, on the earlier work of Marie Clay (Clay, 1979).

Basically, Clay argues that in learning to read children learn various strategies for predicting and working out unknown vocabulary. Learning to read is seen as a process of making mistakes (often referred to as reading errors or miscues) and gradually developing efficient strategies using contextual cues (which relate to meaning and syntax), graphophonic cues (which relate to the visual and auditory patterns of letters and words) and self-monitoring (including self-correction). It is important to stress that mistakes are to be expected and that making mistakes is an important part of the process of learning to read.

Clay emphasizes the importance of providing reading material at an appropriate level such that the child is encountering some unfamiliar words but knows enough words to be able to make good predictions, even if these are miscues. The right level of reading material can be broadly assessed by checking the child's rate of reading accuracy, counting self-corrections as correct words. If this rate is below 80% the text is too difficult, if the child is reading at over 95% accuracy it is clearly too easy. At a rate between 90% and 95% accuracy promotion to the next level should be seriously considered. Thus an ideal level for children learning to read, with all the advantages of making mistakes, is between 80% and 90% accuracy.

This approach also stresses the need for careful monitoring of the child's response to the text so that the teacher can readily work out if the child is making average, or even rapid, progress and if he or she is using efficient predictive strategies. Miscues can be analysed to check their similarity to the text along graphophonic, syntactic and semantic dimensions, providing an indicator of the child's use of appropriate predictions about the text.

Clay (1979) further suggests that the child's rate of self-correction is associated with good reading progress. This is seen as another indicator that the child is reading actively in that he or she is able to 'solve' problem words independently. In her research she showed that the most able quarter of her sample self-corrected at a rate between 25% and 33% whereas the least able quarter self-corrected at a rate of only 5%.

As a developmentalist, Clay paid particular attention to text level and monitoring of reader performance using running records. Working in the same department at Auckland University, Glynn and McNaughton built on her work from a behaviour analytic perspective and emphasized the role of error attention and feedback. McNaughton (1987, 1988) argues that error-free learning is inappropriate and that attention to a reading error, contrary to an obvious prediction from behavioural theory, actually progressively leads to the child making fewer errors. Low-progress readers, in particular, benefit from receiving feedback following an error (McNaughton and Delquadri, 1978). The delaying of attention to errors by five seconds leads to more self-correction and an increase in the child's reading accuracy (McNaughton and Glynn, 1981).

Beginning readers, and those experiencing difficulty in learning to read, need support from a reading teacher or tutor. As individuals learn to read, by gaining better predictive skills and strategies, they gradually manage increasingly more difficult reading material with less support and so become independent readers. Specifically, when using the 'Pause, Prompt and Praise' procedures, the reading tutor must ensure, at minimum, that:

(1) the child is provided with an appropriate level and type of text,
(2) the child's progress is carefully monitored with respect to the text using running records or simple miscue analysis and
(3) that the teacher or tutor listens to the reading and gives appropriate feedback.

Although the whole research project and technique is often referred to as 'Pause, Prompt and Praise' (including all three of the above factors), in fact 'Pause, Prompt and Praise' describes the third aspect—that is the teacher's feedback in response to the reading. This is summarized in Figure 6.1 (McNaughton *et al.*, 1987).

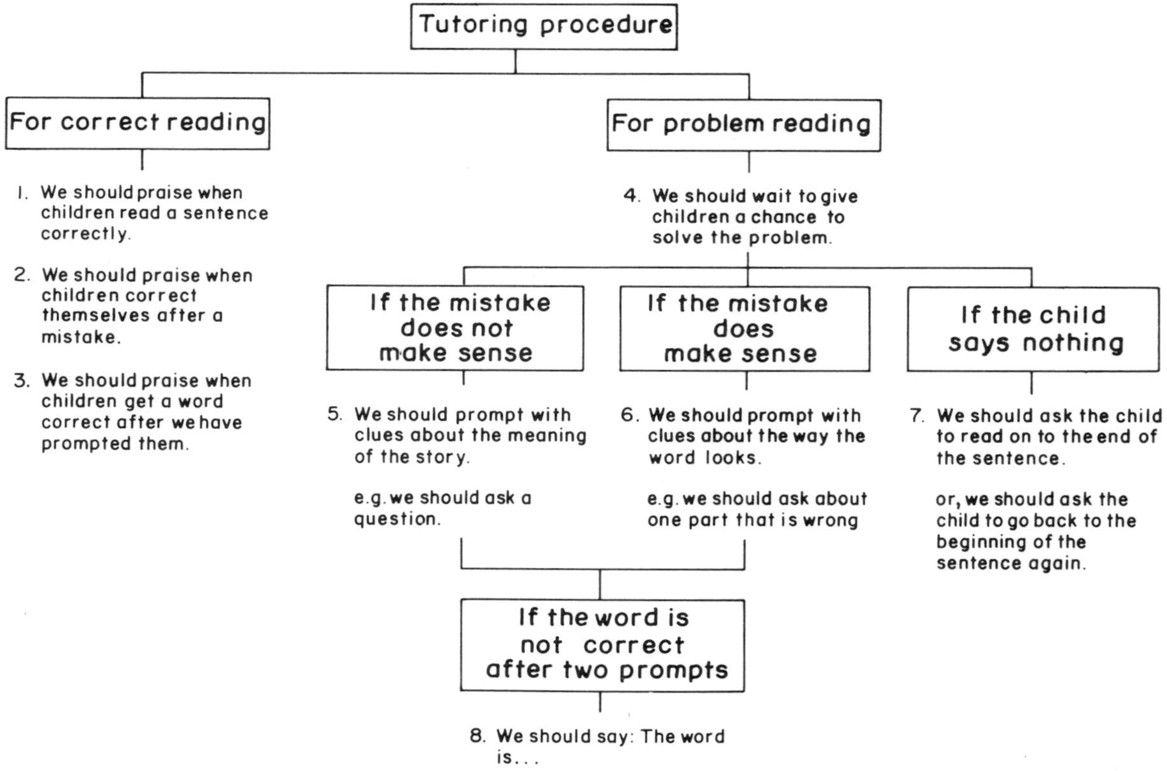

Tutoring procedure
For correct reading
For problem reading
1. We should praise when children read a sentence correctly.
2. We should praise when children correct themselves after a mistake.
3. We should praise when children get a word correct after we have prompted them.
4. We should wait to give children a chance to solve the problem.
If the mistake does not make sense
If the mistake does make sense
If the child says nothing
5. We should prompt with clues about the meaning of the story.
e.g. we should ask a question.
6. We should prompt with clues about the way the word looks.
e.g. we should ask about one part that is wrong
7. We should ask the child to read on to the end of the sentence.
or, we should ask the child to go back to the beginning of the sentence again.
If the word is not correct after two prompts
8. We should say: The word is...


FIGURE 6.1. Instruction sheet for training peers in the 'Pause, Prompt and Praise' procedures

*Pausing.* When the child makes an error or hesitates it is important for the teacher or tutor to pause for at least five seconds or until the child reaches the end of the sentence. This allows the child a reasonable opportunity either to correct the error or, after five seconds, to work out the word with the help of a clue or prompt from the tutor. Pausing is difficult for most reading tutors, but it is a key factor in responding helpfully to the child who is learning to read. It is particularly hard where the child is a low-progress reader and where the teacher or tutor wants to provide as much help as possible. Our research has shown that teachers very rarely pause in this way (although they often claim that they do) and teachers of low-progress readers are even less likely to pause before supplying the correct word (Wheldall *et al.*, 1989).

*Prompting.* If, after pausing for five seconds, the child has made either no response or has made an error the tutor then prompts. The type of feedback or prompt given depends on the nature of the error. If the child's error has not made sense then the prompt should be aimed at providing clues about the meaning or context of the story; for example, a question like 'Do you think the word would be "horse" when the story is about the place where we live?' Often the child's miscue makes sense but the word is still not correct. For example the child may read 'may' where the word is 'might'. In examples like these the tutor's prompt should be aimed at helping the child to look again at the graphical features of the word, that is, how it looks. However, should the child hesitate and still make no attempt, the tutor may either ask the child to read on to the end, or to read again from the beginning of the sentence. Often this additional context provided by the other words in the sentence will help the child to work out the unknown word. In many cases this type of prompt is sufficient for children to determine the correct word. In the few instances where children are not able to correct these errors after one or two prompts it is suggested that they are told the word. This prevents the interruptions to the child's reading from becoming too long.

*Praising.* Finally, teachers or tutors should reinforce appropriate reading behaviour with verbal praise. Such reinforcement should be used both contingently and selectively. It is important to note that the praising of correct reading should be in the form of a specific, descriptive comment rather than just a comment like, 'Good boy'. For example, 'Good work David; you corrected "rabbit" all by yourself' tells David exactly what he is being praised for and so the praise is contingent upon specific reading behaviours. It is important to reinforce children for appropriate, independent reading behaviours such as self-correcting or working out a word following a prompt as well as for, say, reading a whole sentence or paragraph correctly.

The first research study evaluating the effectiveness of the Pause, Prompt and Praise procedures was carried out in Mangere, an Auckland suburb, in 1978. It was called the Mangere Home and School Project and it involved the intensive study of 14 families (McNaughton, Glynn and Robinson, 1981; 1987). Low progress readers aged 8 to 12 years with reading deficits from two to five years were tutored at home three times a week for 10 to 15 minutes by either their parent or an older sibling. Books of appropriate difficulty and interest level were selected and provided by the project. Continual monitoring from tapes of children's reading enabled the researchers to supply books of increasing difficulty levels as children's accuracy improved. After 10 to 15 weeks results showed that children, on average, made nearly six months' reading progress, despite the fact that they had been making little or no progress before the project, as the single subject design methodology demonstrated. On average their rate of self-correction nearly doubled.

The original study clearly showed that parents were able to change their own natural tutoring style following training and feedback from the researchers. Typically, as untrained tutors, parents rarely commented on correct reading or the child's attempts to solve unfamiliar words. They tended not to pause but rather to provide the child with the correct word immediately following the child's hesitation or error. In summary, as untrained tutors working with their own children with reading difficulties, they did not pause or prompt or praise. Interestingly, the data collected showed that their untrained tutoring had little effect on their children's reading. However, following training in these methods and regular feedback sessions from the researchers, parents learned to delay their attention to children's errors (pause), to provide appropriate prompts or cues instead of simply telling their child the word and to increase greatly their use of praise.

The Mangere Home and School Project was so successful with children who were older, low-progress readers that the techniques were subsequently presented on New Zealand Television, and a booklet for parents was widely distributed (Glynn *et al.*, 1979). The original study has now been successfully replicated several times (Glynn and McNaughton, 1985), in New Zealand, Australia and in the United Kingdom. Twelve studies completed up to 1985 involved a total of over 100 tutors and 98 children between the ages of seven and 12. All the subject children had marked deficits in reading skills which varied from six months to as much as five years with a mean of about two years. Following training in implementing the procedures, parents made gains in their use of pausing, prompting and praising of the order of two or three times their pre-training rates. Reported gains in children's reading ranged from 1.5 to 11.0 months in reading age per month of tutoring. For children who are of upper primary age and older, and who are up to five years behind in their reading, the responsive social context provided by the Pause, Prompt and Praise procedures results in major reading gains.

## PEER-TUTORING USING 'PAUSE, PROMPT AND PRAISE'

Our programme of research on peer-tutoring in the UK began in 1981. These studies were the first to research 'Pause, Prompt and Praise' procedures specifically with peer tutors. The first (unpublished) study was a small-scale pilot investigation of peer tutoring. Three groups of three seven-to eight-year-old children took part in the study. They were all less delayed in their reading skills than the children in the original Mangere study, being only about six to 18 months behind in terms of reading age for accuracy. One group was not tutored, a second group was tutored by untrained peers while the third group was tutored by peers trained in the 'pause, prompt and praise' method. The peer tutors were six 10–11-year-old pupils from the same school of at least average reading ability. Children in both tutored groups received about 30 individual tutoring sessions of about 10 to 15 minutes each over a period of 10 weeks.

One child from the 'trained tutor' group dropped out halfway through the study and this made overall comparisons difficult to interpret. What was clear, however, was that peers could be effectively trained to use all three components of the 'Pause, Prompt and Praise' procedure. Another interesting point which arose from this study is whether young children of this age who are not very far behind with their reading really need trained tutoring of the kind provided by the 'Pause, Prompt and Praise' procedures. We will return to this point again shortly. The results of this study were equivocal but it served as a valuable introduction to the rigours of this methodology and the practicalities of its implementation.

Our second UK study involving peer-tutors (Wheldall and Mettem, 1985) was, however, highly successful. We were able to demonstrate large gains made by 12-year-old low progress readers when tutored by 16-year-olds trained in the 'Pause, Prompt and Praise' procedures. In brief, eight 16-year-old, low achieving pupils were trained to tutor reading using these procedures. It is interesting to note that these 16-year-olds had been in the remedial department earlier in their school careers and were still regarded as poor readers (mean reading age about 9 : 9) but they were around 12–18 months, in terms of reading age, ahead of the pupils they tutored. The effectiveness of training such tutors was investigated through a tutorial programme in which these older pupils then tutored eight 12-year-old pupils from the remedial department who were on average three to four years behind their chronological age in terms of reading age. The programme consisted of 24 tutorial sessions each of 15 to 20 minutes three days per week over eight weeks. Two matched control groups of remedial readers were also included in the study. One consisted of eight pupils tutored by a group of eight similar but untrained 16-year-old tutors. These tutors, who were also poor readers, tutored during the same sessions and used the same materials but were not trained in the Pause, Prompt and Praise procedures. They were instructed, in general terms, to be kind and supportive and to help their tutee read the book supplied. The second control or comparison group consisted of a third group of remedial readers who read silently, without a tutor, for the same amount of time as the other groups.

Analyses of the tutoring sessions revealed important differences in tutoring behaviour between the trained and untrained peer tutors. Attention to errors in both groups was very similar at around 75% but for delayed attention to errors (pausing) the picture was markedly different. Whereas the trained tutors paused following 58% of reader errors, tutors in the control group virtually did not pause at all. Prompting very seldom occurred in the untrained control group and was never successful when it did. In contrast, trained tutors used prompts in 27% of their attention to errors and were successful in 49% of these prompts. Finally, use of praise was observed on average 8.8 times per tutor per session in the trained tutor group but hardly ever in the control tutor group. From these results it can reasonably be claimed that the experimental tutor group was trained reasonably successfully in the 'Pause, Prompt and Praise' procedures, although pausing and prompting was not as high as can be achieved with parent tutors.

Turning next to the performance of the tutees, it was found that children in the experimental (trained tutoring) group self-corrected around 20% of their errors but for the control (untrained tutoring) group this figure never rose above 10%. Moreover, the experimental group progressed through a total of 36 book levels during the programme compared with 29 levels for the tutored control group and 24 levels for the untutored control group. Finally, the experimental group of tutees, who had a mean pre-test reading age of 8 years 4 months, made a mean gain of six months in reading accuracy by the end of the programme. The tutees of control group I who had received tutoring from untrained tutors made a mean gain of 2.4 months. The pupils of control group II who read silently without a tutor made a mean gain of 0.9 months. The gains made by the control groups were not significantly different from each other, but the experimental group's gains were highly significant compared with both of the control groups ($p<0.005$). Half of the tutees in the experimental group made gains in excess of six months while none of the tutees in either of the control groups made such gains. This study clearly showed that older, low-progress readers could be successfully tutored by peers, providing the tutors had been given adequate training in these rigorous tutoring procedures.

The original Wheldall and Mettem study has been described in some detail since the following four studies, which confirm and extend these findings, share similar aims and are predicated on basically the same methodology. In essence, in attempting to demonstrate the effectiveness of peer tutoring of reading using 'Pause, Prompt and Praise' procedures, the performance of both tutors and tutees is compared, before, during and following the period of tutoring. More specifically, the tutoring behaviours of the tutors and the reading behaviours of the tutees form the basis of comparisons between experimental and control groups. In all four studies, the experimental groups comprised tutors who were specifically trained to use the 'Pause, Prompt and Praise' tutoring procedures with their tutees. The main control groups comprised tutors who were not trained to use 'Pause, Prompt and Praise' and who received only general advice as to how to tutor their tutees. Again this took the form of encouragement to be warm and supportive, in the style of relaxed reading, but was not very specific. In the first of the studies, a second control or comparison group was included which comprised readers at a similar level of reading performance to the tutees in the experimental and control groups but who did not receive any peer-tutoring during the course of the study. This series of replication studies will be reported in more detail in a forthcoming paper.

The first replication study was carried out in a small Junior school in the West Midlands, serving a large council housing estate. The 11-year-old fourth year pupils of average or above average reading ability were selected as peer tutors. The study also involved 15 low-progress readers from third and fourth year classes aged nine to 11 years who were, on average, just over two years behind in their reading. The 15 low-progress readers were randomly allocated to three groups. Both tutored groups (trained and untrained) experienced six weeks of tutoring of three half-hour sessions per week, i.e. 18 sessions in all.

All tutees and tutors were tested on the Neale Analysis reading test just prior to and again following the six-week period of tutoring. It should be noted, however, that a further two weeks elapsed before post-testing making a total of two months between testings. The experimental 'Pause, Prompt and Praise' group made a mean gain of 6.2 months for reading accuracy, whereas the control group receiving untrained tutoring gained 3.0 months and the untutored comparison group 2.0 months. Similarly, for reading comprehension, the experimental group gained 8.4 months, the control group 4.4 months and the comparison group 3.4 months. All experimental subjects gained at least six months for both accuracy and comprehension over the two-month period between testings, with the exception of one child who gained only five months for accuracy but 13 months for comprehension. In the other two groups only one child in each group made a gain of six months or more and this was only for comprehension (for accuracy no one gained more than four months). Another indicator of reading progress is promotion to higher book levels. The results for this indicator parallel those for reading age. The experimental group on average progressed 6.2 levels, the control group 4.2 levels and the comparison group 2.6 levels.

The two groups of tutors also made large gains in reading age but there were no differences between the two groups. Mean gains for both groups for accuracy and comprehension averaged between six and seven months. It can thus be seen that peer tutoring clearly benefits tutors as well as tutees but that the form of tutoring they employ may be less critical to their gains. Note that the tutors were average or above average readers and that such tutors, as well as such tutees, may not need trained tutoring in Pause, Prompt and Praise to progress. We will return to this point later.

We turn now to the results based on analyses of the taped tutor–tutee reading interactions. Recordings were made prior to training (baseline) and following training in the 'Pause, Prompt and Praise' procedures. Attention to errors was high in both groups, at over 80% during both baseline and experimental phases. During the baseline phase there was little evidence for 'pause', 'prompt' or 'praise' tutor behaviours in either group, as we have come to expect, and, partly as a result of this, low levels of self-correction on the part of tutees were observed. This picture did not change markedly for control group tutors during the intervention phase.

Following training in the 'Pause, Prompt and Praise' procedures, however, the tutoring behaviours of the experimental group of tutors changed markedly. Delayed attention (pausing) was given in response to 56% of tutee errors, being partly responsible for the increase in tutee self-corrections to 20%. A total of 67% of tutee errors were responded to with appropriate forms of prompt and 64% of such prompts were successful in eliciting a correct response from the tutee. Finally, praise, which was virtually non-existent during baseline, now averaged five statements per session. This study thus clearly showed that fourth year junior school pupils can be taught to tutor third and fourth year low-progress peers to good effect, yielding appreciable gains for both tutees and tutors. This provides additional support for the view that peer-tutoring programmes are also beneficial for tutors.

Our second replication study in the series, carried out in a comprehensive school in the West Midlands with older children comprised a simple comparison of the effects of trained and untrained tutoring. Ten fourth year secondary school pupils aged 14 to 15 years volunteered to tutor ten second year low-progress readers aged 12 to 13 years who were between three and five years behind in their reading. Tutors and tutees were randomly allocated to two groups. One group of tutors was trained to use the 'Pause, Prompt and Praise' procedures while the other group received only general advice. Both groups of low-progress readers were tutored for 15 minutes, three times per week for five weeks. All tutees were tested on the Gapadol reading comprehension test (designed for use with older children) prior to and following the five week tutoring programme. In brief, the group receiving trained tutoring made a mean gain of 11½ months of reading age whereas the control group gained seven and a half months on average. All five low-progress readers in the trained tutoring group made gains of at least ten months compared with only two pupils in the untrained group.

The reading performance of the tutors was not measured in this study but again there were clear differences in tutoring behaviour. No instances of pausing, prompting or praising were recorded in either group prior to training and, as expected, there was little change in the behaviour of the untrained group over the tutoring programme. For the trained tutors, however, average levels of tutoring behaviours increased during the programme. Pausing averaged 62% and prompting 72% (successful on 73% of occasions). Praise averaged 6.4 instances per session and tutees self-corrected on 30% of available occasions.

The third replication study was also carried out in a comprehensive school in the West Midlands and again involved a comparison of two randomly allocated groups of six tutors and tutees. The tutors were 12 15-year-old fourth year pupils who tutored 12 first-year pupils aged 11 to 12 years with an average reading age of about eight years. They were thus three to four years behind in reading. The trained and untrained tutors tutored their low-progress readers for 26 sessions over eight weeks. Attention to errors was high, averaging over 90%, in both groups of tutors over the programme but tutoring behaviours in the untrained group remained at very low levels. Training was successful in changing the behaviour of the trained group, however, with pausing averaging 85% over the programme, prompting 55% (92% successful) and praise averaging 3.5 instances per session. Tutee self-corrections for this group averaged 40% as against 11% in the other group, suggesting that the changes in tutor behaviour were bringing about changes in reader behaviour as a result. Testing prior to and following the tutoring programme on Neale Analysis showed that the low-progress readers in the trained tutoring group made average gains of seven months in reading accuracy and 21 months in reading comprehension compared with only two months and ten months respectively for the untrained group. Again, in this study, tutors were not tested but the results confirm the effectiveness of the 'Pause, Prompt and Praise' procedures in bringing about rapid progress in reading skills in low-progress readers.

The fourth replication study is particularly interesting since it was not so successful! This study, carried out in a large middle school in the West Midlands, involved 20 13-year-old tutors and 20 nine- to ten-year-old tutees who were, on average, one year nine months behind in reading. Again the children were allocated randomly to trained and untrained groups and a tutoring programme of 27 sessions was implemented over nine weeks. For both groups, attention to errors was high, averaging over 70%, over the programme but tutoring behaviours in the untrained group, as in the other studies, remained at low levels. In the trained group, pausing averaged 71% over the programme, prompting averaged 76% (64% successful) and praise averaged four instances per session. Tutee self-corrections for this group averaged 38% as against 19% in the untrained group. Testing prior to and following the tutoring programme on Neale Analysis showed that the low-progress readers in both groups made average gains of seven months in reading accuracy. For reading comprehension, the trained group gained 12 months on average whereas the untrained group gained nine months.

The results of this last study were similar to those obtained from another of our unpublished studies which evaluated a parent tutoring programme with high progress young readers. Three groups, each of seven pupils, were involved this time. The children were aged from 5 : 6 to 7 : 6 with reading ages in advance of chronological age by as much as two-and-a-half years. One group was an untutored comparison group, one group was tutored by their parents who were given only general tutoring advice whilst the third was tutored by their parents who had been trained to use 'Pause, Prompt and Praise'. Pre-training (baseline) and post-training measures of parental tutoring behaviours were obtained from both tutored groups.

Briefly, the results again showed that tutors (this time parents) could be readily trained to use the 'Pause, Prompt and Praise' procedures. Before training, rates for pausing, prompting and praising were very low in both groups of parents but following instruction in the methods, the trained group paused after nearly 90% of hesitations or errors, prompted nearly 50% of the time (with 60% success) and used six times as much praise. The group of parents given only general advice made only marginal gains in these skills. Interestingly enough, however, the results showed that for these young, skilled readers trained parental tutoring using 'Pause, Prompt and Praise' led to no greater gains in reading age than the general tutoring advice given to the other group of parents.

Our interpretation of the results from these last two studies is that, in contrast to the low-progress readers in the earlier studies, these readers may have already learned a range of independent strategies for predicting unknown words, and for self-correction of errors. For these readers, additional trained tutor input may be quite unnecessary. All they appear to need is for someone to hear them read on a regular basis.

## CONCLUSION

From the studies completed to date we can begin to draw tentative conclusions. It appears that peers can learn to use 'Pause, Prompt and Praise' procedures relatively quickly and easily. Peer tutors have also been shown to gain in reading skill as a result of their tutoring. However, it seems that children who are making good or average (or even a little below average) progress do not really need trained peer tutoring using Pause, Prompt and Praise. Simply having someone hear them read regularly from appropriate level material appears to be enough. 'Pause', 'Prompt' and 'Praise' tutoring is unlikely to be detrimental to their progress but it is not necessary for such independent readers. Setting up a 'Pause, Prompt and Praise' peer tutoring programme requires some initial effort from teachers and also provision for continual monitoring of the behaviour of both tutors and tutees. Consequently, it should be employed only when it is cost-effective to do so.

For older, low progress readers about to enter or already attending Secondary school, however, it is a different matter. For pupils such as these, whose reading is delayed by at least two years, trained peer tutoring using 'Pause, Prompt and Praise' has been shown consistently to be extremely effective and clearly superior to untrained tutoring.

We reiterate that the issue of book level is critical. If children can read only three or four words from a ten word sentence there is little chance of them being able to utilize contextual cues whereas if they know eight or nine of the ten words their chances of predicting the unknown words are much higher, especially when given a contextual prompt. If, however, children can read nearly every word in the book they have little chance to make progress in this important skill of predicting unrecognized words from contextual and graphophonic cues. The implication of this is that book level is at least as important as the tutoring methodology; in fact, the effectiveness of the tutoring methods is contingent upon appropriate book level. Prompting (especially contextual prompting) will be minimally effective where error rates are high, and cannot occur at all if no errors are made.

We would like to emphasize the all-important role of skilled, trained teachers in successfully implementing 'Pause, Prompt and Praise' peer tutoring. We are keen to see tutoring skills 'given away' to non-professional tutors but are reluctant to allow benefits to be 'thrown away' by insufficient attention to detail, especially with regard to initial placement and promotion in book level. In our view, the teacher should be responsible for these aspects of the programme.

Recent research in New Zealand (Henderson and Glynn, 1986) further emphasizes the important role of the teacher in giving feedback to tutors. As with many programmes teaching new tutoring or other skills to non-professionals, the use of feedback to maintain the newly trained tutoring skills must be considered. The feedback model proposed also follows a 'Pause, Prompt and Praise' procedure. The teacher identifies instances of both good and inappropriate responses by the tutors in their use of 'Pause, Prompt and Praise' with the struggling reader. They then pause to allow the tutor to recall and explain what occurred. If the tutor finds this difficult, the teacher then provides a prompt. The teacher subsequently praises the tutor for their efforts. Provision of consistent feedback to peer tutors is a vital component of the success of these programmes. In future training, this feedback model should ensure both better initial learning and subsequent maintenance of the 'Pause, Prompt and Praise' tutoring procedures.

Far from demeaning the reading teacher or 'taking bread from the teachers' mouths', there is, clearly, an important, professional and skilled role for the teacher to play in establishing and monitoring peer-tutoring programmes. As well as taking the initiative in publicizing the approach and setting schemes in motion the teacher will be responsible for training peer-tutors, for record keeping, for initial placement and subsequent promotion of children to appropriate book levels, for giving feedback on tutoring performance and so on. Peers are a valuable resource for the effective tutoring of reading to low progress readers but the success or failure of any such tutoring programmes will hinge upon the professional skills of teachers.

## REFERENCES


Bennett, N. (1988). Review of Topping, K., 'The Peer Tutoring Handbook', *British Journal of Educational Psychology*, **58**, 366.

Clay M. (1979). *Reading: the Patterning of Complex Behaviour*. (2nd edition). Auckland: Heinemann Educational Books.

Glynn, T. (1987). More power to the parents: behavioural approaches to remedial tutoring at home. In Wheldall, K. (ed.) *The Behaviourist in the Classroom*. London: Allen & Unwin.

Glynn, T., and McNaughton, S. S. (1985). The Mangere home and school remedial reading procedures: continuing research on their effectiveness, *New Zealand Journal of Psychology*, **14**, 66–77.

Glynn, T., McNaughton, S. S., Robinson, V., and Quinn, M. (1979). *Remedial Reading at Home: Helping you to Help your Child*. Wellington: NZCER.

Hamilton, M. (1987). *Literacy, Numeracy and Adults*. London: Adult Literacy and Basic Skills Unit.

Henderson, W., and Glynn, T. (1986). A feedback procedure for teacher trainees working with parent tutors of reading, *Educational Psychology*, **6**, 159–177.

Limbrick, E., McNaughton, S. S., and Glynn, T. (1985). Reading gains for under-achieving tutors and tutees in a cross-age tutoring programme, *Journal of Child Psychology and Psychiatry*, **26**, 939–953.

Lindsay, G., Evans, A., and Jones, B. (1985). Paired reading versus relaxed reading: a comparison, *British Journal of Educational Psychology*, **55**, 304–309.

McNaughton, S. (1987). A history of errors in the analysis of oral reading behaviour, *Educational Psychology*, **8**, 21–30.

McNaughton, S. (1988). *Being Skilled: Socialisation of Learning to Read*. London: Methuen.

McNaughton, S., and Delquadri, J. (1978). Error attention tutoring in oral reading. In Glynn, T., and McNaughton, S. (eds), *Applied Behaviour Analysis in New Zealand*. Auckland: Department of Education, University of Auckland.

McNaughton, S. S., and Glynn, T. (1981). Delayed versus immediate attention to oral reading errors, *Educational Psychology*, **1**, 57–65.

McNaughton, S. S., Glynn, T., and Robinson, V. (1981). *Parents as Remedial Tutors: Issues for Home and School*. Wellington: NZCER.

McNaughton, S. S., Glynn, T., and Robinson, V. (1987). *Pause, Prompt and Praise: Effective Tutoring for Remedial Reading*. Birmingham: Positive Products.

Morgan, R., and Lyon, E. (1979). 'Paired Reading': a preliminary report on a technique for parental tuition of reading retarded children, *Journal of Child Psychology*, **20**, 151–160.

Pumphrey, P. (1987). A critique of paired reading, *The Paired Reading Bulletin*, **3**, 62–66.

Topping, K. (1987a). Peer tutored paired reading: outcome data from ten projects, *Educational Psychology*, **7**, 133–145.

Topping, K. (1987b). Paired reading makes a comeback! *Special Children*, March, 14–15.

Topping, K. (1988). *The Peer Tutoring Handbook: Promoting Co-operative Learning*. London: Croom Helm.

Wheldall, K., and Glynn, T. (1988). Contingencies in contexts: a behavioural interactionist perspective in education, *Educational Psychology*, **8**, 5–19.

Wheldall, K., and Glynn, T. (1989). *Effective Classroom Learning: a Behavioural Interactionist Approach to Teaching*. London: Basil Blackwell.

Wheldall, K., and Mettem, P. (1985). Behavioural peer tutoring: training 16-year-old tutors to employ the 'pause, prompt and praise' method with 12-year-old remedial readers, *Educational Psychology*, **5**, 27–44.

Wheldall, K., Wenban-Smith, J., Morgan, A., and Quance, B. (1989). Reading: how do teachers typically tutor? Unpublished manuscript, Centre for Child Study, University of Birmingham.

Winter, S. (1988). Paired reading: a study of process and outcome, *Educational Psychology*, **8**, 135–151.

CHAPTER 7

# Computer-based Learning: the Social Dimensions

PAUL LIGHT* and AGNÈS BLAYE†

*Centre for Human Development and Learning, The Open University, Milton Keynes, MK7 6AA, UK*

†*Centre de Recherche en Psychologie Cognitive, Université de Provence, Aix-en-Provence, France*

## INTRODUCTION

This chapter concerns the cognitive consequences of peer interaction in the context of educational microcomputer use. The computer has, in the course of its recent appearance on the educational scene, acted as a multi-faceted mirror, reflecting the whole gamut of educational and psychological theories concerning the development of children's thinking. Moreover, the computer has not only lent itself well to assimilation into a wide variety of educational contexts, it also has the potential to transform those contexts.

Without attempting a comprehensive review, we propose to examine some of the broad issues surrounding individualized versus group microcomputer use, to offer an overview of the available experimental literature, and to take a look at some of the possibilities for future development in this field. We will restrict ourselves to situations of 'direct' face-to-face interaction, while acknowledging that the use of networking, of electronic mail and conferencing would all deserve a place in any full discussion of the social dimensions of children's computer use.

Children Helping Children
Edited by H. C. Foot, M. J. Morgan and R. H. Shute

## THE COMPUTER AS AN EDUCATIONAL TOOL: CONCEPT TO REALITY

There are a number of distinct frameworks within which the computer has been envisaged as contributing to education. One of these is the Piagetian constructivist framework, developed in this context most effectively by Papert (1980). Papert's seminal work with LOGO has done a great deal to shape microcomputer use, especially at younger age levels. He saw in programming a distinctive route toward the development of generalizable problem-solving skills ('powerful ideas'), and emphasized the individual constructive activity of the child in acquiring such skills. While Papert's vision was not of the child-computer dyad as *isolated* from other learners, there was little room for any analysis of the social dimensions of the learning process. Programming in a high level language such as LOGO requires the pupils to have a precise and formal representation of all the necessary steps to a particular goal. The essence of Papert's view was that the writing, testing and 'debugging' of programs offers a uniquely powerful resource for the development of abstract thought and high level problem-solving abilities. The intellectually constructive aspect of computer use, then, is to be found in the creative engagement of the child with the computer program.

While this perspective has been an influential one, the majority of contemporary school computer use is of a very different ilk. Surveys such as that by Jackson, Fletcher and Messer (1986) confirm that most computer use in primary schools involves 'drill and practice' software. The pedagogical perspective here is that the computer can provide a level of routine individual tutoring which the busy classroom teacher cannot. Any given educational task can be broken down into its elements and the individual child can be taken through a carefully graduated series of subtasks embodying these elements. The child can progress at his or her own pace, being given lots of practice to establish full mastery of each subtask. From this perspective one of the main virtues of the computer is its facility for providing direct and immediate feedback, shaping performance and ensuring a progressive build-up of understanding.

From this standpoint, the computer can be seen as an infinitely patient teaching assistant, a descendent of the Skinnerian 'teaching machine' of an earlier era. Indeed it has been said of this kind of usage that it amounts to employing the technology of the 1980s to embody the curriculum of the 1950s (Baker, 1985). While the principles of programmed learning proved difficult to implement in the then-available technology, the computer with its speed and flexibility offers these principles a new lease of life.

The recent development of intelligent tutoring systems provides a new way to harness the educational potentialities of computers. What characterizes 'drill and practice' and other non-intelligent computer-assisted learning software is the lack of flexibility which results in all pupils having to undergo essentially the same teaching sequence. By contrast, an intelligent tutoring system offers the possibility of generating the teaching sequence 'online' during the educational interaction (Elsom-Cook, 1987). As a result the teaching sequence is tailored to the requirements of each pupil.

An essentially individualistic view of the learning process is fundamental to the tradition which stretches from programmed learning to intelligent tutoring systems, and *progress* in this domain has largely been measured in terms of increasingly flexible and accurate tailoring of the software to the needs of the individual learner. This in turn has provoked concern about the dangers, supposedly inherent in information technology, of losing out on the social and interactional aspects of the learning process. The worrying image of the socially isolated and withdrawn child, hunched over a computer for hours at a time, is one which has considerable currency (Baker, 1985).

The reality, at least for the early school years in North America and the UK, appears to be very different. For what may prove temporary and pragmatic reasons, the indications are that, far from reducing socially interactive learning, computers in the classroom *increase* the opportunities for such learning. This is especially true in respect of child–child interaction. The most obvious factor here is the scarcity of computer hardware in schools. The survey mentioned earlier by Jackson *et al.* (1986) indicated that in the Primary sector the level of provision averaged less than one computer per class. Moreover, whereas over most curricular areas the teacher has vastly more expertise than the pupils, this is often not true in respect of computers. Here, knowledgeable pupils often become valued sources of information for other children in the class (Sheingold, Hawkins and Char, 1984).

The net result of these factors is that much educational computer work takes place within relatively autonomous *groups* of pupils. Indeed, Jackson *et al.*'s (1986) survey showed that primary school teachers saw learning to interact in groups as one of the main *advantages* of computer use in schools. The view of computer-related activities as incentives to social interaction has been supported by many systematic observations of work on the computer in the classroom (e.g. Hawkins, 1983; Hawkins *et al.*, 1982). Sheingold, Hawkins and Char (1984) reviewed a number of early studies which point to the conclusion that work with computers promotes both a high level of task-related interaction and a high probability of children calling on one another (rather than the teacher) for help. Far from preventing peer interaction, then, computer work in schools may perhaps offer a peculiarly effective environment for interaction between learners.

## EMPIRICAL STUDIES OF COMPUTER USE BY CLASSROOM GROUPS

Classroom-based observational studies have suggested a similar picture for activities specific to computers (e.g. programming and word processing) and for traditional activities transferred to the computer (e.g. most drill and practice and non-intelligent CAL—Computer-Assisted Learning—software).

Cummings (1985), on the basis of an Australian study of children using a variety of CAL programs, concluded that the computer can and does provide an effective motivator for groupwork. In particular he saw computer-based work as supplying the context for the kind of genuine discussion between children which the Bullock Report (1975) considered so necessary, but which is so difficult to achieve in teacher-centred classrooms. Broderick and Trushell (1985), observing 10-year-old children using word processors, described a wealth of positive and mutually supportive interactions amongst the children. Proponents of LOGO in recent years (e.g. Hoyles and Sutherland, 1986; Hughes, McLeod and Potts, 1985; Hawkins, 1983; Hawkins *et al.*, 1982) have offered detailed observational support to the view that children working with LOGO in pairs or small groups typically show high levels of spontaneous interaction. Indeed, Hoyles and Sutherland see this as one of the major strengths of this approach to learning mathematics. They suggest that it is the context of social interaction which pushes the children towards adopting an objective attitude to the task in hand. Their ongoing studies are attempting to validate this claim through a fine-grained analysis of the interaction actually going on between pairs of children working together on LOGO over a prolonged period of time.

Hawkins and colleagues (1982) describe the interaction between pupils when they work with LOGO as sometimes taking the form of sustained collaboration on a joint project, sometimes taking the form of children seeking help and advice from one another when they are in difficulties, and sometimes involving children just 'stopping by' at the computer in passing. Not surprisingly, patterns of interaction are affected by the kind of software in use. Crook (1987) for example, observed that a piece of CAL software involving maze-solving tended to produce turn-taking on the part of the children. Another piece of software involving series completion produced more differentiated interaction, with discussion of competing hypotheses. The richest discussion was promoted by an adventure game, though differences in reading ability were limiting. Similarly in word processing, children's very limited keyboard skills imposed severe restrictions on the interaction (Crook, 1986).

Though suggestive, these kinds of studies cannot definitively establish the effects of such interaction upon individual children's learning. In the next section we turn to more artificial, experimental studies which have sought to do this.

## EXPERIMENTAL STUDIES

One series of experimental studies has stemmed from the mainly American tradition of social-psychological research rooted in the work of Lewin and Deutsch on group dynamics and cooperation. These studies put their emphasis on cooperative organization of groups, tasks and rewards (e.g. Johnson and

Johnson, 1986; Johnson, Johnson and Stanne, 1986) and deal mainly with CAL tasks. For example, Johnson and Johnson describe a study in which 14-year-olds worked in groups of four on a geography simulation task on the computer. In some groups the pupils were given individual goals, independently of one another. In other groups the children within the groups were instructed to work competitively, to see who was best. In the third type of group the children were instructed to work cooperatively, being assigned to specific roles in rotation. The third condition produced significantly higher levels of individual achievement on a number of measures than did either of the other two. Both the cooperative and the competitive conditions produced more positive expressed attitudes towards computers than did the individualized condition.

Johnson and colleagues suggest that such benefits of cooperation may be more evident with more complex and exploratory software of the kind they used. However, rather similar advantages for pupils working in cooperative pairs have been found with relatively simple drill and practice software (Mevarech, 1987). Twelve-year-olds were studied working alone or in pairs of similar ability on arithmetic drill and practice programs. All children were individually post-tested. Those who had worked in pairs achieved significantly better results, and this was especially true amongst the low-achieving children. However, in another rather similar study involving computer-based instruction in Hebrew, only marginal and non-significant differences favouring homogeneous pairs over individuals were found (Mevarech, Stern and Levita, 1987).

Another variable which could potentially play an important role is group size. Trowbridge (1987) observed 13- and 14-year-olds working on CAL software designed to teach them about electrical circuits. The pupils worked either one, two, three or four to a computer. Measures of interactional behaviour taken from videotapes of the sessions indicated that children working in twos or threes engaged in the highest levels of interaction, though those working in threes were more likely to show competitive interaction. The pairs were the most mutually supportive. The children working in pairs made the fewest incorrect entries and formulated higher quality responses than those working in the other conditions, though post-tests failed to show significant superiority in individual learning outcome.

Whereas the work we have discussed thus far has mainly emphasized social motivational and attitudinal concomitants of interaction, treating cognitive attainments simply as an outcome measure, another body of (mainly European) experimental work has attempted a more cognitively oriented analysis of the interaction. For example, Fletcher (1985) has attempted to analyse the role of the verbalization which typically accompanies collaborative work. In a study with 9–11-year-olds, children worked on a computer simulation game either as individuals or in groups of three. Amongst the individuals, some were instructed to work silently while others were asked to talk aloud. On most measures, the groups performed substantially better than the silent individuals.

The requirement to verbalize reasons for decisions, etc., led to some improvement amongst the children working alone, leading Fletcher to conclude that overt verbalization may have at least some part to play in group facilitation of performance. However, there was no individual post-test on the task in this study, and a post-test measure of verbal knowledge concerning the task indicated no significant differences between the conditions.

Experimental studies have also been carried out involving rather more 'computer-specific' activities such as programming. Programming the computer can be thought of as a highly technical chore which, mercifully, computer users have to concern themselves with less and less these days. But it can also be thought of as the activity which most fully embodies the educational potentialities of the microcomputer. We saw this earlier with Papert, who envisaged the writing, running, debugging and developing of LOGO programs as an activity which distilled and rendered accessible to the young child a whole range of powerful, abstract ideas. Indeed, as Colbourn and Light (1987) noted, the claims Papert made for the cognitive benefits of programming (especially in terms of the child's metacognitive ability to reflect upon and articulate his or her own problem-solving abilities) bear a distinct resemblance to claims which have been made for the cognitive benefits of peer interaction. So what can we say about the effectiveness of bringing these two phenomena together and employing peer interaction in the service of learning to program?

We saw earlier that classroom observation work involving LOGO indicates its potential for supporting high levels of task-related social interaction, though the evidence that it promotes the generalizable problem-solving skills envisaged by Papert is less than convincing (Clements, 1987; DES, 1987; Kliman, 1985). For present purposes the key question is whether there is any experimental evidence that child–child interaction facilitates the learning of programming concepts and skills. There appear to have been relatively few systematic studies in this area.

One such study involved 11- and 12-year-old children learning to use a programming language called microPROLOG (Colbourn and Light, 1987; Light, Colbourn and Smith, 1987). The children worked in class groups of eight over a number of sessions. Each group of eight pupils was given access to either two, four or eight microcomputers. No differences were found between these conditions in terms of children's individual grasp of microPROLOG at post-test. A significant difference between the design of this study and those of most others we have discussed is that, although in one condition the children had a microcomputer each, they were working within a group of eight pupils and could interact freely with one another. Videotapes of selected sessions indicated little difference in levels of interaction in the 'individual', 'two to a machine' and 'four to a machine' conditions. This perhaps serves to highlight the artificiality of experimental studies in which the 'control' condition involves children working alone at the computer with no access at all to their fellow students.

Faced with this difficulty, one way forward is to rely on trying to *correlate* the amount or quality of interaction which particular learners engage in and their particular learning outcome. Webb, Ender and Lewis (1986) adopted this approach in a study of 11- to 14-year-olds learning BASIC programming in pairs over a number of sessions. They looked for evidence that the quality of social interaction and discussion in which children engaged during learning could predict achievement in terms of eventual individual programming skills. Measures were taken of the frequency of such behaviours as giving and receiving explanations, asking questions and getting replies, and verbalizing aloud. Correlations with learning outcome were calculated, partialling out variations in initial ability level. The results showed that many of the interaction measures were significantly positively correlated with some (though not all) of the learning outcome measures.

Perhaps the most systematic and theoretically coherent body of experimental work on the cognitive consequences of peer interaction has been that associated with Doise, Mugny and Perret-Clermont in Geneva and Neuchatel (see Doise, this volume). While this work has not been concerned with computer-based learning, it has exercised considerable influence on work in this field. Doise and colleagues typically used a three-step experimental design involving an individual pre-test, an intervention session in which children work either alone (the control condition) or in groups (usually pairs) and finally an individual post-test. The studies which established this tradition (see for example Doise and Mugny, 1984; Perret-Clermont, 1980) involved children in the age range 5–7 who, in Piaget's terms, were in the process of mastering concrete operational modes of thought. Where working in pairs facilitated subsequent individual performance the mediating process was characterized as 'socio-cognitive conflict', i.e. conflict between differing wrong answers based on partial centrations, embodied socially in the differing perspectives of the two children. The social dimension of the situation was seen as providing the impetus towards resolving the conflict. Such resolution could be achieved by transcending the different centrations to arrive at a more advanced 'decentred' solution.

This analysis has been adapted by a number of researchers interested in peer-facilitation effects on non-Piagetian tasks, and several of these have involved computer-based work (Blaye, 1988; Fraisse, 1987; Light *et al.*, 1987). In these cases, the reason for using the computer was principally that it offered advantages in controlling and manipulating task presentation, so as to facilitate detailed study of interactional effects. In some cases these manipulations involve the software, in some the hardware.

As an example of a software manipulation, Fraisse (1985, 1987) followed up a series of studies on recursive reasoning with 11- and 12-year-olds by pitting children, either alone or in pairs, against the computer. When the 'computer-opponent' was programmed to give poor (in fact random) answers the children working in pairs discussed their ideas and showed superior learning to those children who worked alone. But when the 'computer-opponent' was programmed to give perfect answers every time, the children in effect used the computer to check out their hypotheses, did not interact much with their partners, and showed no peer-facilitation of performance.

The effects of different types of hardware and interface devices upon interactive learning has not been extensively studied as yet (Wilton and McClean, 1984). However, Scaife (1987) has begun to analyse children's performance with various kinds of input devices. Most such devices have clearly been designed with a single user in mind. However, it is possible to exploit them for cooperative usage, and this has been done in a number of experiments.

Blaye (1988) reports a series of studies in which 5- and 6-year-olds worked on a form/colour matrix filling task either individually or in pairs. Although the task might have been expected to engender conflicts of centration, the children working in pairs showed only a low frequency of verbal disagreement, and there was little to suggest that such disagreements were conducive to learning. Nevertheless, experience in pairs did in some studies lead to greater individual progress than working alone. This was particularly true with a version of the task where the interaction in the pairs was structured so that one child indicated his or her choice with a lightpen and the other had to key in his or her assent via the keyboard before the instruction would be accepted by the computer.

A rather similar procedure for preserving the engagement of both children with the task was used by Light *et al.* (1987). Here pairs and individuals were presented with a problem-solving task on the computer. Superiority of the pairs condition (as judged in terms of individual post-test performance) was only shown when the keyboard was modified so as to require corresponding key entries from both partners to activate a response. Despite rather little verbal interaction of any kind, this 'dual key' condition, resulting in joint participation of both children in every move, was associated with clear peer facilitation of individual performance. As with Blaye (1988), the most likely mechanism underlying progress seems to be the destabilization of initial inefficient solution strategies, creating novel intermediate stages on the basis of which the children could see their way through to more efficient solutions.

Light and Glachan (1985) and Light and Foot (1987) have reported a number of studies of problem-solving on the computer which suggest that both the likelihood of peer interaction benefits and the underlying mechanisms vary considerably from task to task. For example, whereas benefits in the 'Tower of Hanoi' task seemed to accrue from the essentially non-verbal disequilibration process referred to above, explicit verbal justification of choices seemed to be an important factor in a 'Balance Beam' task. Disagreement and argument about moves proved a good predictor of learning outcome in the code-breaking game 'Master-mind'.

It is clear from these and other studies that pairs or groups of children working at the computer do not always perform better than individuals, and even when they do this advantage is not always reflected in individual learning outcome. On the other hand it is worth remarking that *contrary* results, favouring the individual over the group, do not seem to appear in this literature. The studies we have reviewed either favour learning in groups or indicate no difference in outcome. There are no indications from these studies that, for example, the reduced 'hands on' experience associated with group use of the computer entails any disadvantages to the learner.

As to the mechanisms of group facilitation, where it occurs, it is apparent that the concept of socio-cognitive conflict which inspired much of the recent work in this field is far from adequate to explain all the effects observed. Much remains to be done in explicating the processes involved. We have seen in some of the studies that we have been considering that manipulations of computer hardware and software can be used as a way of influencing the nature of the socio-cognitive activity and hence the outcome of the interaction. How far can this be taken? To what extent can we envisage the computer actively supporting interaction amongst learners or participating as a full interactive partner in the learning process? These are some of the issues to which we shall turn in the final section of this chapter.

## PROSPECTS: THE SOCIAL INTERFACE

As we noted at the outset of this chapter, the goal of intelligent tutoring systems has often been expressed in terms of *individualizing* the learning process (Elsom-Cook, 1988), and to this extent it may seem to be very much opposed in spirit to any consideration of social processes in learning. But this is not necessarily the case. Woolf (1988) recently noted the 'most surprising' observation that certain experimental intelligent tutoring systems have been shown to be very effective when used with quite heterogeneous *groups* of students (in this case adults). Hennessy and colleagues are presently developing an arithmetic tutor specially designed to be used by pairs of children (Hennessy *et al.*, 1987).

To pick up the idea touched upon at the end of the previous section, it is possible to envisage an intelligent tutor not only coping with pairs of learners but also as being itself a *member* of such a pair, i.e. a partner in the learning process. If it is the case that children learn certain things in and through peer group interaction, then can this process itself be modelled? The possibility of the computer playing the role of a working companion to the child, interacting in such a way as to maximize the child's learning, has recently surfaced in the Intelligent Tutoring literature. For example, Chan and Baskin (1988) propose a system in which the computer plays both the role of teacher and the role of a companion who 'learns' to perform the task at about the same level as the child, and who exchanges ideas with the child as they work together on the same material.

Many problems stand in the way of implementing such a system, not the least of which is our very imperfect understanding of how 'real' learning companions help one another. While there is a long way to go, there are real signs of convergence with some of the work being undertaken by developmental psychologists working in this field. For example, Blaye, Farioli and Gilly (1987), using Blaye's matrix filling task mentioned earlier, experimented with a condition in which the child proposed an entry for a given cell and the computer 'partner' proposed an alternative choice. The alternative selected was based on a diagnosis of the child's proposal—if it reflected a centration on one dimension of the matrix the computer-partner suggested an (equally wrong) alternative based on the other dimension of the matrix. The results were not impressive—in fact as we have seen, Blaye's (1988) other studies seriously question the power of socio-cognitive conflict as a mechanism for progress on this task—but the basic design illustrates well the close convergence of work in cognitive science and developmental psychology at the present time.

Similar issues arise in respect of computer-based 'help' facilities. Researchers in this area seem to be confronted with two basic observations. Firstly, children are typically very ready to use their peers as sources of help when faced with computer tasks. Secondly, when help facilities are available on the computer itself, the children seem to show little interest in them and benefit little from their use (Messer, Jackson and Mohamedali, 1987; Turner, 1988). These apparently conflicting results again point to the need to integrate psychological research on peer facilitation with software design work.

We need to be able to specify the ways in which children solicit and gain help from those around them while working at the computer, and then to use this knowledge of socially mediated help to inform the design of machine-based help. In the realm of adults, the need for research on learners' informal support networks when working with computers is increasingly being recognized, as indeed are the potential implications of such research for the design of effective software-based help (e.g. Bannon, 1986; O'Malley, 1986). Hopefully, similar research with children will generate progress towards more adaptive and 'helpful' software for children (whether working individually or collectively) before too long.

It is striking, given the inherently individualistic assumptions about the learning process which informed so much of the early work in the field of educational computing, that the social dimension of computer-based learning has come so clearly to the fore. It should allay the fears of any who still see the computer as necessarily a threat to social processes in learning. We concur with a recent OECD report that 'there is every prospect for more rather than less interchange among learners thanks to the new information technologies' (1987, p. 105). We hope that we have said enough to indicate why psychologists interested in 'children helping children' should be interested in educational computing. It is an area where more psychological research on the social foundations of learning is sorely needed, and where such research has a real chance of influencing children's educational experience.

## ACKNOWLEDGEMENTS

The writing of this chapter was facilitated by a joint ESRC/CNRS grant to Professor Paul Light and Professor Michel Gilly (Université de Provence) and by a grant to Dr Agnès Blaye from the Fondation Fyssen, Paris.

## REFERENCES

Baker, C. (1985). The microcomputer and the curriculum: a critique, *Journal of Curriculum Studies*, **17**, 4.

Bannon, L. (1986). Helping users help each other. In D. Norman and S. Draper (eds), *User Centred System Design*. Hillsdale, N.J.: Erlbaum.

Blaye, A. (1988). Confrontation socio-cognitive et résolution de problème. Unpublished doctoral thesis, University of Provence.

Blaye, A., Farioli, F., and Gilly, M. (1987). Microcomputer as a partner in problem solving, *Rassegna di Psicologia*, **4**, 109–118.

Broderick, C., and Trushell, J. (1985). Problems and processes—Junior School children using wordprocessors to produce an information leaflet, *English in Education*, **19**, 2.

Bullock, A. (1975). *A Language for Life*. London: HMSO.

Chan, T-W., and Baskin, A. (1988). 'Studying with the Prince': the computer as learning companion. Paper presented to IT-88 Conference, Montreal, June, 1988.

Clements, D. (1987). A longitudinal study of the effects of LOGO programming on cognitive abilities and achievement, *Journal of Educational Computing Research*, **3**, 1.

Colbourn, C. J., and Light, P. H. (1987). Social interaction and learning using micro-PROLOG, *Journal of Computer Assisted Learning*, **3**, 130–140.

Crook, C. (1986). The use of a word-processor to support writing as a joint activity. Paper presented at second European Developmental Psychology Conference, Rome, September.

Crook, C. (1987). Computers in the classroom: defining a social context. In J. Rutkowska and C. Crook (eds), *Computers, Cognition and Development*. Chichester: Wiley.

Cummings, R. (1985). Small group discussions and the microcomputer, *Journal of Computer Assisted Learning*, **1**, 149–158.

DES (1987). Aspects of the work of the Microelectronics Education Programme. Department of Education and Science, London.

Doise, W., and Mugny, G. (1984). *The Social Development of the Intellect*. Oxford: Pergamon Press.

Elsom-Cook, M. (1987). Intelligent computer-aided instruction research at the Open University. CITE Technical Report No. 10. The Open University.

Elsom-Cook, M. (1988). Guided discovery tutoring and bounded user modelling. In J. Self (ed.), *Artificial Intelligence and Human Learning*. London: Chapman & Hall.

Fletcher, B. (1985). Group and individual learning of junior school children on a microcomputer based task, *Educational Review*, **37**, 251–261.

Fraisse, J. (1985). Interactions sociales entre pairs et découverte d'une stratégie cognitive chez des enfants de 11 ans. Unpublished Doctoral Thesis, University of Provence.

Fraisse, J. (1987). Etude du rôle pertubateur du partenaire dans la découverte d'une stratégie cognitive chez des enfants de 11 ans en situation d'interaction sociale, *Bulletin de Psychologie*, **382**, 943–952.

Hawkins, J. (1983). Learning LOGO together: the social context. Tech. Report 13, Bank St. College of Education, New York.

Hawkins, J., Sheingold, K., Gearhart, M., and Berger, C. (1982). Microcomputers in schools: impact on the social life of elementary classrooms, *Journal of Applied Developmental Psychology*, **3**, 361–373.

Hennessy, S., Evertsz, R., Ellis, D., Black, P., O'Shea, T., and Floyd, A. (1987). Design specification for 'Shopping on Mars'. CITE report 29, *Institute of Educational Technology*, The Open University.

Hoyles, C., and Sutherland, R. (1986). Using LOGO in the mathematics classroom. *Computers in Education*, **10**, 61–72.

Hughes, M., MacLeod, H., and Potts, C. (1985). Using LOGO with Infant School children, *Educational Psychology*, **5**, 3–4.

Jackson, A., Fletcher, B., and Messer, D. (1986). A survey of microcomputer use and provision in primary schools, *Journal of Computer Assisted Learning*, **2**, 45–55.

Johnson, D., and Johnson, R. (1986). Computer assisted cooperative learning, *Educational Technology*, January 1986.

Johnson, R., Johnson, D., and Stanne, M. (1986). Comparison of computer assisted cooperative, competitive and individualistic learning, *American Educational Research Journal*, **12**, 382–392.

Kliman, M. (1985). A new approach to Infant and Early Primary Mathematics. DAI Research Paper 241, Department of Artificial Intelligence, University of Edinburgh.

Light, P. H., Colbourn, C. J., and Smith, D. (1987). Peer interaction and logic programming: a study of the acquisition of micro-PROLOG. ESRC Information Technology and Education Programme, Occasional Paper ITE/17/87.

Light, P. H., and Foot, T. (1987). Peer interaction and microcomputer use, *Rassegna di Psicologia*, **4**, 93–104.

Light, P. H., and Foot, T., Colbourn, C., and McClelland, I. (1987). Collaborative interactions at the microcomputer keyboard, *Educational Psychology*, **7**, 13–21.

Light, P. H., and Glachan, M. (1985). Facilitation of problem solving through peer interaction, *Educational Psychology*, **5**, 217–225.

Messer, D., Jackson, A., and Mohamedali, M. (1987). Influences on computer-based problem solving. *Educational Psychology*, **7**, 1.

Mevarech, Z. (1987). Learning with computers in small groups: cognitive and social processes. Paper presented at 2nd European Conference for Research on Learning and Instruction, Tubingen, W. Germany, September, 1987.

Mevarech, Z., Stern, D., and Levita, I. (1987). To cooperate or not to cooperate in CAI: that is the question, *Journal of Educational Research*, **80**, 164–167.

OECD (1987). Information Technologies and Basic Learning. Organisation for Economic Cooperation and Development, Paris, 1987.

O'Malley, C. (1986). Helping users help themselves. In D. Norman and S. Draper (eds), *User Centred System Design*. Hillsdale, N.J.: Erlbaum.

Papert, S. (1980). *Mindstorms: Children, Computers and Powerful Ideas*. Brighton: Harvester Press.

Perret-Clermont, A.-N. (1980). *Social Interaction and Cognitive Development in Children*. London: Academic Press.

Scaife, M. (1987). Sensorimotor learning in children's interactions with computerised displays. Final report to ESRC, No. C08250010.

Sheingold, K., Hawkins, J., and Char, C. (1984). "I'm the thinkist, you're the typist": the interaction of technology and the social life of classrooms. Tech. Report 27, Bank St. College of Education, New York.

Trowbridge, D. (1987). An investigation of groups working at the computer. In Berger, K. Pezdek and W. Banks (eds), *Applications of Cognitive Psychology: Problem Solving, Education, and Computing*. Hillsdale, N.J.: Erlbaum.

Turner, T. (1988). Cognitive development through child-computer interaction using HELP facilities. Unpublished paper, Department of Psychology, University of Southampton.

Webb, N., Ender, P., and Lewis, S. (1986). Problem solving strategies and group processes in small groups learning computer programming, *American Educational Research Journal*, **23**, 243–261.

Wilton, J., and McClean, R. (1984). Evaluation of a mouse as an educational pointing device, *Computers and Education*, **8**, 455–461.

Woolf, B. (1988). Representing complex knowledge in an intelligent machine tutor. In J. Self (ed.), *Artificial Intelligence and Human Learning*. London: Chapman & Hall.

PART II

# Cooperative Learning

CHAPTER 8

# Cooperative Learning and Helping Behaviour in the Multi-ethnic Classroom

SHLOMO SHARAN

*Professor of Educational Psychology, School of Education, Tel-Aviv University, Tel-Aviv, Israel*

## INTRODUCTION

The values or behaviour we seek to impart to the younger generation through the school should be implemented in the manner in which students actually experience life in school, and not through verbal exhortation alone. The axiom that the school must practise what it preaches sounds like a principle that we should be able to take for granted. Yet, a close look at the nature of instruction practised in most classrooms today in Western countries, and the impact of that instruction on students, quickly reveals that there is a wide gap between proclamations about the goals of schooling on the one hand, and the means employed for achieving these goals on the other. Schools generally do not demonstrate a highly coordinated relationship between means and ends. This lack of means–ends coordination is one feature of the organizational structure of schools as loosely coupled systems (Weick, 1976). What we wish to stress here is that the loosely-coupled nature of schools appears not only in their organizational structure at the school-wide or even system-wide level, such as lack of curricular coordination between different subject-matter areas, or the absence of systematic problem solving by committees of teachers, but at the level of the classroom as well. The instructional methods employed in classrooms

Children Helping Children
Edited by H. C. Foot, M. J. Morgan and R. H. Shute

are not calculated to achieve the academic or social goals for which schools publicly proclaim to strive (Sarason, 1983).

The gap between means and ends in classroom instruction is nowhere more glaringly evident than in the realm of inter-pupil interactions in the classroom. Schools claim to be the major setting outside the family for socialization of the young. Yet the instructional methods practised in most classrooms today foster behaviour that is predominantly competitive and individualistic, not at all oriented toward pro-social and cooperative modes of behaviour with peers. Pupils are told to be helpful and considerate of others, but classroom practices do not cultivate cooperation, and pupils are reprimanded for cheating or copying when they share their school work with their classmates. Instruction is aimed at the pupils as an aggregate of individuals, rather than as a cohesive group that maintains a communication network designed to achieve common goals by utilizing the personal resources of everyone present. In the prevailing system, pupils are socialized into a set of classroom norms that value individual achievement without regard for the good of the group, and even at the expense of others. Observational studies of peer interaction in traditional classrooms (Hertz-Lazarowitz, 1983; Hertz-Lazarowitz *et al.*, 1984; Hertz-Lazarowitz *et al.*, 1989) reveal that only 13% of students' interactive behaviour in elementary school classrooms, and 16% of their interactive behaviour in secondary classrooms were of a pro-social character, i.e. cooperative or helping behaviour.

A fundamental premise of cooperative learning, derived from John Dewey's (1916, 1938) philosophy of education, states that the values and goals of schooling, in both the academic and social realms, should constitute an essential part of the methods and procedures of instruction practised at the classroom level. In order to exert genuine influence on pupils' behaviour, these experiences *must form* part of the central activities of the school, which are instruction and learning. If a programme for developing pro-social behaviour is merely an appendage to the regular school programme, such as a once-a-week discussion of social issues, its effects will be virtually negligible. The authors of cooperative learning methods have designed their methods to work through, and not alongside, the curriculum of the school (Johnson and Johnson, 1987; Sharan *et al.*, 1980; Sharan and Sharan, 1976; Slavin, 1983, 1986; Slavin *et al.*, 1985). The pro-social effects of cooperative learning on students are documented by extensive experimental research conducted in hundreds of classrooms at all levels of public schooling (Hertz-Lazarowitz and Sharan, 1984).

This chapter presents a short outline of four major cooperative learning methods, followed by a summary of research studies that evaluated the effects of cooperative learning experiences on pupils' helping behaviour in multi-ethnic classrooms. The thumbnail descriptions of the cooperative learning procedures offered in this chapter are intended to give readers an indication of how the different cooperative learning methods structure mutual assistance among classmates as part of the on-going learning process in the classroom. Before proceeding, some comments are needed about the relevance of cooperative learning for promoting positive cross-ethnic relationships in the multi-ethnic classroom.

Ever since its inception in the early 1970s, cooperative learning has been employed to foster positive social relations among peers in the ethnically/racially desegregated classroom. Cooperative learning was conceived as fulfilling the basic conditions for positive inter-group relations set forth by Gordon Allport years earlier in his seminal work on prejudice (Allport, 1954). Allport's essential conditions are: direct face-to-face contact between members of different ethnic or racial groups, where the contact is between persons of equal status, or where the contact situation itself provides for equal status of the participants, where the contact occurs under the auspices of the relevant institution, and where the contact leads to the perception of common interests or goals (Allport, 1954, p. 281).

Cooperative learning in the ethnically heterogeneous classroom is a convenient setting for face-to-face contact between pupils from different ethnic backgrounds. They study together in small groups within the larger classroom. In these groups relatively intimate, non-superficial interaction around learning tasks is made possible and encouraged. The work of the group is structured so that each pupil can make a contribution to the collective group goal, thus creating conditions for pupils to achieve status in their peer group.

These conditions differ markedly from the competitive atmosphere prevailing in the classroom taught with the whole-class method (teacher presentation and pupil recitation) where students vie for the teacher's attention and praise, and where their contributions are constantly being compared with those of more able classmates. Moreover, the cooperative learning groups encourage mutual exchange and assistance among pupils. Such behaviour increases friendly relations with groupmates and greater mutual acceptance based on their common interests and individuality as persons instead of focusing on their ethnic differences. Several recent publications have carried our understanding of learning in cooperative groups and its implications for inter-ethnic relations far beyond the ground covered by Allport and his students in the previous two decades (Brewer and Miller, 1984; Miller and Harrington, 1990; Miller and Brewer, 1986). The central emphasis of this later work is to design the cooperative groups to allow for inter-ethnic relationships based on the personal characteristics of the individuals involved rather than on their group identity.

## COOPERATIVE LEARNING: AN OUTLINE OF FOUR MAJOR METHODS

Four different methods constitute the main repertoire of cooperative learning, although other methods are constantly evolving. These four methods have also been the subject of a very substantial amount of empirical research.

**Student teams—achievement divisions (STAD)**

This method, proposed by Robert Slavin (1986), is carried out in five stages.

1. *Direct instruction*

The teacher presents academic material, usually in the typical lecture-discussion (question-and-answer) approach. The study unit must be clearly defined. Pupils know that they will be tested on this unit and that their test scores constitute their contribution to the overall score of their study group.

2. *Teams*

Study groups are set up following teacher presentation of the material. The groups are composed of four pupils representing each of three levels of achievement (high, medium, low) in the class, as well as each of the different ethnic groups in the class. Group members assist each other in understanding and reviewing the materials taught by the teacher. The teacher gives each group work sheets that focus the group's attention on specific questions and other exercises that help the pupils master the material. Each group engages in discussions, exchange of information and answers to questions, and in correcting any misunderstandings regarding the study material. Each group member is helped to reach full mastery of the academic material.

3. *Quizzes*

After the teams have completed their study of the material, the pupils are given a quiz to be answered individually, without any assistance from others.

4. *Individual progress score*

The purpose of this approach to scoring is to give each pupil a goal that is within reach, but on condition that the pupil is prepared to invest considerable effort in reaching this goal and to demonstrate improvement over past levels of performance. A scoring system was devised whereby each pupil is given a mean score calculated from scores on similar tests, and the present score consists of the number of points that exceed that mean score. Those points become part of the study group's total score. In this fashion, each pupil is scored in comparison with his/her own earlier achievement, and not on the basis of comparison with other classmates.

5. *Team recognition*

Each study group receives a weekly achievement score based on all the contributions of all its members during the week. The group with the highest score in the class can be awarded with a special citation, its score can be published in a classroom weekly newspaper, or any other appropriate form of recognition. Group scores can also be accepted as part of the individuals' scores.

**Jigsaw**

The Jigsaw method was devised by Elliot Aronson and colleagues (Aronson *et al.*, 1978). It is implemented in four stages.

(1) The class is divided into small groups of five pupils, and each member takes a number from 1 to 5. Each pupil receives a portion of the learning task that corresponds with his or her number so that all groups have the same task, and all pupils with the same number throughout the class have the same portion of the task. Obviously the entire task itself consists of five separate parts, each one having a degree of integrity even though it is part of a larger whole.
(2) The pupils leave their home groups and form new 'expert' groups consisting of everyone in the class with the same number. The purpose of the new groups is to afford their members an opportunity to clarify and master the material, and to have members assist each other in planning how to present and explain the material to the other members of their home group. At various points in the existence of these groups the pupils participate in a number of team-building exercises intended to improve interpersonal communication and collaboration within the group.
(3) Pupils return to their home groups and instruct the other members in that portion of the material for which they are responsible. This process continues until they have all presented their portion and the group has been taught the entire task.
(4) The class is tested on its mastery of the task. The test is answered individually, without consulting with others.

The original Jigsaw method has undergone several revisions by various authors, as described recently by Slavin (1986).

**Learning together**

This approach to cooperative learning was proposed by David and Roger Johnson (1987; see also Johnson, Johnson and Holubec, 1986). The Johnsons' method is best conceived as consisting of several components rather than of stages. Basically, this approach calls upon teachers to provide small groups of pupils with one learning task, which frequently appears on one work-she and all of the group members must participate in completing the task. The gro must produce a single product, and each pupil learns all of the mater associated with the task. Moreover, each pupil must agree with the nat of the group's product. The group receives one grade or reward for product.

The teacher is asked to develop the pupils' skills for working together i group. Most of these skills deal with interpersonal communication, and th acquisition requires practice as a participant in a group.

The Johnsons described their cooperative learning method in somewh general terms, but it seems clear that pupil interdependence within groups formed primarily by virtue of the fact that each group is given only one ta that must be completed collectively, whatever the task may be. Each pupil m sign his or her name on the final group product to indicate agreement with formulation. In a recent summary, the Johnsons emphasized the following poi as the conditions necessary for productive group learning (Johnson and Johnsc 1990):

(1) Clearly perceived positive interdependence.
(2) Considerable face-to-face interaction.
(3) Felt personal responsibility to achieve the group's goals.
(4) Frequent use of relevant interpersonal and group skills.
(5) Periodic and regular group processing.

## Group investigation

Group investigation has a long history of development, and is rooted in Dewe philosophy of education that stressed learning as social inquiry, in Kurt Lewi approach to group dynamics, in Herbert Thelen's book on groups at wo (Thelen, 1954), and in the educational experiment of Alice Miel at Teach College, Columbia University (Miel, 1952). The classroom instructional meth presented here was developed by this author and collaborators (Sharan a Hertz-Lazarowitz, 1980; Sharan and Sharan, 1976). The method can conceived as consisting of six stages.

### *Formation of interest groups*

Pupil participation in identifying subtopics of a broader topic (which is genera determined by the teacher) for group study, and the division of the class in small groups according to the pupils' interest. Group composition by inter is subject to the constraint that all groups must be heterogeneous in terms gender and ethnic background. Teachers may wish to present a lesson th provides students with a basis for further study.

*Division of labour: Choosing sub-topics*

Once in groups, pupils further identify different aspects of the group topic which each member or pair of members selects as their personal portion of the larger group task for which they are responsible. Teachers assist the groups in planning what they wish to study about their topic and in implementation. Teachers assist the groups in the location of appropriate sources for learning about their topic. Students are encouraged to employ a variety of sources for gathering the information needed, including books, interviews, experiments, visits to sites, measurements, etc.

*Implementing the plan*

Pupils gather information according to the plan developed in stage 2. Each group member makes some unique contribution to the group goal. Pupils exchange information and discuss ideas, problems and plans. They analyse their information and decide how to combine their work into a single group product. Interdependence is created through division of labour in carrying out a multifaceted study project that is divisible into various parts. The implementation stage is the single longest stage of the group's work, and is directed by the group's plan regarding the nature of the product it seeks. The teacher is always aware of the group's progress and needs.

*Preparation of a group report*

The groups in the class decide on the nature of their final report to be made to the class. One guiding principle should be to avoid lectures as much as possible. Pupils should be encouraged to use innovative and interactive forms of reporting, such as skits, demonstrations, experiments, learning centres where their classmates carry out various tasks, simulations, exhibitions, models, quiz shows, dramatizations, mock TV programmes, etc. It is often useful to form a steering committee where representatives of all the groups in the classroom present their groups' plans, get feedback from the teacher, enlist the teacher's assistance in providing resources, set a class schedule for presentations, follow each group's progress in the preparation of its report, etc.

*Group presentation to the class*

Each group presents its work to the class in an interesting fashion, as suggested in stage 4. Presentations should provide for maximum involvement of class members. Classmates can also contribute to the evaluation of each group's presentation.

*Evaluation*

Different approaches to evaluation can be employed simultaneously. It is recommended that the pupils be involved in carrying out evaluations, such as contributing to the preparation of questions for an examination (each group can be asked to prepare two or more questions that will appear on a test), filling out evaluation sheets at the end of a presentation, participating in scoring their classmates' answers to the questions contributed by their group, etc. The goal is to incorporate the evaluation into the learning process. This contrasts with the usual situation in which the evaluation constitutes an event separate from, and coming after the conclusion of, the learning process. Moreover, the exclusive purpose of the traditional approach to evaluation is to give the teacher information about what the pupils remember, and not to contribute to their ability to understand more about what they had learned.

Obviously, the four methods described here differ considerably from one another and, consequently, can exert different impacts on students. The variations in the structure and procedures of the methods have been discussed elsewhere, and will not be elaborated on here (Kagan, 1985; Sharan, 1980). Clearly, there is a wide range of methods for implementing mutual assistance among pupils in school during the pursuit of academic goals. Indeed, helping one's peers on a fairly equal-status basis (not just as a tutor or tutee) becomes one of the primary vehicles for conducting the process of learning.

## REVIEW OF RESEARCH

Several reviews of research on the effects of cooperative learning on cross-ethnic relations have been published (Johnson, Johnson and Maruyama, 1983, 1984; Sharan, 1980; Slavin, 1983). We will focus on some of the critical studies, as well as on research that appeared subsequent to those reviews.

### Cooperative learning and academic achievement in the multi-ethnic classroom

The study of academic achievement in classrooms conducted with the Jigsaw method (Lucker *et al.*, 1976) was one of the first experiments reported to use cooperative learning in multi-ethnic classrooms. The black children in six fifth and sixth grade classrooms benefited academically from this experience in comparison with their racial peers who studied in five traditionally-taught classes. However, the white students in the cooperative classes did not perform any better than did their peers in the control classes. This study raised the problem, not completely resolved to this day, of whether cooperative learning benefits all pupils, or has a differential effect on pupils from different ethnic/racial backgrounds. Does it generally contribute more to the achievement of lower-class, minority group children than to the white majority group (in the United States)? We will return to examine these questions and others in the course of this review.

Slavin (1978) reported two studies with his STAD method, two of which dealt with academic achievement in biracial classes. Forty percent (25) of the students in this study were white and 60% (37) were black. One black female teacher taught the two seventh grade English classes in this study, and each team within the class had the same racial composition. Slavin found that, academically, the black students learned much more in the small-group setting than their peers in the control class. The white students learned only marginally more in the cooperative learning class, similar to the results reported by Lucker *et al.* (1976).

In a more extensive experiment involving 424 seventh and eighth grade students in 12 English classrooms, 38.7% were black, 0.9% were oriental and the rest were white. Classes were randomly assigned to treatments (experimental or control) and each teacher taught one cooperative and one matched traditional classroom (control). In this study no race by treatment effects were found, nor were there any main effects for academic achievement (Slavin, 1978). We will return to this study later when we discuss the effects of cooperative learning on cross-ethnic/race social relations. In a follow-up study of the effects of the STAD method, Slavin (1979) found that there were still more cross-ethnic friendships in the cooperative than in the control classes.

Two extensive field experiments were conducted by this author and colleagues on the effects of the Group Investigation method on pupils in mixed-ethnic junior high-school classes in Israel (Sharan *et al.*, 1984; Sharan and Shachar, 1988). Both studies assessed these effects on a range of cognitive and social variables.

The first study encompassed 31 teachers of Literature and English as a second language in seventh grade classes from three junior high schools, all located in the same general neighbourhood near Tel-Aviv serving the same lower middle class population. Over 800 pupils participated in this study, 42% of whom were from Jewish families who had come to Israel from Western countries, including Europe, North and South America and South Africa, while 58% of the children were from Jewish families who came to Israel from the Muslim countries of the Middle East. Teachers of English and Literature were randomly assigned to one of three treatment groups: the Group Investigation method, STAD and frontal whole-class teaching. All teachers participated in a series of 10 workshops where they acquired instructional skills relevant to the method they were being called upon to implement in their classrooms during the experiment. The purpose of conducting workshops in frontal teaching was to ensure that teachers' skills in this group were 'fine tuned' and to give them equal attention and a sense of the importance of their classes' contribution to this experiment. All the teachers met to decide upon the curricular materials in their subject that would be taught during the course of the experiment. The teachers also were active participants in constructing the achievement tests to be administered to their students.

Results from this study in terms of cross-ethnic relationships will be discussed later in this chapter. Here we will limit ourselves to findings about the academic achievement of pupils from the two ethnic groups. Pupils in both cooperative learning methods (Group Investigation and STAD) achieved higher scores in English than did their peers in the frontal classes. This was true despite the fact that the teachers who used direct whole-class teaching were far more experienced in this method than were the cooperative learning teachers in their methods, which they had acquired for the purpose of this experiment. The achievement tests in English evaluated primarily the students' understanding of spoken language (they were asked to indicate the correct answer on their paper in response to questions which were tape-recorded in advance to ensure uniform administration to all students), as well as their knowledge of various principles of grammar. There were no findings of interactions between ethnicity and achievement, or between the students' initial level of achievement and progress during the course of the experiment (four months): pupils from both ethnic groups and from three levels of initial achievement exhibited the same degree of progress in learning English. These results do not corroborate earlier reports to the effect that cooperative learning was more suited for lower-class and minority pupils than for pupils from the middle-class and majority group.

Findings on achievement in Literature were quite different. The Literature test was comprised of questions at high and low levels of learning, according to Bloom's taxonomy (Bloom, 1956). Students in the STAD and whole-class method did better on low-level questions than did those in the Group Investigation classes, while the latter excelled on the questions that assessed high-level learning more so than the students in both the STAD and traditionally-taught classes. Again, the results did not reveal interaction effects for ethnicity with any instructional method (Sharan *et al.* 1984).

A second experiment in multi-ethnic classes was conducted with all nine of the eighth-grade classes in History and Geography in a junior high school (Sharan and Shachar, 1988). Sixty-seven percent ($N = 236$) of the students in these classes came from middle-class Western families. Many of the fathers in these families were college graduates, or even pursued academic careers. Approximately 33% ($N = 115$) of the pupils were from lower-class, Middle-Eastern families where most of the parents had completed less than eight grades of schooling. The primary purpose of this experiment was to assess the effects of Group Investigation (in five classes, $N = 197$) and of traditional whole-class instruction (in four classes, $N = 154$) on the children's spoken language (in Hebrew). We also sought to determine if cooperative learning affected lower-class, minority-group children's language usage when conversing with their peers from both Western and Middle-Eastern background. Academic achievement and the pupils' social interaction were evaluated as well. Again, discussion of cross-ethnic interaction will be postponed to a later section of this chapter. We will concentrate here on the children's academic achievement and language usage as a function of instructional method.

Findings from the achievement data, gathered before and after the study of a given curricular unit in History and a unit in Geography, reveal that pupils in the classes taught with the Group Investigation method received much higher scores on both achievement tests than their peers in the whole-class method. Indeed, the difference in achievement scores of the students from classes taught with either of the two methods approached 1.5 standard deviations. This was true for pupils from both ethnic groups. Of considerable importance is the finding that the mean scores of the Middle-Eastern children in the G–I classes exceeded those of the Western children in the whole-class form of instruction, quite apart from the difference in progress from the pre- to post-test scores. Nevertheless, the achievement gap between the two ethnic groups within each method was not closed. These findings appeared in both the low-level and high-level questions on the achievement test. The histograms in Figure 8.1 illustrate the change in achievement scores that occurred in the classes taught with the different methods for pupils from the two ethnic groups.

It should be emphasized again that the teachers in the cooperative learning classes acquired their skills in group-centred instruction by participating in a series of workshops conducted in advance of the experiment, and they had no

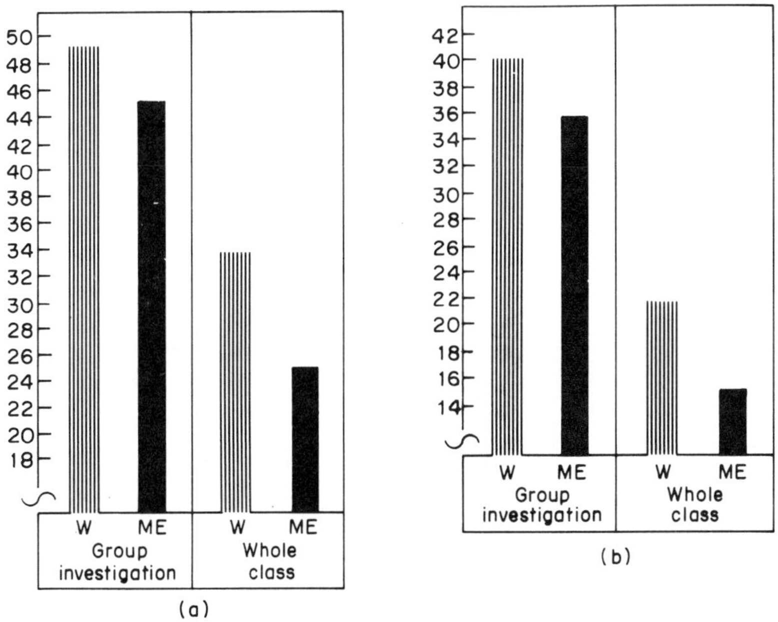


FIGURE 8.1. (a) Mean difference scores on achievement test in History of Western and Middle-Eastern pupils from the Group Investigation and Whole-Class methods. (b) Mean difference scores on achievement test in Geography of Western and Middle-Eastern pupils from the Group Investigation and Whole-Class methods

previous exposure to this approach to instruction. On the other hand, teachers of the whole-class method had 10 years of experience teaching in this fashion. Results from the same study about the pupils' spoken language are of particular interest. Pupils were chosen at random, three from each of the two ethnic groups, and asked to conduct a 15-minute discussion on a topic taken from their current study of history, and 15 minutes (on another day) on a topic from geography. Twenty-seven such groups were videotaped, three groups from each of the nine classes. The videotapes were scored by judges who were completely 'blind' as to the class from which the students came as well as to the purpose of the study.

There was a main effect for number of words per turn of speech spoken by pupils who had studied in the classes taught with the Group Investigation method. Also, the lower-class children who had studied in the cooperative learning classes used as many words per turn of speech during the 30-minute discussion as did the Western, middle-class pupils who had studied in the classes taught with the whole-class method. Pupils from Middle-Eastern background who came from the G–I classes took more turns to speak than their ethnic peers from the classes taught with the whole-class method. On the measure of the frequency of 'turns of speech' taken during the discussion, the Western and Middle-Eastern pupils who had studied in the cooperative learning classes were almost equal. The students who had studied with the whole-class method displayed a different pattern altogether: their data (Figure 8.2) revealed a vast

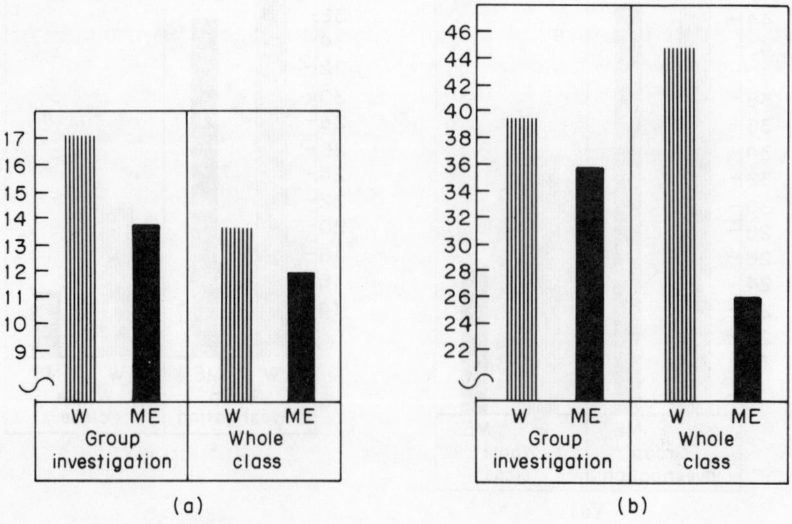


FIGURE 8.2. (a) Mean number of words per turn spoken by Western and Middle-Eastern Pupils from Group Investigation and Whole-Class methods during the group discussion. (b) Mean number of turns taken by Western and Middle-Eastern Pupils from Group Investigation and Whole-Class methods during the group discussion

difference in the number of turns taken by pupils from Western and Middle-Eastern backgrounds, with the Western students dominating the discussions almost to the point where the Middle-Easterners 'couldn't get a word in edgewise'. It should be remembered that these discussions were held outside the classroom and not in the presence of the teacher.

Clearly, the cooperative learning classes created a more symmetrical set of interchanges among these students from the two ethnic groups so that they all shared 'air time'. By contrast, whole-class instruction places the lower-class children at a distinct disadvantage and the middle-class students monopolize the situation, virtually to the exclusion of their lower-class peers. While it is unlikely that the lower-class children from the cooperative classrooms in this study suddenly increased their vocabulary, it is evident that they were more prepared to express themselves and less inhibited in their speech after experiencing cooperative learning than when they had been exposed to the competitive whole-class teaching. It is likely that the format of teacher presentation followed by pupil recitation 'on stage' while the entire class looks on, and only when called upon by the teacher, is not conducive to many pupils expressing themselves freely.

When pupils are able to converse with one another in their learning groups, and help each other, their speech patterns take on a different character from those which are ordinarily observed in the traditional classroom where the teacher is the central figure. Whole-class instruction is not very hospitable to lower-class children whose entire intellectual performance, including their speech, is markedly stifled in this environment. Nor does this kind of environment offer middle-class children optimal learning conditions.

The results of the study under discussion point to the extent to which all of the students, and the lower-class students in particular, can benefit substantially from a change in classroom teaching style. That change calls for the use of teaching methods that employ structured peer collaboration and interaction in small groups, within the regular classroom, as the main strategy for the pursuit of learning.

## Cooperative learning and cross-ethnic relations

In an early study, the effects of cooperative learning on race relations were evaluated in classes taught with the Jigsaw method (Blaney *et al.*, 1977). A total of 304 white and black students participated in this experiment, in which the Jigsaw method was implemented three times a week for six weeks. The fifth and sixth grade students were asked to evaluate their racial peers, the extent to which they felt liked by their classmates, liking for school, self-esteem, and their interest in cooperative or competitive activities with classmates. Fifty-three multi-ethnic groups (of five or six pupils per group) were composed of members from different racial groups, academic achievement levels, and gender.

A significant increase was found from the pre- to the post-test measures on 'liking for one's own group' without any decrease in liking for other members of the class. In light of this finding the authors concluded that the Jigsaw method has potential for 'mitigating school desegregation problems'. White pupils in the cooperative learning classes registered greater liking for school than their peers taught with the whole-class method. Black pupils who studied in all classes indicated a decline in their liking for school, although the decline was less marked in the classes with cooperative learning than in those taught with the whole-class method. All pupils in the Jigsaw classes also responded more cooperatively when asked if they preferred to help or to outdo their classmates on school work, and whether they felt they could learn something from other pupils in the class.

It must be noted that due to the absence of direct measures of intergroup friendships in this study, the inference that the Jigsaw method contributed to improved cross-racial attitudes or perceptions seems unwarranted. However, a later study conducted in Canada (Ziegler, 1981) with a variation of the Jigsaw method (called Jigsaw II, described by Slavin, 1986) did find more cross-ethnic selections of friends in the cooperative classes in contrast with classes taught with the whole-class method. The latter study included children from families who had immigrated to Canada from Europe, the islands of the Caribbean, and white native-born Canadian children in the city of Toronto.

Hansell and Slavin (1981) carried out an experiment in 12 seventh and eighth grade classrooms with the STAD method. The experiment lasted ten weeks. The investigators wished to learn about the extent to which relatively close or superficial relationships were formed between students from different ethnic/racial groups in the cooperative as compared with the traditional classes. The first six nominations of the pupil's friends in the class, on an open-ended sociometric questionnaire, were considered by the investigators to indicate relatively close friends, as were reciprocal nominations. Students named seventh or later in the list were considered to be distant friends. The results showed that STAD led primarily to significant increases in reciprocated and in close friendships, only secondarily to distant friendships, and even less to unreciprocated nominations.

In an experiment conducted in sixth grade classrooms, 230 students (of whom 66% were white, 34% black) studied with the STAD method for 12 weeks. The investigators (Slavin and Oickle, 1981) found gains in white friendships toward the black children but no differences in black friendships toward the whites compared with the control (whole-class) classrooms.

An extensive experiment with STAD and with TGT (Teams, Games Tournaments is a method similar to STAD except that it includes a face-to-face tournament between representatives of the different groups in the class) was conducted by Kagan and colleagues in California (Kagan *et al.*, 1985). Thirty-five student teachers at the University of California at Riverside were assigned at random to elementary classes, grades 2 through 5, to teach according to one of three methods: TGT, STAD or Whole-Class. Over 900 pupils participated in this experiment which continued for several years, but the data reported here were gathered during the first year of the study. The ethnic composition of the classrooms included 66% whites, 20% children from Mexican background and 13% blacks.

One of the dependent variables assessed in this study was the pupils' 'cooperativeness' measured by their decisions to share resources with others or to keep them for themselves. In general, participation in the TGT or STAD classes resulted in students making many more cooperative decisions, i.e. greater willingness to share their property with others, than their peers who were in the classes taught with the Whole-Class method. In the fourth through sixth grade classrooms this finding was typical of students from all ethnic/racial groups. In grades 2 through 4, the finding of greater cooperativeness was true for the minority-group children, but the white children's decisions did not differ as a function of instructional method.

Another finding of interest emerged in the data of the fourth and fifth grade classes taught with the Whole-Class method. All of the students, including those from the two minority groups of blacks and Mexicans, were more willing to share their resources with white children than they were with members of their own groups. Thus, the white children clearly constituted the higher status group in the eyes of everyone in the class. This was not true in the classes conducted with STAD and TGT where the minority group children enjoyed much higher social status, i.e. they were selected more as friends (Kagan *et al.*, 1985). The phenomenon of pupils from the majority ethnic group occupying a high-status position (asymmetrical cross-ethnic relations) appears to be the typical state of affairs in desegregrated classrooms conducted with the traditional Whole-Class method. That condition can be altered, though not necessarily completely eliminated, through the use of cooperative learning methods (Amir *et al.*, 1978; Cohen, 1984; Miller and Brewer, 1986; Johnson, Johnson and Maruyama, 1984; Miller and Harrington, 1989; Sharan *et al.*, 1984; Sharan and Rich, 1984; Slavin, 1983).

The experiment reported by Weigel, Wiser and Cook (1975) encompassed 324 pupils in the seventh and eighth grades, of whom 231 were whites, 54 blacks and 39 children of Mexican background. The experiment lasted for seven months, during which the classes were taught in a manner that closely resembles, in most of its procedures, the Group Investigation method of cooperative learning. The one exception was that there was some competition between the groups in the classroom. Otherwise, the pupils collected information on their group topic, conducted small-group discussions on the material they gathered, and prepared group reports that presented a summary of their work.

Results from this experiment show that cooperative learning positively affected the white and Mexican students' cross-ethnic and cross-racial friendship choices, but it did not affect the selections made by the black students. Nor did the

Mexican students change their selections of their black classmates. White students were mentioned in 20% of the selections made by black students when the whites constituted 60% of the classroom populations.

The number of interpersonal conflicts among students was registered by observers. It was found that 90% of the interpersonal conflicts that occurred among pupils who studied in the classes taught with the Whole-Class method were between children from different ethnic groups, while only 45% of the conflicts among pupils in the cooperative learning classes occurred between children from different ethnic groups. Finally, 56% of the total amount of helping behaviour among pupils in the cooperative classes occurred between pupils from different ethnic groups, while only 36% of the helping behaviour observed among pupils in the traditional classes was cross-ethnic. Cooperative learning brought about positive changes in the relationships between children from the various ethnic groups.

A meta-analysis was performed of the research findings about the effects of cooperative learning on ethnic relations in the heterogeneous classroom (Johnson, Johnson and Maruyama, 1983, 1984). The authors identified 31 studies on inter-ethnic attraction among pupils who had participated in cooperative learning experiments. The results of this analysis strongly support the claim that cooperative learning exerts positive effects on interethnic/racial relationships in the classroom. Moreover, an experiment conducted by some of the same investigators (Johnson *et al.*, 1983) found that fourth grade students ($N=48$) from cooperative learning classes even maintained more cross-ethnic/racial relationships during learning activities (supported each other's learning activities) as well as during free time in the classroom than their peers from classes with Whole-Class instruction. However, it must be pointed out that the teacher was present in the situations in which these relationships were observed, even though they were observed during free time in the class, and not during a lesson. Similar results were also reported in another study as well with fourth grade students ($N=51$) (Johnson and Johnson, 1981).

Little evidence has been published to date documenting the nature of inter-ethnic or cross-racial relationships outside school as a function of the kind of instruction the pupils experience inside school. Nor has it been demonstrated as yet that cross-ethnic relations developed among specific pupils in the classroom carry over to relationships with pupils who were not in the classroom together. Thus far there is not much evidence to support the expectation that social experiences related to classroom life can effect changes in broad social phenomena, such as race/ethnic relations, even though such changes might occur in the lives of some children as individuals as a result of their schooling. One study (Warring *et al.*, 1985) with fourth grade children ($N=51$), conducted approximately one hour a day for 11 days, found that the students in cooperative groups without intergroup competition elected (on a pencil-and-paper measure) to have more cross-ethnic peers as companions for out-of-school activities than students who participated in cooperative groups with intergroup competition.

The studies mentioned above in the section on academic achievement, that were conducted by this author and colleagues in Israel, also evaluated the effects of the Group Investigation method on the social relationships of children from different ethnic groups. Both experiments (Sharan *et al.*, 1984; Sharan and Shachar, 1988) employed observations of behaviour during the performance of a group task as a central measure of the social interaction among group members in general, and among members from different ethnic groups in particular. These measures were taken after the pupils had studied for several months in cooperative learning classes or in those taught with the Whole-Class approach.

In one experiment (Sharan *et al.*, 1984), pupils were selected at random to form six-person groups (three of Western, three of Middle-Eastern ethnic background). Several groups were selected from each of the 30 classrooms that participated in this experiment, 10 classrooms in each of the three instructional methods of Group Investigation, STAD and Whole-Class teaching. All in all there were 63 groups (numbering more than 390 pupils) who were observed working on the construction of a model of a person from pieces of Lego. Two observers sat next to each group recording the behaviour of each member once every five minutes over a period of 30 minutes. The observers had no information about the classroom from which the students came, about the plan of the experiment or about the nature of the teaching methods employed in the experiment.

Analysis of the data revealed that pupils in the Group Investigation classes demonstrated many more cross-ethnic cooperative acts and far fewer competitive cross-ethnic acts during their work than did their peers from the classes taught with the other two methods. Pupils from the Whole-Class method displayed the largest number of competitive acts of all groups in this study. In fact, the number of competitive acts performed by the pupils from the Whole-Class method was identical to the number of cooperative acts in their behaviour. On the other hand, pupils from the cooperative learning classes displayed twice as many cooperative acts during the performance of this task than competitive ones. Indeed, there was no objective cause to behave competitively in these groups. The investigators encouraged the students in each group, before and during their work, to cooperate with one another. There can be little doubt that the traditional whole-class format of instruction stimulates considerable competition among classmates and cultivates behavioural patterns that do not support cooperation with, or offering help to, others.

Of particular interest here is how student helping behaviour is related to ethnic relations in the class. The initiative for offering help to other group members from a different ethnic group was equally distributed among students from both the Western and Middle-Eastern groups for those students who had studied in the Group Investigation classes. Moreover, the number of initiatives of offering help within one's own ethnic group or to members of the other group was completely symmetrical among students from the Group Investigation method, and neither of the ethnic groups appeared to enjoy any degree of superior status in this respect. Among students from the other two instructional methods the picture was quite different. In the groups from both STAD and Whole-Class teaching the Western students received twice the number of helping acts directed to them than did the students of Middle-Eastern background: Western background students addressed twice as many cooperative statements to other Westerners than they did to Middle-Eastern students, while Middle-Eastern students addressed cooperative statements to their own ethnic peers only 60% as often as to Western students in their groups. Thus, both STAD and Whole-Class instruction, in terms of the measures employed here, left the asymmetrical ethnic relationships typically found in the multi-ethnic classroom virtually untouched, while the Group Investigation method had a distinct and positive impact on these relationships.

The second experiment (Sharan and Shachar, 1988) conducted in all the eighth grade classes (9) in a junior high school also asked ethnically mixed groups of six students to perform a group task and recorded their behaviour as the basis for assessing social relations in the group. In this case three groups were formed at random from the students in each of the nine classes and asked to conduct two 15-minute discussions (as described above in the section on academic achievement). All of the discussions were videotaped and the students' behaviour was categorized by judges on the basis of a predetermined set of criteria. In this fashion it was possible to use 100% of the students' behaviour during the group tasks as the basis for generating the data, rather than making 'live' recordings once every few minutes, as is generally done by on-the-spot observers.

Findings from analyses of these data were as follows: the Western students received more cooperative statements than did the Middle-Eastern students regardless of which teaching method they had experienced. Nevertheless, there were large and significant differences in the cooperative behaviour of the students who had been exposed to the different teaching methods, Group Investigation or Whole-Class. Students from Middle-Eastern and Western background who were in the Group Investigation classes addressed the same number of cooperative statements to members of the other group (i.e. Western to Middle-Eastern equalled Middle Eastern to Western). Also, the number of such statements addressed by the Western children to other members of their own group did not differ substantially from the number of statements that Middle-Eastern children addressed to the Western children in their groups. To this extent there was a high degree of symmetry created in the groups from the Group Investigation classes.

On the other hand, there was a large gap between the number of statements addressed by Middle-Eastern to Western students compared with the number of statements they addressed to members of their own group. That means that, among students from the Group Investigation classes, the Middle-Eastern students occupied equal status with the Western students in the eyes of the Western students but not in their own eyes! They still treated themselves as having lower status than the Western students, even after being in the cooperative classrooms. By contrast, the picture that emerged from the data gathered from the students in the Whole-Class method is very different, and quite negative. The Western students addressed their own ethnic peers twice as often as they offered help to Middle-Eastern students. For their part, the Middle-Eastern students offered help to Western students more than three times as often as they did their own ethnic peers. Consequently, the lower-class, Middle-Eastern pupils remain at a distinct disadvantage in the classroom taught with the whole-class method both in terms of the way they are treated by members of the other ethnic group, and in terms of the way they relate to members of their own group. This situation is made particularly clear by the histograms in Figure 8.3.

## Constructive controversy

A promising development in the cooperative learning literature has focused on the effects of controversy among pupils within cooperative learning groups

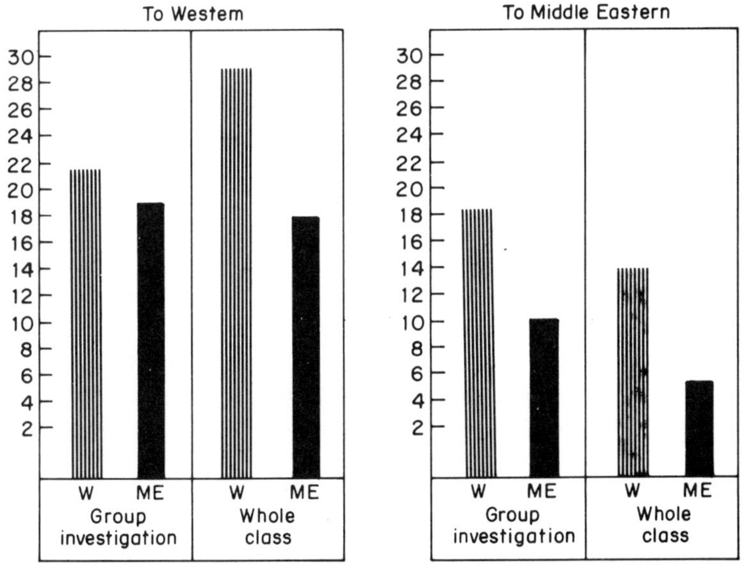


FIGURE 8.3. Mean number of cooperative statements addressed to Western and to Middle-Eastern pupils from Group Investigation and Whole-Class methods by Western and Middle-Eastern pupils in the discussion groups

in the classroom. It is unreasonable to assume that pupils working together in small groups will always agree and collaborate smoothly and efficiently without conflict. Moreover, differences of opinion and perspective have been cited by many students of cognitive functioning to provide an impetus for more critical and higher-level consideration of problems. Cooperative learning was conceived by several investigators as providing an opportunity for students to examine ideas from different points of view (Nijhof and Kommers, 1985; Sharan and Hertz-Lazarowitz, 1980).

David and Roger Johnson have experimented with what they call constructive conflict within the context of cooperative learning (Johnson and Johnson, 1979; 1986). One of these experiments was conducted in desegregated classrooms (Johnson, Johnson and Tiffany, 1984). Seventy-two sixth grade students were assigned, on a stratified random basis controlling for gender, reading level and ethnicity, to one of three conditions: controversy, debate and individualistic learning. Each learning group in the controversy condition was divided into two pairs, each pair given a position either in favour or against a topic in wild-life conservation. In the debate condition, each member of a learning group was given a pro- or con- position to represent in a debate with the other three members of the group. In the individualistic condition each student was given both the pro- and con- material and asked to study it. The students participated in sessions lasting 55 minutes per day for 11 days, and the students in each of the three conditions worked in a separate classroom.

Several dependent variables were assessed as a function of experimental condition. The investigators wished to ascertain whether structured controversy over academic subject matter aggravates or alleviates cross-ethnic hostility and rejection; how students from different ethnic groups evaluate the experience of controversy; and to what extent students will incorporate others' ideas into their own arguments after experiencing the controversy or the debate condition.

Results indicated that controversy promoted (i) the most cross-ethnic exchanges about the assigned subject matter, (ii) the most active search for information about the topic, (iii) the greatest amount of re-evaluation of one's position in order to incorporate the opponent's arguments, (iv) the most liking for the subject matter, (v) the highest self-esteem and (vi) the most accepting and supportive relationships among minority and majority group students. The debate condition promoted higher levels of functioning on these dependent variables, and the individualistic condition the lowest levels. The investigators concluded that structured academic conflicts with strong cooperative elements may facilitiate effective desegregation. The limited scope and duration of this experiment, as well as the laboratory-like conditions under which it was carried out, indicate that it is necessary to replicate this study under conditions more similar to classroom learning before the results can be accepted as applying to the cooperative classroom.

**Pupils' status in the multi-ethnic, cooperative classroom**

The structure of conventional classroom life perpetuates the social status ordering of the society at large, thus impeding the academic and social integration of lower-class and minority group children in school. For the past two decades, Elizabeth Cohen and her students have been experimenting with various methods for intervening in the multi-ethnic classroom in order to create conditions for equal status interaction between members of the different ethnic groups (Cohen, 1980, 1984). During the past few years, Cohen and associates have developed a method that uses cooperative learning groups in elementary school classrooms that is called 'Finding Out', a bilingual (English and Spanish) approach to the development of thinking skills. A series of activities are carried out by four or five children who work together on science and mathematics concepts in different learning centres located in the classroom. Teachers cultivated a set of cooperative norms among these 2nd to 4th grade students by using a series of training games. The norms included asking questions of classmates, listening to others, helping others without actually performing their task for them, explaining to others, showing other people how things work, and giving others what they need. Pupils were also assigned specific roles in their groups, such as facilitator, checker, reporter, clean-up supervisor and safety officer. The roles were rotated.

A study of the effects of these procedures on children compared their interactions with those demonstrated by children in the same grades some years earlier who experienced learning in the same learning centres but without the use of the group management techniques and helping norms (Cohen, Lotan and Catanzarite, 1990). All children interacted more with one another, and the effect of status on interaction patterns was decidedly weakened, though not eliminated. High-status children were still more likely to offer assistance to others, and perceived themselves as more competent, than low-status children. The low-status children also made sizeable gains in learning. More children chose lower-status classmates as best friends and as being good at mathematics and science, and a smaller percentage of pupils chose high-status classmates on these questions in the Spring than had done so in the Fall of the previous year. Other findings reported in this study support the claim that the treatment had a variety of positive effects on the status structure of the class, distinctly reducing the status advantage of some children over others though, again, this advantage was not totally eliminated. All in all, the study demonstrates the effectiveness of various norms of helping behaviour in small groups for counteracting the adverse effects of social status for children's social and academic adjustment in the multi-ethnic classroom.

In a unique meta-analysis of 21 cooperative learning experiments in mixed-ethnic classrooms, Miller and Davidson-Podgorny (1987) examined some of the consequences for cross-ethnic relations of different approaches to the implementation of cooperative learning. In addition, the authors distinguished different theoretical approaches to understanding intergroup relations in order to relate these theories to research on the effects of cooperative learning. These various theories and their application to cooperative learning research cannot be reviewed here, and the reader is referred to the excellent chapter by Miller and Davidson-Podgorny. Their meta-analysis showed once again that there can be little doubt that cooperative learning improves intergroup relations in mixed-ethnic classrooms. Nevertheless, the critical components of cooperative learning that foster improved inter-group relations remain to be identified, and the various methods of cooperative learning differ considerably in terms of their practical procedures.

The meta-analysis focused on six moderator variables or features of the various cooperative learning models. These moderator variables, and their consequences for improving intergroup relations, are as follows:

(1) *Task structure*. Tasks that specifically require all group members to contribute to the final group product, i.e. tasks that involve interdependence, are associated with more benefit than those that do not require interdependence.
(2) *Reward structure*. Interdependent rewards are allocated to teams, individualistic rewards are given to individual group members, such as individual test scores. (No effect of reward structure on intergroup relations was found.)
(3) *Task role assignment*. Students are, or are not, formally and randomly assigned to specific task roles in the group. The studies that include random assignment to roles are associated with greater benefit than those with no role assignment, and hence, choice of sub-topic or role by students can have implications for their status in the group.
(4) *Task content*. Experiments that use academic materials from language, arts and social studies are contrasted with those using maths and science curricula. Greater benefit for group relations derive from studies that use the latter subjects rather than the former.
(5) *Publicized performance*. Participants' academic performance is made known to the class by means of a newsletter or bulletin board, or else such notice is not present in the study. No differences were found on this variable for promoting ethnic relations.
(6) *Ethnic representation on teams*: Greater benefit is associated with groups where the different ethnic groups present in the class are represented equally than with groups with unequal ethnic representation.

## CONCLUSION

From the research cited in this review, it appears justifiable to conclude that cooperative learning positively affects children's academic learning and ethnic relations in terms of their behaviour in school, and that traditional whole-class instruction is certainly not the teaching method to be preferred in desegregated classrooms. The patterns of cross-ethnic cooperation acquired during classroom learning carry over to the children's relationships with their classmates when they work together on a collective task outside the classroom, but still in the school. This change in interpersonal relationships in the school is of considerable importance for the process of schooling itself. It creates conditions which make it possible for lower-class and minority group children to play an active role in classroom learning, and where they have more opportunity for receiving help and support from their peers. Positive relationships of this kind are supported by the social norms cultivated by the cooperative learning methods. Desegregation might prove to be a barren administrative act if these goals could not be accomplished. On the other hand, expecting schools to change the nature of the social processes that characterize entire societies seems to be asking far too much. It is as if we hang our hopes of social salvation on one institution called the school and demand that the school save us from ourselves (Sarason, 1983).

We must focus on achieving what is within the realm of possibility at this time and not allow the process of schooling to continue into the future in the same manner as it has been implemented in the past. If we are concerned with the nature of our children's schooling, then we must concern ourselves with the nature of instruction in school and how teachers perform their professional task. Concern for children in school by necessity means concern with teaching. Again, the essence of this position has been incisively formulated by Seymour Sarason:

> The assumption that teachers can create and maintain those conditions which make school learning and school living stimulating for children without those same conditions existing for teachers, has no warrant in the history of man (Sarason, 1976, pp. 123–124).

To ignore the teacher is to ignore the children. To improve schooling means to change instruction to more socially productive and intellectually stimulating forms of teaching than that which is currently practised in the majority of schools.

What begins as a review of research on children helping children in school must end, it appears to me, with some awareness of the enormity of the challenge that confronts us when we approach the subject of changing teachers' instructional practices (Sharan and Hertz-Lazarowitz, 1982; Sharan and Sharan, 1987). Therein lies the key as to how we can teach a large number of children to grow up helping each other through life.

## REFERENCES

Allport, G. (1954). *The Nature of Prejudice*. Cambridge, Mass.: Addison-Wesley.
Amir, Y., Sharan, S., Bizman, A., Ribner, M., and Ben-Ari, R. (1978). Attitude

change in desegregated Israel high schools, *Journal of Educational Psychology*, **70**, 63–70.

Aronson, E., Stephen, C., Sikes, J., Blaney, N., and Snapp, M. (1978). *The Jigsaw Classroom*. Beverly Hills, Calif: Sage Publications.

Blaney, N., Stephan, S., Rosenfield, D., Aronson, E., and Sikes, J. (1977). Interdependence in the classroom; a field study, *Journal of Educational Psychology*, **69**, 121–128.

Bloom, B. (ed.) (1956). *Taxonomy of Educational Objectives: The Cognitive Domain*. New York: Longmans, Green and Co.

Brewer, M., and Miller, N. (1984). Beyond the contact hypothesis: Theoretical perspectives on desegregation. In N. Miller and M. Brewer (eds), *Groups in Contact: The Psychology of Desegregation*. Orlando, Florida: Academic Press, 281–302.

Cohen, E. (1980). Design and redesign of the desegregated school: Problems of status, power and conflict. In W. Stephan and J. Feagin (eds), *School Desegregation: Past, Present and Future*. New York: Plenum Publishing Corporation, 251–280.

Cohen, E. (1984). The desegregated school: problems in status, power and interethnic climate. In N. Miller and M. Brewer (eds), *Groups in Contact: The Psychology of Desegregation*. Orlando, Florida: Academic Press, 77–96.

Cohen, E., Lotan, R., and Catanzarite, L. (1990). Treating Status problems in the cooperative classroom. In S. Sharan (ed.), *Cooperative Learning: Theory and Research*. New York: Praeger Publishing Co., 203–229.

Dewey, J. (1916). *Democracy and Education*. New York: Macmillan.

Dewey, J. (1938). *Experience and Education*. New York: Macmillan.

Hansell, S., and Slavin, R. (1981). Cooperative learning and the structure of interracial friendships, *Sociology of Education*, **54**, 98–106.

Hertz-Lazarowitz, R. (1983). Pro-social behavior in the classroom, *Academic Psychology Bulletin*, **5**, 319–338.

Hertz-Lazarowitz, R., Baird, H., Webb, C., and Lazarowitz, R. (1984). Student–student interactions in science classrooms: a naturalistic study, *Science Education*, **68**, 603–619.

Hertz-Lazarowitz, R., Fuchs, I., Sharabany, R., and Eisenberg, N. (1989). Students' interactive and non-interactive behaviours in the classroom: a comparison between two types of classrooms in the city of the Kibbutz in Israel, *Contemporary Educational Psychology*, **14**, 22–32.

Hertz-Lazarowitz, R., and Sharan, S. (1984). Enhancing prosocial behavior through cooperative learning in the classroom. In E. Staub, D. Bar-Tal, J. Karylowski and J. Reykowski (eds), *Development and Maintenance of Pro-social Behavior*. New York: Plenum Publishing Corporation, 423–443.

Johnson, D., and Johnson, R. (1979). Conflict in the classroom, *Review of Educational Research*, **49**, 51–61.

Johnson, D., and Johnson, R. (1981). Effects of cooperative and individualistic learning experiences on interethnic interaction, *Journal of Educational Psychology*, **73**, 444–449.

Johnson, D., and Johnson, R. (1986). Academic conflict among students: controversy and learning. In R. Feldman (ed.), *The Social Psychology of Education*. Cambridge: Cambridge University Press, 199–231.

Johnson, D., and Johnson, R. (1987). *Learning Together and Alone*. Englewood Cliffs, New Jersey: Prentice-Hall. (2nd edition).

Johnson, D., and Johnson, R. (1990). Cooperative learning and achievement. In S. Sharan (ed.), *Cooperative Learning: Theory and Research*. New York: Praeger Publishing Co., 23–37.

Johnson, D., Johnson, R., and Holubec, E. (1986). *Circles of Learning: Cooperation in the Classroom*. Edina, Minnesota: Interaction Book Company.

Johnson, D., Johnson, R., and Maruyama, G. (1983). Interdependence and interpersonal attraction among heterogeneous and homogeneous individuals: A theoretical formulation and meta-analysis of the research, *Review of Educational Research*, **68**, 446–452.

Johnson, D., Johnson, R., and Maruyama, G. (1984). Goal interdependence and interpersonal attraction in heterogeneous classrooms: a meta-analysis. In N. Miller and M. Brewer (eds), *Groups in Contact: The Psychology of Desegregation*. Orlando, Florida: Academic Press 187–212.

Johnson, D., Johnson, R., and Tiffany, M. (1984). Structuring academic conflicts between majority and minority students: hindrance or help to integration, *Contemporary Educational Psychology*, **9**, 61–73.

Johnson, D., Johnson, R., Tiffany, M., and Zaidman, B. (1983). Are low achievers disliked in a cooperative situation? A test of rival theories in a mixed-ethnic situation, *Contemporary Educational Psychology*, **8**, 189–200.

Kagan, S. (1985). Dimensions of cooperative classroom structures. In R. Slavin, S. Sharan, S. Kagan, R. Hertz-Lazarowitz, C. Webb, and R. Schmuck (eds), *Learning to Cooperate, Cooperating to Learn*. New York: Plenum Publishing Co., 67–96.

Kagan, S., Zahn, G., Widaman, K., Schwarzwald, J., and Tyrrell, G. (1985). Classroom structural bias: impact of cooperative and competitive classroom structures on cooperative and competitive individuals and groups. In R. Slavin, S. Sharan, S. Kagan, R. Hertz-Lazarowitz, C. Webb, and R. Schmuck (eds), *Learning to Cooperate, Cooperating to Learn*. New York: Plenum Publishing Co., 277–312.

Lucker, G., Rosenfield, D., Sikes, J., and Aronson, E. (1976). Performance in the interdependent classroom: a field study, *American Educational Research Journal*, **13**, 115–123.

Miel, A. (1952). *Cooperative Procedures in Learning*. New York: Teachers College, Columbia University.

Miller, N., and Brewer, M. (1986). Social categorization theory and team learning procedures. In R. Feldman (ed.), *The Social Psychology of Education*. Cambridge: Cambridge University Press, 172–198.

Miller, N., and Davidson-Podgorny, G. (1987). Theoretical models of intergroup relations and the use of cooperative teams as an intervention for desegregated settings. In C. Hendrick (ed.), *Group Processes and Intergroup Relations*. Newbury Park, Ca.: Sage Publications, 41–67.

Miller, N., and Harrington, H. (1990). A situational identity perspective on cultural diversity and teamwork in the classroom. In S. Sharan (ed.), *Cooperative Learning: Theory and Research*, New York: Praeger Publishing Co., 39–75.

Nijhof, W., and Kommers, P. (1985). An analysis of cooperation in relation to cognitive controversy. In R. Slavin, S. Sharan, S. Kagan, R. Hertz-Lazarowitz, C. Webb, and R. Schmuck (eds), *Learning to Cooperate, Cooperating to Learn*. New York: Plenum Publishing Corporation, 125–145.

Sarason, S. (1976). *The Creation of Settings and the Future Societies*. San Francisco: Jossey-Bass.

Sarason, S. (1983). *Schooling in America: Scapegoat and Salvation*. New York: The Free Press.

Sharan, S. (1980). Cooperative learning in small groups: recent methods and effects on achievement, attitudes and ethnic relations, *Review of Educational Research*, **50**, 241–271.

Sharan, S., Hare, P., Hertz-Lazarowitz, R., and Webb, C. (eds) (1980). *Cooperation in Education*. Provo, Utah: Brigham Young University Press.

Sharan, S., and Hertz-Lazarowitz, R. (1980). A Group-Investigation method of cooperative learning in the classroom. In S. Sharan, P. Hare, C. Webb, and R. Hertz-Lazarowitz (eds), *Cooperation in Education*. Provo, Utah: Brigham Young University Press, 14–46.

Sharan, S., and Hertz-Lazarowitz, R. (1982). Effects of an instructional change program on teachers' behaviour, attitudes and perceptions, *The Journal of Applied Behavioral Science*, **18**, 185–201.

Sharan, S., Kussell, P., Hertz-Lazarowitz, R., Bejarano, Y., Raviv, S., and Sharan, Y. (1984). *Cooperative Learning in the Classroom: Research in Desegregated Schools*. Hillsdale, New Jersey: Lawrence Erlbaum and Associates.

Sharan, S., and Rich, Y. (1984). Field experiments on ethnic integration in Israeli schools. In Y. Amir and S. Sharan (eds), *School Desegregation*. Hillsdale, New Jersey: Lawrence Erlbaum and Associates, 189–217.

Sharan, S., and Shachar, H. (1988). *Language and Learning in the Cooperative Classroom*. New York: Springer Publishing Co.

Sharan, S., and Sharan, Y. (1976). *Small Group Teaching*. Englewood Cliffs, New Jersey: Educational Technology Publications.

Sharan, Y., and Sharan, S. (1987). Training teachers for cooperative learning, *Educational Leadership*, **45**, 20–25.

Slavin, R. (1978). Student teams and achievement divisions, *Journal of Research and Development in Education*, **12**, 39–49.

Slavin, R. (1979). Effects of bi-racial learning teams on cross-racial friendships, *Journal of Educational Psychology*, **71**, 381–387.

Slavin, R. (1983). *Cooperative Learning*. New York: Longman.

Slavin, R. (1986). *Using Student Team Learning*. Baltimore, MD.: Center for Research on Elementary and Middle Schools, The Johns Hopkins University.

Slavin, R., and Oickle, E. (1981). Effects of cooperative learning teams on students' achievement and race relations: treatment by race interactions, *Sociology of Education*, **54**, 174–180.

Slavin, R., Sharan, S., Kagan, S., Hertz-Lazarowitz, R., Webb, C., and Schmuck, R. (eds), (1985). *Learning to Cooperate, Cooperating to Learn*. New York: Plenum Publishing Corporation.

Thelen, H. (1954). *Dynamics of Groups at Work*. Chicago: The University of Chicago Press.

Warring, D., Johnson, D., Maruyama, G., and Johnson, R. (1985). Impact of different types of cooperative learning on cross-ethnic and cross-sex relationships, *Journal of Educational Psychology*, **77**, 53–59.

Weick, K. (1976). Educational organizations as loosely coupled systems, *Administrative Science Quarterly*, **21**, 1–19.

Weigel, R., Wiser, P., and Cook, S. (1975). Impact of cooperative learning experiences on cross-ethnic relations and attitudes, *Journal of Social Issues*, **31**, 219–245.

Ziegler, S. (1981). The effectiveness of cooperative learning teams for increasing cross-ethnic friendship: additional evidence, *Human Organization*, **40**, 264–268.

CHAPTER 9

# Teacher-mediated Versus Peer-mediated Instruction: a Review of Educational Advantages and Disadvantages

CHARLES R. GREENWOOD, JUDITH J. CARTA, and DEBRA KAMPS

*Juniper Gardens Children's Project, Bureau of Child Research, University of Kansas, Kansas City 66102, USA*

## INTRODUCTION

During the last fifteen years, major advances have occurred in what we know about student learning and effective instructional practices. These advances have taken place in large part because of a shift in the type of variables researchers have chosen to study with respect to both academic achievement and social competence. Research conducted prior to 1970 extensively examined classroom learning relative to *unalterable* variables such as levels of teacher experience, available school resources, socioeconomic status, etc. More recent research, however, has focused on *alterable* variables such as classroom ecological arrangements, teacher behaviours, and student behaviours that transpire in the classroom during lessons (e.g. Bloom, 1980; 1984). These studies are directed at questions regarding *what is done* and *what needs to be done* during instruction to produce optimal growth in students' learning. Findings from these studies address the specific teaching practices which create classroom processes (e.g. the opportunity to learn a subject matter or to actively engage in a learning task), that in turn lead

Children Helping Children
Edited by H. C. Foot, M. J. Morgan and R. H. Shute

to accelerated gains in students' performance on measures of achievement or social competence.

The primary purpose of this chapter is to compare teacher- and peer-mediated approaches to instruction. As we will illustrate, the processes of effective teaching may be orchestrated within both approaches. Our strategy in this chapter will be to review examples of both teacher-mediated and peer-mediated approaches to teaching and characterize the salient differences among them.

A secondary purpose of this chapter is to discuss the advantages and disadvantages of both approaches. A premise of this chapter is not that one approach is necessarily better than the other, rather that what is of interest is how peer mediation may be used to support various instructional goals and to enhance learning. Each approach has advantages and disadvantages that powerfully affect its potential contribution to teaching and student learning. Because of recent trends in education that have increased the heterogeneity of student abilities within classrooms (e.g. Slavin, Madden, and Leavey, 1984), we presume that many readers will be interested in peer-mediated methods as alternative options in support of the need to individualize instruction. But first, we define some terms.

In this chapter, we define *mediation* to mean the act of providing instructional services directly to the student. These services may range from incidental peer help and support for a task to the provision of routine direct instruction in a subject matter (e.g. Greenwood, Carta, and Hall, 1988; Kalfus, 1984). Traditionally, instruction has been teacher mediated. However, when a teacher arranges for students to be directly taught or supervised by peers for some period of instructional time, we enter the world of peer mediation. Thus, for the purposes of this review, methods that employ peer monitors, peer tutors, peer helpers, or peer teams are those employing *peer mediation*.

Throughout this chapter, we will frequently refer to practices, processes, and products in relation to teacher- and peer-mediated approaches. *Practices* are those specific teaching procedures and methods used to plan, organize, and guide the delivery of instruction. *Processes* are those observable features of the classroom environment that reflect the immediate implementation of a practice. *Products* refer to the growth in student performance typically based on either pre-test-to-post-test measures of educational outcome (e.g. achievement tests) or continuous curriculum-based measures (e.g. oral reading rates).

## EFFECTIVE INSTRUCTIONAL PROCESSES

Recent research has revealed a number of instructional processes related to academic outcomes. While these effective processes have been reviewed by many (e.g. Anderson, Evertson, and Brophy, 1982; Christenson, Thurlow, and Ysseldyke, 1987; Rosenshine and Stevens, 1986), Berliner (1988) has focused on seven specific factors shown by past research to powerfully affect whether or not learning as measured by achievement tests will occur. Those factors include: engaged time, time management, success rate, academic learning time, monitoring, structuring, and questioning. Each of these will be briefly discussed below.

### Engaged time

The time students spend making active academic responses such as writing, reading (i.e. aloud or silently), or talking about academic subjects is considered *engaged time*. Engaged time has been consistently demonstrated to be a positive correlate of academic achievement (e.g. Rosenshine and Stevens, 1986; Greenwood, Delquadri, and Hall, 1984). However, it is also known that there are individual student variations within and across regular and special education classrooms in the amount of engaged time (Carta, Greenwood, and Robinson, 1987; Fisher *et al.*, 1978; Rotholz, Kamps, and Greenwood, 1989). Within one hour allocated to reading instruction in a classroom, the actual amount of engaged time in reading might be as little as 10 minutes for one student or as much as 55 minutes for another. The level of engagement in a classroom is highly related to the arrangement of the classroom ecology and the way in which that design sets the stage for and reinforces academic interactions between teachers, students, and academic materials. For example, a classroom in which the teacher stands in front of the class lecturing to students is designed to produce large amounts of passive attention from students. Such an instructional arrangement inherently limits the amount of active engagement that can take place, that is, the amount of direct student participation. In contrast to lecturing, teaching strategies that mediate high levels of active engagement include peer tutoring and cooperative learning groups.

### Time management

In industry, time is money. In education, time is the opportunity to learn. When time is lost in a classroom, it results in missed opportunities. Unfortunately, in a classroom time is easily lost. For example, transition from one activity to another, that is, the time it takes for students to move to their places and get ready for instruction, can result in the loss of large percentages of the classroom day (e.g. Carta, Greenwood, and Robinson, 1987). Time lost due to inefficient transitions is inversely correlated with achievement gains (e.g. Leinhardt, 1980). Fisher and his colleagues (1978) noted that in one class in which the school day was 300 minutes, 76 minutes or about 25% of the day was spent in transition. In this classroom, instruction was delivered within learning centres where small groups of students spent time in each learning centre at different points of the day. Unfortunately, students spent more than an hour a day commuting between centres.

Teachers may employ simple techniques to reduce the loss of time. For example, in one study, Kuergleis, Deutchman, and Paine (1980) used a timing and feedback approach. Students were told that their transitions were being timed and were challenged to meet or beat an announced criterion time. Times between activities which were often as high as 20 minutes were reduced to between 30 seconds and 2 minutes.

**Success rate**

Another instructional variable that has been shown to have powerful effects on achievement is the rate of successful completion of tasks. In his review of several studies, Rosenshine (1983) determined that in the initial phases of learning, during small group work and recitation, students should experience success rates of approximately 75% or greater. When doing independent seatwork and homework assignments, students should perform rapidly, smoothly, and almost always correctly (Brophy, 1983). Yet some studies have determined that in some classrooms, students spend 100% of their time making errors (e.g. Fisher *et al.*, 1978). These researchers reported that time spent making errors was negatively correlated with achievement.

**Academic learning time**

Academic learning time (ALT) combines engaged time, time management, and success rate. According to Berliner (1988), ALT is the:

> time engaged with materials or activities related to the outcome measure being used (often an achievement test), during which a student experiences a high success rate (p. 15).

More simply, academic learning time is the time spent on material similar to that on which the student will be tested. This variable simply emphasizes the point that students must be more than engaged or active during the course of the day. If achievement gains are to occur, students must exhibit high levels of engagement on tasks that promote the skills to be assessed by evaluation measures (Anderson, Evertson, and Brophy, 1979; Fisher *et al.*, 1978; Gersten, Carnine, and Williams, 1981). Rosenshine and Stevens (1986) listed several techniques for increasing student success rate during academic exercises. Among them are: (a) breaking down instruction into smaller steps that allow students to master each step before proceeding on to subsequent steps, (b) providing students with teacher-monitored practice prior to independent seatwork activities so that students' errors can be corrected before they become part of students' repertoires, and (c) providing independent practice opportunities of sufficient length and frequency to enable all students to master skills to the point of overlearning.

## Monitoring

Monitoring means determining if a student is performing correctly through a process of asking questions and giving feedback. This task, whether undertaken by teachers or peers, is critical in today's classrooms where a good portion of the students' day is spent working independently. Students have been shown to make the greatest academic gains in classrooms in which the level of monitoring is high (Fisher *et al.*, 1978). Students who are not monitored during independent seatwork often spend less time engaged as compared with students who receive higher levels of monitoring.

## Structuring

'It is not surprising that students who do not have a clear handle on what they are to do easily find ways to do nothing.' (Berliner, 1988, p. 18). If teachers are to be effective, they need to communicate to students what they are expected to do and why. This type of structuring affects both student attention and level of success in lessons. Emmer, Evertson, and Anderson (1980) compared two groups of classrooms. Teachers in one group were clearly better managers and provided a greater degree of structure. These teachers communicated objectives, directions, and content more clearly, adapted instruction to students' interests and skill levels, and explained to students the reasons for learning particular materials. Students whose teachers provided more structure exhibited greater on-task behaviour, and by the end of the year, realized greater achievement gains than students whose teachers provided less structure.

## Questioning

Questioning in the classroom, as it affects student achievement, has been approached on at least two levels, i.e., frequency and cognitive level. The literature is most clear with regard to question frequency, that is, high levels of lower order questions are correlated positively with student achievement (Brophy, 1986; Brophy and Evertson, 1976). Christenson *et al.* (1987) postulated that this may be the case because teachers with high rates of questioning are frequently more active teachers in general and have well-managed classes.

The literature is mixed, however, on the issue of cognitive level on student achievement. Some authors have suggested that there are no academic advantages to teachers asking students higher level questions such as those that test a student's ability to analyse and evaluate (Christenson *et al.*, 1987). Other researchers contend just the opposite, that teachers who ask higher-order questions have students who achieve considerably more (Redfield and Rousseau, 1981).

To conclude this discussion of effective instructional processes, the literature provides several yardsticks for evaluating teaching whether it be teacher-mediated or peer-mediated. Among these process yardsticks are the following:

1. Do students spend most of their time engaged in active academic responses (i.e. writing, reading, academic talk, asking, and answering questions)?
2. Is time used efficiently with a minimum amount of time being spent in transition between activities?
3. Are students' error rates kept to a minimum?
4. Do students spend most of their time engaged in successful responses on tasks that are related to what will be tested?
5. Are students frequently monitored to determine if they are engaged and performing correctly?
6. Are lessons structured so that students know what they are to do and why?
7. Are students frequently asked questions that test their knowledge and comprehension?

Clearly, within both peer-mediated and teacher-mediated practices, a range of methods exist that orchestrate all of these processes. However, some teacher-mediated practices and the quality of their implementation may stray considerably, thus adversely affecting these processes. The same holds true for peer-mediated instruction. We now describe four exemplary practices known to orchestrate these effective processes. The first two, *Direct Instruction* and *Mastery Learning* are primarily teacher-mediated. The second two, *Cooperative Learning Groups* and *Classwide Peer Tutoring* are peer-mediated. All four practices have been demonstrated highly effective in producing gains in students' measured levels of academic achievement.

## EFFECTIVE INSTRUCTIONAL PRACTICES

### Mastery Learning

Mastery learning is a class of strategies based on the premise that learning is a function of the amount of time engaged with learning tasks relative to the amount of time needed to learn a task. A key assumption is that the amount of time needed varies with each individual. Students who spend too little engaged time master only a part of the curriculum (Carroll, 1963). Mastery learning programmes typically involve organizing the curriculum into short units of material and frequently testing students' performance over the material. Advancement to new material is dependent on mastery standards and criteria (e.g. 90% correct). Critical elements of mastery learning include:

1. Clearly specified instructional objectives.
2. Small units of learning related to instructional objectives.
3. Short tests which assess each student's performance on objectives.
4. Predetermined performance standards which indicate whether students have achieved mastery on objectives.

5. Clear communication with students regarding what content is to be mastered and how it is to be learned.
6. Corrective procedures for students failing to meet pre-set standards.
7. Monitoring of students' corrective activities until all students have achieved the predetermined standard of mastery (Anderson, 1984).

Examples of mastery learning programmes are the *Learning for Mastery* (LFM) program (Bloom, 1968) and the *Personalized System of Instruction* (PSI) (Keller, 1968). While sharing the mastery feature in common, these two programmes differ with respect to the learning activities employed. In the LFM approach, the teacher is more likely to use traditional lecture and teacher/student discussion methods of teaching. In order to obtain the increased time and practice necessary to reach mastery, students are expected to use their study time in class and at home. Thus, progress over the content to be learned in LFM is group paced. In PSI, however, a written curriculum is developed in lieu of lectures or discussion, and students may move through the sequence of written units at their own pace. Independent study of the material is the primary method of teaching. The instructor or sometimes peer proctors (i.e. students having mastered the units of material), check students' tests, discuss their errors, and provide direction for additional study.

Obviously, both of these mastery learning approaches create many of the effective instructional processes previously discussed. Foremost among them is the use of structure, that is, communication of learning expectations, and the monitoring of student performance (Anderson, 1984). Critics have suggested that mastery approaches place heavier time demands on teachers and as the result of breaking content into small learning units may produce fragmentation of knowledge and skills (e.g. Arlin and Webster, 1983; Buss, 1976). Nonetheless, mastery approaches have been found to produce greater gains in achievement and cognitive skills than non-mastery methods (Bloom, 1984).

### Direct instruction

Direct Instruction (DI) is a teacher-mediated practice based on the premise that 'For all students to learn, both the curriculum and teacher presentation of these materials must be clear and unambiguous.' (Gersten, Carnine, and Woodward, 1987, pp. 48–49). The primary goal of DI is the efficient acquisition of academic skills that are durable and generalizable. Critical elements of direct instruction include the following:

1. Clearly specified and sequenced learning objectives.
2. An explicit scripted step-by-step instructional strategy.
3. Development of mastery on each skill.

4. Design of instructional materials that reduce the likelihood of student errors and misunderstanding.
5. Gradual fading from teacher-mediated activities toward independent work.
6. Use of systematic practice across a range of examples.
7. Cumulative review and integration of newly learned concepts with previously mastered material (Gersten *et al.*, 1987).

DI is implemented by teachers who refer frequently to scripted lesson plans to direct their teaching behaviour. Lessons are presented to small groups composed of students of relatively homogeneous ability. These groups also engage in independent seatwork using workbooks, worksheets, and readers/text materials in the DI format. During direct instruction groups, teachers employ both group and individual communications with students. For example, teachers use both verbal directives and physical signals to prompt students' response. These strategies ensure participation and active engagement with the individual tasks presented within lessons. Frequent unit testing is employed and material is directly retaught when students fail to reach mastery criteria.

DI places a heavy emphasis on all the previously identified effective processes of teaching including academic learning time and structure in particular (e.g. Berliner, 1988). The use of small group instruction with unison responding is designed to give each student the greatest number of response opportunities. Instruction is rapidly paced, deliberately fashioned to maintain student attention and to increase the amount of material covered in a lesson. In DI, the use of classroom aides, volunteers, and peers is also employed to maximize individualized practice and feedback.

In spite of its widely acknowledged positive effects (e.g. see Stallings and Stipek, 1986), criticism has been levelled at DI because of its use of scripted lessons and its perceived emphasis on rote skills rather than higher-order conceptual learning (see, for example, Calfee, 1986). Yet, the evidence for the effectiveness of the practice of DI is overwhelming (Gersten *et al.*, 1984; Meyer, 1984; Stebbins *et al.*, 1977). In recent years, DI programmes have appeared covering topics such as earth science, creative writing, and logical and critical thinking (Carnine, 1988). Not only have both short- and long-term positive effects of DI been demonstrated, these effects have similarly been documented for low-income, disadvantaged and special education students (Gersten, 1985; Gersten, Woodward, and Darch, 1986; Kennedy, 1978).

**Cooperative learning groups**

Cooperative learning is a class of peer-mediated practices in which small teams of four to six children work together in order to earn rewards based on the collective performance of their team. Many variations of cooperative learning groups have been developed, for example, *Learning Together* (Johnson and

Johnson, 1983), *Team Assisted Individualization* (TAI) (Slavin, Madden, and Leavey, 1984), *Cooperative Integrated Reading and Composition* (CIRC) (Madden, Slavin, and Stevens, 1986), *Teams–Games–Tournaments* (TAT) (DeVries and Slavin, 1978), *Jigsaw* (Aronson *et al.*, 1978) and *Group Investigation* (Sharan and Sharan, 1976).

The critical elements of cooperative learning group strategies are:

1. Teacher instruction, to introduce new material.
2. Team practice, to allow children to learn from each other.
3. Team recognition, to give all students the opportunity to be winners and thus, relieving motivational problems that low-ability students may have.
4. Group rewards and cooperative peer relations, to give students experience in working interdependently and facilitate mutual friendships (Custer, and Osguthorpe, 1983; Stallings and Stipek, 1986).

Cooperative learning group strategies take advantage of the fact that, when students earn reinforcement based on their combined effort rather than just their own, natural sources of peer help, tutoring, encouragement, and peer pressure are produced (e.g. Greenwood and Hops, 1981; Johnson and Johnson, 1974; McCarty *et al.*, 1977). Not only do cooperative learning groups differ in the use of rewards, they also differ according to variations in the learning tasks (e.g. group tasks versus individualized tasks), task ability levels within groups (e.g. homogeneous versus heterogeneous ability), and the degree to which interactions by team members are scripted by the teacher or are free to vary according to the natural interactions within teams (Wilcox, Sbardellati, and Nevin, 1987). Use of cooperative learning groups are typically integrated with periods of time in which the teacher provides direct instruction to introduce new material or to review material covered.

TAI, for example, is a cooperative learning group practice applied to mathematics instruction. In TAI, students are organized into four or five member teams heterogeneously distributed by students' mathematics ability levels. Thus, high and low ability students are always present on each team. Students work within these teams on individualized curriculum materials at their own rate. Team members may help each other when problems arise. Team members handle most of the checking of work and management tasks inherent in an individualized, self-paced curriculum. Students who attain mastery on quizzes add to their weekly teams' score. At the end of each week, students are rewarded with certificates based on the average number and accuracy of units completed by all team members.

Several elements of effective teaching are inherent in TAI and other forms of cooperative learning group strategies. First, reinforcing students for the number of successfully completed units of material sets the occasion for high levels of student engagement and academic learning time. Effective management of time is emphasized through the careful structuring of classroom activities. High levels of success are maintained by grouping students according to a range of skill level and the natural effects of peer monitoring. Student progress is assessed using a structured hierarchy of the skills being taught.

Many studies have documented the positive effects of cooperative learning groups on both achievement and attitudinal variables (see reviews by Johnson, Johnson, and Scott, 1978; Johnson *et al.*, 1986; Johnson *et al.*, 1981; Sharan, 1980; Slavin, 1984). While generally favourable, the research on the effectiveness of cooperative learning groups, has also shown mixed results (e.g. Bryan, Cosden, and Pearl, 1982). Many factors have been suggested to explain the mixed results. For example, some studies have reported that the skill level of team members or the actual academic and social exchanges within the group may mediate the eventual outcomes as opposed to just the use of group rewards (Webb, 1982). Other researchers have suggested that cooperative learning groups may benefit some children (e.g. low achievers or members of minority groups) more than others (Edwards, DeVries, and Snyder, 1972; Lucker *et al.*, 1976). In addition, some content areas may lend themselves better than others to a cooperative learning groups' approach. Sharan (1980) indicated that subject matter requiring high level cognitive skills may not be appropriate for use in cooperative learning group practices.

Another factor that may powerfully determine the effectiveness of cooperative learning groups is the specific group reward structure that is in place (Greenwood and Hops, 1981). Studies have documented that practices which create the opportunity for students to work together but fail to reward group performance result in lower academic achievement than when students work independently (Johnson, Johnson, and Scott, 1978; Slavin, 1980).

### Peer tutoring

Peer tutoring has historically been a practical means of providing extra help to particular students, a means of individualizing instruction, and a means for facilitating social skills development (e.g. Wagner, 1982). In most situations, peer tutoring allows students to obtain 'extra instruction, practice, repetition, or clarification of a concept that enables them to succeed in the general classroom curriculum' (Jenkins and Jenkins, 1981; 1988, p. 339; Young, Hecimovic, and Salzberg, 1983). According to Greenwood *et al.*, 1984, tutoring compared with teacher-mediated instruction increases the time students spend engaged in relevant academic behaviours (e.g. academic talk, reading aloud, writing, etc.), that are related to learning specific academic tasks.

Central elements in most peer tutoring programmes are:

1. Selection of peer partners or partner pairing procedures.
2. Tutoring roles that involve tutor and tutee interactions (e.g. task presentation,

error correction strategies, presentation of new material, point systems, positive reinforcement, etc.).
3. Regularly scheduled tutoring sessions.
4. Adapted materials for use within a peer tutoring arrangement.
5. Frequent testing to evaluate learning.
6. Teacher monitoring of tutoring activities.

Classwide peer tutoring (CWPT), for example, is a form of same-age, intra-class, peer tutoring (Greenwood, Delquadri, and Carta, 1988; Heron *et al.*, 1983). It has been successfully applied to passage reading, reading comprehension, mathematics, and spelling instruction. CWPT involves the entire class in tutoring. Students are either randomly assigned or loosely matched by ability to partners each week (e.g. Heward, Heron, and Cooke, 1982). Pairs are assigned to teams that compete for the highest point total resulting from daily scheduled tutoring sessions. Unit mastery is checked at least weekly using teacher prepared tests. New content to be learned and new teams and tutoring pairs are formed on a weekly basis. Variations of CWPT have been reported by Delquadri *et al.* (1986), Heward, Heron, and Cooke (1982), Maheady and Harper (1987), and Maheady, Sacca, and Harper (1988).

CWPT contains several of the effective processes that have been discussed. Most prominent among these are engagement and academic learning time. In the most successful tutoring programmes, a high degree of structure is provided with frequent teacher monitoring of tutoring situations. Students are trained in the procedures necessary to act as tutors and tutees. On a given day, they know precisely whom to tutor, what material is to be covered in the tutoring sessions, how to correct errors, and how to award points for correct responding. Monitoring by the teachers is continuous and weekly assessments are provided so that students receive feedback on their level of mastery.

Other forms of peer tutoring, such as cross-age and/or cross-ability inter-class tutoring involve the use of older/higher skilled tutors who work with younger, lower skilled tutees (Jenkins and Jenkins, 1981; Johnson and Bailey, 1974). These programmes are most often organized around a group of upper grade students who come into the classroom or a special resource room setting to tutor younger students (see Greer and Polirstok, 1982). Cross-age or cross-ability tutoring arrangements have included the use of nonhandicapped students as tutors for handicapped students (Carlton, Litton, and Zinkgrof, 1985). However, the most recent work has demonstrated the feasibility and the benefit of employing special education students as tutors for special education students (e.g. Cook *et al.*, 1985; Brown, Fenrick, and Klemme, 1971; Greenwood *et al.*, 1988; Osguthorpe and Scruggs, 1986).

Peer tutoring has been widely reported as effective in increasing students' academic performance (e.g. Cohen, Kulik, and Kulik, 1982; Jenkins and Jenkins, 1988; Greenwood, Delquadri, and Hall, in press; Pigott, Fantuzzo, and Clement,

1986; Young, 1981) and social interaction (e.g. Maheady and Sainato, 1985; Wilcox, Sbardellati, and Nevin, 1987). Positive effects have been reported both for the tutor and the tutee (e.g. Dineen, Clark, and Risley, 1977).

However, tutoring also has some of the same drawbacks that have been identified for other effective practices. Foremost among these is its limited use in teaching higher level conceptual skills. While some studies have documented the success of tutoring for improving reading comprehension (e.g. Greenwood, Delquadri, and Hall, 1984), most of the evidence for its effectiveness has been based on the acquisition of rote skills such as oral reading, spelling words, reading rate, mathematics facts, and vocabulary (see Delquadri *et al.*, 1986). Another potential drawback is that the content for tutoring sessions, as in some forms of mastery learning and cooperative learning groups must be developed or adapted by the teacher. While this may be an advantage in that the peer tutoring system may operate to support whatever curriculum the classroom teacher is already using, it nonetheless leaves the programme vulnerable to poorly sequenced materials or teachers who are unable or unwilling to appropriately structure the curriculum into forms suitable for tutoring.

To this point, we have argued that (a) research has identified particular instructional processes that are related to increased academic products and (b) that a number of effective practices exist for orchestrating these processes. Effective classroom processes and their responsible teaching practices stand in marked contrast to what we often find in classrooms which employ traditional teacher-mediated approaches.

In the United States particularly, teacher-mediated approaches centre on the use of basal reading or mathematics curricula. Basal programmes are commercially produced curricula. These programmes, in reading for example, employ a central text which contains a series of stores that introduce new vocabulary and provide the basis for students' reading practice. These programmes provide a teacher's manual which contains advice concerning how to organize the students and various learning activities relative to the teaching of reading.

Unfortunately, conventional basal programmes have been widely criticized as unsystematic and often ambiguous (Gersten, Carnine, and White, 1984; Vargas, 1984). Additionally, basal programmes are often not sound technological practices, that is, what teachers do when implementing a basal programme is often observed to vary widely from classroom to classroom. This is because the programmes give advice concerning implementation but do not actually script what is to be said or done. Consequently, there are often wide differences in the processes produced by teachers who are attempting to employ the same practice.

The materials and ecological arrangements employed to aid conventional instruction, such as overhead projectors, lectures, and teacher/student discussions, and independent seatwork also frequently fail to provide students with sufficient opportunities to respond (e.g. Carta, Greenwood, and Robinson, 1987) and necessary academic learning time (e.g. Gettinger and White, 1979).

Lastly, much of conventional instruction fails to conform to high standards of implementation quality and fidelity. Consequently, many students in conventional teacher-mediated programmes are at risk for lower academic outcomes than could otherwise be obtained. We now turn our attention to the research which has sought to compare the relative effectiveness of teacher-mediated with peer-mediated instruction.

## RESEARCH COMPARING TEACHER- VERSUS PEER-MEDIATED INSTRUCTION

There are few, if any, adequate comparisons in the literature in which just the teacher versus peer components of instruction have been examined. Instead, most studies have compared total systems of instruction, that is, the mediator plus other components of instructional practice (e.g. the sequencing of the curriculum, error correction, reinforcement, etc.). Thus, it is not possible to know the specific contribution of just peer or teacher roles. The literature does demonstrate, however, the relative merit of total systems of instruction. For example, research conducted by Bloom and his students (e.g. Bloom, 1984), indicated that the optimal teaching/learning arrangement was one-to-one tutoring provided by a highly skilled tutor. Across several studies he and his graduate researchers reported that one-to-one tutoring produced achievement effect sizes as large as 2.00, or as high as two standard deviations above the control group mean. (Effect sizes larger than 0.25 of a standard deviation have been described as educationally significant effects.) In these studies, the control group teachers employed conventional teacher-mediated, lecture-oriented instruction to teach the same content.

Jenkins *et al.* (1974) compared one-to-one cross-age peer tutoring with conventional teacher-led, small group instruction. In this study, students with learning disabilities and mental handicaps were participants. The task taught included oral reading, work recognition, spelling, and mathematical facts. The authors reported that the tutoring procedures were significantly more effective than the teacher-mediated method.

Greenwood *et al.* (1984) reported that disadvantaged elementary students learned more spelling words, vocabulary items, and mathematical facts when they were taught using classwide peer tutoring (CWPT) than they did when the teacher designed and directly mediated their instruction. This finding was subsequently replicated in spelling for 211 inner-city students whose teachers alternated between teacher designed/mediated instruction and CWPT methods of instruction. Teacher-mediated procedures included use of a spelling textbook with word lists and vocabulary exercises to be completed, chalkboard discussions of new word lists, group oral spelling with teacher assistance, self study, and home assignments to study the words.

More recently, Greenwood, Delquadri, and Hall (in press) reported that inner-city students whose teachers employed CWPT in the first four grades to teach reading, arithmetic, and spelling gained significantly more on each subtest of the Metropolitan Achievement Test than did an equivalent control group. At the end of fourth grade, the means of the peer tutoring group exceeded those of the control by 0.37 (arithmetic), 0.57 (reading) and 0.60 (language) standard deviations.

Based on classroom observation data, it was also demonstrated that the CWPT intervention significantly increased students' active engagement with learning tasks compared with levels produced during the teacher-mediated procedures (Greenwood, Delquadri, and Hall, in press; Greenwood *et al.*, 1984). Similar findings have been reported for improvements in the reading fluency of students with learning disabilities in special education programmes (Greenwood, Delquadri, and Hall, 1984).

Slavin and his colleagues reported increased academic gains for students whose teachers implemented cooperative learning teams. For example, Slavin, Leavey, and Madden (1984) reported that team assisted individualization (TAI) significantly increased the mathematics achievement of a sample of suburban elementary students compared to a control group whose teachers implemented the conventional instruction. Control teachers used a single pace in their instruction and made few adaptations for learners with handicaps. In this study, mainstreamed students with learning handicaps in the TAI programme gained 0.52 grade equivalents more in computation skills than control groups did over a 6-month intervention period. Students without handicaps gained 0.42 grade equivalents more than controls.

In two other studies, Slavin, Madden, and Leavey (1984) compared TAI and Individualized Instruction (II) to traditional instruction using texts, whole-class lectures and group-paced instruction supplemented by teacher-directed small mathematics groups. TAI and II students gained twice that achieved by the control group on the mathematics computation subscale of the Comprehensive Test of Basic Skills. However, TAI students did equally as well as the II group. TAI teachers also reported fewer behavioural problems with students than did the controls.

Another report compared the reading achievement gains of student groups whose teachers used cooperative integrated reading and composition (CIRC) versus traditional reading instruction (Madden, Slavin, and Stevens, 1986; Stevens *et al.*, 1987). Traditional instruction consisted of a basal reading series in a three reading group arrangement followed by workbook and worksheet seatwork study. In language arts and writing, teachers used whole-class instruction based on published texts selected from the school district's adoption list. Results indicated that students gained significantly higher scores on the reading and language subscales of the California Achievement Test at post-test than did controls. Additionally, CIRC students performed better on measures of oral reading and written expression. Analyses also indicated that CIRC was effective for students of all ability levels including mainstreamed students.

Collectively, these studies comparing peer-mediated instruction with conventional teacher-mediated instruction demonstrated that forms of peer-mediated instruction were generally more effective than teacher-mediated programmes (e.g. basal curricula, teacher-designed instruction, etc.). It was also evident that peer-mediated programmes produced greater levels of important classroom processes as well as gains in measured achievement. Based on this research, peer mediation is clearly a viable instructional alternative. However, it does carry with it costs and constraints that do not accompany conventional teacher-mediated instruction. We now turn to a discussion of the advantages and disadvantages of peer-mediated instruction.

## THE ADVANTAGES AND DISADVANTAGES OF TEACHER- VERSUS PEER-MEDIATION

Peer mediation offers a number of advantages compared with conventional teacher-mediated instruction in facilitating and creating processes known to result in academic products (see Table 9.1).

TABLE 9.1. Advantages and disadvantages of peer- and teacher-mediated instructional approaches

| | Mediator | |
|---|---|---|
| Teacher factor | Teacher | Peer |
| *Advantages* | | |
| Pupil/teacher ratio | High | Low |
| Engaged time | Variable | High |
| Opportunities to respond | Low | High |
| Opportunities for error correction | Low | High |
| Immediacy of error correction | Delayed | Immediate |
| Opportunities for help and encouragement | Few | Many |
| Opportunities for both competitive and cooperative learning experiences | Few | Many |
| Motivation | Teacher support | Peer plus teacher support |
| *Disadvantages* | | |
| Peer training requirements | Few | Many |
| Quality control requirements | Few | Many |
| Content coverage | Good | Variable |
| Peer selection | Not required | Required |
| Curriculum adaptations | Few | Many |
| Costs | High | Low |
| Ethical concerns | Few | Increased |

**Pupil/teacher ratio**

As previously discussed, pupil–teacher ratio is a major constraint on the extent to which any student's programme may be individualized, that student responding can be directly supervised, that student errors may be detected and corrected, and that student progress may be reinforced. At the most basic level, the advantage of peer mediation is the creation of more favourable pupil–teacher ratios. Consequently, the goals of individualization, response supervision, error correction, and reinforcement are more likely to be achieved. In classrooms where peer tutors or cooperative learning groups are employed, each student may have his or her own teacher for at least the period of time in which peer-mediated instruction is conducted. This is not the case in conventional, teacher-mediated instruction.

**Engaged time**

Compared to traditional forms of teacher-mediated instruction, research confirms that peer-mediated teaching increases time on academic tasks. Task behaviours such as writing of spelling words, solving mathematical equations, oral reading, task completion, etc. are reliably produced by peer tutoring programmes. For example, Greenwood *et al*. (1984) reported that engaged time averaged from 15% to 35% during conventional teacher instruction versus 45% to 75% during CWPT. Tutee's engaged time was increased because of the rapid and sustained task demands created by the tutor and the motivational factors associated with peer interaction and/or group reward contingencies.

**Opportunities to respond**

A major advantage of peer-mediated instruction is that it provides increased opportunities to respond (Greenwood *et al*., 1984; 1987) compared with conventional teaching. Furthermore, peer-mediated instruction provides an additional context in which students may use their academic knowledge. The conventional contexts for the use of academic knowledge are teacher–student discussions, worksheets, workbooks or other written tasks, computer tasks, or structured projects. Peer-mediation adds peer interactions in which students may employ both their academic and social knowledge with each other (e.g. Kohler, 1986; Kohler *et al*., 1985). Additionally, many peer tutoring formats employ task trials in which students are required to employ a rapid sustained response rate (e.g. a timed writing task) or discrete trial task presentations (e.g. spelling word practice), during which tutees are requested to respond at a rate as high as 5 to 10 times per minute (e.g. Kohler, 1986). Thus, the pace of peer-mediated instruction is generally higher.

In comparison, conventional teaching formats typically provide relatively fewer direct response opportunities. Furthermore, much of conventional instruction (e.g. seatwork), is self-paced, that is, the student determines the rate at which new tasks (e.g. problems, words read, etc.), are attacked and assignments completed. Consequently, the pace of conventional instruction is typically less than peer-mediated instruction.

### Opportunities for error correction

Peer-mediated methods, compared with conventional teacher methods, typically employ procedures that lead to frequent error identification and practice of the correct response. Because of the one-to-one pupil–teacher ratio in peer tutoring, for example, tutors are in a position to monitor and supervise directly the academic responding of the tutee. Error identification is supported in peer tutoring by the use of peer selection (tutors who have learned the task they are teaching), the use of answer keys (tutors correct tutee responses to a criterion), or through answer challenge procedures (tutors earn points for identifying tutee errors and providing correct answers). In addition to identifying errors, most peer-mediated procedures include procedures for practising the correct response. These procedures have ranged from direct modelling of the correct response and word supply, to extensive positive practice including spelling a word, looking it up in the dictionary, using it in a sentence, etc.

### Immediacy of error correction

In addition to increased opportunities for receiving error correction in peer-mediated instruction, the immediacy of feedback and practice of correct responses is also an important factor. Immediacy of feedback and correction has long been acknowledged as a positive contributor to the rate of learning (Brophy, 1986; Rosenshine, 1983). Because tutors directly monitor tutee responding, they are in a position to immediately interrupt as soon as errors occur. Thus, the delay between emission of an error and corrective feedback is dramatically reduced. Consequently, tutees have greater opportunities to practice correct responses following errors. In teacher-mediated instruction, such as lecture or seatwork, feedback on errors is either delayed or non-existent.

### Opportunities for help and encouragement

Help from a peer tutor or a team member may be both frequently obtained and spontaneously provided, whereas help in conventional teacher methods may be infrequent and delayed. In many tutoring programmes, for example, tutors and tutees engage in teaching interactions that are designed around specific teaching strategies. However, it has been our experience that tutors at times spontaneously provide the necessary help and instruction outside of the strategy that clears up a particular problem a student may be having. Tutors also provide the necessary and timely prompts that assist the tutee in sustaining good progress on a task during a lesson.

> Many tutors instruct their tutees to 'write faster',
> Some tutors provide encouragement while tutees work: 'I know you can get this one Billy' or 'You know the answer John, think hard',
> Some tutors provide direct help: 'No, that's close but you're still missing a letter that goes without the 'i' and the 't'.'
> Tutors also provide direct praise, 'Good job writing the words fast!' or 'A hundred and fifty-one points, that's wonderful Joe.' (Kohler *et al.*, 1985).

## Opportunities for competitive and cooperative learning

Peer-mediated instruction, compared with conventional teacher-mediated instruction, provides a context for students to work together to achieve a common goal. This may be a common goal to simply work through a tutee's learning task (e.g. reading passage), or a combination of goals including completing work tasks, earning of points or grades, and/or determining of a winning pair or team. Peer tutoring establishes

> 'An atmosphere where children overtly encourage and support academic accomplishments of their peers.', and where
> 'students encourage and expect their peers to contribute their best performance toward the effort, 'sure to earn a lot of points today' or as a tutor told her tutee, 'I'm going to make sure you work hard today' (Kohler *et al.*, 1985).

## Motivation

In peer-mediated instruction, motivation may be supplied by both teacher and peers. In teacher-mediated instruction, only teacher forms of influence typically operate to support instructional goals. Conventional forms of teacher motivational influences include use of interesting learning tasks or teacher praise and approval. Peer mediation adds to these the motivational aspects of peer interaction (e.g. novelty, excitement about new partners, winning teams, peer approval, and peer pressure). Peer-mediated instruction provides a convenient means of tapping the positive side of peer group influence, which in most teacher-mediated classrooms unfortunately, tends to support undesirable social behaviours rather than the teacher's instructional goals (Greenwood and Hops, 1981).

## Peer training requirements

Peer-mediated approaches vary in the degree to which they structure or script teaching interactions, hence they vary in the amount of training required for the interactants. Conventional forms of teacher-mediated instruction require little if any such training of the students. Peer tutoring strategies, for example those that require the tutor to employ a specific set of instructional behaviours, have been reported more effective than those that only create pairs and then leave the tutoring procedures entirely to the discretion of the tutor (e.g. Niedermeyer, 1970). Unfortunately, when structured interactions between tutor and tutee are employed, training requirements are increased.

In regular classroom settings, tutors are typically trained in the instructional practices they are to provide. Training may centre on the materials to be used, how to present an item and how to sort through the possible responses the tutee may give, how to identify errors, how to correct errors, how to provide positive reinforcement, and what records of the tutee's performance are to be kept. When used within special education settings, tutor training may also necessarily include other areas of information. For example, if nonhandicapped peers are to participate as tutors for handicapped tutees, it may be important that they receive some orientation related to the handicaps their tutees have and how they may affect tutoring interactions. It may also be important that potential tutors have an opportunity to observe handicapped children prior to initiating a tutoring programme.

In a tutoring programme targeted at students with autism, Whorton *et al.*, (1989) provided an orientation for fifth grade students that described the behavioural characteristics of autism. This was followed by demonstrations and practice sessions which modelled strategies to be employed in the event of inappropriate tutee behaviours. Additionally important for some applications may be modifications in materials so that task presentations may be completed effectively by persons with limited or developing motor skills (Brown, Fenrick, and Klemme, 1971). For example, Kohler (1987) reported using circular wire supports to enable preschool aged tutors to efficiently present and remove task cards in discrete trial tutoring. Without the support, tutors tended to drop the cards or present them so that they could not be seen.

## Quality control

Peer-mediated systems may fail dramatically in the absence of sensitive mechanisms for monitoring and maintaining the fidelity of tutor's or team members' component instructional behaviours. Peer-mediated instruction changes the teacher's role from one of *delivery of instruction* to one of *monitoring and shaping of peer-teaching activities*. Monitoring of tutoring, for example, has typically focused on curriculum-based tests of student learning (e.g. oral reading rates, weekly tests), products stemming from tutoring sessions (e.g. written work produced, points earned, etc.), and teacher observations of tutoring interactions.

In CWPT, for example, the teacher is required to give bonus points and praise to tutors and tutees who are observed to be engaged in specific 'tutoring behaviours'. In cases in which point cheating has been observed in tutoring programmes (Maheady and Harper, 1987), consequences must be provided which reduce the probability of this problem in the future, and thus, reduce the risk of programme failure.

## Content coverage

As mentioned earlier, a major obstacle to wide-scale use of peer mediation compared with conventional instruction is the problem of continuous input of new content to be learned, as prior material is mastered. The rate of academic growth in a content domain is a function of the rate at which new content is mastered over a semester and over a school year (Borg, 1979). Students who master 25 units of material compared with those who master 15 units within the same semester will certainly demonstrate greater academic gains on a summative achievement test covering all material taught.

Peer-mediated systems that rely exclusively on tutors skilled in the specific content area may be prone to obsolescence when tutees master the content taught. As many teachers know, once a tutee has learned the skills from the tutor, the relationship is essentially finished (Gerber and Kauffman, 1981). This can be a major barrier to the maintenance of any tutoring strategy over time and it may limit the content that can be covered in a tutoring programme. This problem has shaped the thinking of many teachers concerning tutoring and consequently many consider peer tutoring only a temporary procedure for remediating the skills of one or two students. To remove this limitation, either a new tutor with more advanced skills is needed or a strategy that empowers tutors to teach new skills and new content is required in order to maintain the system.

Many successful peer-mediated programmes use mastery-like systems for defining, organizing, and sequencing content to handle the problem of tutor obsolescence. For example, Heward, Heron, and Cooke (1982), simply defined the universe of all sight words to be a content domain for classwide peer tutoring. Students were pre-tested on these materials and those words in need of teaching were identified for each student. These words were then organized into manageable lists and taught over subsequent weeks. Because tutors had the answers and could check tutee responses, it was possible for tutors to cover the entire domain of material with their tutees. Thus, the problem of tutor obsolescence was avoided.

## Peer selection

A traditional concern in peer mediation strategies is selection of the optimal tutors or set of team members. In peer tutoring, the optimal tutor is one with both the academic and social skills necessary to teach a set of skills to a peer without any teacher assistance. However, optimal tutors are scarce resources and those available in a classroom or a school are quickly utilized. Consequently, most partner pairing strategies seek to provide tutees with a tutor sufficiently skilled in the task to be learned or at least skilled in the instructional method to be employed. Many options are available and include *cross-age or cross-skill tutoring; same-age, cross-skill tutoring*; and *same-age, same-skill tutoring*.

The use of heterogeneous ability classroom teams in cooperative learning groups and the tutor huddle, for example, have been used to ensure that students always have access to a peer likely to have the answer or with the ability to provide help or more elaborate explanations of the subject matter. In the tutor huddle described by Cooke, Heron, and Heward (1983), tutor–tutee pairs each belong to a team headed by a student most skilled in the content to be taught. New material is presented and reviewed by the team leader in the team huddle before tutoring occurs each day. Questions are also answered by the leader and in some cases the leader's responses may be challenged by team members. In some cases, random pairing may be appropriate when the tasks being tutored are supported by materials and answer keys which enable every tutor to adequately teach, correct, and supervise the responding of the tutee.

### Curriculum adaptations

To our knowledge, there exists no commercially available curriculum designed for use within a peer-mediated approach to instruction. However, tutoring or cooperative learning group procedures are highly adaptable to the classroom objectives and materials found in most classroom and school settings. As previously mentioned, adaptations usually take the form of organizing basal materials into shorter units so that they can be used as task materials during tutoring sessions. In this process, teachers must examine their instructional objectives and relate them to the units of material and their sequencing over time. Maheady, Sacca, and Harper (1988) noted that development of these units for a junior high social studies class was the most time-consuming aspect of the entire programme.

### Cost

The start-up costs of peer mediation relative to teacher mediation are potentially high and may prove prohibitive. Start-up costs include planning time, teacher training, consultation, peer group or peer tutor training, and monitoring to ensure quality control. General issues to be solved include the problem of a limited number of best tutors, and finding and adapting the curriculum to make it appropriate for a peer mediation format of instruction.

After start-up costs are considered (e.g. design, planning, material development, etc.), the costs of operating most tutoring programmes appear to be relatively less than methods depending on more salaried adult staff (e.g. teachers or aides). For example, Armstrong *et al.* (1979) reported that a cross-age tutoring programme employing high school students as tutors was equally effective in teaching younger handicapped learners in Vermont as was a paraprofessional programme, and it was three times less costly. According to Levin, Glass, and Meister (1984), tutoring programmes were more cost effective in terms of academic gain per dollar spent, than alternative options such as increasing learning time or computer-assisted instruction.

## Ethical concerns

Lastly, the use of peer-mediated instruction raises three areas of ethical concern not necessarily raised by conventional teacher instruction. These are (a) the issue of accountability, (b) peer competence, and (c) informed consent (see Greenwood, 1981). In the area of accountability, procedures must be in place that establish that both tutees and tutors are benefiting from peer-mediation and are not in any way negatively affected by it. For example, a typical concern is that highly skilled tutors should not be short-changed by frequent tutoring assignments that reduce their learning of more difficult material or that otherwise reduce their time to learn a subject matter. Similarly, lower-skilled students should not be stigmatized by always being the tutee or lower ability learner in a tutoring programme.

In the area of tutor competence, a question often asked is related to the ability of the tutor to effectively teach the desired material. Are the materials, training, and procedures effective? In other words, are tutors able to fluently carry out their role and does the role relate directly to improvements in tutees' performance? Similarly, are the gains made by students as large as those expected of conventional methods of instruction? Parents and administrators are particularly interested in these questions.

In the area of informed consent, the concern is that tutors have been told exactly what is required of them and that they are aware of the effects that their tutoring may have on their relationships with their classmates? In cooperative learning programmes, an initial concern may be the effects of negative peer pressure or the pressure on lower achieving students to perform at levels expected by their team members. Furthermore, it is important that tutors have the opportunity to decide not to tutor if they find it difficult or aversive. In the case of tutors assigned to work with students with disabilities, are the tutors' knowledgeable about the disability and how it may affect both the tutees' performance and their interaction with the tutors? Lastly, is it assured that the appropriate persons know about the procedures to be employed and have they approved the fact that peers are to be used in the ways intended?

## IMPLICATIONS AND CONCLUSIONS

Peer-mediated instruction is obviously an increasingly sophisticated instructional technology. It is a set of strategies that may be used to create the instructional processes known to be necessary for optimizing students' performance on standardized achievement tests. Across a number of studies, peer-mediated strategies of various types have been demonstrated to be as effective or more effective than the traditional teacher-mediated practices against which they were compared. Peer-mediated instruction has been effective with students in regular classroom programmes across a range of subject matter areas. It has also been effective with special students when either regular education peers or handicapped peers have been employed as tutors (Cook *et al.*, 1985; Whorton *et al.*, 1989).

Unlike conventional, teacher-mediated instruction, peer-mediated procedures reduce the problem of unwieldy pupil/teacher ratios and create a more favourable climate for the individualizing of instruction. It supports practices and processes (e.g. students' engagement, academic learning time, etc.), that have been demonstrated to optimize students' academic and social gains. It also supports the integration of students with diverse academic and social abilities within the same classroom. Compared with conventional instruction, it directly enlists the naturally existing sources of peer group influence and motivation in direct support of the academic and social goals of the teacher, the classroom, and the school.

The use of peer-mediated approaches, however, entails a number of additional costs, responsibilities, and ethical concerns not evident in conventional teacher-mediated instruction. These costs are primarily in terms of the additional time and effort relative to starting up a program (i.e. planning and design). In our opinion, these costs may well be worth the investment compared with the costs of many alternatives that are teacher- or computer-mediated (e.g. Levin, Glass, and Meister, 1984), or to systems such as Direct Instruction, wherein curriculum purchase costs at the local school level in the USA at least, may be prohibitive.

We expect that future work will increasingly explore the integration of well-designed curricula with peer-mediated practices. As Direct Instruction has developed from a delivery model focused on small teacher-directed groups initially, to now also include seatwork and homework activities, so too peer-mediated methods will see a greater definition and integration with the best features of curriculum design. We expect to see more sophisticated hierarchical skill sequencing of materials and short units, as in Direct Instruction, which will ultimately replace the basal curricula. The eventual product may comprise the best of Direct Instruction materials together with the best of peer-mediation in a comprehensive, integrated system of instruction. In the meantime, however, for those teachers interested in creating an interesting, exciting, and productive instructional climate for their students, peer-mediated approaches are clearly an alternative that should be considered.

## ACKNOWLEDGEMENTS

This chapter was prepared with the support of grant HD03144 from the National Institute of Child Health and Human Development to the Bureau of Child Research, University of Kansas.

## REFERENCES

Anderson, L. M., Evertson, C. M., and Brophy, J. (1979). An experimental study of effective teaching in first-grade reading groups, *The Elementary School Journal*, **79**, 193–222.

Anderson, L. M., Evertson, C., and Brophy, J. (1982). *Principles of Small-Group Instruction in Elementary Reading* (Occasional paper No. 58), Institute for Research on Teaching, Michigan State University, East Lansing, MI.

Anderson, L. W. (1984). Instruction and time-on-task: a review. In L. W. Anderson (ed.), *Time and School Learning*, pp. 143–163. New York: St Martin's Press.

Arlin, M., and Webster, J. (1983). Time costs of mastery learning, *Journal of Educational Psychology*, **75**, 187–195.

Armstrong, S. B., Conlon, M. F., Pierson, P. M., and Stahlbrand, K. (1979). *The Cost Effectiveness of Peer and Cross-Age Tutoring*, Paper presented at the Annual Meeting of the Council for Exceptional Children, Dallas, TX.

Aronson, E., Stephan, C., Sikes, J., Blaney, N., and Snapp, M. (1978). *The Jigsaw Classroom*. Beverly Hills, CA: Sage.

Berliner, D. C. (1988). The half-full glass: a review of research on teaching. In E. L. Meyen, G. A. Vergason, and R. J. Whelan (eds), *Effective Instructional Strategies for Exceptional Children* pp. 7–31. Denver, CO: Love Publishing.

Bloom, B. S. (1968). *Learning For Mastery: Evaluation Comment 1* (Occasional Report No. 9), UCLA Center for the Study of Evaluation, Los Angeles, CA.

Bloom, B. S. (1980). The new direction in educational research: alterable variables, *Phi Delta Kappan*, February, 352–356.

Bloom, B. S. (1984). The 2 sigma problem: the search for methods of group instruction as effective as one-to-one tutoring, *Educational Researcher*, **13**, 4–16.

Borg, W. R. (1979). Teacher coverage of academic content and pupil achievement, *Journal of Educational Psychology*, **71**, 635–645.

Brophy, J. (1983). Classroom organization and management, *The Elementary School Journal*, **83**, 265–286.

Brophy, J. E. (1986). Teacher influences on student achievement, *American Psychologist*, **41**, 1069–1077.

Brophy, J. E., and Evertson, C. M. (1976). *Learning From Teaching: A Developmental Perspective*. Boston: Allyn and Bacon.

Brown, L., Fenrick, N., and Klemme, H. (1971). Trainable pupils learn to teach each other, *Teaching Exceptional Children*, **4**, 18–24.

Bryan, T., Cosden, M., and Pearl, R. (1982). The effects of cooperative goal structures and cooperative models on LD and NLD students, *Learning Disability Quarterly*, **5**, 415–421.

Buss, A. R. (1976). The myth of vanishing individual differences in Bloom's mastery learning, *Instructional Psychology*, **3**, 4–14.

Calfee, R. (1986, May). *Compensatory Reading*. Paper presented at the Office of Educational Research and Improvement Conference on Effects of Alternative Designs in Compensatory Education, Washington, DC.

Carlton, M. B., Litton, F. W., and Zinkgrof, S. A. (1985). The effects of an interclass peer tutoring program on the sight-word recognition ability of students who are mildly mentally retarded, *Mental Retardation*, **23**, 74–78.

Carnine, D. (1988, July). *Direction Instruction*, Presentation made at the Field Initiated Project Director's Meeting, Office of Special Education Programs, US Department of Education, Washington, DC.

Carroll, J. (1963). A model for school learning, *Teachers College Record*, **64**, 723–733.

Carta, J. J., Greenwood, C. R., and Robinson, S. (1987). Application of an ecobehavioral approach to the evaluation of early intervention programs. In R. Prinz (ed.), *Advances in the Behavioral Assessment of Children and Families*, Vol. 3, pp. 123–155. Greenwich, CT: JAI Press.

Christenson, S. L., Thurlow, M. L., and Ysseldyke, J. E. (1987). *Instructional Effectiveness: Implications For Effective Instruction of Handicapped Students* (Monograph No. 4), Instructional Alternatives Project, University of Minnesota, Minneapolis, MN.

Cohen, P. A., Kulik, J. A., and Kulik, C. L. (1982). Educational outcomes of tutoring, *American Educational Research Journal*, **19**, 237–248.

Cook, S. B., Scruggs, T. E., Mastropieri, M. A., and Casto, G. C. (1985). Handicapped students as tutors, *Journal of Special Education*, **19**, 483–492.

Cooke, N. L., Heron, T. E., and Heward, W. L. (1983). *Peer Tutoring: Implementing Classwide Programs in the Primary Grades*. Columbus, OH: Special Press.

Custer, J. D., and Osguthorpe, R. T. (1983). Improving social acceptance by training handicapped students to tutor their non-handicapped peers', *Exceptional Children*, **50**, 175.

Delquadri, J., Greenwood, C. R., Whorton, D., Carta, J. J., and Hall, R. V. (1986). Classwide peer tutoring, *Exceptional Children*, **52**, 535–542.

DeVries, D., and Slavin, R. (1978). Teams-games-tournaments (TGT): review of ten classroom experiments, *Journal of Research and Development in Education*, **12**, 28–38.

Dineen, J. P., Clark, H. B., and Risley, T. R. (1977). Peer tutoring among elementary students: educational benefits to the tutor, *Journal of Applied Behavior Analysis*, **10**, 231–238.

Edwards, K., DeVries, D., and Snyder, J. (1972). Games and Teams: a winning combination, *Simulation and Games*, **3**, 247–269.

Emmer, E. T., Evertson, C. M., and Anderson, L. M. (1980). Effective classroom management, *Elementary School Journal*, **80**, 219–231.

Fisher, C. W., Filby, N. N., Marliave, R. S., Cahan, L. S., Dishaw, M. M., Moore, J. E., and Berliner, D. C. (1978). *Teaching Behaviors, Academic Learning Time and Student Achievement* (Technical Report V-I), Final Report of Phase III-B, Beginning Teacher Evaluation Study, Far West Laboratory for Educational Research and Development, San Francisco, CA.

Gerber, M., and Kauffman, J. M. (1981). Peer tutoring in academic settings. In P. Strain (ed.), *The Utilization of Peers as Behavior Change Agents*, pp. 155–188. New York: Plenum.

Gersten, R. (1985). Direct instruction with special education students: a review of evaluation research, *Journal of Special Education*, **19**, 15–29.

Gersten, R., Becker, W., Heiry, T., and White, W. A. T. (1984). Entry IQ and yearly academic growth of children in direct instruction programs: a longitudinal study of low SES children, *Educational Evaluation and Policy Analysis*, **6**, 109–121.

Gersten, R., Woodward, J., and Darch, C. (1986). Direct instruction: a research-based approach to curriculum design and teaching, *Exceptional Children*, **53**, 17–31.

Gersten, R. M., Carnine, D. W., and White, W. A. T. (1984). The pursuit of clarity: direct instruction and applied behavior analysis. In W. L. Heward, T. E. Heron, J. Trap-Porter, and D. S. Hill (eds), *Focus on Behavior Analysis in Education*, pp. 38–57. Columbus, OH: Charles Merrill.

Gersten, R. M., Carnine, D. W., and Williams, P. B. (1981). Measuring implementation of a structured educational model in an urban school district, *Educational Evaluation and Policy Analysis*, **4**, 56–63.

Gersten, R. M., Carnine, D. W., and Woodward, J. (1987). Direct instruction research: the third decade, *Remedial and Special Education*, **8**, 48–56.

Gettinger, M. and White, M. A. (1979). Which is the stronger correlate of school learning?: time to learn or measured intelligence, *Journal of Educational Psychology*, **71**, 405–412.

Greenwood, C. R. (1981). Peer-oriented behavioral technology and ethical issues. In P. Strain (ed.), *The Utilization of Peers as Behavior Change Agents*, pp. 327–360. New York: Plenum.

Greenwood, C. R., Carta, J. J., and Hall, R. V. (1988). The use of peer tutoring strategies in classroom management and educational instruction, *School Psychology Review*, **17**, 258–275.

Greenwood, C. R., Carta, J. J., Walker, D., Arreaga-Mayer, C., and Dinwiddie, G. (1988). Special education curriculum and instruction: peer tutoring, *International Encyclopedia of Education: Research and Development* (Supplement I). New York: Pergamon.

Greenwood, C. R., Delquadri, J., and Carta, J. J. (1988). *Classwide Peer Tutoring*. Delray Beach, FL: Educational Achievement Systems.

Greenwood, C. R., Delquadri, J., and Hall, R. V. (1984). Opportunity to respond and student academic performance. In W. L. Heward, T. E. Heron, J. Trap-Porter, and D. S. Hill (eds), *Focus on Behavior Analysis in Education*, pp. 55–88, Columbus, OH: Charles Merrill.

Greenwood, C. R., Delquadri, J., and Hall, R. V. (in press). The longitudinal effects of classwide peer tutoring, *Journal of Educational Psychology*.

Greenwood, C. R., Dinwiddie, G., Bailey, V., Carta, J. J., Dorsey, D., Kohler, F. W., Nelson, C., Rotholz, D., and Schulte, D. (1987). Field replication of classwide peer tutoring, *Journal of Applied Behavior Analysis*, **20**, 151–160.

Greenwood, C. R., Dinwiddie, G., Terry, B., Wade, L., Stanley, S., Thibadeau, S., and Delquadri, J. (1984). Teacher- versus peer-mediated instruction: an ecobehavioral analysis of achievement outcomes, *Journal of Applied Behavior Analysis*, **17**, 521–538.

Greenwood, C. R., and Hops, H. (1981). Group contingencies and peer behavior change. In P. Strain (ed.), *The Utilization of Classroom Peers as Behavior Change Agents*, pp. 189–259. New York: Plenum.

Greer, R. D., and Polirstok, S. R. (1982). Collateral gains and short-term maintenance in reading and on-task responses by some inner-city adolescents as a function of their use of social reinforcement while tutoring, *Journal of Applied Behavior Analysis*, **15**, 123–139.

Heron, T. E., Heward, W. L., Cooke, N. L., and Hill, D. S. (1983). Evaluation of classwide peer tutoring systems: first graders teach each other sight words, *Education and Treatment of Children*, **6**, 137–152.

Heward, W. L., Heron, T. E., and Cooke, N. L. (1982). Tutor huddle: key element in a classwide peer tutoring system, *Elementary Education Journal*, November, 115–123.

Jenkins, J. R., and Jenkins, L. M. (1981). *Cross Age and Peer Tutoring: Help for Children with Learning Problems*. The Council for Exceptional Children, Reston, VA.

Jenkins, J. R., and Jenkins, L. M. (1988). Peer tutoring in elementary and secondary programs, *Focus on Exceptional Children*, **17**, 1–12.

Jenkins, J. R., Mayhall, W. F., Peschka, C. M., and Jenkins, L. M. (1974). Comparing small group instruction and tutorial instruction in resource rooms, *Exceptional Children*, **40**, 245–250.

Johnson, D. W., and Johnson, R. T. (1974). Instructional goal structure: cooperative, competitive or individualistic, *Review of Educational Research*, **44**, 213–240.

Johnson, D. W., and Johnson, R. T. (1983). Effects of cooperative, competitive, and individualistic learning experiences on social development, *Exceptional Children*, **49**, 323–329.

Johnson, D. W., Johnson, R. W., and Scott, L. (1978): The effects of cooperative and individualized instruction on students' attitudes and achievement, *Journal of School Psychology*, **104**, 207–216.

Johnson, D. W., Johnson, R. T., Warring, D., and Maruyama, G. (1986). Different cooperative learning procedures and cross-handicap relationships, *Exceptional Children*, **53**, 247–252.

Johnson, D. W., Maruyama, G., Johnson, R., Nelson, D., and Skon, L. (1981). Effects of cooperative, competitive and individualistic goal structures on achievement: a meta-analysis, *Psychological Bulletin*, **89**, 47–62.

Johnson, M., and Bailey, J. S. (1974). Cross-age tutoring: fifth graders as arithmetic tutors for kindergarten children, *Journal of Applied Behavior Analysis*, **7**, 223–232.

Kalfus, G. R. (1984). Peer mediated intervention: a critical review, *Child and Family Behavior Therapy*, **6**, 17–43.

Keller, F. S. (1968). "Good-Bye Teacher . . .", *Journal of Applied Behavior Analysis*, **1**, 79–89.

Kennedy, M. (1978). Findings from the follow through planned variation study, *Educational Researcher*, **7**, 3–11.

Kohler, F. W. (1986). *Classwide Peer Tutoring: Examining Natural Contingencies of Peer Reinforcement*, Doctoral Dissertation, Department of Human Development and Family Life, University of Kansas, Lawrence, KS.

Kohler, F. W. (1987, May). *Peer-Mediation in the Integrated Classroom: A Presentation of Research at the LEAP Preschool*, Symposium presented at the Thirteenth Annual Convention of the Association for Behavior Analysis, Nashville, TN.

Kohler, F. W., Richardson, T., Mina, C., Dinwiddie, G., and Greenwood, C. R. (1985). Establishing cooperative peer relations in the classroom, *The Pointer*, Summer, 12–16.

Kuergleis, B., Deutchman, L., and Paine, S. (1980). *Effects of Explicit Timings on Students' Transitions*. Direction Instruction Follow Through Project, University of Oregon, Eugene, OR.

Leinhardt, G. (1980). Transition rooms: promoting maturation or reducing education?, *Journal of Educational Psychology*, **72**, 55–61.

Levin, H., Glass, G., and Meister, G. (1984). *Cost-Effectiveness of Four Educational Interventions* (Report No. 84-All). Institute for Research in Educational Finance and Governance (IFG), Stanford University, Stanford, CA.

Lucker, G., Rosenfield, D., Sikes, J., and Aronson, E. (1976). Performance in the interdependent classroom: a field study, *American Educational Research Journal*, **13**, 115–123.

Madden, N. A., Slavin, R. E., and Stevens, R. J. (1986). *Cooperative Integrated Reading and Composition: Teacher's Manual*. Baltimore, MD: Johns Hopkins University Center for Research on Elementary and Middle Schools.

Maheady, L., and Harper, G. (1987). A classwide peer tutoring program to improve the spelling test performance of low-income, third- and fourth-grade students, *Education and Treatment of Children*, **10**, 120–133.

Maheady, L., Sacca, M. K., and Harper, G. F. (1988). Classwide peer tutoring program with mildly handicapped high school students, *Exceptional Children*, **55**, 52–59.

Maheady, L., and Sainato, D. (1985). The effects of peer tutoring upon the social status and social interaction patterns of high and low status elementary students, *Education and Treatment of Children*, **8**, 51–65.

McCarty, T., Griffin, S., Apolini, T., and Shores, R. E. (1977). Increased peer teaching with group-oriented contingencies for arithmetic performance in behavior-disordered adolescents, *Journal of Applied Behavior Analysis*, **10**, 313.

Meyer, L. A. (1984). Long-term academic effects of the direct instruction project follow through, *Elementary School Journal*, **84**, 380–394.

Niedermeyer, F. C. (1970). Effects of training on the instructional behaviors of student tutors, *Journal of Educational Research*, **64**, 119–123.

Osguthorpe, R. T., and Scruggs, T. E. (1986). Special education students as tutors: a review and analysis, *Remedial and Special Education*, **7**, 15–26.

Pigott, H. E., Fantuzzo, J. W., and Clement, P. W. (1986). The effects of reciprocal peer tutoring and group contingencies on the academic performance of elementary school children, *Journal of Applied Behavior Analysis*, **19**, 93–98.

Redfield, D. L., and Rousseau, E. W. (1981). A meta-analysis of experimental research on teacher questioning behavior, *Review of Educational Research*, **51**, 237–245.

Rotholz, D. A., Kamps, D., and Greenwood, C. R. (1989). Ecobehavioral assessment and analysis of special education settings for students with autism, *Journal of Special Education*, **23**, 59–81.

Rosenshine, B. V. (1983). Teaching functions in instructional programs, *The Elementary School Journal*, 335–352.

Rosenshine, B., and Stevens, R. (1986). Teaching Functions. In M. C. Wittrock (ed.), *The Handbook of Research on Teaching*, pp. 376–391. New York: Macmillan.

Sharan, S. (1980). Cooperative learning in small groups: recent methods and effects on achievement attitudes and ethnic relations, *Review of Educational Research*, **50**, 241–271.

Sharan, S., and Sharan, Y. (1976). *Small-Group Teaching*. Englewood Cliffs, NJ: Education Technology Publications.

Slavin, R. (1980). Effects of student teams and peer tutoring on academic achievement and time on task, *Journal of Experimental Education*, **48**, 252–257.

Slavin, R. (1984). Students motivating students to excel: cooperative incentives, cooperative tasks, and student achievement, *Elementary School Journal*, **85**, 53–64.

Slavin, R. E., Leavey, M. B., and Madden, N. A. (1984). Combining cooperative learning and individualized instruction: effects on student mathematics achievement, attitudes and behaviors, *The Elementary School Journal*, **84**, 409–422.

Slavin, R. E., Madden, N. A., and Leavey, M. (1984). Effects of team assisted individualization on the mathematics achievement of academically handicapped and nonhandicapped students, *Journal of Educational Psychology*, **76**, 813–819.

Stallings, J. A., and Stipek, D. (1986). Research on early childhood and elementary school teaching programes. In M. C. Wittrock (ed.), *The Handbook of Research on Teaching*, pp. 727–753. New York: Macmillan.

Stebbins, L. B., St. Pierre, R. G., Proper, E. C., Anderson, R. B., and Cerva, T. R. (1977). *Education as Experimentation: A Planned Variation Model* (Vols IV A–D). Cambridge, MA: Apt Associates.

Stevens, R. J., Madden, M. B., Slavin, R. E., and Farnish, A. M. (1987). Cooperative integrated reading and composition: two field experiments, *Reading Research Quarterly*, **22**, 433–453.

Vargas, J. S. (1984). What are your exercises teaching?: an analysis of stimulus control in instructional materials. In W. L. Heward, T. E. Heron, J. Trap-Porter, and D. S. Hill (eds), *Focus on Behavior Analysis in Education*, pp. 126–144. Columbus, OH: Charles Merrill.

Wagner, L. (1982). *Peer Teaching: Historical Perspectives*. Westport, CT: Greenwood Press. Webb, N. (1982). Peer interaction and learning in cooperative small groups, *Journal of Educational Psychology*, **74**, 642–655.

Whorton, D., Walker, D., Locke, P., Delquadri, J., and Hall, R. V. (1989). Increasing academic skills of students with autism using fifth grade peer tutors, *Education and Treatment of Children*, **12**, 38–51.

Wilcox, J., Sbardellati, E., and Nevin, A. (1987). Cooperative learning groups aid integration, *Teaching Exceptional Children*, **20**, 61–63.

Young, C. C. (1981). Children as instructional agents for handicapped peers: a review and analysis. In P. Strain (ed.), *The Utilization of Classroom Peers as Behavior Change Agents*, pp. 305–326. New York: Plenum.

Young, C. C., Hecimovic, A., and Saltzberg, C. L. (1983). Tutor–tutee behavior of disadvantaged kindergarten children during peer teaching, *Education and Treatment of Children*, **6**, 123–135.

Vargas, E.S. (1984). What are your exercises teaching? an analysis of stimulus control in instructional materials. In W. L. Heward, T. E. Heron, J. Trap-Porter, and D. S. Hill (eds), *Focus on Behavior Analysis in Education*, pp. 126–144. Columbus, OH: Charles Merrill.
Wagner, L. (1982). *Peer Teaching: Historical Perspectives*. Westport, CT: Greenwood Press. Webb, N. (1982). Peer interaction and learning in cooperative small groups. *Journal of Educational Psychology*, **74**, 642–655.
Wharton, D., Walker, D., Locke, P., Delquadri, J., and Hall, R. V. (1989). Increasing academic skills of students with autism using fifth grade peer tutors. *Education and Treatment of Children*, **12**, 38–51.
Wilcox, J., Sbardellati, E., and Nevin, A. (1987). Cooperative learning groups aid integration. *Teaching Exceptional Children*, **20**, 61–63.
Young, C. C. (1981). Children as instructional agents for handicapped peers: a review and analysis. In P. S. Strain (ed.), *The Utilization of Classroom Peers as Behavior Change Agents*, pp. 305–326. New York: Plenum.
Young, C. C., Hecimovic, A., and Salzberg, C. L. (1983). Tutor–tutee behavior of disadvantaged kindergarten children during peer teaching. *Education and Treatment of Children*, **6**, 123–135.

CHAPTER 10

# Cooperative Learning Among Special Students

ADRIAN F. ASHMAN and JOHN ELKINS

*Fred and Eleanor Schonell Special Education Research Centre, University of Queensland, St Lucia, Queensland 4067, Australia*

## INTRODUCTION

When we were attending school, perhaps too many years ago, competition was a prominent feature of the school environment. Students were graded and sometimes assigned to their seats in the classroom according to their level of achievement. The most academically competent students often were seated in the back row of the class, and the least competent occupied the front row, usually within ruler-reach of the teacher's desk.

Even in 'enlightened' schoolrooms in which teachers 'managed' learning using Skinnerian principles, the external signs of competition were visible, translated into stars, checkmarks, and other indications of success displayed for all to see on wall charts and class progress boards. It was not easy to overlook who were the achievers and who were not. For students with learning or developmental disabilities in these situations, open competition generally meant failure, both inside and outside of the classroom (Elkins, 1987).

Today, support for cooperation among students can be seen in the adoption of mixed ability teaching by some schools rather than streaming students into homogeneous classes (Bailey and Bridges, 1983; Sands and Kerry, 1982). In the area of literacy, cooperative approaches have become popular. Instead of

Children Helping Children
Edited by H. C. Foot, M. J. Morgan and R. H. Shute

teacher-directed instruction in reading and writing, students are expected to act as the first source of assistance to others. Cambourne (1987) quotes a student's comment to illustrate the different classroom organization.

> I guess I learn a lot from talking with other kids. Sometimes I talk with the teacher, but you're only supposed to do that when others in the class haven't been able to help you. Usually I just have a go and then share my go with someone else. In this class you can always put hard things away and come back to them later when you learn a bit more about how it's done. (p. 43)

However, not all classrooms are structured so that students *expect* the first level of assistance to be provided by other students.

Atwell (1987) noted that attempts to foster collaborative writing in junior high school students often produce negative consequences for the students because teachers in other classes regard cooperation as 'cheating'. Nonetheless, she observed that students who had experienced collaborative writing continued the practice despite official opprobrium. She noted that 'students became avariciously adept at passing a new kind of forbidden note, a draft to which they wanted a friend to write a response' (p. 37).

## COOPERATIVE LEARNING

The notion of students working together on projects, and assisting each other on difficult tasks has become a regular part of school life even though it may not be the dominant mode. Particularly outside the classroom, teamwork is an important part of sporting activities. At home, cooperation is also an essential element, regardless of the level of competence of children. Siblings help and support siblings, and in the case of a family containing a child with special needs, brothers and sisters have much to contribute in terms of care and education (Senapati and Hayes, 1988).

Within the classroom, there are many activities that can enhance student participation in the teaching and learning process. Brainstorming, feedback, and sharing sessions in large and small groups are important strategies that can lead to an improvement in the 'quality of school life'. The cohesiveness or friction existing within the class group, the degree of student involvement in the learning process, teacher support, clarity of class and school rules, teacher control and the degree of innovation apparent within the teaching strategies are all factors to be considered by the teacher. These, together with attitudinal variables appear to have an influence not only on the quality of school life in terms of cooperation, but also on learning outcomes (Fraser, 1986).

Cooperation between students is a key element of specific teaching strategies such as classwide peer tutoring (Delquadri *et al.*, 1986), reciprocal teaching (Palincsar, Brown, and Martin, 1987), or Process-based Instruction (Ashman and Conway, 1989). Cooperation was introduced to the education literature in the mid-1970s as a teaching strategy designed to improve social interaction between students, and the resulting movement is often referred to as Cooperative Learning (Johnson and Johnson, 1974, 1975).

Cooperative Learning involves the organization of the classroom activities and structure so that cooperation between students is necessary to attain mutually attractive objectives. The approach requires students to perceive individual needs for assistance, the acceptance of skills and experience in collaborative efforts, and the regular monitoring of individual contributions to the group activities.

Reviews of the Cooperative Learning literature indicate general support from teachers and point to consistent successes in improving social behaviour, especially with non-disabled students (Lloyd *et al.*, 1988). While Cooperative Learning researchers may prescribe the nature of the peer contacts, the interactions desired and expected, and make these contingent upon rewards, many teachers implement similar procedures within their classrooms without necessarily pursuing the Johnson and Johnson (1974) model.

In general, reports of cooperative classroom endeavours have indicated an improvement in student productivity, and the development of a more favourable classroom climate (Cohen, Kulik and Kulik, 1982). Smith (1987) also reported that his students perceived several advantages in the use of Cooperative Learning over other teaching strategies. These included the opportunity to share ideas, to achieve better quality products, to gather information from more diverse sources, to generate more ideas, to open up lines of communication between students, to stimulate interest in curriculum tasks and to improve self-confidence.

The success of cooperative learning activities depends upon the skill of the teacher in developing students' skills in contributing ideas, providing useful feedback to others, organizing time and priorities, and remaining on-task. The key to the success of Cooperative Learning appears to be the students' knowledge that success depends upon the involvement of others. As Smith (1987) commented '. . . students must realize that they will sink or swim together' (p. 664). However, other cooperative teaching and learning strategies may not demand the shared commitment of students.

In the past, most instructional materials have been provided on an individual basis, thus predisposing classroom activities toward either whole group or individual/parallel activities (see Wagner, this volume). In recent years, computers have become widespread in schools, but often they are fewer in number than the size of the student groups who need to use them at the one time. Thus many teachers have approached computer and word processor use in the classroom as small group activities. Indeed, if students are required to work individually, they may well compete for restricted opportunities to use the equipment, and undesirable consequences are likely for low ability or unassertive students. Pekin (1988) noted that support for cooperative learning tasks with the computer can be found in the research literature (Johnson and Johnson, 1985a; Watt and Watt, 1986) and in the reports of teachers (Carr, 1986;

Dale, 1986; Martin, 1986). Students within groups can discuss some tasks to obtain consensus, can assign roles and responsibilities within the group, ensure through evaluation that all students participate and contribute, and that there is some corporate responsibility for individual learning.

## THE NATURE OF LEARNING AND INSTRUCTION

Having considered briefly some contextual aspects of cooperation, we turn now to the nature of learning and teaching. Instruction and learning are complementary activities. Learning is not simply the result of teachers presenting information. It involves the complex interaction of ecological variables (classroom climate, use of space and time, and the involvement of the student in the instructional process), curriculum variables (the sequence of content, the use of teaching aids), direct teaching variables (keeping students on-task, organization of input, quality and quantity of feedback), and learner variables (Leinhardt and Putnam, 1987; Marsh, Price, and Smith, 1983). As such, the study of cooperative teaching and learning practices within special classes or with exceptional students requires consideration of the nature of instruction for students with special needs.

Current teaching practices with special education students are based upon the assumption that special programme options are more likely to satisfy the needs of students than the provision of regular class instruction. The implication of this assertion is that, through special programmes, students receive more intensive instruction (e.g. teacher attention) than would be provided in other settings. Indeed, the more time students spend on-task, the greater will be the achievement.

Two studies have provided some data concerning the form of instruction (quality or quantity) provided to students with a learning difficulty (e.g. a specific problem with reading, mathematics or spelling) or a mild intellectual disability (i.e. a person with an IQ of 55 and inappropriate social skills for his or her age). The first study examined the quality of instruction and the second the quantity of instruction.

Sindelar *et al.* (1986) observed the instructional behaviour of teachers of mildly intellectually disabled and learning disabled students. Teachers spent approximately 80% of in-class time on instructional activities (similar to studies of regular classes). Of this time, teachers of intellectually disabled students spent approximately 60% on teacher-directed activities, whereas only 40% of allocated time was devoted to teacher-directed activities in the classes for learning disabled students. More importantly, time spent in independent instructional activities was unrelated to achievement gains, contrary to results from regular class programmes (see for example, Fisher *et al.*, 1978); learning disabled students benefited more from observing classmates' interactions.

Ysseldyke *et al.* (1987) reported a study in which regular students and those with a learning difficulty, a mild intellectual disability, or a behaviour disorder were observed over an entire school day. Ysseldyke *et al.* reported several interesting findings. First, few differences were noted between the amount of time allocated to student groups across curriculum area during the typical school day, though students with an intellectual disability were allocated less time for science, and had more free time than students in all other groups. The researchers also noted that intellectually disabled students received a greater proportion of time devoted to academic instruction in special classes than peers in regular classes. However, significantly less time was allocated to academic instruction of intellectually disabled students in self-contained classes than for similar students in special or regular classes.

Ysseldyke *et al.* do not provide information in regard to the quality of the instruction received by the various groups of students. However, they concluded that it appears that students with an intellectual disability can do little more than maintain their relative position of handicap if access to flexible programming alternatives is limited and if options do not address areas of instructional needs. One study has addressed the issue of instructional differences. Sindelar *et al.* (1986) reported that teachers devote different proportions of instructional time to different activities, and that students with special needs respond in different ways to certain strategies. For example, learning disabled children benefited more from watching classmates interact with their teacher than other students in the same circumstances.

## Social skill development

Social skill deficits are one of the more pervasive problems encountered by teachers of students with learning and intellectual disabilities. These deficits are observed in all categories of students with special needs. They appear in the early years and become more prominent and serious with increasing age. While social skills deficits *per se* are the major cause of concern with students with a behaviour disorder, their impact upon learning and other intellectual domains causes social skill training to be among the more important non-academic programmes introduced in special class environments.

Numerous programmes have been devised to ameliorate social skill deficits in exceptional children. These have included teacher involvement in management programmes, developing behaviour change through modelling and role playing activities, and other peer-oriented interventions. Having their peers initiate social interactions with exceptional children as a treatment for their social skills deficits was used because of various observed limitations of teacher-mediated interventions, notably the short period of implementation. Consequently, teachers have come to realize the value of using peers as change agents to overcome the limitations associated with reliance on teachers as the sole agent of change.

## Generating independent learning skills

Perhaps one of the most important areas of development in the domain of intellectual skills related to the classroom is that of independent learning and problem solving. Some ten years ago, cognitive researchers devoted considerable energy to the development of information processing strategies which would enhance students' learning. Initially, the focus of attention was improvement in the students' use of memory aids and strategies. However, over the past decade, researchers have turned their attention to the development of superordinate processes (such as planning and organizational strategies, and a knowledge of one's own cognition, i.e. metacognition).

The reason behind this shift in emphasis was the realization that students needed more than just the skill of organizing information. They also needed to be aware of *how* they organized information, and how skills could be applied to a variety of tasks, or in various situations. In other words, they needed the capability of adaptation (see for example, Belmont, Butterfield, and Ferretti, 1982). Such superordinate activities imply a self-management component which challenges the individual to set goals, plan for goal achievement, test the plan, evaluate the effectiveness of the plan, and amend the plan if it is not successful.

Researchers have explored various aspects of students' self-management skills in both laboratory and classroom settings. These have included self-instruction, self-recording, self-monitoring, and self-regulation in learning disabled and intellectually disabled students.

Self-instruction has been the focus of cognitive behavioural instruction techniques, the most prominent of these being verbal self-instruction (Meichenbaum and Goodman, 1971). These approaches are based upon the premise that students can be taught to work through a series of self-instruction steps to facilitate learning and problem solving. Five stages are commonly involved in cognitive behaviour managements approaches: cognitive modelling, in which the instructor models the self-instruction behaviour; overt external guidance, in which the student performs the task while the teacher provides the instructions; overt self-guidance, in which the student performs the activity while providing the instructions out aloud; faded self-guidance, in which the student whispers instructions while performing the activity; and covert self-instruction, in which the student performs the task while using internal (or private) language (Ashman and Conway, 1989).

Such self-instruction techniques have been used with students experiencing difficulties in specific academic areas such as reading and mathematics, and with students with a mild intellectual disability, though many of these approaches have also included other self-generated monitoring components (Brown, Campione, and Barclay, 1979).

The major issue associated with self-instruction techniques is the concern with the robust nature of the intervention. While researchers have argued that these techniques are effective for improving attention and academic skills through the provision of routines for selecting, producing, monitoring, and modifying important trained cognitive strategies (Litrownik *et al.*, 1978; Rooney, Hallahan, and Lloyd, 1984; Ryan, Short, and Weed, 1986), others have shown less enthusiasm for the technique (Borkowski and Varnhagen, 1984; Leon and Pepe, 1983; Snider, 1987).

Borkowski and Varnhagen (1984), for example, used mildly intellectually disabled students to examine strategy maintenance and generalization following traditional strategy training and following a self-instruction format which provided strategy initiation and modification routines. Borkowski and Varnhagen focused attention on reading comprehension and specifically on paraphrasing and serial anticipation skills. Both processes appear to be important for understanding a theme and recalling the plot of a story. The anticipation strategy included monitoring and self-testing aspects.

The results of their study showed that students using the self-instruction format did not demonstrate performance superior to the students involved in the traditional strategy training programme. They concluded that the potential effectiveness of any self-instruction package appears to be dependent upon the inclusion of detailed strategy-relevant information or a set of executive skills missing from the students' existing repertoire. One additional limitation of self-instructional techniques appears to be the reliance on teacher-designed and teacher-imposed instruction sequences which pay little attention to how individual students would prefer to undertake the learning activity.

Snider (1987), in her conclusion of a review of self-monitoring research with learning disabled students, provides support for Borkowski and Varnhagen's findings. Snider stated that self-monitoring appears to increase students' on-task behaviour in classroom activities. However, research has not shown that self-monitoring leads to academic gains. She suggested that the consequence of much self-monitoring research is teaching students how to pay attention. While this might be effective if the student possesses the necessary prerequisite skills, it does not lead to a change in academic behaviour unless the student knows the importance of the content.

## Expanding students' involvement in the learning process

Strategy plus metastrategy training has become an important innovation in instruction of students with special needs. This has extended researchers' involvement in areas such as cooperative learning through peer interactions. The importance of metacognition in any learning activity (including collaborative learning activities) appears to be well-established. This process involves the ability to make evaluations and to control the outcomes of one's cognitive activities. Within the cooperative learning context, instruction in superordinate processes can enhance students' understanding of the manner in which learning and problem solving occurs. Emphasis on metacognition (in particular) has been explored in the cooperative learning context in order to gauge the improvement in acquisition of information by the students involved.

In one study, Larson *et al.* (1985) examined the relative contribution of metacognitive versus elaborative activity to reading performance during cooperative learning. This study used college students as subjects; however, the results are of some interest to us at this point. They suggested that an *emphasis on metacognitive activity* facilitated cooperative learning but did not help transfer, while an *emphasis on elaborative activity* facilitated transfer to individual learning behaviour. It seems that students can assist each other in correcting errors and detecting important information. Larson *et al.* suggested that the lack of transfer related to the metacognition condition arose from the lack of direct instruction focusing on improvement of individual skills. On the other hand, elaboration involved the personalization of content, and may have provided the stimulus for exploring ways in which strategies might be transferred to tasks outside the training context.

Other writers have emphasized the need to use students as a teaching resource in the classroom. Graham and Harris (1988) proposed that teachers should strive to create a supportive classroom climate which is conducive to skill development (in their case, writing). They argued that teachers should attempt to develop a sense of community to promote sharing and collaboration among students with special needs. Activities that promote cooperation include reading composition to other students, editing written work, brainstorming on a topic, and the introduction of assignments that promote collaboration. Graham and Harris also suggested that teachers should become engaged in the cooperating experience by sharing their creative writing with students.

The value of peer interactions in developing problem-solving skills has also been explored. In a series of two studies, Light and Glachan (1985) used the Tower of Hanoi puzzle to establish whether peer interaction would lead to better individual performance than when students worked alone. They showed that in the collaborative condition (moving puzzle pieces jointly), students produced more efficient problem solutions than in the individual condition, though advantage was only gained by children who showed evidence of a strategic approach at the beginning of the study.

In a second study, a structured integration condition (students moved the pieces in the puzzle jointly), an unstructured interaction (no requirement to move pieces jointly), and an instruction condition (researcher directed movement of pieces but without justification) were introduced. In this study, only the structured interaction condition led to significant gains by the students. In the unstructured condition, most of the moves were made by one student without consultation with the other. In other words, there was no peer tutoring or collaborative activity involved, and the opportunity to resolve conflicts was not available. In a third and fourth study, Light and Glachan used variants of the parlour game, Mastermind, to examine the quality of verbal interactions between students in dyads. They found a positive relationship between the character of the verbal interactions and the progress made by students on the cooperative task.

These studies have suggested that using a peer-oriented teaching or learning condition alone may not necessarily lead to improvement in performance or gains in academic achievement. Rather, it might be concluded that specific conditions may need to be met before the value of collaborative group work can be realized, or perhaps, justified.

Finally, in this section we explore the effectiveness of student-controlled study conditions. Graham and Freeman (1985) examined the spelling performance of students with a learning disability under three experimental conditions: directed study, student-controlled study, and teacher-monitored study. Spelling involves the purposeful memorization of a vocabulary and it is not clear whether student-controlled or idiosyncratic methods for studying spelling will lead to useful performance gains (cf., Graham and Miller, 1979).

Results of the study showed that students' performance on the spelling task improved as a result of adult-imposed plans and procedures. Students who were taught a task-specific strategy and instructed to use the procedure independently performed more competently on the immediate recall of spelling words than students who worked independently. This result indicated that students do not have a problem in learning how to regulate their study behaviour. Graham and Harris (1988) argued that the study showed that students with learning problems should not be allowed to devise their own study plans as they are unlikely to generate effective strategies on their own.

In terms of working together in peer tutoring activities, it would still be possible for the students to generate inefficient strategies, so teacher monitoring of the learning activity would be necessary to identify and rectify inappropriate or inaccurate student instruction and feedback. However, as the Graham and Harris study showed, once the efficient strategy had been established, student-controlled interventions can be as effective as those controlled by teachers.

## LESSONS FROM THE REGULAR CLASSROOM

Peer tutoring has been described as a teaching and learning process. It involves the exposure of students to material to be learned, together with rehearsal of curriculum tasks to improve retention and, in some cases, the development of superordinate cognitive skills (Collier, 1980). In other words, peer tutoring is a context in which students learn to learn.

The explicit goal of peer tutoring is usually that of academic gain for the tutee. However, as has been shown in numerous studies, the tutor can also benefit from the tutoring experience. What contributes to these gains?

Four factors have been proposed by Cohen (1986) as major contributors to the success or otherwise of peer tutoring activities. These include:

1. the individualized nature of peer tutoring which improves upon the teacher to student ratio typically found in the regular (and special) classroom;
2. the positive effect of modelling which increases the similarity factor and enhances the possibility of identification;
3. the likelihood of encouraging the use of tangible, social, academic and moral reinforcements, leading to an increase in tutee motivation; and,
4. the potency of a peer as a means of providing instruction and reinforcement in the most effective manner (e.g. using student- rather than teacher-language).

Besides the stated advantages of peer tutoring as a means of improving the academic skills of students, there are several advantages in terms of the social benefits. Peer tutoring has been suggested as a means of promoting interactions between students, a means of developing social skills such as listening, understanding, providing feedback, and of resolving differences. For the tutor, Cohen (1986) claimed that peer tutoring trains empathy, management and organizational skills, persistence, concentration, setting standards, and taking responsibility. These academic and social benefits, however, are not automatic gains from peer tutoring.

While the majority of peer tutoring studies have shown positive gains from the cooperative teaching activity, some writers have been less than enthusiastic about the possible advantages to both the tutor and the tutee. McKellar (1985) recognized that there is wide variation in the behaviours used by students in a tutoring dyad. She argued that students have a general understanding of what is involved in teaching or tutoring which is, in part, determined by training as a tutor, or through the classroom teacher's modelling. McKellar examined the specific behaviours which untrained college students used when they were engaged in tutoring and the relationship between behaviour and performance.

McKellar found that tutors imitate those behaviours which have been modelled for that person, though the most frequent behaviours exhibited by either the tutor or the tutee were not among the behaviours which generally predict success. Typically, there is a positive correlation between achievement and the giving and receiving of explanations and elaborations. For the tutee, the most important factor is the development of relationships between the new information and that which the tutee already possesses. When the tutor elaborates upon the content and relates it to other experiences and ideas with which the students are familiar, both gain. McKellar found that the only tutee behaviour predictive of the tutees' scores was asking for clarification, which implies an evaluation by the tutee that certain information was not clear. Such active involvement of the tutee in evaluating what was being taught may also have involved comparison and association between what was already in the tutee's memory and the information being presented at the time.

One significant point raised by McKellar relates to the special education context, namely, the inclusion of inaccurate or incorrect instruction or explanations by the tutors. Few peer tutoring researchers comment upon the extent to which incorrect information is given to the tutee by the tutor, though it is a concern in programmes in which both students are of low ability. In a special education classroom, it is likely that many instances of incorrect information or explanations could occur in peer tutoring situations when supervision is less frequent than tutoring. For instance, in a study by Bar-Eli and Raviv (1982), tutoring occurred three times a week while the experimenter only made weekly visits to supervise, advise and assist.

The question of whether peer tutoring works or not appears to have been resolved many times over. Both teachers and researchers have documented the advantages to both tutors and tutees in terms of improvement in academic performance and social skills. Harvey and Johnston (1986) for instance, reported a case of cross-age tutoring using Grade 5 children to assist Grade 2 students with oral reading. Harvey and Johnston asked the older children to write down their thoughts about their tutoring activities. Their comments demonstrated enthusiasm for the programme with changes occurring in the tutors' learning style, their ability to interact with younger children and to break down the segregation of the sexes.

A somewhat more structured approach to peer tutoring in the reading domain grew from the doctoral work of Manzo (1968). His ReQuest procedure was designed to encourage students to formulate their own questions about the material they were reading, thereby developing an active inquiring approach which would enhance students' reading independence. While Manzo only focused upon teacher–student interactions, the procedure has many similarities with those more recently developed.

Manzo's approach involved a teacher and student reading sections of text together and taking turns asking and answering questions about the material. The teacher modelled good questioning behaviour, provided feedback to the student about the child's questions and evaluated the effectiveness of questions in terms of their purpose. He proposed six steps: (a) preparing appropriate material and questions which would aid prediction; (b) developing the student's readiness for the strategy by explaining the purpose of the reading activity; (c) developing students' questioning behaviour by alternating the 'instructional role' between teacher and student; (d) developing students' predictive behaviours; (e) reading silently through the story to verify predictive questions; and, (f) introducing follow-up activities that encourage the student to manipulate the ideas presented in the story.

Reciprocal Teaching appears to be the peer tutoring extension of Manzo's approach, emphasizing varying degrees of teacher assistance depending upon the student's competence, active participation of the student in the teaching–learning process, and the gradual withdrawal of teacher support as the novice develops independent reading skills (called 'scaffolding'), and the provision of feedback to the student concerning the effectiveness of the strategies being used.

The evidence for the success of reciprocal teaching has been demonstrated in numerous studies, and the technique has been shown to be successful in increasing comprehension scores of children with reading difficulties. The foci of attention in reciprocal teaching are four strategies: questioning, summarizing, clarifying, and predicting, representing the activities manifested by successful, strategic readers. Palincsar and Brown (1987) have described reciprocal teaching within the framework of peer instruction, emphasizing not only the strategies used by successful readers, but also the typical teacher–student interactions that characterize peer tutoring activities.

Palincsar and Brown indicate that four strategies are typical of successful readers. They rephrase information and seek relationships among the ideas presented and they are alert to breakdowns in comprehension. A *predicting* strategy is employed as a before-reading activity when the reader activates knowledge which enables the anticipation of content. *Questioning* and *summarizing* represents strategies that are useful during the act of reading. When employed after reading, questioning and summarizing provide a means of consolidating information and ascertaining that what has been read has also been integrated. *Clarifying* occurs on many levels. Students use clarifying strategies during the activity of reading, focusing on words or material that are not immediately clear.

These four strategies are important for focusing students' attention on the content being presented in the written passage, and also are involved in the monitoring procedure which maintains contact with comprehension. Palincsar and Brown (1988) have emphasized the collaborative learning nature of reciprocal teaching which takes place in the socially relevant context typically undertaken in small groups in which students are jointly working on the understanding of reading material. Palincsar and Brown stated that students are often in an advantaged position to help one another on a reading task since they are more likely to experience the same difficulties, and to generate their own effective solutions.

Other small group instruction alternatives have addressed curriculum areas other than reading. For example, Tripp (1979a) considered corporate thinking which occurred in the context of small group discussions. He used data from an evaluation of de Bono's (1971) CoRT thinking skills materials, and aimed to codify group discussion both in form and content. Analysis proceeds via a matrix of statements and their occurrence which enables the flow of ideas to be mapped, and subsidiary analyses to be undertaken (such as balance of argument, process, judgement and content). While aspects of Tripp's technique are tantalizingly vague, it does point the way to a richer investigation of how students teach each other through discussion. Tripp (1979b) also considered small group discussions to be valuable for slower students.

Bickel and Bickel (1986) draw attention to the influence of ways in which children are grouped. While they did not elaborate on these in the context of students teaching students, the following factors should receive further consideration: (a) the number and size of groups in relation to student characteristics and subject content, and (b) how and when group membership is changed.

The effects of grade level and perceived ability on social interaction in groups of children who were not familiar with each other were examined by Dembo and McAuliffe (1987). They found that actual status (grade) produced more effect than induced status (assigned bogus ability), but that both produced social interaction benefits, including helping behaviours. However, students did not prefer to ask for help from either type of high status students, who also tended to respond negatively to help offered by low status students. There were also complex interactions in heterogeneous groups, particularly for students of mixed status (i.e. high/low grade and low/high 'ability'). One implication of this study is that pre-existing status effects might be reduced by suggesting that success on new tasks is unrelated to known abilities. However, this may lead to complex and not entirely desirable outcomes. Dembo and McAuliffe suggest focusing on task-relevant abilities to minimize defensiveness by students of mixed status, but note that low ability students may need to be encouraged to seek help in order to maximize their interactional participation in the group.

## SPECIAL STUDENTS AS INSTRUCTORS AND LEARNERS

The current movement in special education is toward the integration of students with special needs into mainstream or regular classes. The problem for the teacher becomes one of providing appropriate instruction within a classroom in which the range of student abilities is very wide. Including a student with a learning or intellectual disability in classwide academic activities can be a major concern. Students may be left out of classroom activities for which a higher level of achievement is required than they possess, or they may not remain on-task when the teacher's attention is drawn to other students.

Some variations in cooperative learning procedures discussed earlier have been introduced to help recognize the contribution of low achieving students (Slavin, 1985a). Johnson and Johnson (1985b) claim that low achieving children consistently benefit from cooperative learning and that their gains are achieved without detriment to high achievers, who do no worse, and often benefit also. However, Webb (1985) noted that irrespective of their own ability, the most able students on a particular task in a group will function as 'explainer'. Slavin (1985b) noted that cooperative learning was particularly beneficial in heterogeneous mathematics classes, where because of the sequential nature of learning, teachers otherwise tend to move at the pace of the slowest student.

In discussing special education, Sapon-Shevin (1978) has argued that the competitive environment increases the apparent differences between students, while cooperation makes a virtue of them. It may prove that the clearer reward structure which pertains in competitive situations will give better results for special education students than cooperative approaches. This conjecture leads to testing whether group rewards would enhance learning in cooperative situations.

As far as can be ascertained, students with special needs have not been consulted about their preferences for competitive/cooperative learning. This situation stands in contrast with regular school students who have been shown to favour or dislike both competition and cooperation independently (Owens and Stratton, 1980). Thus, some children may favour working individually, some competition but not cooperation, others the reverse while all modes are favoured by the remainder. It seems important for the preferences of special education students to be determined if they are to be involved in peer or cross-age teaching situations. Moreover, as students prepare to move from school to engage in work and to live in the community, there may be special need for them to be able to operate effectively with others. Thus, housekeeping in a group home may require cooperative decision-making and problem-solving and this may be fostered by school learning structures in which students 'teach' each other. Likewise, work teams in factory enclaves, restaurants or in contract cleaning or landscaping are examples of employment situations in which individual job skills alone are insufficient. Certainly some research in these areas seems overdue.

As indicated by several writers, peer tutoring is not a new phenomenon having been reported as an instructional technique for several centuries (Osguthorpe and Scruggs, 1986; Wagner, this volume). Indeed, the benefits to both tutor and tutees have been reported consistently in the literature, in both cross-age and peer-tutoring configurations. There are three approaches that have been adopted for use with exceptional students. One involves the use of a regular (non-disabled) student to assist a disabled student. A second approach has been to develop peer tutoring dyads of disabled students (in some cases, the more able helping the less able). A third approach has capitalized upon the benefits accruing to the tutor by using disabled students to instruct young, non-disabled students. In the following two sections we will describe these approaches to the use of students as tutors, highlighting the methods and the results of research.

## Non-disabled students helping disabled peers

The technique of using non-disabled children to assist disabled peers has been employed by teachers at all age levels, from preschool to high school. The success of a programme appears to be based upon the effectiveness of the *activity* of tutoring, in other words, what the tutors do to limit the variability of the disabled students' performance.

In some cases, practitioners have described the benefits of interactions between preschool children in terms of integration, with an emphasis being given to the socialization aspects of students helping others (see for example, Baxter, 1988). In other cases, dyadic peer interactions have provided the opportunity for researchers to evaluate the effect of modelling socially appropriate interactions and their long-term benefits.

In one such example, Guralnick and Groom (1987) systematically paired 3- and 4-year-old intellectually disabled and non-disabled children in a series of dyadic play interactions. Each of the children was paired with two others from the playgroup, and each pair was brought together four times over the duration of the study. Mildly handicapped children were paired with younger non-disabled children matched in terms of developmental level, with non-disabled children matched in terms of chronological age, and with other disabled peers. Mixed and same age pairings for the non-disabled children were also arranged.

The researchers found that the interactions of the disabled children improved significantly when they were paired with older children who were not disabled. Positive interaction increased and solitary play decreased for the disabled children, apparently brought about by the more active role taken by the non-disabled children in organizing and managing the interactions. When matched with other disabled peers, and with younger children of equivalent mental age, the disabled children's interactions did not show qualitative improvements.

At levels above the preschool, training in school-related activities has been predicated upon the difficulties encountered by students with intellectual disabilities in solving curriculum-related tasks and problems. Several studies have investigated whether students with a mild intellectual disability can learn to solve curriculum tasks when normal peers act as tutors. In one such study, Lancioni (1982) trained 12 normal 3rd and 4th graders to work as tutors with six mildly disabled students on problems dealing with quantity using the four arithmetic operations (addition, subtraction, multiplication, and division). The results of the study showed that children with simple pre-arithmetic skills and low reading skills could be taught by peers to solve quantity problems. Of interest was the finding that the disabled students were able to isolate distracting information and could solve problems correctly when the problems were presented in a different manner or form, thus increasing their independence from both the context and cues associated with the training.

At the high school level, normal peers have also been engaged in peer tutoring activities with 'slow learners'. Haisley, Tell, and Andrews (1981), for example, argued that curriculum requirements at the high school level place a considerable demand upon disabled students (e.g. changing classes, subject, teachers, emphasis on adaptability, organization, task completion and success). Haisley, Tell, and Andrews developed a peer tutoring programme using Grade 8 and 9 students focused upon the engagement of students with the task and increasing opportunities for tutees to learn. Tutors were taught behaviour management, and other skills relating to task analysis, designing teaching activities, direct instruction and communication.

While little information is given in regard to the ability level of the tutees in the Haisley, Tell and Andrews study (tutees being identified as mainstreamed handicapped students), the results presented by the authors show tutees increased their on-task behaviour during teacher-led activities, when working independently, and during group work to a greater extent than the control students. Moreover, the anecdotal comments of tutees, tutors, and teachers attested to the success of the programme.

Classwide peer tutoring programmes have been introduced in mainstream, resource, and self-contained classes for students with special needs (e.g. mildly intellectually disabled, behaviour disordered), and constitute an extension of peer tutoring programmes in which only one or two children with special needs are tutored. Classwide programmes provide a general structure into which peer tutoring can be placed within the context of the breadth of classroom activities.

In one study, a classwide programme provided direct, individualized instruction to students in a class containing a student with Down's syndrome, and another identified as learning disabled (Cooke *et al.*, 1982). Tutors began the instruction session by gathering in 'tutor huddles' to familiarize themselves with the information to be taught to their tutees (e.g. sight words). All children (except the child with Down's syndrome) were involved in this activity as all acted as tutors using materials developed by the classroom teacher based upon a pre-test. The tutors took turns presenting the material they would be responsible for teaching to the other tutors in the huddle. Tutors in the huddle confirmed the correct responses required or helped identify the material a tutor may not have known and the teacher circulated around huddles giving assistance where it was needed.

After the huddles, partners joined together to work through the material, one tutor presenting the information first, providing the tutee with practice and supportive feedback as necessary. At a predetermined time, the roles changed and the tutor became the tutee. Once completed, the roles changed back and a testing phase began during which time the tutor presented all words again, identifying successful learning and sight words which would remain in a current teaching stack. Cooke *et al.* (1982) reported that all children made substantial gains, including the student with Down's syndrome (though the student never tutored), and were able to learn on average nine new words per week.

The effectiveness of classwide peer tutoring programmes has been reported by Delquadri and his colleagues (Delquadri *et al.*, 1986; Hall *et al.*, 1982). In another recent study, classwide student tutoring teams were used in a programme with mildly intellectually disabled and non-disabled secondary school students. The programme based upon the Delquadri *et al.* approach, operated in a mathematics subject at the Grade 9 and 10 level and a multiple baseline design across setting was used to examine the effects of peer tutoring. Maheady,

Sacca and Harper (1987) reported that there were immediate and systematic increases in the students' performance on the weekly mathematics tests for all students involved in the study, virtually eliminating failing grades. Maheady and Harper (1987) used class-wide peer tutoring with low-income 3rd and 4th grade students to boost scores on spelling tests. However, the techniques used required only low level instruction, with tutor children dictating words to be spelled, and tutees wrote or spelled words aloud. Other oral interactions were confined to praising or supplying correct spelling. It seems that little high-level teaching occurred, though the obvious effectiveness of the strategy suggests that teachers may overlook the potency of simple behavioural techniques of the kind routinely used by special educators. Yet children themselves can easily be trained to deliver such instruction quite effectively. As the authors pointed out:

> peer tutoring is a combination of instructional strategies shown to be effective by previous applied behavioral researchers. High opportunity to respond, rapid pacing, immediate error correction, praise for correct responses, reinforcement for correcting errors, earning of points, and posting and feedback on daily performance were integral parts of this intervention. The success of peer tutoring, we believe, is that it is an efficient means to combine all of the elements described above into a single instructional practice. (p. 131)

**Special students as tutors**

The benefits of peer tutoring in special education have been considered under the heading of tutee benefits and tutor benefits. Perhaps most attention has been given in the special education literature to instructional situations in which the tutee has been a special education student. In this area, emphasis is given primarily to improvement in academic skills as a result of tutoring programmes.

One of the more useful analyses of peer tutoring was provided by Osguthorpe and Scruggs (1986). In their meta-analysis, they examined 26 studies in which special education students were used as tutors of (predominantly) special education peers. While Osguthorpe and Scruggs highlighted the variability in research methodologies (with associated weaknesses), their examination of the effectiveness of tutoring and being tutored across learning disabled, intellectually disabled, and behaviourally disordered classification generally concluded that special education students have much to gain from instruction by their peers.

Of the 26 studies considered, 23 reported treatment effects including improvement in social skills and the consolidation of academic content for the tutors, and improvement in academic skills for the tutees. One typical example of the effectiveness of peer tutoring with special education students was provided in a two-part study by Scruggs and Osguthorpe (1986). In their investigation, they examined the relative advantage of cross-age and peer-tutoring interventions using the same dependent measures.

In the first study, Scruggs and Osguthorpe engaged learning and behaviourally disordered students across Grades 1 to 6 in a cross-age tutoring programme. Their results indicated that the tutees made significant gains over the control group children on a reading diagnostic test and both tutors and tutees made gains on a test of word analysis strategies (for example, syllabification, use of graphemic and phonological cues). On the attitude-to-school instrument, tutees gained significantly (when compared with tutors and control students). In the second study, learning and behaviourally disordered Grade 2 to 5 students were involved in a peer tutoring programme. The same dependent measures were used as in the first experiment, and again students in the experimental group showed significant gains on a test measuring number of words correctly read, though gains on the Woodcock–Johnson word-attack skills subtest were not replicated. No attitude changes were reported. Scruggs and Osguthorpe suggested that their investigations indicated the positive effects of both cross-age and peer tutoring interventions. While such results provide some indication of academic and attitudinal gains resulting from the peer interaction, they are relatively narrow in their generality.

In another recent study, Maheady, Harper, and Sacca (1988) reported on a classwide peer tutoring system (CWPT) which was used in a resource room for adolescents with mild disabilities (mean IQ = 76). The study used two groups (Grade 9, $n = 8$; Grades 10–12, $n = 12$) in an ABAB design. Students were randomly allocated to teams and to dyads within teams. Groupings and pairings were changed each fortnight. Each student tutored the other for 15 minutes (i.e. 30 minutes per day) using 30-item study guides which were changed each week. Tutors asked questions from the guides and checked oral and written responses. Points were awarded for correct responses and tutees wrote out answers for items on which they were incorrect. Tutors were awarded points for good tutoring. Individual and team scores were charted and displayed and points were awarded for a weekly quiz.

Baseline procedures were standard teaching but used the same study guides and quizzes. The mean improvement noted was 18%, sufficient to eliminate failing grades. Withdrawal of CWPT indicated a drop in test performance to baseline levels.

A 10-item rating of CWPT by the 20 students indicated substantial support for the approach, with few indicating dissatisfaction or opposition. Thus, social benefits were apparent in addition to the academic gains directly sought.

Cross-age tutoring has an additional facet, namely, the use of disabled students as tutors of non-disabled peers. In most cases, the various studies that have addressed reverse-role tutoring have focused upon improvements in social skills, or increasing the socialization of the disabled students (see for example, Custer & Osguthorpe, 1983; Eiserman and Osguthorpe, 1985).

In a recent study, Grade 4 to 6 learning and behaviourally disordered students were trained to be tutors of Grade 1 non-disabled children in a 14-week programme. Top and Osguthorpe (1987) pre- and post-tested all children on a test of reading achievement and on several self-esteem measures. The special education students were able to develop effective tutoring skills, thus allaying the fears of parents that the task would be too emotionally and academically demanding.

The results of the study were similar to those reported by Scruggs and Osguthorpe (1986) in the area of academic skills in that both tutors and tutees made significant gains in reading achievement when compared to the control group children. The data dealing with self-concept were less convincing. The investigators reported that the tutors' perception of their teaching skills improved, but there were no changes on the measures of self-esteem. This is not surprising since it is somewhat naive to believe that 16 hours of tutoring would effect a change on a personality characteristic that is thought to develop over a person's lifetime.

The apparent value of peer involvement is not necessarily limited to mild (or educational) disabilities or to school age persons. Moderately and severely intellectually disabled young adults have been involved successfully in peer tutoring/training activities in workshop settings for several years. While it is true that supervisors (non-disabled craftsmen) often provide the bulk of training, disabled workers often are used as models when an employee is receiving training on a new task. In one study, Wacker and Berg (1985) verified the efficacy of using intellectually disabled persons to teach peers work-related skills.

Their project involved two 19-year-old individuals (one moderately and the other severely intellectually disabled) in a programme in which they each taught three other peers to perform various complex assembly line tasks. The two trainers were taught to provide instruction using correct procedures and performance, and to provide appropriate responses when their tutee had performed the selected task correctly. Following the training phase of the project, the tutors monitored the performance of their three tutees who worked independently at separate work stations.

This study is consistent with the many others that have shown benefits accruing to both tutors and tutees. Perhaps the most important implication in this workshop study was the independence of the two trainers both during the instruction, and the monitoring phases. Staff did not need to intervene to maintain the training process. This is an important contribution to workshop settings in which cost and training effectiveness is important, and the development of a pleasant and supportive environment is a key element to efficient workshop operation.

In general, approaches such as those described above provide evidence of the success of students helping others in a variety of instructor/learner configurations. The review of literature raises several important points. First, the studies show that peer tutoring can operate successfully in special tutoring programmes. Perhaps more important have been those studies in which peer tutoring has been introduced in whole classroom groups where teachers have no specific training in working with special education students.

Second, where peer tutoring occurs, there appears to be little need for teachers to provide instruction additional to the usual class schedule. Students can learn to teach effectively, and in doing so, effect academic change in the tutees, and behavioural changes in themselves.

Third, tutoring appears to have a positive impact on students' performance on a variety of dependent measures including teacher-developed tests. However, the majority of studies have evaluated the success of peer tutoring on a very restricted range of measures and over a very short timeframe. There is little evidence, if any, to show the long-term effects of peer tutoring.

## REDEFINING THE LEARNING ENVIRONMENT

Perhaps the most significant contribution of peer tutoring programmes is the movement toward changing the traditional teaching methods and strategies typically employed by classroom teachers in the mainstream. While peer tutoring is hardly an educational innovation, its use in regular and special classroom settings is far from widespread. The approach may suffer the same fate as other initiatives at the hands of teachers who may not be willing to abandon known and effective teaching methods merely because it is a new approach (Cowie and Rudduck, this volume; Sheinker, Sheinker, and Stevens, 1984).

Perhaps one of the limiting factors relating to the general use of systematic peer tutoring approaches has been the lack of data showing the benefits of peer tutoring over other forms of educational innovation. Even where it is possible to convince teachers of the value of peer tutoring, it may be impossible to coordinate cross-age or reverse-role tutoring in schools in which timetabling and scheduling is a major limiting factor.

While the empirical evidence for peer tutoring has shown advantages over (presumably) usual classroom teaching practices, only one paper has reviewed peer tutoring along with other non-traditional methods. Lloyd *et al.* (1988) examined the literature related to the effectiveness of four intervention approaches, namely, Cooperative Learning (Johnson and Johnson, 1975), prereferral, teacher consultation, and peer-mediated interventions (e.g. peer management, tutoring, and modelling).

Lloyd *et al.* commented that reports about the potential for peer-mediated procedures were optimistic though they expressed reservations about the nature of the peer tutoring literature. Their most substantial criticism addressed the lack of a programmatic approach to research. They argued that, in many instances, the continuation of innovative programmes is dependent upon the continuation of a research project that is administered outside the school. They concluded that researchers have been able to address and resolve the easy questions which relate to the effectiveness of the procedures with some students, under some conditions. The more difficult task is establishing the limitations of the various procedures.

The only resolution to this question is the long-term evaluation of peer tutoring which has become an integral, and continuing part of the classroom teaching practice. One might argue that in mainstream classes, developing a peer tutoring programme may be more appropriate and feasible in curriculum areas in which brainstorming and group discussions are considered commonplace (e.g. social studies, English literature) than in more prescriptive curriculum areas, such as mathematics. Moreover, peer-mediated teaching and learning may be more manageable in special education contexts in which achievement and progress through a curriculum and annual promotion through the grades are less heavily emphasized.

The development of student-mediated teaching and learning methods appears to have three advantages for special education students, whether in the role of tutor or tutee. First, the literature suggests that gains in some curriculum areas are likely as a result of cross-age and peer tutoring. While most attention has been given to reading achievement, it would seem unlikely that benefits would be limited to that skill area.

Second, there are obvious advantages to be gained in the area of social development. The literature points to changes in socialization and increased acceptance of special education students by their non-disabled peers (Osguthorpe and Scruggs, 1986; Yogev and Ronen, 1982).

Third, there are gains to be made in terms of increasing the learning and problem-solving independence of special students through the development of higher level skills that are associated with the role of instructor (e.g. questioning, metacognition). Ashman and Conway (1989) have developed an instructional programme designed to increase the students' knowledge, skills, and independence using teacher- and student-mediated instructional strategies.

The basis of the programme is the development of a systematic and planned approach to information presentation (by the instructor) and acquisition (by the student). Peer tutoring plays an important role. To exemplify the instructional role of students in this process, we have provided an example of a peer tutoring session which is taken from a videotape record. In this session, Michael (one of the more able students in the special class) is working with six classmates.

*Michael:* Stacey, how would you set this sum out?
*Stacey:* Well, I'd put the 60 down first.
*Michael:* What's that for?
*Stacey:* The bike. Then I'd put the 12 down under it for the record (Michael writes as she talks), but I forgot to put the plus sign, so I'd put that in.
*Michael:* Where would I put that?
*Stacey:* Beside the . . . the record.

*Michael:* There? (Michael puts the sign in the wrong place).
*Stacey:* No, in the middle (points).
*Michael:* Kylie, what would you do next?
*Kylie:* Add it up!
*Michael:* Righto, nought and two?
*Kylie:* '2'.
*Michael:* '6' and '1'?
*Kylie:* '7'.
*Michael:* Now what?
*Kylie:* Put 'Spent' beside it.
*Michael:* Okay, we've forgotten one thing. What are we adding up?
*Kylie:* A record and a bike.
*Michael:* Yeah, but what are we using?
*Kylie:* (Pauses) Oh, okay, we forgot the dollar sign.
*Michael:* John, what would you do next?
*John:* Ah—get how much you was paid, and what was left over from that amount we spent.
*Michael:* How much was I paid?
*John:* $140—you take it away, don't you? Ah, and put $72 where that thing is. Put a line, now add it up. '2' and '0' is '2'.
*Michael:* No, we're taking it away!
*John:* Oh yeah. You gotta carry and you gotta borrow one and take one back.
*Michael:* Where do I have to borrow from?
*John:* From the nought.
*Michael:* But I can't borrow from the nought because there's nothing to borrow from.
*All:* From the '7'.
*Michael:* So I put one there, and one there (Michael writes a small '1' in front of the '0', and '1' in front of the '7'). Right, now I got 10, take away '2'. What's that?
*John:* Ah, that's '9', '8'.
*Michael:* Ah, Julie, what do I have to do now?
*Julie:* Ah, '4', take away the '7'.
*Michael:* Can you do it though?
*Julie:* No.
*Michael:* So what do I have to do?
*Julie:* You have to borrow and pay back (Michael marks in the two small 1s).
*Michael:* Righto, what's '14' take away '8'?
*Julie:* Wait. There, '6'.
*Michael:* Stacey, what do you have to do now?
*Stacey:* Now you add it up . . . the last one.

*Others:* No you don't.
*Terry:* That's nought.
*Michael:* No, shush, hang on . . . what you have to do is take '1' away from '1' which is nought, and we put the '$' sign and we write 'left' here. That's sixty-eight bucks. Almost $70. Do you all understand?
*John:* I don't know about the '17', I think you forgot to carry the '17'.
*Michael:* No. What you do, right, is nought take away 2. You can't do, '10' to top, '10' to bottom, '8', can't do, '10' to the top, '10' to the bottom. '14' take away '8', that's '6'. That's not '17', it's '8'.

The interaction described above provides clear evidence of the value of peer tutoring. Instruction similar to the example above demonstrates that a student who has consolidated a particular skill can transfer this knowledge effectively to peers. In this case, Michael was able to consolidate three-column-addition and subtraction-with-carrying with a small group of peers while the classroom teacher worked with another student who was learning a lower level skill.

Of course, there are few teachers who would be prepared to make peer tutoring the most common instruction method employed in their classrooms. At the primary school level, teachers are dealing with students who need input in terms of curriculum content to expand their knowledge base. In the high school, teachers may be reluctant to introduce a strategy which reduces the teacher's control over classroom events and student behaviour. There is no implication here that peer tutoring should be the modal form of instruction. Indeed, effective teaching demands flexibility in strategy use, and applying didactic and student-maintained methods as deemed appropriate. Another example of the use of these various teaching strategies within a reading context is found in Wood (1988).

## CONCLUSION

Our conclusion to this review of literature in the special education domain is straightforward. Peer tutoring is a valuable tool in the classroom teacher's store of instructional strategies. Teaching by students has the capability of generating positive learning outcomes across academic and social domains. The major limitation we perceive emanating from the research findings is the lack of generality of any specific peer tutoring approach outside the context of the relevant studies. Moreover, our experience has shown that the dynamics in one classroom may differ markedly from those in another, making the one-to-one transposition of any peer tutoring approach difficult. This statement may provide a warning to those who wish to adopt existing approaches (e.g. reciprocal teaching, CWPT), but it should not restrict the use of peer tutoring procedures by practitioners or researchers.

One aspect we consider worthy of greater exploration is a more careful examination of the qualitative outcomes of cooperative learning where special needs students are involved. This may help generate hypotheses for testing in future studies in which more variables are manipulated experimentally than in research up to the present time. It would be useful, for example, to determine the critical or essential elements that cause change in both academic achievement and social relationships. For the moment, we support the inclusion of cooperative learning as one among many teaching strategies for the special education teacher.

## REFERENCES

Ashman, A. F., and Conway, R. N. F. (1989). *Cognitive Strategies in Special Education*. London: Routledge.

Atwell, N. (1987). *In The Middle: Writing, Reading and Learning with Adolescents*. Portsmouth, NH: Heinemann.

Bailey, C., and Bridges, D. (1983). *Mixed Ability Teaching: A Philosophical Perspective*. London: Allen & Unwin.

Bar-Eli, N., and Raviv, A. (1982). Underachievers as tutors, *Journal of Educational Research*, **75**, 139–143.

Baxter, R. (1988). The integration of very young, physically handicapped children into child care centres. In A. F. Ashman (ed.), *Integration 25 Years On* (Exceptional Child Monograph No. 1), pp. 85–92, Fred and Eleanor Schonell Special Education Research Centre, St. Lucia, Queensland.

Belmont, J. M., Butterfield, E. C., and Ferretti, R. P. (1982). To secure transfer of training instruct self-management skills. In D. K. Detterman and R. J. Steinberg (eds), *How and How Much Can Intelligence be Increased?* pp. 147–154. Norwood, N.J: Ablex.

Bickel, W. E., and Bickel, D. D. (1986). Effective schools, classrooms and instruction: implications for special education, *Exceptional Children*, **52**, 489–500.

Borkowski, J. G., and Varnhagen, C. K. (1984). Transfer of learning strategies: contrast of self-instructional and traditional training formats with EMR children, *American Journal of Mental Deficiency*, **88**, 369–379.

Brown, A. L., Campione, J. C., and Barclay, C. R. (1979). Training self-checking routines for estimating test readiness: generalization from list learning to prose recall, *Child Development*, **50**, 501–512.

Cambourne, B. (1987). Liberating learners. In J. Hancock and B. Comber (eds), *Independent Learners*. North Ryde, NSW: Methuen.

Carr, P. (1986). Grouping students for task-sharing in activity based classroom. In N. Ellerton (ed.), *Mathematics: Who Needs What? Proceedings of the 1986 Mathematical Association of Victoria Conference*, pp. 55–58.

Collier, K. G. (1980). Peer-group learning in higher education: the development of higher order skills, *Studies in Higher Education*, **5**, 55–62.

Cohen, J. (1986). Theoretical considerations of peer tutoring, *Psychology in the Schools*, **23**, 175–186.

Cohen, P. A., Kulik, J. A., and Kulik, C. C. (1982). Educational outcomes of tutoring: a meta-analysis of findings, *American Educational Research Journal*, **19**, 237–248.

Cooke, N. L., Heron, T. E., Heward, W. L., and Test, D. W. (1982). Integrating a Down syndrome student into a classwide peer tutoring system, *Mental Retardation*, **20**, 22–25.

Custer, J. D., and Osguthorpe, R. T. (1983). Improving social acceptance by training handicapped students to tutor their nonhandicapped peers, *Exceptional Children*, **50**, 175.

Dale, M. (1986). Cooperative learning for effective mainstreaming, *The Computing Teacher*, **8**, 35–37.

de Bono, E. (1971). *The Use of Lateral Thinking*. Toronto: Holt.

Delquadri, J., Greenwood, C. R., Whorton, D., Carta, J. J., and Hall, R. V. (1986). Classwide peer tutoring, *Exceptional Children*, **52**, 535–542.

Dembo, M. H., and McAuliffe, T. J. (1987). Effects of perceived ability and grade status on social interaction and influence in cooperative groups, *Journal of Educational Psychology*, **79**, 415–423.

Elkins, J. (1987). Education without failure? Education for all?, *The Exceptional Child*, **34**, 5–19.

Eiserman, W. D., and Osguthorpe, R. T. (1985, April). Increasing social acceptance: mentally retarded students tutoring regular class peers, Paper presented at the Annual Meeting of the Council for Exceptional Children, Anaheim, CA.

Fisher, C. W., Berliner, D. C., Filby, N. N., Marliave, R., Cohen, L. S., Dishaw, M. M., and Moore, J. (1978). *Teaching and Learning in Elementary Schools: A Summary of the Beginning Teacher Evaluation Study*, Far West Regional Laboratory for Educational Research and Development, San Francisco.

Fraser, B. J. (1986). *Classroom Environment*, London: Croom Helm.

Graham, S., and Freeman, S. (1985). Strategy training and teacher- vs. student-controlled study conditions: effects on LD students' spelling performance, *Learning Disability Quarterly*, **8**, 267–274.

Graham, S., and Harris, K. R. (1988). Instructional recommendations for teaching writing to exceptional students, *Exceptional Children*, **54**, 506–512.

Graham, S., and Miller, L. (1979). Spelling research and practice: a unified approach, *Focus on Exceptional Children*, **12**, 1–16.

Guralnick, M. J., and Groom, J. M. (1987). Dyadic peer interactions of mildly delayed and nonhandicapped preschool children, *American Journal of Mental Deficiency*, **92**, 178–193.

Haisley, F. B., Tell, C. A., and Andrews, J. (1981). Peers as tutors in the mainstream: trained "teachers" of handicapped adolescents, *Journal of Learning Disabilities*, **14**, 224–226, 238.

Hall, R. V., Delquadri, J., Greenwood, C. R., and Thurston, L. (1982). The importance of opportunity to respond in children's academic success. In E. Edgar, N. Haring, J. Jenkins, and C. Pious (eds), *Mentally Handicapped Children: Education and Training*, pp. 107–140, University Park Press, Baltimore, MD.

Harvey, G., and Johnston, W. (1986). Peer tutoring in oral reading, *Australian Journal of Remedial Education*, **18**, 5–7.

Johnson, D. W., and Johnson, R. T. (1974). Instructional goal structure: cooperative, competitive, or individualistic, *Review of Educational Research*, **44**, 213–240.

Johnson, D. W., and Johnson, R. T. (1975). *Learning Together and Alone: Cooperation, Competition, and Individualization*, Englewoods Cliffs, NJ: Prentice-Hall.

Johnson, D. W., and Johnson, R. T. (1985a). Cooperative learning: one key to computer assisted learning, *The Computing Teacher*, **8**, 11–15.

Johnson, D. W., and Johnson, R. T. (1985b). The internal dynamics of cooperative learning groups. In R. E. Slavin, S. Sharan, S. Kagan, R. Hertz-Lazarowitz, C. Webb, and R. Schmuck (eds), *Learning to Cooperate, Cooperating to Learn*, pp. 103–124. New York: Plenum.

Lancioni, G. E. (1982). Employment of normal third and fourth graders for training retarded children to solve problems dealing with quantity, *Education and Training of the Mentally Retarded*, **17**, 93–102.

Larson, C. O., Dansereau, D. F., O'Donnell, A. M., Hythecker, V I., Lambiotte, J. G., and Rocklin, T. R. (1985). Effects of metacognitive and elaborative activity on cooperative learning and transfer, *Contemporary Educational Psychology*, **10**, 342–348.

Leinhardt, G., and Putnam, R. T. (1987). The skill of learning from classroom lessons, *American Educational Research Journal*, **24**, 557–587.

Leon, J. A., and Pepe, H. J. (1983). Self-instructional training: cognitive behavior modification for remediating arithmetic deficits, *Exceptional Children*, **50**, 54–60.

Light, P., and Glachan, M. (1985). Facilitation of individual problem solving through peer interaction, *Educational Psychology*, **5**, 217–225.

Litrownik, A. J., Cleary, C. P., Lecklitner, G. L., and Franzini, L. R. (1978). Self-regulation in retarded persons: acquisition of standards for performance, *American Journal of Mental Deficiency*, **83**, 86–89.

Lloyd, J. W., Crowley, E. P., Kohler, F. W., and Strain, P. S. (1988). Redefining the applied research agenda: cooperative learning, prereferral, teacher consultation, and peer-mediated interventions, *Journal of Learning Disabilities*, **21**, 43–52.

McKellar, N. (1985). Behaviors used in peer tutoring, *Journal of Experimental Education*, **26**, 163–167.

Maheady, L., and Harper, G. F. (1987). A classwide peer tutoring system to improve the spelling test performance of low-income, third- and fourth-grade students, *Education and Treatment of Children*, **10**, 120–133.

Maheady, L., Harper, G. F., and Sacca, K. (1988). A classwide peer tutoring system in a secondary resource room program for the mildly handicapped, *Journal of Research and Development in Education*, **21**, 76–83.

Maheady, L., Sacca, M. K., and Harper, G. F. (1987). Classwide student tutoring teams: the effects of peer-mediated instruction on the academic performance of secondary mainstreamed students, *Journal of Special Education*, **21**, 107–121.

Manzo, A. V. (1968). Improvement of Reading Comprehension through Reciprocal Questioning, Unpublished Doctoral Dissertation, Syracuse University, New York.

Marsh, G. E., Price, B. J., and Smith, T. E. C. (1983). *Teaching Mildly Handicapped Children: Methods and Materials*. St. Louis, MO: C. V. Mosby.

Martin, M. (1986). Cooperative learning: my solution for teaching mathematics for yet another ten years. In N. Ellerton (ed.), *Mathematics: Who Needs What? Proceedings of the 1986 Mathematical Association of Victoria Conference*, pp. 103–106.

Meichenbaum, D. K., and Goodman, J. (1971). Training impulsive children to talk to themselves, *Journal of Abnormal Psychology*, **77**, 115–126.

Osguthorpe, R. T., and Scruggs, T. E. (1986). Special education students as tutors: a review and analysis *Remedial and Special Education*, **7**, 15–26.

Owens, L., and Stratton, R. G. (1980). The development of a cooperative, competitive and individualized learning preference scale for students, *British Journal of Educational Psychology*, **50**, 147–161.

Palincsar, A. S., and Brown, A. L. (1987). Enhancing instructional time through attention to metacognition, *Journal of Learning Disabilities*, **20**, 66–75.

Palincsar, A. S., and Brown, A. L. (1988). Teaching and practising thinking skills to promote comprehension in the context of group problem solving, *Remedial and Special Education*, **9**, 53–59.

Palincsar, A. S., Brown, A. L., and Martin, S. M. (1987). Peer interaction in reading comprehension instruction, *Educational Psychologist*, **22**, 231–253.

Pekin, M. (1988). Cooperative learning activities for your favourite software, *Computerchat*, April, 20–22.

Rooney, K. J., Hallahan, D. P., and Lloyd, J. W. (1984). Self-recording of attention by learning disabled students in the regular classroom, *Journal of Learning Disabilities*, **17**, 360–364.

Ryan, E. B., Short, E. J., and Weed, K. A. (1986). The role of cognitive strategy training in improving the academic performance of learning disabled children, *Journal of Learning Disabilities*, **19**, 521–529.

Sands, M., and Kerry, T. (1982). *Mixed Ability Teaching*. London: Croom Helm.

Sapon-Shevin, M. (1978). Another look at mainstreaming: exceptionality, normality, and the nature of difference, *Phi Delta Kappan*, **59**, 119–121.

Scruggs, T. E., and Osguthorpe, R. T. (1986). Tutoring intervention within special education settings: a comparison of cross-age and peer tutoring, *Psychology in the Schools*, **23**, 187–193.

Senapati, R., and Hayes, A. (1988). Sibling relationships of handicapped children: a review of conceptual and methodological issues, *International Journal of Behavioral Development*, **11**, 89–115.

Sheinker, A., Sheinker, J. M., and Stevens, L. J. (1984). Cognitive strategies for teaching the mildly handicapped, *Focus on Exceptional Children*, **17**, 1–15.

Sindelar, P. T., Smith, M. A., Harriman, N. E., Hale, R. L., and Wilson, R. J. (1986). Teacher effectiveness in special education programs, *Journal of Special Education*, **20**, 195–207.

Slavin, R. E. (1985a). An introduction to cooperative learning research. In R. E. Slavin, S. Sharan, S. Kagan, R. Hertz-Lazarowitz, C. Webb, and R. Schmuck (eds), *Learning to Cooperate, Cooperating to Learn*, pp. 5–15. New York: Plenum.

Slavin, R. E. (1985b). Team-assisted individualization: combining cooperative learning and individualized instruction in mathematics. In R. E. Slavin, S. Sharan, S. Kagan, R. Hertz-Lazarowitz, C. Webb, and R. Schmuck (eds), *Learning to Cooperate, Cooperating to Learn*, pp. 177–209. New York: Plenum.

Smith, R. A. (1987). A teacher's view on cooperative learning, *Phi Delta Kappan*, **68**, 663–666.

Snider, V. (1987). Use of self-monitoring of attention with LD students: research and application, *Learning Disability Quarterly*, **10**, 139–151.

Top, B. L., and Osguthorpe, R. T. (1987). Reverse-role tutoring: the effects of handicapped students tutoring regular class students, *The Elementary School Journal*, **87**, 413–423.

Tripp, D. H. (1979a). Changes in children's corporate thinking, Paper Presented at 49th ANZAAS Congress, Auckland, New Zealand.

Tripp, D. H. (1979b). The use of the CoRT thinking project with exceptional children: some outcomes of the UK Evaluation, *The Exceptional Child*, **26**, 71–81.

Wacker, D. P., and Berg, W. K. (1985). Use of peers to train and monitor the performance of adolescents with severe handicap, *Education and Training of the Mentally Retarded*, **20**, 109–122.

Watt, D., and Watt, M. (1986). Logo quilt: a collaborative learning project, *The National Logo Exchange*, **5**, 1–2.

Webb, N. M. (1985). Student interaction and learning in small groups: a research summary. In R. E. Slavin, S. Sharan, S. Kagan, R. Hertz-Lazarowitz, C. Webb, and R. Schmuck (eds), *Learning to Cooperate, Cooperating to Learn*, pp. 147–172. New York: Plenum.

Wood, K. (1988). Guiding students through informational text, *The Reading Teacher*, **41**, 912–920.

Yogev, A., and Ronen, R. (1982). Cross-age tutoring: effects on tutors' attributes, *Journal of Educational Research*, **75**, 261–268.

Ysseldyke, J. E., Thurlow, M. L., Christenson, S. L., and Weiss, J. (1987). Time allocated to instruction of mentally retarded, learning disabled, emotionally disturbed, and nonhandicapped elementary students, *Journal of Special Education*, **21**, 43–55.

CHAPTER 11

# Learning from One Another: the Challenge

HELEN COWIE and JEAN RUDDUCK

*Division of Education, Arts Tower (Floor 12), University of Sheffield, Sheffield, S10 2TN, UK*

## INTRODUCTION

Recognition of the value of learning cooperatively in small groups is not new. Sharan (1988), for example, indicates that this form of learning and instruction has been used by Jewish scholars in the Yeshiva for the past two millennia and argues that their methods have the same underlying principle:

> that students make knowledge their own, not by repeating what they heard, but by exploring ideas through intense conversations with others with whom they quite often disagree. These discussions afford the participants the opportunity to think and rethink, formulate and reformulate their ideas, using what they know, what they think and what they hear, until they reach some sense of completeness about their own thoughts and understanding. (Sharan, 1988, p. 2)

Recently, there has been a widespread renewal of interest in developing cooperative learning methods for the education of young people. Graves and Graves (1988), writing in the newsletter of the International Association for the Study of Co-operation in Education (IASCE), a network of educators committed to the dissemination of knowledge about cooperation in education, refer to work in Israel, Greece, Hungary, Russia, the Netherlands, France,

Children Helping Children
Edited by H. C. Foot, M. J. Morgan and R. H. Shute

Britain, the Philippines, Australia, South Africa, Canada and the United States. These educators, despite their differing backgrounds, all express a belief in the potential which cooperative learning methods offer for enhancing pupils' understanding, for facilitating interpersonal skills and for creating a climate of community in the classroom.

In Britain, Her Majesty's Inspectorate (HMI) have been actively promoting group work in schools in the belief that it increases children's motivation, develops responsibility and initiative, and creates a context for effective learning (HMI, 1982, 1983, 1985). Most recently, many of the new General Certificate of Secondary Education (GCSE) syllabuses now require group work as one of the ways of learning that pupils in most subject areas should experience.

There is also a political justification for the development of cooperative learning amongst young people (Aronowitz and Giroux, 1986; Harber and Meighan, 1989; Salter and Tapper, 1981). The skills which are fundamental to group work, such as the ability to acknowledge the range of perspectives which may be brought to bear on an issue, form the basis of democracy (Bridges, 1979). At a time when there are many pressures from minority groups within our society for rights and justice, there is a growing feeling in some quarters that it is the responsibility of schools to give their pupils, regardless of gender, social class or ethnic background, the confidence and the ability to make their voices heard within their own community and in society at large.

A belief in the effectiveness of cooperative learning has also come from industry. Industry's support for cooperative group work in schools arises from a concern to prepare young people for the world of work where, so the argument goes, it makes economic sense to have employees who can work effectively in teams and who experience personal satisfaction in the work which they do. Through the forging of school–industry links, teachers have been increasingly encouraged to give their students the direct experience of how industry works. The development of active learning strategies has played a central part in this movement. Organizations such as the School Curriculum Industry Partnership (SCIP) have promoted a 'process' approach where the focus is experiential rather than didactic. Cooperative learning, with its emphasis on participant activity in small groups, is now widely used in recent curriculum initiatives in Britain such as the Technical and Vocational Education Initiative (TVEI) and the Certificate of Pre-Vocational Education (CPVE). Teachers on these courses are encouraged to move away from traditional didactic methods. For example, in one educational programme for 14–16-year-olds on the theme of 'enterprise', the variety of roles appropriate to each stage in the course is outlined as follows:

> As the programme unfolds and develops the teacher becomes more consultative and finally peer and layman, listening to groups who are 'expert' on their own ideas. Control becomes less overt and less necessary. En route the roles of catalyst, arbitrator, troubleshooter, confidante, fellow learner and signposter are necessary. The responsibility of 'getting things done' shifts continuously and increasingly onto the

participants themselves. Teacher control must therefore be subtle and acceptable to the groups. (Gibb, 1985, p. vii).

## RESEARCH PERSPECTIVES ON COOPERATIVE LEARNING

Researchers have attempted a more precise analysis of claims that cooperative learning has positive effects on outcomes as wide-ranging as academic achievement, inter-group relations, and self-esteem (Johnson and Johnson, 1982, 1987; Slavin, 1983; Slavin *et al.*, 1985). In general, their verdicts confirm the intuitions of practitioners in the classroom, but they are more cautious in interpreting the particular effects of different kinds of group work on children's thinking, social behaviour and emotional response. On the basis of his own research and of a meta-analysis of other studies, Slavin has concluded that cooperative group work can offer 'a coherent alternative means of organising the classroom for instruction in fundamental curriculum areas' (Slavin, 1987, p. 1161). But he also stresses that there are inevitable differences of approach within this large and growing field with its varying definitions of cooperative learning. It is not enough simply to distinguish cooperative learning approaches from traditional methods. Cooperative learning methods differ widely in their underlying philosophy and in the forms which they take in practice.

Slavin distinguishes two major theoretical perspectives, *developmental* and *motivational*. From the developmental perspectives, it is the interaction amongst peers working together on a task which increases their achievement. Cooperative learning is successful because, by discussing issues with others, students experience cognitive conflicts (see Doise, this volume). Faulty reasoning is shown up and, as a result of imbalance between their own and others' logic, they arrive at a higher level of understanding (Damon, 1984). Learning arises from the opportunity within the group to hear different arguments, to debate on issues and to develop a critical awareness of one's own and others' points of view. Furthermore, ideas are generated through the process of peer interaction. Extrinsic rewards, from the developmental perspective, are unnecessary.

Supporters of the motivational perspective focus instead on the reward or goal structures under which group members work. It is the cooperative goal structures, they argue, where groups are rewarded for their performance *as a group*, that promote higher achievement and enhanced interpersonal relationships (Johnson and Johnson, 1982; Slavin, 1983). Extrinsic rewards in the form of grades, praise, extra time at break or some reward which has been chosen by the students themselves may be given for a single group product, such as a group presentation, a report, or a solution to a problem. Johnson and Johnson (1975) call this 'positive reward interdependence'. Either everyone in the group receives the reward or no one does and, they stress, it is important that groups who do not 'reach the criteria' do not get the reward (p. 128). Alternatively, group rewards may be given for the sum of individual learning performance. In Student Teams Achievement Divisions (STAD) (Slavin, 1983), students work on a topic in teams and are then quizzed individually. Quiz scores are turned into team scores through a weighting system which takes into account previous performance by individuals. The reward is given to the team with the highest score. In Teams–Games–Tournaments (TGT) (DeVries and Slavin, 1978) students in groups of four or five study work sheets together and question one another to check that the material has been learned. A tournament is then held in which individual representatives of each group compete with one another. Points are awarded on these individuals' performance and the reward is given to the most successful team. The Jigsaw method (Aronson, 1978) is designed to make students work interdependently by splitting a task into four or five sections. Each student has access to only part of the material to be mastered and must therefore work with others in order to fit together all the pieces of the 'jigsaw'. Students work in 'expert' groups in which they study one section; they then return to their teams and teach the material which they have mastered to other members of their team. Finally, students individually are tested on their knowledge of all aspects of the topic. Here there is interdependence of task but not of reward.

Slavin (1987) carried out a meta-analysis of 46 empirical investigations into cooperative learning and achievement. The 46 studies investigated group work across the curriculum among students of different ages and from a variety of social backgrounds. Sixty-three per cent of the studies showed statistically significant gains for experimental as opposed to control groups. In only 2% of the studies did control students achieve more highly than experimental students. Slavin found little to support the argument that peer interaction alone led to increased achievement and concluded that 'two elements are required to make cooperative learning more effective than traditional instruction: *group rewards* and *individual accountability*' (p. 1164). At the same time, Slavin also acknowledged the need to utilize peer interaction and suggested a reconciliation between the developmental and motivational perspectives:

> Under the right motivational conditions, peers can and, more important, *will* provide explanations in one anothers' proximal zones of development and will engage in the kind of cognitive conflict needed for disequilibration and cognitive growth. (Slavin, 1987, p. 1166)

## THE NEGOTIATION OF MEANING

Some researchers, who are also committed to cooperative group work, focus as much on the *process* of learning as on measurable outcomes such as those identified in Slavin's meta-analysis. On that basis they would claim that cognitive and social processes interact in complex ways. Their emphasis is on coming to understand how pupils in cooperative groups begin to explore and negotiate their own meanings through the processes of dialogue, active participation and engagement in issues of significance to the learners. Using interview data and observations of groups in action, several researchers (e.g. Barnes, 1976; Cowie and Rudduck, 1988; Salmon and Claire, 1984; Stenhouse, 1970) have attempted to make a qualitative analysis of the processes at work when students learn cooperatively from one another.

This approach places central emphasis on the idea that the learning process is about the negotiation of meaning rather than its transmission, and that it is firmly rooted in personally significant issues, human settings and social relationships. In the words of Salmon (1988, p. 60), 'just as the knowledge that every teacher offers is essentially personal . . . so, in learning, pupils construct an understanding which is theirs alone.' Group work, from this standpoint, creates a context in which the active construction of meanings can take place through dialogue in contexts which allow for a range of perspectives and which give to the learner a say in what is to be learned. In sharp contrast with the traditional view that there is a single formulation of understanding, as presented by knowledgeable experts, cooperative learning strategies offer to pupils the opportunity to define issues in their own words and to move towards understanding in terms of their own concepts and at their own pace; furthermore, cooperative group work gives young learners the chance to construct meanings and understandings from their own experience in an active way.

There are a number of ways in which this approach to learning can be investigated. We present three examples to illustrate the insights to educators which may be offered by qualitative studies—the work of Lawrence Stenhouse on the handling of controversial issues in the humanities classroom, Douglas Barnes's explorations of pupil talk, and the study of classroom collaboration by Phil Salmon and Hilary Claire. Each study has a different emphasis, but the researchers share a belief that people come to know and to understand through a process of dialogue and face-to-face interaction about topics of personal concern to the learners.

## The Humanities Curriculum Project (HCP)

Stenhouse (1970, revised 1983) developed a strategy for handling controversial issues in which the teacher had a key role as a member of the discussion group. The problem in secondary schooling, as Stenhouse perceived it, was that pupils for the most part work independently and are continually in competition with one another for grades, praise and recognition. Classroom analysis studies consistently showed that a high percentage of classroom talk was teacher talk and that a high percentage of questions asked by the teacher were closed questions, designed to test pupils' recall of factual material and providing little opportunity for pupils to respond in thoughtful ways. Stenhouse saw such teaching as offering a view of the teacher as one who protects young people from the complexities of knowledge by holding out safety nets. His starting point was the need to find a way of respecting the rights of young people to intellectual honesty and independence, in particular the right to enquire into and deepen their understanding of controversial social issues. He saw face-to-face discussion as a fitting strategy for exploring such issues in that it supports the interplay of various perspectives and permits individual members of a group to arrive at their own understandings in the light of evidence that has been critically examined by the group. In Stenhouse's discussions the teacher acts as 'neutral chairperson', and, in accepting this role, the teacher expresses a procedural commitment not to endorse any single perspective on an issue by disclosing his or her own view. The teacher's authority is not therefore used to assert meaning but to foster the critical search for meaning. In the discussions, the teacher acts as a model of an enquirer, as a listener and respectful questioner. The teacher is also the guardian of intellectual and interpersonal standards of enquiry. Aware that teachers would find it difficult to relinquish familiar patterns of classroom behaviour, the project offered the support of a strong self-monitoring framework. Teachers were encouraged to tape discussions and listen to them, bearing in mind questions such as these:

- To what extent do you interrupt pupils while they are speaking? Why and to what effect?
- What proportion of silences are interrupted by you?
- Are you consistent and reliable in chairing? Are all the pupils treated with equal respect?
- Do you habitually rephrase and repeat pupils' contributions? If so, what is the effect of this?
- Do you press towards consensus?
- Is there any evidence of pupils looking to you for rewards rather than to the task?
- Do you generally ask questions to which you think you know the answer?

The transfer from whole-class teaching to discussion-based learning was not easy. Many teachers disliked the role of neutral chairperson. Some argued that pupils would think that the teacher did not care about an issue if he or she did not express a personal view. Some claimed that they were failing as teachers if they did not give a positive lead to their pupils. Others felt that they were distancing themselves from pupils if they did not join in the discussion. Pupils too found it more comfortable to cling to habits of dependence on the teacher and often resisted the idea that it might be legitimate to learn from one another.

But evidence from the evaluation of the project suggested that most pupils, once they had understood the reasons for neutrality on the part of the chairperson, appreciated the fact that the teacher was listening to them and giving them time to explore ideas for themselves. They made comments like: 'she actually believes such and such—but she doesn't let her view get in the way of our discussion' or 'Miss is talking too much and getting too interested in the group. As chairman, she shouldn't talk, you know, as much, leaving it to the group to argue between themselves'.

Stenhouse pointed out the need to acknowledge the confusion experienced by pupils when the norms of classroom behaviour are suddenly changed and a new mode of learning introduced. Teachers cannot take it for granted, he concluded, that pupils will understand what an innovation means, what it implies for their relationships with one another, what new kinds of behaviour will be accepted in the classroom, or what model of knowledge the innovation endorses. An alternative may be for the teacher to negotiate the meaning of the new strategies with the pupils and so help them to engage in this process with one another. In fact, Stenhouse argued, it is the negotiation of new meanings or shared meanings which is central to the process of change in schools.

The Humanities Curriculum Project offered a clearly articulated and definitive code of practice for learning through discussion-based group work. Although the method itself was too challenging at the time for many teachers to adopt, it has exerted a strong influence on much teaching since then. Various curriculum projects initiated in the 1970s under the aegis of the Schools Council, both in science and arts/humanities subjects, endorsed the use of discussion-based group work, and there has undoubtedly been an impact on teachers' consciousness of alternative ways of learning.

## LEARNING THROUGH TALK

In secondary schools teacher talk rather than pupil talk has long been seen as the basis of 'real' learning. Barnes and his colleagues (Barnes, Britton and Rosen, 1969; Barnes, 1976) were amongst the most influential challengers of this tradition. On the basis of his detailed observations of the interactions which took place between secondary school teachers and their pupils, Barnes indicated the extent to which teacher-centred talk can devalue the language of children, can stifle genuine enquiry and discourage the development of thinking processes. In accord with Stenhouse he noted that many questions asked in class are 'closed', requiring a factual type of response (e.g. 'Does anyone know of any books which Homer wrote?' or 'This is what we call a mortar, this bowl. Does anyone know what we call the other thing which we are going to pound it with?'). Clearly there is a place for questions of this nature, but Barnes observed that entirely 'open' questions scarcely ever occurred. Furthermore, he found very little evidence that children were encouraged to make connections between personal experience and classroom learning:

> Those children who come up from primary schools ready to explore personal experiences aloud and to offer anecdotal contributions to discussion cease to do so within a few weeks of arrival. Clearly they learn in certain lessons that anecdotes are held by teachers to be irrelevant. It can be hypothesised that they begin to take

TABLE 11.1. Poem for discussion

WARNING
When I am an old woman I shall wear purple
With a red hat which doesn't go, and doesn't suit me,
And I shall spend my pension on brandy and summer gloves
And satin sandals, and say we've no money for butter.
I shall sit on the pavement when I'm tired
And gobble up samples in shops and press alarm bells
And run my stick along the public railings
And make up for the sobriety of my youth.
I shall go out in my slippers in the rain
And pick the flowers in other people's gardens
And learn to spit.

You can wear terrible shirts and grow more fat
And eat three pounds of sausage at a go
Or only bread and pickle for a week
And hoard pens and pencils and beermats and things in boxes.

But meanwhile we must stay respectable
And must not shame the children; they mind more
Even than we do, being noticeable.
We will keep dry with sensible clothes and spend
According to good value, and do what's best
To bring the best for us and for our children.

But maybe I ought to practise a little now?
So people who know me are not too shocked and surprised
When suddenly I am old, and start to wear purple.

Jenny Joseph



part in each new subject by taking in their teacher's behaviour as a reciprocal element in their own role as learners, so that his voice becomes one 'voice' in their own internal dialogues. (Barnes, Britton and Rosen, 1969, pp. 25–26)

Barnes argued that a key aspect of the learning process grows out of personal relationship, and he recommended as an alternative to the 'straitjacket' of traditional teaching the use of small interacting groups which can facilitate each individual's ability to take responsibility for his or her learning.

In order to test his hypothesis, Barnes explored the use of small, highly interactive groups which gave pupils more freedom to construct their own meanings and to work things out in their own way—activities which had usually been discouraged in traditional teacher-centred classrooms.

Four groups of 12- to 13-year-old pupils were set three interpretative tasks—scientific, literary and historical—as follows:

TABLE 11.2. Examples of 'closed' and 'open' responses to the poem

*'Closed' responses*
Group IV typically makes responses like 'No' which discourage the exploration of ideas in the poem:

A: Do you think she would eat three pounds of sausages at a go and only bread and pickle for a week?
B: No.

* * * *

R: What do you think the poem's about, Tony?
A: Er . . . someone who's fairly young . . . er . . . who's got children or grandchildren.
J: Well, what do you think it means by saying 'spend my money on brandy and summer gloves and satin sandals'?
R: She'll waste her money. (long pause)
J: What does she mean . . . And say 'we've no money for butter'?
R: Well, she means . . . waste the money on some things and then just have no money for other things . . . which are necessary.

Here the pupils approach the poem as if it had one right answer. There is no scope for discussion of their own and other people's self-indulgence which might give insights into the middle-aged woman's longings. The overall evaluation of the poem is that 'It's all childish', in a tone of disparagement.

*'Open' responses*
Group III, by contrast, makes frequent use of the hypothetical mode, e.g. 'What if?', 'Sounds as if . . . ', 'I wonder . . . ' and 'Perhaps':

F: 'When I am an old woman I shall wear purple with a red hat which doesn't go and doesn't suit me. I shall spend my pension on brandy and summer gloves'.
P: Sounds as if she's obstinate.
F: Sounds as if she's sick of being young as well.
L: Well, she's got her ideas of being old hasn't she already. Don't think she'll *be* like that though.
All: No.
L: 'I'll gobble up samples in shops and press alarm bells'. I wonder what she wants to press alarm bells for.
F: Perhaps she wants to be naughty as well as show off.

This group keeps referring to the text but for a different reason from Group IV. They seem to be trying to construct a meaning for themselves, testing ideas out against their own experience and against other parts of the poem.

(1) Discussion about a scientific experiment: the pupils were asked to do some simple experiments about air pressure (e.g. sucking liquid through a straw) and then to discuss amongst themselves exactly what happened and why it happened.
(2) Discussion of a poem (see Table 11.1): the pupils read *Warning*, a poem about a middle-aged woman, and were asked to 'talk about the poem in

any way you want to'. Understanding of the poem required the pupils to try to take the perspective of someone whose experience was very different from their own.

(3) Discussion about the founding of Saxon settlements. The pupils were shown a picture of rough, uncultivated land and were asked 'What would a Saxon family do when they approached English shores in order to settle?'. The groups were encouraged to construct in imagination the conditions under which a settlement would have been made.

When the teacher withdrew and deliberately left the pupils to work together in groups, it was clear that a new communication system appeared. Instead of relying on the expert teacher to help them out of difficulties, the pupils were faced with a situation where they had to negotiate some new strategies.

Barnes found that the small discussion groups varied greatly in their capacity to speculate, to think tentatively, to formulate hypotheses, and to share perspectives (see Table 11.2). For example, one group 'saw' the picture of the Saxon settlement differently after they had discussed the problems faced by settlers; by contrast, another group, faced with the same picture of uncleared land, said that the settlers should simply 'start farming', indicating that they had not yet made a connection between what they could see and the task of making it ready for planting.

Barnes concluded that the quality of discussion is not determined solely by the ability of pupils. It also depends on the task, familiarity with the subject, confidence, and knowing what is expected. The language used in the groups was often informal but, as Barnes points out:

> When we consider children working in small groups, we tend to compare their discussion with an idealised teacher–pupil dialogue, forgetting how often this falls below the ideal even for an experienced teacher, and forgetting too that it compels most of the class to listen in silence. Moreover, the very presence of a teacher alters the way in which pupils use language, so that they are more likely to be aiming at 'answers' which will gain approval thus using language to reshape knowledge. Only the most skilful teaching can avoid this. (Barnes, 1976, p. 78).

Barnes's argument held in essence that small group talk has the exploratory character necessary for personally meaningful learning. The kind of active exploration which can happen where groups of equals talk among themselves is greatly constrained, he argued, by a didactic teaching style which presupposes that the inexpert pupils receive the correct formulation of an issue in the words of an expert teacher. Barnes concluded that, in the absence of the teacher, pupils were more likely to adopt a speculative stance to test out the limits of their knowledge and to re-shape ideas collaboratively. They often drew on their own experience as a way of helping the group to arrive at an understanding of the matter under discussion.

Barnes's ideas were controversial at the time, but, especially in the area of English teaching, it is now accepted practice that groups of students without their teacher work collaboratively to explore new ideas and formulate their own meanings.

## CLASSROOM COLLABORATION

Barnes's work indicated how small group discussion could help pupils to relate their own personal knowledge, perceptions and experiences to the processes of learning and understanding. He was able to observe his groups under carefully controlled conditions, one at a time. Salmon and Claire (1984) carried out their investigation into the effect of collaborative group work on pupils' learning in normal classroom settings. They worked with teachers who were committed to a cooperative approach and who, like Barnes, rejected the passive role assigned to pupils by the traditional model of education. Central to this research was the view that social relationships and shared personal meanings form the basis of learning.

A strong influence on the thinking behind the study came from the work of George Kelly, in particular his concepts of *commonality*—the degree of similarity between the perceptions of different individuals—and *sociality*—the extent to which people understand one another's views (Kelly, 1955). As Salmon and Claire point out, 'pupils do not always interpret classroom events in the way that their teacher does' and 'classroom communication, if it is to be effective, must depend on mutual understanding'. They argued that classroom learning involves the meeting of a number of different frames of reference—the teacher's and the pupil's. Collaborative learning modes make the pupils' frame of reference central, in direct contrast to traditional modes. The goals of people involved in collaborative learning, therefore, relate to commonality and sociality between teacher and pupils, and among pupils:

> Far from seeing children's relationships as irrelevant to classroom practice, or as a source of potential disruption in learning, the collaborative ethos presupposes the need to build learning experiences out of the positive feeling between children. (Salmon and Claire, 1984, p. 4)

Salmon and Claire spent two years exploring collaborative learning modes in four classrooms—design and technology, social studies, humanities and drama—in two comprehensive schools. Both schools were inner-city, mixed and multi-ethnic. The authors combined observation of lessons with evaluation of pupils' and teachers' frames of reference; their concern was with the degree of commonality and sociality which existed between teachers and their pupils. The teachers who took part in the study were all committed to a teaching style which emphasized common goals and mutual understanding.

Two major themes emerged from the study—the meaning of learning and the meaning of social relationships within these classrooms. The authors concluded that the two are inextricably intertwined and that, for the pupils especially, lessons are essentially social situations. This intertwining is illustrated in some detail by the kind of learning which takes place in different areas of the curriculum.

However, committed as the teachers were to the principles of collaborative learning, they still found a number of powerful constraints which prevented them from putting these ideals into practice. Mac, the design and technology teacher, believed that, by working collaboratively, pupils would become more imaginative and capable of solving design problems. He was disappointed to discover that pupils expected to be given a series of exercises in which they followed instructions individually in order to produce a useful object. He also believed that, by creating a classroom environment in which qualities of kindness, sensitivity and tolerance were valued, he would be able to adopt a more human and less unequal relationship with his pupils than would be found in more traditional, teacher-centred classrooms. In reality, as interviews and classroom observations showed, there was less 'mutuality' than he thought in his class. He interacted far more naturally with the boys and did not seem to be aware of the powerful gender barriers which existed in his class. The design and technology work which the boys did in school made sense to them because it had some bearing on out-of-school activities. This integration did not happen for the girls, largely because there was a strong sense that the subject was irrelevant to their gender roles. So, with the boys only, sociality and commonality did seem to be achieved by collaborative learning methods. Mac had achieved some of his aims and had become aware of barriers which prevented greater 'mutuality' developing amongst the members of this class.

Even more formidable barriers to classroom collaboration appeared in the fourth year social studies class, a multi-ethnic group of boys taught by Islay, a young woman with a strong belief in the value of a personal approach to teaching. The social studies course, designed to be of interest to pupils in a multi-ethnic classroom, was about cultural conflicts experienced by North American Indians. Islay aimed to 'draw on the personal resources for learning inherent in young people' (Salmon and Claire, 1984, p. 74) by emphasizing course-work and oral work rather than formal written examinations. But the members of her class were extremely alienated from the educational system and saw school as a place where pupils took little responsibility for their own learning. Generally their attitudes towards teachers were negative. Although in their social life outside school they valued the qualities which Islay hoped to develop through the social studies course, they could not see their relevance to the classroom. School work was 'extraneous and mechanical rather than personal and creative' and they often seemed to prefer set work, written work and work which could be marked, to activities which demanded a more personal response from them.

Interaction with peers was seen as incompatible with learning. The presence of friends did not enhance learning.

How did collaborative learning fare in such a setting? Islay believed that she achieved her aim of getting the boys to listen to one another's points of view in a constructive way. Supportive social relationships were formed and the pupils maintained an atmosphere of tolerance towards one another. Although the friendships tended to be formed within ethnic groupings, there was no sign of racial tension in this class. Islay's positive feelings were reciprocated. She shared her own personal experiences with the class and some at least of the boys revealed their feelings to one another.

However, the class retained a very narrow view of what constituted 'learning'. Only written assignments were perceived as 'real work' and tended to be carried out individually. Group discussion was not taken seriously except as a rehearsal for the oral examination. At no point in the two years of the study did the group use talk for the exploration of ideas arising from course content. There was no evidence that the boys made links between their own personal lives and the content of the social studies course.

Salmon and Claire suggest that one reason for the failure to learn collaboratively may be that the boys in this class had a long history of working and failing within a traditional framework. The ideas of autonomy, initiative and critical thinking were quite alien to them. Interviews with the pupils revealed a mismatch between the teacher's positive expectations of them and their own very pessimistic view of their life chances. However, by encouraging the social relationships within the class, Islay affirmed their value for the boys, even though she did not succeed in linking them to school learning. Islay's approach was certainly valuable to the boys as people and may have increased their mutual sociality. But Salmon and Claire conclude that 'the level of commonality between their views of schooling and Islay's philosophy was too low to enable them to integrate their classroom learning with their social relationships' (Salmon and Claire, 1984, p. 91).

One might be tempted to conclude that the collaborative approach to learning was inappropriate in real life school settings, but this is not the conclusion of Salmon and Claire. They are aware that individual initiatives by enthusiastic teachers can only have limited impact on a whole school system. In fact, the authors argue that 'it is the potentialities in collaborative learning methods for the fostering of commonality and sociality between teachers and pupils, and between pupils themselves, which are ultimately crucial in forestalling personal alienation from school education' (p. 239).

The studies by Stenhouse, by Barnes and by Salmon and Claire highlighted personal and social barriers which operate against the most effective use of cooperative group work. In the next section, we explore how group work was experienced by some of teachers and pupils in our own study.

## TEACHERS' PERCEPTIONS OF COOPERATIVE GROUP WORK

Despite the body of evidence, both from research findings and from educational practice, which confirms the value of creating classroom contexts where pupils learn from one another, it still seems to be hard for many teachers and pupils to accept the legitimacy of arriving at an understanding based on these kinds of experiences. One of the difficulties is that it can be very threatening to pupils to be placed in a situation where there is not the security that the right answer will, in the end, be revealed by the teacher. Exploratory thinking often involves pain, frustration and confusion, especially in its early stages. Many learners seem to be unnerved by tentativeness, thrown by uncertainty.

Our extensive interviews with teachers reveal widespread anxiety about their own capacity to deal with the challenge of cooperative group work in the classroom. Even teachers who are committed to group work may face criticism and hostility from sceptical colleagues. The following heated exchange took place at a school-based in-service course on group work. The three Science teachers (who will be referred to as David, Peter and Jerry) are by no means atypical and they express some common fears and doubts as they respond to a tape-recording, made by a colleague from the English department, of a group of girls discussing a poem. The tape-recording illustrates many of the points made by Barnes. The girls have demonstrated the role of pupil talk in sharing responses, exploring meaning and in forming tentative hypotheses. Their discussion is part of a process which eventually results in a written assignment. To the English teacher, there is nothing especially radical about this way of working; it is part of his normal approach to teaching within the General Certificate of Secondary Education (GCSE) syllabus. But the Science teachers differ widely in their response. David is positively in favour of group work as an approach to learning; Peter rejects it absolutely; Jerry, after initial scepticism, tentatively considers its value.

*David*: I do go along with what's been said. However, I got the general feeling that they were discussing in a sensible manner which is a positive thing. Nobody larking about, nobody cracking jokes, and so forth.

*Peter*: (loudly) Exactly! They were discussing it with the tape recorder, not with each other. They were in a room on their own. If I was to do group work in Science, I can't say 'You go in that group. You go in that group and take a tape recorder'. It's totally false, totally false! A contrived situation.

*David*: I think you're being very silly, Peter. I would imagine like most people that when the tape is there you are very self-conscious at the beginning, but I am convinced that a lot of that discussion was quite genuine. They were genuinely searching for things. And the kids were actually prepared to put themselves on the line with one another.

*Peter*: I don't understand that. That will not happen in a formal classroom situation, putting kids round a table and saying, 'Let's perform'.

*David*: You wouldn't do that. You would prepare people for it and use it as part of a programme. It is not an end in itself. It is a means to an end. It's a technique and the sort of discussion that is going on there, why shouldn't it go on in a small group in Science? How do we know that doesn't go on if we don't listen?

*Peter*: You take a typical group where you have 24 kids where you split them up into 6 groups of 4. Now in any typical group that I teach, there are at least 5 or 6 disruptive kids in that unit. I would doubt that you would get any serious conversation going on in that class.

*Jerry*: (tentatively) We actually have tried this method in Science. We find a problem and we sit in groups and get them to work out how to do an experiment, how to select the equipment, what they make of the results. We didn't do it quite like this (i.e. with a tape recorder) but we did do it in small groups.

*Peter*: There's nothing wrong with them discussing but if it's a planned experiment the written exercise is done on an individual basis.

*Jerry*: I don't see anything wrong with them discussing.

*Peter*: In the old-fashioned terminology, it is cribbing. Yes cribbing! In an examination, you might as well say, 'Instead of having a formal exam, just sit next to each other?'

In this case, the differences were not resolved and each teacher stayed with his own point of view. Perhaps the tentative teacher, Jerry, experienced enough support from David to encourage him to work on the strategies which he was beginning to develop within a traditional framework. But Peter's hostility is a sign of the defensiveness aroused by the idea that pupils might be involved in the negotiation of meaning and in the construction of understanding. He recognizes that cooperative group work poses a strong challenge to the traditional whole-class approach that he is familiar with and probably operates well. He understands that it would demand from him a radical reformulation of educational principles: he is not yet ready to accept such a challenge. Peter holds the view that most of his pupils are incapable of participating sensibly in a discussion; moreover, he does not consider the possibility that he might offer them positive guidance in exploring an alternative learning strategy. There are many practical ways in which he could equip his pupils with the skills which would help them to engage in this kind of activity. And if he stopped to listen to his English colleague, he could hear about successful attempts to do just that. However, it is more likely that his doubts will be mirrored by his own students. Without commitment on the part of the teacher, the method may fail, so reinforcing the belief that traditional methods are best.

## PUPILS' VIEWS ON LEARNING FROM ONE ANOTHER

Pupils are also threatened by group work and those whose predominant experience has been in traditional classrooms share this mistrust of their own capacity to formulate meaning in their own words and at their own pace. They are highly likely to reject group work as a legitimate way of working and so give a powerful message to the teacher who experiments with a new method. Here are some typical statements made by young people with very little experience of working cooperatively in school (Cowie and Rudduck, 1988):

> 'No you wouldn't learn really much if you were in groups all the time because a lot of people just mess about when you're in groups. If every lesson were in groups, you wouldn't learn much.'
>
> 'Talking is not real work.'
>
> 'Your opinion (in History) doesn't matter because it's happened and it's all written down.'
>
> 'You're not gaining anything really because you're all talking together.'
>
> 'When you're in groups with your mates, you have a joke and you have a laugh but you don't do much work.'
>
> 'Well you can't spend too much time hanging around discussing things when you've got an exam in June . . . If you're working for an exam it's quite nice to discuss things but underneath you're thinking, 'I want the work. I want to have the whole thing together so I can revise it all . . . '

Talk is a distraction from the main business of writing: if you do it too much 'you end up in the last two minutes scribbling'. While these pupils accept that peers may offer a pleasant social context, they find little intellectual stimulation from collaboration with others in their age group and may be suspicious that others might 'steal my ideas' or 'use me as a resource and then get the credit'. Peers, from this standpoint, do not offer a sufficient challenge to their thinking, and may not even be trustworthy.

Teachers who introduce cooperative group work into their classes often meet with initial difficulties as pupils encounter educational demands which they have rarely met before. The attempt by Helen, an Art teacher, to help her pupils develop a language of critique gives a vivid illustration. Her 5th year pupils had no experience at all of discussing how judgements in art are made. When Helen told them that examiners reached their decisions about a piece of work through a process of discussion and that sometimes they disagreed with one another, the pupils were disturbed to think that 'the experts' might not always have 'the right answer'. The task of finding words to criticize one another's paintings was not easy for them but there was evidence, when Helen legitimized their participation in initial evaluation, that they did have the potential for developing a personal and critical response to art:

> Neatness . . . textures, shading, something like that. The textures she's using are good. I don't know whether she's using shading or pencil. It's all I can say. I'm not really good at textures.

> I like this shape here and that pattern—the way she shades it and blends it in. It's colourful. I like it. It's blended dark bits and light bits.

In putting forward hesitant responses to one another's paintings, some pupils shared their anxieties about hurting a person's feelings or letting personal relationships interfere with an aesthetic judgement. It also emerged that some worried about the dangers of peers copying their ideas. Still others fell back on ridicule and derision as a form of criticism ('It's rubbish!' or 'Look at that! It's got a blue leg!') But the main barrier seemed to be their lack of a vocabulary of art and a reluctance to consider that their views, as opposed to the views of an examiner, might have any validity. It was with relief that many of them returned to the familiar activity of getting on with their own work instead of 'just talking about it'.

Where pupils have had a positive experience of group work, it is more likely that they will express strong support for it as a method. Here two girls, Nicola and Joanne, discuss a humanities module; their teacher, Mr W, had successfully worked to create a cooperative classroom in which the pupils explored a diversity of viewpoints in the context of conflict in Northern Ireland:

*Nicola*: Well, you learn that other people have got ideas as well as you and maybe they can think something better than you. Or find a way to do it differently.

*Joanne*: Yes, I like their different views.

*Nicola*: I think that discussion is a very important part of learning. (She uses the example of N. Ireland) I still don't agree with killing people to get what they want, but I can appreciate why they do it, which is something I couldn't do before.

*Joanne*: As we're getting older Mr W's saying to us, 'Well you're this age now and you should be able to think for yourselves'.

*Nicola*: I mean, once you leave school you're not going to have teacher behind you saying you've got to think like this.

Two boys, Maxwell and Mark, consider how the process of coming to understand different perspectives on the situation in Northern Ireland, has affected their capacity to formulate an opinion using the information available. Their discussion grows out of the approach which they have been encouraged to adopt by Mr W, and Maxwell begins by challenging the use of materials prepared by Mr W for the module:

*Maxwell*: Oh yes, we were presented with enough information, but putting it down on paper it don't work, because it's hard to read something that you don't understand and put it in your own words.

*Mark*: Like if we haven't lived there, we don't know that fear. How can we write about it?

*Maxwell*: That's what we've been doing—just using information that Mr W knows instead of asking someone that had actually experienced it and then working from that. Rather like you are now. (He refers to the work of the interviewer.) Like you are now. You're working off us! Well, instead of doing that, we're working from booklets and secondary sources . . .

*Mark*: Yes but that's what we're looking at. We're in England now, aren't we? We're looking at papers and news reports, that's all that we can get about N. Ireland. In a way this course has opened up our eyes an awful lot. We didn't know as much as we know now because at night, you know, well documentary comes on, World In Action, and it's just a bloke in a tie, posh voice, two kids, big house, speaking about Northern Ireland.

*Maxwell*: Yes. Now we can't just sit and watch it.

These pupils are beginning to experience at first hand the process of working towards a real understanding of the many interrelated social, political and historical factors which underlie a complex situation. But at a more personal level, the negotiation of meaning is also opening their eyes to another critical issue— the extent to which they can choose between being spectators or actual participants in forming views of their own social world. They are beginning to develop the confidence to challenge rather than simply to accept ideas. They are asking for more explanation about what they are learning and more feedback on what they have done.

## LEARNING FROM ONE ANOTHER

How can teachers help their pupils to work effectively with one another? As we have seen, first attempts may well not be successful since young people are being asked to tackle unfamiliar and threatening tasks. But this in itself should not lead teachers to abandon the approach. There are distinct qualities of cooperation which most pupils can learn and there are guidelines for creating a cooperative classroom which will work in most settings. With experience and with the support of teachers and members of the peer-group, pupils can develop the qualities which will help them to solve problems, to complete tasks and to interact effectively with others.

At risk of sound evangelical, we would argue that our experiences of talking with teachers and observing examples of good practice have led us to the view that teachers and students can work together to help one another face personal fears and anxieties about tentativeness. By ensuring that group members understand the importance of participation, supportiveness and turn-taking, groups can learn to be tolerant as members search for the right words to capture an experience or encompass an idea. Empathic awareness of the other person's feelings, an essential ingredient of effective cooperation, can also play a key role in exploring the processes of controversy and conflict. Pupils learn by challenging one another as they reformulate points of view and practise the skills of constructive criticism. (Appropriate examples of school and classroom studies illustrate these issues in Cowie and Ruddock, 1988).

With the growing interest by educators in the potential which group work offers, there have arisen a number of publications which offer guidance to teachers for putting the idea of cooperative learning into practice. These range from very prescriptive exercises and lesson plans to more flexible case studies which may encourage teachers to adapt cooperative learning strategies to their own particular settings.

Such ways in which teachers can create a cooperative classroom are well-documented in the literature. Jaques (1984) gives innovative alternatives to the traditional seminar and tutorial in higher education. The effective use of role play and simulation in secondary schools is described in a number of books for secondary school students. Seely (1978), Brandes and Phillips (1978) and Brandes (1982) give many practical ideas for exercises and strategies which promote communication, heighten sensitivity, break down barriers between group members, and enable groups to work on qualities such as confidence, self-awareness, decision-making, trust and assertiveness. There is also a large literature on life skills development. Hopson and Scally (1981) and Kirk (1987) suggest ways in which teachers can develop new teaching strategies in order to implement programmes of personal development across the curriculum. There are books on cooperative games, notably those by Orlich (1978; 1982). Johnson and Johnson (1987) and Johnson *et al.* (1984) give practical guidelines to teachers who would like to implement appropriate group goal structures in their classrooms. This is by no means an exhaustive list, but it gives some sense of the variety of strategies which come under the umbrella of cooperative learning.

## CONCLUSION

Cooperative learning is now being widely promoted as an effective way of working and learning together. It is recognized to be democratic rather than authoritarian, collaborative rather than competitive, and valued because, amongst other things, it demonstrates the possibility of integrating personal concerns with academic learning. But the experience of pioneers in this field has also shown that, even though the climate of opinion is shifting, there are many difficulties involved in implementing group work in schools.

In this chapter, we have outlined some of the barriers, both personal and organizational, which have to be overcome by teachers who try to implement cooperative group work in the classroom. Traditional concepts of what constitutes 'real learning' are firmly held by many teachers and pupils. The organizational patterns which are strong in most educational institutions make it hard for innovations to take root. Hargreaves (1988) argues that teacher-centred instruction has been a creative response by teachers to cope with work place conditions, conflicting expectations and structural arrangements over which they have little influence and he explains the persistence of this method of teaching in terms of 'situationally controlled choice'.

We have argued the case for co-operative group work as a way of learning which promotes the capacity to negotiate meaning and which acknowledges the existence of multiple perspectives on any issue. But this idea in itself challenges traditional ways of working and opens up the possibility of a different balance of power. Other aspects of cooperative group work also pose threats to traditional values. For example, cooperative strategies devised by working-class pupils may not be valued by teachers because they challenge the traditional structure of secondary schools (Dunn, Rudduck and Cowie, 1989).

Educators need to consider their own attitudes towards cooperative group work and to develop a deeper understanding of its implications. Only when these issues are unravelled and understood will the enormous potential which pupils have for learning from one another become more than a largely untapped resource.

## REFERENCES


Aronowitz, S., and Giroux, H. (1986). *Education Under Siege*. London: Routledge & Kegan Paul.

Aronson, E. (1978). *The Jigsaw Classroom*. Beverly Hills: Sage.

Barnes, D. (1976). *From Communication to Curriculum*. Harmondsworth: Penguin.

Barnes, D., Britton, J., and Rosen, H. (1969). *Language, the Learner and the School*. Harmondsworth: Penguin.

Brandes, D. (1982). *Gamesters' Handbook Two*. London: Hutchinson and Company.

Brandes, D., and Phillips, H. (1978). *Gamesters' Handbook*, London: Hutchinson and Company.

Bridges, D. (1979). *Education, Democracy and Discussion*. Windsor: NFER.

Cowie, H., and Rudduck, J. (1988). *Learning Together, Working Together*. London: British Petroleum Education.

Damon, W. (1984). Peer education: the untapped potential. *Journal of Applied Developmental Psychology*, **5**, 331–343.

DeVries, D., and Slavin, R. (1978). Teams–Games–Tournaments: review of ten classroom experiments. *Journal of Research and Development in Education*, **12**, 28–38.

Dunn, K., Rudduck, J., and Cowie, H. (1989). Co-operation and the ideology of individualism in schools. In C. Harber and R. Meighan, (eds), *Democratic Education: Management and Curriculum Issues*. Ticknall: Education Now Books.

Gibb, A. (1985). *Enterprise: an Educational Resource. 14–16 Version*. Durham: Durham University Business School 'Enterprise' Project.
Graves, N., and Graves, T. (1988). Co-operative learning round the world, *International Association for the Study of Co-operation in Education (IASCE) Newsletter*, **9**, 1, 7–17.
Harber, C., and Meighan, R. (eds) (1989). *Democratic Education: Management and Curriculum Issues*, Ticknall: Education Now Books.
Hargreaves, A. (1988). Teaching quality: a sociological analysis, *Journal of Curriculum Studies*, **20**, 3, pp. 211–231.
HMI (1982). *Education 5–9*. London: HMSO.
HMI (1983). *9–13 Middle Schools: an Illustrative Study*. London: HMSO.
HMI (1985) *Education 8–12 in Combined Middle Schools*. London: HMSO.
Hopson, B., and Scally, M. (1981). *Lifeskills Teaching*. London: McGraw-Hill.
Jaques, D. (1984). *Learning in Groups*. London: Croom Helm.
Johnson, D. W., and Johnson, R. T. (1975). *Learning Together and Alone*. Englewood Cliffs, NJ: Prentice-Hall.
Johnson, D. W., and Johnson, R. T. (1982). *Joining Together: Group Theory and Group Skills*. Englewood Cliffs, NJ: Prentice-Hall.
Johnson, D. W., and Johnson, R. T. (1987) *Learning Together and Alone, Second edition*. Englewood Cliffs, NJ: Prentice-Hall.
Johnson, D. W., Johnson, R. T., Holubec, E., and Roy, P. (1984) *Circles of Learning*. Minnesota: Interaction Book Company.
Kelly, G. (1955). *The Psychology of Personal Constructs*. New York: Norton.
Kirk, R. (1987). *Learning in Action*. Oxford: Basil Blackwell.
Orlich, R. (1978). *The Co-operative Sports and Games Book*. New York: Pantheon.
Orlich, R. (1982). *The Second Co-operative Sports and Games Book*. New York: Pantheon.
Salmon, P. (1988). *Psychology for Teachers*. London: Routledge & Kegan Paul.
Salmon, P., and Claire, H. (1984). *Classroom Collaboration*. London: Routledge & Kegan Paul.
Salter, B., and Tapper, T. (1981). *Education, Politics and the State*. London: Grant McIntyre.
Seely, J. (1978). *In Role*. London: Edward Arnold.
Sharan, S. (1988). *The Group-Investigation Approach to Co-operative Learning: Theoretical Foundations*. Unpublished Paper, University of Tel Aviv.
Slavin, R. (1983). *Co-operative Learning*. New York: Longman.
Slavin, R. (1987). Developmental and motivational perspectives on co-operative learning: a reconciliation, *Child Development*, **58**, 1161–1167.
Slavin, R., Sharan, S., Kagan, S., Hertz-Lazarowitz, R., Webb, C., and Schmuck, R. (1985). *Learning to Co-operate, Co-operating to Learn*. New York: Plenum.
Stenhouse, L. (1970). *The Humanities Project: an Introduction*, Heinemann Books: revised by J. Rudduck (1983). Norwich: University of East Anglia Press.

PART III

# Social and Clinical Issues

CHAPTER 12

# Children Helping Children in the Family: Developmental Perspectives on Sibling Relationships

CATHERINE R. COOPER and LINDA ST. JOHN

*Board of Studies in Psychology, Clark Kerr Hall, University of California at Santa Cruz, Santa Cruz, California 95064, USA*

## INTRODUCTION

This chapter considers the nature of sibling helping in the family from the point of view of recent theoretical and empirical perspectives on close relationships and development. Traditionally, sibling research has focused on the effects of sibling constellation variables such as birth order and age spacing on the development of children as individuals (Lamb, 1982; Sutton-Smith and Rosenberg, 1970). The little work that has concerned the sibling relationship has tended to focus on negative qualities such as rivalry (Irish, 1964). In recent years, however, developmental, social, and clinical psychologists have developed more powerful causal accounts of close relationships by moving beyond structural variables. These scholars are mapping how both overt behavioural patterns and subjective experiences in relationships are influenced by cognitive and affective qualities of their members, characteristics of the interaction between them, and features of the wider social, cultural, and physical environment. Further, these scholars have begun to investigate how relationships may serve as templates or models in the construction of future ones (e.g. Hartup, 1986; Kelley *et al.*, 1983; Sroufe and Fleeson, 1986).

Children Helping Children
Edited by H. C. Foot, M. J. Morgan and R. H. Shute

This chapter proceeds in three parts, each building on these newer approaches to the study of relationships. It begins with an analysis of sibling helping from a relational perspective, then examines developmental patterns in early childhood, middle childhood, and adolescence. For each age period, we first consider current research that bears upon sibling helping, then how self and relational development affect siblings, and finally, how siblings' family experiences may account for individual differences in their helping. In the third and closing section, we consider the role that culturally-held values may play in siblings' helping.

## RELATIONAL PERSPECTIVES ON SIBLING HELPING

Sibling relationships are both unique and complex. They are likely to be the most stable and long-lasting of all relationships (Cicirelli, 1982, 1987), yet siblings have no choice in selecting one another. Early psychoanalytic work emphasized the role of sibling rivalry in personality development (Schacter, 1982), while more recent work has increasingly documented the complex, often ambivalent feelings of companionship, loyalty, and protectiveness that co-exist with rivalry and conflict in sibling relationships (Abramovitch *et al.*, 1986; Dunn and Kendrick, 1982; Furman and Buhrmester, 1982).

Similarly, recent analyses of helping in children's relationships reveal a paradoxical interplay between helping and rivalry: children's helping, linked in theory to empathy, altruism, teaching, and other prosocial behaviours, may be neither helpful nor appreciated. For example, Bryant (e.g. Bryant, 1982; Bryant and Crockenberg, 1980) found that in middle childhood, older sisters' comforting, sharing, and help-giving were contingent on their younger sisters' requesting and accepting help; in turn, such helping often elicited expressions of anger from younger sisters. As Bryant (1982, p. 103) notes, 'in fact, helping was the only prosocial behavior that correlated positively with conflictual and competitive/achievement-related sibling behaviour dimensions'.

A second example of this paradox is seen in the work of Krappman and Oswald (1986), who found in naturalistic observations in elementary school and playground settings that almost half of children's spontaneous helping was treated as problematic by at least one party. Help had often not been requested, and recipients often denigrated either the quality of the help given or the child giving it. Krappman and Oswald posit that children's helping may produce an imbalance of power that the helper may exploit and the recipient may try to counteract.

We wish to argue in this chapter that this paradox can be understood by viewing helping in terms of the dynamics of the relationship in which it occurs rather than as a skill or behaviour of an individual. Recent developmental and clinical work has emphasized the significance of individuality and connectedness within family relationships as a context for child and adolescent development, not only of individual personality characteristics such as self-esteem and identity, but also of interpersonal competence such as perspective taking and negotiation skill (Cooper, Grotevant, and Condon, 1983; Grotevant and Cooper, 1985, 1986).

At the core of our model is the proposition that central to all relationships, including marital, parent–child, sibling, and peer relations, is the interplay between the two dimensions of individuality and connectedness. Individuality is reflected by self-assertion, seen in the expression of one's own point of view, and by separateness, seen in expressions of distinctiveness of the self from others. Connectedness is reflected by expressions of acknowledgement, respect for, and responsiveness to the views of others.

The second proposition of the model is that children's and adolescents' experiences in parent–child relationships differing in these qualities affect their self-development and their relational development beyond the family (Cooper and Ayers-Lopez, 1985). Patterns of parent–child communication reflecting individuality and connectedness have been found to be associated with measures of adolescents' perceived self-competence (Cooper and Carlson, 1988), identity exploration (Cooper, Grotevant, and Condon, 1983), and peer negotiation and role-taking skill (Cooper, Grotevant, and Ayers-Lopez, 1989; Cooper and Carlson, 1989). Such work suggests that the opportunities to have a point of view that differs from others while enjoying mutual support are key qualities of well-functioning families.

From this perspective, both the behavioural expression and meaning of helping between siblings will differ as a function of the nature of their relationship. If it provides connectedness while preserving individuality, then helping would be predicted to be both sought and received in functional patterns. However, if the relationship does not offer siblings the means for maintaining their individual integrity and sense of self, then helping might be experienced by both as a way to control and exploit the vulnerability of the recipient. Moreover, according to this model, differences in the capacities of siblings to enjoy both individuality and connectedness in their relationship can be traced to their experiences within the family, especially in parent–child relationships.

We will now consider how helping functions in the context of other dynamics in sibling relationships during early childhood, middle childhood, and adolescence.

## EARLY CHILDHOOD

### Sibling helping

Although sibling interactions in early childhood are marked by both parent-like helping and teaching as well as peer-like play and rivalry (Abramovitch, Corter, and Lando, 1979; Dunn, 1983), sibling relationships during this period are at their most asymmetrical with regard to status. At this age, a two-year age gap is associated with dramatic differences in linguistic, social, cognitive, and motor skills. Reported birth order differences in siblings' behaviour may simply reflect developmental differences between them (Vandell, Minnett, and Santrock, 1987). Consequently, early childhood could be considered the least peer-like period in the history of sibling relationships; as siblings age, their relationships have been reported as becoming increasingly egalitarian (Cicirelli, 1987).

In early childhood, age is a powerful predictor of prosocial behaviour within the sibling relationship. Reports of naturalistic home observations have shown that older siblings initiate more prosocial interactions such as helping and invitations to play than their younger siblings, but also more aggression (Abramovitch *et al.*, 1986; Berndt and Bulleit, 1985; Dunn and Kendrick, 1982). Towards the end of this period, the asymmetry begins to diminish as younger siblings show more prosocial behaviour and less imitation while older siblings become less dominating.

Outside the home, preschool children have been found to be more prosocial and playful with peers than at home with their siblings. Comparing siblings' behaviour at home and school, Berndt and Bulleit (1985) found few associations. However, they did find that children with siblings close to their own age (who might be seen as more peer-like) initiated similar levels of prosocial and aggressive behaviour with their siblings and with peers. In contrast, children with siblings more dissimilar in age showed no relationship between their aggressive and prosocial initiations at home and school. Interestingly, the more help this latter group received from their siblings, the less they were observed to receive from peers at school. As with the findings of Bryant and Crockenberg (1980) and Krappman and Oswald (1986), these patterns suggest the need to consider the meaning of helping in the sibling relationship rather than simply how frequently one child exhibits behaviour that adults consider prosocial.

### The contribution of self and relational development

In studies of the development of self-understanding, young children typically view themselves and others in concrete behavioural terms. Their self-judgements are expressed as descriptions of their own specific abilities, such as running fast or working puzzles (Harter and Pike, 1984). Similarly, in describing reasons for their choice of friends, young children cite their friends' behavioural characteristics or the activities they enjoy together. (Although older children increasingly value psychological characteristics in friendships such as loyalty and trust, shared activities continue to be a key feature of friendships, especially for males [Cooper and Ayers-Lopez, 1985; Cooper, Marquis, and Edward, 1986].)

The work of Dunn and her colleagues (e.g. Dunn, 1988; Dunn and Kendrick, 1982; Dunn and Munn, 1987) has illuminated how young siblings develop self and relational capacities in the family that bear on their helping and cooperative skills. In longitudinal work, Dunn and her colleagues have conducted home observations of spontaneous daily activites and interactions among middle- and working-class mothers and their children, beginning when the second-born sibling was between 14 and 36 months of age. As she notes, young children:

> not only fight, argue, and laugh at the misfortunes and misdeeds of others; they also cooperate with others in play at an astonishingly early age, and with an appreciation of the other's goals and mood that is impressive and delightful to observe. Their ability to cooperate in play with a sibling well before they are two years old far outstrips what might have been expected on the basis of studies of children in more formal settings or with less familiar companions (Dunn, 1988, p. 108).

This work has documented that very young children both offer unsolicited help to their siblings and participate in cooperative play involving shared goals. The negotiated character of successful helping is shown by the finding that at 36 months, almost half of younger siblings' unsolicited offers to help their older siblings (while the latter were engaged in solitary activities) were not accepted.

In the process of pursuing their own interests and securing their rights as individuals, young children become attuned to social rules and a kind of intuitive moral order. Just as sibling conflict, including annoying, teasing, taunting, and sabotage, all increase during the second year, so too does a sense of individual responsibility increase as children begin to defend others' attributions of their blame. Thus, Dunn's work indicates that both the sense of an individual self and of relational helping develop apace in the context of emotional, relational, and cognitive interchanges in the family.

## Sources of individual differences in sibling helping

Individual differences in self and relational development during early childhood are increasingly traced to differences in experiences in the family. Dunn and Kendrick (1982) have linked individual differences in siblings' helping and conflict to their mothers' helping older siblings to differentiate and understand their younger siblings' experiences. Given the typical focus of young children on concrete behaviours of themselves and others, this parental assistance in conceptualizing the psychological experiences of others would appear critical.

Parental unavailability can also provide the circumstances for the development of unusual degrees of compensatory sibling loyalty and helping. In their study of German-Jewish children orphaned by the Nazis, Freud and Dann (1951) found less rivalry and competition as well as extraordinarily intense sibling attachments.

In addition, individual differences in children's cooperative behaviour with siblings has been linked to their own siblings' behaviour. Dunn (1988) found that siblings' cooperative behaviours were highly intercorrelated in pretend play as well as other contexts. Moreover, the frequency with which firstborn siblings behaved in a cooperative manner toward their 18-month-old younger siblings predicted the degree to which these younger siblings would act cooperatively six months later. Finally when older siblings displayed greater closeness and harmony and less teasing, distress, and anger in their relationship, the younger sibling became, over time, more cooperative in sibling play.

## MIDDLE CHILDHOOD

### Sibling helping

For school-age children, helping changes as a function of advances in metacognitive development, including the ability to select a behaviour from a repertoire of potential strategies as a function of situational requirements. For example, elementary school children can 'scaffold' the problem-solving of other children by providing hints and guidance as a function of their progress, whereas younger children are more likely simply to demonstrate or announce the solution (Cooper, Marquis, and Edward, 1986). Within the family, siblings show comparable gains in their skills in caretaking and in mediating and providing translations between siblings and others, including parents and other kin (Bryant, 1982; Minuchin, 1978). They also begin to offer instrumental assistance, emotional support, and a 'pioneering' model of competent behaviour with regard to life beyond the family in neighbourhood and school activities (Vandell *et al.*, 1987).

In middle childhood, schoolwork emerges as a new arena of sibling helping. Although most older siblings do help younger ones with their homework, they differ from parents in their teaching strategies by using more concrete and specific instructions and more frequent feedback, which may offer advantages to younger siblings.

Such potential advantages were found by Steward and Steward (1974), who observed three groups of preschool children as they were taught a sorting task: one group was taught by their concrete operational siblings (about 8 years old), one by their formal operational siblings (about 12), and one by their mothers. Sibling teachers in both groups gave more feedback and positive reinforcement and elicited more active responses from their younger siblings than did mothers, with concrete operational siblings giving more negative feedback and eliciting more demands for help than did formal operational siblings. Steward and Steward posit that, compared with mothers, siblings' less mature role-taking skills might make them more likely to restate instructions and verbalize for their own mastery. Their more frequent alerting, elicitations, demands, and negative feedback may also segment the learning process into small cycles; between cycles, younger siblings ask what to do next, thereby increasing their engagement.

Besides formal teaching, children in a wide range of cultures enter apprentice roles in caring for younger siblings. Weisner (1987) provides a vivid description of such socialization for parenthood in Polynesian and African families. In these cultures, children from 7 to 14 years old assume a significant proportion of the responsibilities for nurturing and disciplining their own younger siblings as well as other children. These roles are most often assigned to girls, especially in the context of other domestic chores. As Weisner notes, the assignment of caregiving responsibilities to children of this age reflects adults' attributions that they are now able to manage sequences of domestic routines as well as the family's rules and expectations for acceptable conduct. The costs and benefits for a child in this role during middle childhood are illustrated in the reminiscences of a Kenyan woman from the Abaluyia, a Bantu group:

> The first two children I took care of . . . shared a bed with me and would cry if put to sleep somewhere else. I was called their 'auntie'. They imitated everything I would do . . . I felt so frantic sometimes when they were sick, due to the attachments between us, but could do nothing to help them. But for me, it also brought me closer to their parents (her own brother and sister-in-law), and I learned a great deal about everything connected with child care . . . (the younger child benefits by feeling) that he belongs, that there is a group that appreciates a lot of things it does, that values its noise and appreciates a lot of things not even significant to parents and much older children (Weisner, 1987, pp. 240–1).

In sum, siblings' helping during middle childhood, seen in the areas of school work and household responsibilities, reflects both their maturing cognitive skills and rapport with younger children that appears to derive from their concrete orientation.

**The contribution of self and relational development**

In middle childhood, cognitive changes are also reflected in the dramatic emergence of social comparison as the basis for perceptions of the self. This results in increased concerns about inclusion in social groups, avoidance of embarrassment and rejection, and increased reliance on others, including siblings, for information, support, and gossip (Gottman and Parker, 1986). The co-occurrence of such intense needs and vulnerabilities may account for the ambivalence common in sibling relationships during middle childhood (Brody, Stoneman, and MacKinnon, 1986; Vandell *et al.*, 1987).

This heightened awareness of social comparison also helps explain the intricacies of negotiations regarding helping during middle childhood, including distinctions between necessary and unnecessary help-seeking. At this age, Nelson-Le Gall (1985) has shown that effective help seeking reflects a complex set of both individual capacities and relational dynamics, including being aware of the need for help, deciding to seek help, identifying potential helpers, and using strategies to elicit and negotiate help. Distinguishing necessary or instrumental from unnecessary or excessive requests for help, elementary school children were observed in mathematics and reading task settings in the classroom. The finding that unnecessary help-seeking was more common among unpopular children but not among children of low academic ability suggests that it is but one component of social incompetence. These findings point to relational rather than strictly ability-based origins of helping skill, and the sensitivity that skilled children of this age possess to group norms regarding self-reliance (Nelson-Le Gall and Glor-Scheib, 1986).

### Sources of individual differences in sibling helping

Among the key variables accounting for individual differences in siblings' helping are gender and family functioning in parent–child, marital, and sibling relationships. During both early and middle childhood, many studies of sibling relationships report gender differences. For example, Brody, Stoneman, and MacKinnon (1982), observing siblings' interaction in their homes, found that in early childhood, females played together more often, while males expressed more agonistic behaviour. In middle childhood, female siblings were more likely to exhibit prosocial behaviour, to play together, and to assume the teacher role, whereas male siblings appeared more interested in competitive activity.

With regard to mixed-gender sibling relationships, few systematic developmental studies have been conducted. Certainly, more public neighbourhood and school interactions among school-age boys and girls are marked by gender segregation and rivalry (Maccoby, 1988). The privacy of home may offer mixed-gender siblings a uniquely protected context in which they can relinquish their preoccupation with gender roles and share a richer array of experiences.

Parental child-rearing techniques as well as marital well-being have been found to affect the degree to which older siblings assumed helping, managing, or teaching roles. Brody, Stoneman, and Burke (1987) found that parents' use of authoritative or authoritarian patterns of childrearing were reflected in their children's behaviour with one another. In an observational study conducted in the homes of siblings and their parents, Brody, Stoneman, and Burke (in press) found that for younger siblings, marital conflict was associated with more agonistic behaviour, and low parental conflict with greater prosocial behaviour. With increased conflict, parents became less involved and more inconsistent with their children, especially in families in which the older sibling had highly active temperamental characteristics.

Finally, individual differences in siblings' helping in middle childhood may stem from processes within the sibling relationship, especially their attempts to maintain self-esteem. Tesser, Campbell, and Smith (1985) have argued that to maintain self-esteem, children begin to discount the relevance (to their own self-esteem) of domains in which their siblings excel. Although this de-identification, or differentiation of domains of self-definition between siblings, may allow them to avoid rivalry and even to 'bask in the reflected glory' of their sibling's achievements, it may have costs in addition to benefits. For example, if one sibling excels in school achievement, the other may discount the importance of academic work, and focus on social acceptance or athletic competence. However, a second pathway by which siblings may be able to maintain self-esteem and consequently prosocial behaviour is by experiencing a cooperative family environment. Research by Bryant (1977) has shown that in cooperative rather than competitive relationships, children are less invested in self-enhancement. Thus, sibling rivalry may be attenuated in two ways: through de-identification, which may prove costly to the development of both siblings, or through family experiences which affirm the distinctive competence of each family member.

In sum, middle childhood marks a period of new prosocial competence as well as new potential for rivalry in sibling relationships. Children's experiences in the family, including marital, parent–child, and sibling relationships, affect siblings' opportunities both for the development of the self as well as for teaching, cooperation, and nurturing that can occur in their relationship. In fact, it appears that siblings' self-esteem may enhance their ability to provide nurturance to one another.

## ADOLESCENCE

### Sibling helping

Research on altruistic behaviour during adolescence focuses on the individual helper, documenting, for example, frequencies of helpful acts and their origins in parental modelling and inductive parenting styles (Mussen and Eisenberg-Berg, 1977). Advances in altruism rest on growth in role-taking skills that enable adolescents to differentiate their own feelings and needs from those of others, and eventually not only to coordinate these perspectives, but also to incorporate their awareness of mutuality in relationships in collaborative behaviour, including the negotiation of interpersonal conflict (Selman *et al.*, 1986).

Within the family, adolescents experience greater mutuality with their siblings than with parents. For example, O'Brien (1988) found that both younger (12–16 years) and older (18–23 years) adolescents were more receptive and understanding of their siblings' interventions than those of their parents. Adolescents also expected their siblings to mediate for them with their parents, resulting in greater mutuality and less asymmetry. Siblings were sought as frequently as mothers and more frequently than fathers for emotional support, although mothers served as the most important source of emotional, informational, and material help.

## The contribution of self and relational development

Children moving from middle childhood to adolescence show increasing tendencies to view themselves in more complex and differentiated psychological terms, and to evaluate themselves more on logical, evidential, and autonomous bases and less on the basis of social comparisons (Rosenberg, 1986). These cognitive and emotional changes create new potential for intimacy, as adolescents begin to use close relationships for self-exploration, especially when they can disclose and compare personal information with trust in its confidentiality (Cooper and Ayers-Lopez, 1985). Compared with younger children, adolescents are more likely to define friendship as involving the sharing of thoughts and feelings; they also display greater knowledge of intimate information about their best friends.

During adolescence, sibling relationships also begin to offer helping grounded in mutual psychological understanding rather than simply unilateral donating of services. O'Brien (1988) found that siblings in later adolescence expressed greater intimacy and closeness than those in earlier adolescence. Such findings suggest a decline in social comparison and rivalry, with a *rapprochement* similar to that described by object relations theorists for parent–adolescent relationships during this same period (e.g. Blos, 1979).

## Sources of individual differences in sibling helping

Although adolescent siblings have achieved the developmental potential for providing one another with intimacy and support, these benefits are not universally available. For example, adolescent females interact more, express more connectedness, and feel closer to family members than do males (Baskett and Johnson, 1982; Cooper and Carlson, 1989; Youniss and Smollar, 1985). Adolescent females have also been found to be more likely than males to approach fathers, mothers, and siblings for any kind of support (O'Brien, 1988).

Depending on their family experiences, adolescent siblings may experience less de-identification and enjoy greater closeness. Daniels *et al.* (1985) found that female adolescent siblings with close relationships also had closer relationships with their mothers and peers and participated more equally in family decision-making. In addition, these adolescents were more likely to score higher on measures of emotional adjustment, including prosocial behaviour.

As in middle childhood, adolescent siblings' relationships with their parents have been linked with the rivalry they feel towards one another. In studies of university students from two- and three-child families conducted from a psychoanalytic perspective, Schacter (1982, 1985) has found that two-thirds of siblings report a pattern of 'split-parent' identification, that is, each established a close relationship with a different parent. Such patterns occurred primarily between first- and second-born siblings and more often in same-sex than opposite-sex sibling pairs. Like Tesser, Campbell, and Smith (1985), Schacter views such processes as a defence against rivalry, enabling each child to have a special place within the family. She posits that such differentiation also allows parents to reduce potential competition and comparison with one another by providing each with a special relationship with one child.

## CROSS-CULTURAL PERSPECTIVES

The responsibilities of siblings vary dramatically across cultures, in part as a function of cultural differences in parent–child relationships. One key dimension concerns the degree to which parents demonstrate and encourage egalitarian interactions. In their work comparing family and peer relationships in Kenyan and northeastern US communities, Whiting and Edwards (1988) reported that the typical mother in their US sample tended to conduct exchanges with her children in a verbally explicit way, emphasizing principles of fairness between siblings and negotiating with them as if she and they were of equal social status and as though they were of equivalent status *vis-à-vis* one another. For example, during sibling conflicts, mothers intervened and emphasized the merits of the issue rather than basing their support on natural hierarchies based on age or physical size. In contrast, Whiting and Edwards' observations in Kenya (as well as comparable data from several other African and Asian samples) indicated that mother–child relationships were conducted on more asymmetrical, power-assertive terms. In these communities, siblings were viewed as important as caregivers and accorded power appropriate to such roles.

A second dimension illuminated by cross-cultural work concerns variability in group norms concerning communality and individualism. In studies of Hawaiian-American and Kenyan families, Weisner (1987) has described how children's experiences in shared-caretaking families occur in the context of a stronger sense of family belonging than is typical of middle-class Caucasian urban families. As Weisner notes, these shared-caretaking families

> encourage interdependence (not autonomous independence); responsibility to others (not expectations of services from adults); shared work and functions (rather than particular, specialized tasks); affiliation (not competition and individual achievement); and deference to parents (not egalitarian discussions and family 'democracy') (Weisner, 1987, p. 250).

However, such practices are currently showing changes from communal towards more individualistic values, reflecting changes in economic and demographic conditions. Weisner observes that changes from shared caretaking between parents and older siblings in large family groups towards greater reliance on parental caretaking in small families parallels four ecocultural changes: families moving from agrarian to urban industrial settings, decreasing birth and death rates, increasing involvement of children in school, and a resulting emphasis on the uniqueness and special needs of children. In a comparison of rural and urban Kenyan families, Weisner found that urban mothers expressed concern that such caregiving responsibilities would interfere with their children's individual achievement in school.

Thus, group norms, whether in communities, families, or schools, emphasize individual achievement and self-reliance and consequently devalue helping. Under such circumstances, helping is seen as draining the attentional resources of the helper, while receiving help may be viewed as placing the recipient at risk of appearing and feeling incompetent.

## CONCLUSION

In this chapter, we have argued that siblings have the potential of offering significant positive influence on one another's development. Although sibling helping has often been compared unfavourably in its sophistication with adult skills, the peer-like relationship of siblings appears to afford distinctive opportunities for more spontaneous and mutual relational experiences, including play, rivalry, and shared assistance and support. In early childhood, sibling helping is likely to take the form of functional, task-oriented behaviours; in middle childhood, caregiving, helping with academic work, or mediating with parents; and in adolescence, being a confidante.

However, such potential is not realized in all sibling encounters or relationships. Recent work has shown how peer helping and other prosocial behaviour is associated with parent–child as well as sibling relational patterns promoting both individuality and connectedness. This relational account of differences in sibling helping presented in this chapter departs from traditional structural accounts emphasizing birth order, age spacing, and gender as explanatory factors in sibling development (Minnett *et al.*, 1983; Sutton-Smith and Rosenberg, 1970). Research conducted from the latter perspective has yielded inconsistent findings, and at best, suggests that status variables account for only modest amounts of variance in sibling relational patterns. Future work will productively investigate the mechanisms of attribution as well as behaviours by which helping operates productively in sibling relationships.

Finally, we have found that the most illuminating research on siblings considers sibling relationships in the context of the family and of cultural values concerning the interplay of self and relationships and of individuality and connectedness. Certainly research to date amply demonstrates that in a family, classroom, or culture in which shared benefit is not valued, helping is less likely to occur.

## ACKNOWLEDGEMENTS

The authors gratefully acknowledge the insightful comments of Robert G. Cooper and Campbell Leaper. Work on this chapter was supported by a University of California Faculty Research Grant to Catherine R. Cooper.

## REFERENCES

Abramovitch, R., Corter, C., and Lando, B. (1979). Sibling interaction in the home, *Child Development*, **50**, 997–1003.

Abramovitch, R., Corter, C., Pepler, D., and Stanhope, L. (1986). Sibling and peer interaction: A final follow-up and a comparison, *Child Development*, **57**, 217–229.

Baskett, L. M., and Johnson, S. M. (1982). The young child's interactions with parents versus siblings: a behavioral analysis, *Child Development*, **53**, 643–650.

Berndt, T. J., and Bulleit, T. N. (1985). Effects of sibling relationships on preschoolers' behavior at home and at school, *Developmental Psychology*, **21**, 761–767.

Blos, P. (1967/1979). The second individuation process of adolescence. In P. Blos (ed.), *The Adolescent Passage: Developmental Issues*. New York: International University Press.

Brody, G. H., Stoneman, Z., and Burke, M. (1987). Child temperaments and maternal and paternal perceptions of individual child adjustment: a within-family analysis, *American Journal of Orthopsychiatry*, **57**, 561–569.

Brody, G. H., Stoneman, Z., and Burke, M. (in press). Family system and individual child correlates of sibling behavior, *American Journal of Orthopsychiatry*.

Brody, G. H., Stoneman, Z., and MacKinnon, C. E. (1982). Role asymmetries in interactions among school-aged children, their younger siblings and their friends, *Child Development*, **53**, 1364–1370.

Brody, G. H., Stoneman, Z., and MacKinnon. (1986). Contributions of maternal child-rearing practices and play contexts to sibling interactions. *Journal of Applied Developmental Psychology*, **7**, 225–236.

Bryant, B. K. (1977). The effects of the interpersonal context of evaluation on self- and other-enhancement behavior, *Child Development*, **48**, 885–892.

Bryant, B. K. (1982). Sibling relationships in middle-childhood. In M. E. Lamb and B. Sutton-Smith (eds), *Sibling Relationships: Their Nature and Significance across the Lifespan* (pp. 87–121). Hillsdale, NJ: Lawrence Erlbaum Associates.

Bryant, B., and Crockenberg, S. (1980). Correlates and dimensions of prosocial behavior: female siblings with their mothers, *Child Development*, **51**, 529–544.

Cicirelli, V. G. (1982). Sibling influence throughout the lifespan. In M. E. Lamb and B. Sutton-Smith (eds), *Sibling Relationships: Their Nature and Significance across the Lifespan* (pp. 267–285). Hillsdale, NJ: Lawrence Erlbaum Associates.

Cicirelli, V. G. (1987). Attachment theory and sibling psychological support in old age. Paper presented at the IXth Biennial Meetings of the International Society for the Study of Behavioral Development. Tokyo, Japan.

Cooper, C. R., and Ayers-Lopez, S. (1985). Family and peer systems in early adolescence: new models of the role of relationships in development, *Journal of Early Adolescence*, **5**(1), 9–21.

Cooper, C. R. and Carlson, C. (July 1988). Individuality and connectedness in family relationships during early adolescence. Paper presented at the meetings of the International Conference on Personal Relationships, Vancouver, Canada.

Cooper, C. R., and Carlson, C. I. (1989). The role of family relationships in self-esteem and peer relationships in early adolescence. Paper presented at the meetings of the International Society for the Study of Behavioral Development, Jyvaskyla, Finland.

Cooper, C. R., Grotevant, H. D., and Ayers-Lopez, S. (1989). Links between patterns of negotiation in adolescents' family and peer interaction. Manuscript under editorial review.

Cooper, C. R., Grotevant, H. D., and Condon, S. M. (1983) Individuality and connectedness in the family as a context for adolescent identity formation and role-taking skill, *New Directions for Child Development*, **22**, 43–59.

Cooper, C. R., Marquis, A., and Edward, D. (1986). Four perspectives on peer learning among elementary school children. In E. C. Mueller and C. R. Cooper (eds), *Process and Outcome in Peer Relationships* (pp. 269–300). Orlando, FL: Academic Press.

Daniels, D., Dunn, J., Furstenberg, F. F., and Plomin, R. (1985). Environmental differences within the family and adjustment differences within pairs of adolescent siblings, *Child Development*, **56**, 764–774.

Dunn, J. (1983). Sibling relationships in early childhood, *Child Development*, **54**, 787–811.

Dunn, J. (1988). *The Beginnings of Social Understanding*. Cambridge: Harvard University Press.

Dunn, J., and Kendrick, C. (1982). Siblings and their mothers: Developing relationships within the family. In M. E. Lamb and B. Sutton-Smith (eds), *Sibling Relationships: Their Nature and Significance across the Lifespan* (pp. 39–60). Hillsdale, NJ: Lawrence Erlbaum Associates.

Dunn, J., and Munn, P. (1987). Development of justification in disputes with mother and sibling, *Developmental Psychology*, **23**, 791–798.

Freud, A., and Dann, S. (1951). An experiment in group living. In R. Eisler (ed.), *The Psychoanalytic Study of the Child* (Vol. 6). New York: International Universities Press.

Furman, W., and Buhrmester, D. (1982). The contribution of siblings and peers to the parenting process. In M. J. Kostelnik, A. I. Rabin, L. A. Phenice, and A. K. Soderman (eds), *Child Nurturance, Volume 2. Patterns of Supplementary Parenting*. New York: Plenum.

Gottman, J. M., and Parker, J. G. (eds) (1986). *Conversations of Friends: Speculations on Affective Development*. Cambridge: Cambridge University Press.

Grotevant, H. D., and Cooper, C. R. (1985). Patterns of interaction in family relationships and the development of identity exploration in adolescence, *Child Development*, **56**, 415–428.

Grotevant, H. D., and Cooper, C. R. (1986). Individuation in family relationships, *Human Development*, **29**, 82–100.

Harter, S., and Pike, R. (1984). The pictorial scale of perceived competence and social acceptance for young children, *Child Development*, **55**, 1969–1982.

Hartup, W. W. (1986). On relationships and development. In W. W. Hartup and Z. Rubin (eds), *Relationships and Development*. Hillsdale, NJ: Erlbaum.

Irish, D. P. (1964). Sibling interaction: a neglected aspect in family life research, *Social Forces*, **42**, 279–288.

Josselson, R. (1980). Ego development in adolescence. In J. Adelson (ed.), *Handbook of Adolescent Psychology*. New York: John Wiley.

Kelly, H. H., Berscheid, E., Christensen, A., Harvey, J., Huston, T. L., Levinger, G., McClintock, E., Peplau, L. A., and Peterson, D. (1983). *Close Relationships*. San Francisco: Freeman.

Krappmann, L., and Oswald, H. (1986, September). *"Prosocial" and "antisocial" helping among ten-year old children—Results from a qualitative study in natural settings*. Paper presented at the II European Conference on Developmental Psychology, Rome, Italy.

Lamb, M. E. (1982). Sibling relationships across the lifespan: An overview and introduction. In M. E. Lamb and B. Sutton-Smith (eds), *Sibling Relationships: Their Nature and Significance across the Lifespan* (pp. 123–151). Hillsdale, NJ: Erlbaum.

Maccoby, E. E. (1988). Gender as a social category, *Developmental Psychology*, **24**, 755–765.

Minnett, A. M., Vandell, D. L., Santrock, J. W. (1983). The effects of sibling status on sibling interaction: influence of birth order, age spacing, sex of child and sex of sibling, *Child Development*, **54**, 1064–1072.

Minuchin, S. (1978). *Families and Family Therapy*. Cambridge: Harvard University Press.

Mussen, P. H., and Eisenberg-Berg, N. (1977). *Caring, Sharing, and Helping*. San Francisco: Freeman.

Nelson-Le Gall, S. (1985). Necessary and unnecessary help-seeking in children, *Journal of Genetic Psychology*, **148**(1), 53–62.

Nelson-Le Gall, S., and Glor-Scheib, S. (1986). Academic help-seeking and peer relations in school, *Contemporary Educational Psychology*, **11**, 187–193.

O'Brien, R. W. (1988). *The role of siblings in the development of individuation during adolescence*. Unpublished doctoral dissertation, Catholic University of America, Washington, DC.

Rosenberg, M. (1986). Self-concept from middle childhood through adolescence. In J. Suls and A. G. Greenwald (eds), *Psychological Perspectives on the Self: Vol. 3*. Hillsdale, NJ: Erlbaum.

Schacter, F. F. (1982). Sibling deidentification and split-parent identification: a family trend. In M. E. Lamb and B. Sutton-Smith (eds), *Sibling Relationships: Their Nature and Significance across the Lifespan* (pp. 123–151). Hillsdale, NJ: Erlbaum.

Schacter, F. F. (1985). Sibling deidentification in the clinic: Devil vs. angel, *Family Processes*, **24**, 415–427.

Selman, R. L., Beardslee, W. R., Schultz, L. H., Krupa, M., and Podorefsky, D. (1986). Assessing adolescent interpersonal negotiation strategies: toward the integration of structural and functional models, *Developmental Psychology*, **22**, 450–459.

Sroufe, L. A., and Fleeson, J. (1986). Attachment and the construction of relationships. In W. W. Hartup and Z. Rubin (eds), *Relationships and Development*. Hillsdale, NJ: Erlbaum.

Steward, M., and Steward, D. (1974). Parents and siblings as teachers. In E. Y. Mach, L. C. Handy, and L. B. Hamerlynch (eds), *Behavior Modification Approaches to Parenting* (pp. 193–206). New York: Brunner/Mazel.

Sutton-Smith, B., and Rosenberg, B. (1970). *The Sibling*. New York: Holt, Rinehart & Winston.

Tesser, A., Campbell, J., and Smith, M. (1985). Friendship choice and performance: self evaluation maintenance in children, *Journal of Personality and Social Psychology*, **46**, 561–574.

Vandell, D. L., Minnett, A. M., and Santrock, J. W. (1987). Age differences in sibling relationships during middle childhood, *Journal of Applied Developmental Psychology*, **8**, 247–257.

Weisner, T. S. (1987). Socialization for parenthood in sibling caretaking societies. In J. B. Lancaster, J. Altmann, A. S. Rossi, and L. R. Sherrod (eds), *Parenting across the Life Span: Biosocial Dimensions* (pp. 237–270). New York: Aldine de Gruyter.

Whiting, B. B., and Edwards, C. P. (1988). *Children of Different Worlds: The Formation of Social Behavior*. Cambridge: Harvard University Press.

Youniss, J., and Smollar, J. (1985). *Adolescent Relations with Mothers, Fathers, and Friends*. Chicago: University of Chicago Press.

CHAPTER 13

# Peer Interactions and the Development of Handicapped Children's Social and Communicative Competence

MICHAEL J. GURALNICK

*Director, Child Development and Mental Retardation Centre, WJ-10, University of Washington, Seattle, Washington 98195, USA*

## INTRODUCTION

The preschool years signal for most young children a major transition to a world in which relationships with peers begin to assume a prominent role in their social development. Even with extensive experience with peers as infants and toddlers in day care or in playgroups, the rapid development of cognitive and linguistic structures that occurs between three and five years of age provides the foundation for the establishment of the more extensive and elaborate peer relations that characterize the preschool period (Guralnick, 1986).

The rather remarkable array of research that has been carried out in the field of peer relations in the last 15 years has suggested strongly that these child-child social and communicative interactions have important implications for young children's development (Hartup, 1983). Many researchers and theorists have suggested that child–child interactions foster socialization of aggressive tendencies, contribute to moral development, promote language and communication, and facilitate the development of prosocial behaviours and social-cognitive processes (Bates, 1975; Garvey, 1986; Hartup, 1978, 1983; Rubin

Children Helping Children
Edited by H. C. Foot, M. J. Morgan and R. H. Shute

and Lollis, 1988). Although much of the evidence pertaining to the influence of peers on development is correlational and circumstantial, the fact remains that failure to establish effective peer relationships is predictive of future adjustment problems (Parker and Asher, 1987). Moreover, the nature of peer relationships during the preschool years appears to be a sensitive index of developmental difficulties (Guralnick, 1989).

Fortunately, the vast majority of young children are able to resolve satisfactorily problems encountered in approaching essential peer-related social tasks, such as conflict resolution, entry into a peer group, responding to aggression, and negotiating and sharing. However, this does not appear to be the case for children with handicaps, especially those with general (cognitive) delays (e.g. Guralnick and Groom, 1985, 1987a; Guralnick and Weinhouse, 1984). As will be seen, not only do children with a wide range of disabilities exhibit a disproprortionately high rate of peer interaction problems in comparison with appropriate non-handicapped groups, but the difficulties these children experience appear to be unusual in the sense that the magnitude of their problems far exceeds that which would be expected on the basis of their progress in other developmental domains, particularly cognitive development.

The origins of these peer interaction difficulties for young handicapped children are quite complex and not fully understood, but the foundations for these deficits are likely to be in place well before children reach preschool age. Certainly, a cognitive component is implicated, as many models of peer-related social competence rely extensively on the cognitive abilities of the participants (e.g. Dodge *et al.*, 1986). Krakow and Kopp (1983) have demonstrated how information processing difficulties affect developmentally delayed children's ability to solve problems involving social exchange. Difficulties in detecting and interpreting social cues, as well as processing rapidly changing complex social behaviours of peers, are likely to pose problems for children with a variety of different disabilities.

However, it is apparent that non-cognitive factors can have a significant impact as well. Some insight into the difficulties handicapped children experience can be found in an examination of the historical antecedents of individual differences normally developing children exhibit in both their willingness to engage in peer interactions as well as the quality and effectiveness of those relationships. Although it is beyond the scope of this chapter to explore these factors in any detail, it is now well established that portions of this variability have their origins in early and continuing parent–child interactions.

For example, there now exists a substantial group of studies demonstrating that insecure attachment between parents and infants is associated with lowered initial sociability with peers and difficulties in establishing peer relationships in general (Easterbrooks and Lamb, 1979; Lieberman, 1977; Pastor, 1981; Waters, Wippman, and Sroufe, 1979). Rubin and his colleagues have described some potential developmental pathways that can lead to peer relationship problems. These pathways consider interactions occurring among numerous variables including child characteristics, particularly temperamental variations, family interaction styles, and environmental factors and resources (Rubin, LeMare, and Lollis, in press; Rubin and Lollis, 1988). Recent research has now moved toward an examination of specific aspects of parent behaviour and interactive skills that can directly influence the peer-related social competence of their children, such as social modelling, forms of communicative exchange, and the extent to which parents directly encourage and monitor peer interactions (Ladd and Golter, 1988; MacDonald and Parke, 1984; Putallaz, 1987). In addition, Gottman and Katz (1989) have demonstrated recently the existence of a strong association between marital conflict and social competence with peers. Assessments of physiological indices were consistent with a model suggesting that difficulties encountered by children are related to their ability to control emotional arousal. Indeed, conflict resolution and escalation and de-escalation processes are vital to maintaining extended social interactions with peers (Gottman, 1983). Similarly, MacDonald (1987) suggested that regulation of affect during parent–child play can serve an important role in peer-related social competence.

Given these influences, the question arises as to whether families with handicapped children exhibit patterns that may not be as conducive to the development of their child's peer-related social competence in comparison with families with non-handicapped children. Unfortunately, available evidence suggests that many of the interactions between parents and handicapped children are, in fact, stressed, apparently setting the conditions for reduced levels of competence in relations with peers.

Specifically, the presence of a handicapped child within a family clearly adds an additional element of tension and potential discord (Bristol, 1987; Crnic, Friedrich, and Greenberg, 1983; Farber, 1975). Similarly, difficulties encountered in forming secure attachments also appear to be increased for these families, endangering the quality of parent–child relations (e.g. Stone and Chesney, 1978). Problems encountered in establishing affectively positive parent–child relationships and the formation of more directive communication styles (Crnic, Friedrich and Greenberg, 1983; Cunningham *et al.*, 1981) in families with a handicapped child suggest conditions that will adversely affect future peer-related social competence. Many families do, in fact, make successful adaptations, a circumstance that will vary with available resources and the severity of a child's disability (Beckman, 1983; Crnic, Friedrich and Greenberg, 1983). However, the increased risk of stress and discord remains, and may well serve to alter the ultimate quality and effectiveness of children's peer-related social competence.

Moreover, it appears that opportunities for exchanges with peers for handicapped children decline throughout the preschool years (Lewis, Feiring, and Brooks-Gunn, 1987). Whether the stigmatizing aspects (Goffman, 1963) or perhaps the prevalence of associated behaviour problems (Guralnick and

Groom, 1985) are responsible for this constriction of the social world of handicapped children, it is clear that limitations are imposed on the growth and development of peer relations.

Despite the array of environmental and family factors that may predispose handicapped children to engage in less than ideal peer relations by the time they reach preschool age, the impact of specific and extended experiences with peers themselves cannot be ignored. During the preschool years activities involving peers become more central, and the influence of one's companions may well be able to alter the developmental path established by these early and perhaps continuing experiences.

Accordingly, the purpose of this chapter is to examine the peer relationships of preschool age handicapped children, placing special emphasis on the importance of the characteristics of their companions in regulating essential features of peer-related social competence. A particular focus will be the social and communicative adaptations and accommodations required of young non-handicapped children to interact effectively and appropriately with children different in developmental status. It should be noted that arrangements designed to create highly structured situations usually involving explicit training of one or more peers, such as that which occurs in peer tutoring (see Chapters 4, 5, and 6, this volume), will not be considered here. Rather, the nature and impact of social and communicative interactions as they typically occur in both dyad and group settings will be the focus of this chapter.

First, descriptive information on the nature of handicapped children's peer interactions will be presented. Emphasis in this section will be placed on peer interaction assessment procedures as well as an identification of the nature of specific deficits exhibited by handicapped children. This information will provide a framework for understanding the effects of the impact children's companions may have on peer-related social competence as presented in the remainder of the chapter. It is important to note as well that most of this descriptive and related research has been carried out on children with cognitive delays. As a consequence, the information provided in this chapter will focus primarily on that population of young handicapped children.

This initial section will be followed by a discussion of the impact of the characteristics of one's companions on peer-related social behaviour, focusing primarily on the effects of social exchanges occurring with non-handicapped children. Issues of social integration between children differing in developmental status, the qualitative nature of interactions occurring between handicapped and non-handicapped children, and the appropriateness of social and communicative accommodations and adaptations by non-handicapped children to handicapped children will then be addressed. Finally, systematic manipulations of the characteristics of handicapped children's companions accomplished through changes in the composition of groups as occurs in an effort to modify peer-related social interactions will be analysed.

## HANDICAPPED CHILDREN'S PEER INTERACTIONS

Cross-sectional and longitudinal studies of preschool age handicapped children's peer relations have yielded consistent findings suggesting both specific deficits and atypical developmental patterns. As noted, much of this research has centred on children with a range of developmental (cognitive) delays. In general, the peer interactions of these children have been assessed in free-play situations while interacting with other children with similar delays or disabilities. Since the effects of one's peers on children's social and communicative development is a central theme of this chapter, the unavailability of non-handicapped children (due to segregated environments) and the relatively homogeneous nature of the children with regard to social skills in these settings should be noted. Fortunately, most of the analyses of delayed children's peer relations have been presented within a developmental framework and comparisons have been made with non-handicapped children at equivalent developmental levels.

This section will focus on assessments of the peer relations of young handicapped children as reflected by measures obtained from many different perspectives. Included are global measures of peer-related social interactions, some specific indices of individual peer-related social behaviours, measures of the ability of handicapped children to adjust their communicative interactions to the characteristics of their companions, and process analyses of behaviour request episodes.

### Global measures

Descriptive accounts of the peer-related social competence of both handicapped and non-handicapped children have frequently utilized variations of Parten's (1932) index of social participation. This scale characterizes the global peer interactions of young children as they progress from independent to group play. Concerns do exist with regard to the sequential and hierarchical nature of this scale (Bakeman and Brownlee, 1980; Roper and Hinde, 1978; Rubin, Maioni, and Hornung, 1976; Smith, 1978). However, its widespread use reflects the scale's sensitivity to developmental changes, socioeconomic status, and environmental conditions (e.g. Barnes, 1971; Rubin and Krasnor, 1980; Smith, 1978; Vandenberg, 1981). In addition, the scale has been shown to be sensitive to differences associated with the characteristics of one's peers (Goldman, 1981) and correlates with other indices of peer-related social competence (Rubin, Daniels-Bierness, and Hayvren, 1981).

The most commonly used current version of this scale is the one developed by Rubin and his colleagues (Rubin, Maioni and Hornung, 1976; Rubin, Watson, and Jambor, 1978). The scale consists of 11 mutually exclusive and exhaustive categories. Based primarily on Parten's (1932) social participation scale, the three primary play categories are as follows: (1) solitary play—playing alone, (2) parallel play—playing next to another child, and (3) group play—playing with another child in some mutual fashion (actually a combination of Parten's [1932] associative and cooperative play categories). This scale also yields an additional dimension related to the level of cognitive play in which children are engaged. Specifically, four measures of cognitive play based on the work of Smilansky (1968) are nested within the three social participation categories. Accordingly, whenever children are observed participating in solitary, parallel, or group play, their play is also classified into one of the following: (1) functional—simple repetitive play, (2) constructive—learning to use materials, creating something, (3) dramatic—role taking and pretend play, and (4) games with rules—child behaves in accordance with prearranged rules. The eight remaining categories consist of: (1) unoccupied behaviour—child is not playing, (2) onlooker behaviour—child watches other children but does not enter into play, (3) reading—reading, leafing through a book, (4) rough and tumble—mock and playful fighting, running after one another, (5) exploration—examining physical properties of objects, (6) active conversation—talking, questioning, and suggesting to other children, but not playing, (7) transitional—moving from one activity to another, and (8) adult-directed—any activity with an adult. Typically, the free play sequence is divided up into 10- or 20-second intervals and that category which best describes the child's behaviour for that interval is coded. If solitary, parallel, or group play is coded, one of the four cognitive play classifications is also made. The identity of those peers with whom a particular child interacted is also obtained.

When the naturally occurring peer interactions of handicapped children participating in play with other handicapped children are described within this framework, a pattern emerges suggesting a peer interaction deficit. Specifically, for moderately and mildly delayed preschool age children, a series of cross-sectional and short-term longitudinal studies (Crawley and Chan, 1982; Guralnick and Weinhouse, 1984; Guralnick and Groom, 1985) have documented that delayed children engage in the most advanced form of peer interaction, i.e., group play, only to a very limited extent. In fact, comparisons with non-handicapped samples similar in developmental level suggested that, on average, delayed children participated in group play approximately half as often as would be expected on the basis of their level of cognitive development. Unfortunately, even this figure is somewhat deceptive in that only a small proportion of the delayed children accounted for a majority of the more advanced forms of social play. Moreover, cross-sectional analyses across the preschool years failed to find a trend toward increased participation in more interactive forms of play or a decrease in solitary or parallel types of play. These patterns are highly atypical from a developmental perspective. In addition, these deficits appear to be characteristic of other groups of handicapped children (see Guralnick, 1986) such as those with hearing impairments (Higgenbotham and Baker, 1981).

It is important to note as well that aspects of these peer interaction deficits have been observed in settings which included other non-handicapped children (e.g. Guralnick and Groom, 1987a). As discussed in detail in a subsequent section of this chapter, the simple availability of non-handicapped children may minimize some of the peer relationship difficulties, but the essential features of the deficit remain intact.

## Specific social behaviours

The relative absence of group play for handicapped children found in these studies is especially discouraging since it is this measure that provides the best index of young children's abilities to utilize whatever social skills and social resources are available to them to engage in extended play interactions. The design of intervention programmes requires insight into those specific social skills or social behaviours that might be associated with peer interaction deficits revealed by the more global measures. The simple frequency of social behaviours is not the answer, as this measure appears to be of minor value in identifying children at-risk for problematic peer relations (Asher, Markell, and Hymel, 1981). However, more qualitative approaches that consider both the positive and negative aspects of peer interactions as well as those specific social behaviours and social processes that are associated with peer-related social competence should prove more useful.

One of the most comprehensive and widely utilized scales that focuses on children's individual social behaviours consists of a cluster of behaviours originally developed by White and Watts (1973). Such behaviours include gaining the attention of peers, leading peers in activities, imitating a peer, expressing affection or hostility, competing for an adult's attention or equipment, and following or refusing to follow a peer's requests. The success of social bids (i.e. actually gaining the attention of peers) can also be evaluated using this scale. These individual social behaviours have demonstrated predictive and concurrent validity in relation to peer-related social competence. Specifically, these component behaviours do increase across the preschool years, they correspond with other measures of peer-related social competence such as teacher ratings and peer sociometrics, and they correlate positively with the index of social participation (Connolly and Doyle, 1981; Doyle, Connolly, and Rivest, 1980; Wright, 1980).

When this scale is applied to observations of the free play of developmentally delayed children, an interesting pattern is obtained (Guralnick and Groom, 1985, 1987a; Guralnick and Weinhouse, 1984). Overall, interactions tend to be positive. However, compared to non-handicapped children at similar developmental levels, there is a noticeable absence of those individual social behaviours associated with peer-related social competence (see White, 1980). The limited attempts of mildly delayed children in particular to lead others, to use them as resources, or to show affection appear to restrict opportunities to establish and maintain extended peer interactions. Overall, the lack of directedness in peer play appears to be the most obvious feature distinguishing the play of delayed from non-delayed children.

### Communicative adjustments

The ability to adjust communicative exchanges in accordance with the characteristics of one's companion is an essential feature of peer-related social competence (see Guralnick, 1981a, for discussion). Successful exchanges typically require numerous adjustments in syntactic, semantic, pragmatic, and discourse features of language. By the time young children reach preschool age, these adjustment capabilities are well established, including interactions occurring with companions differing in chronological age (Gelman and Shatz, 1977; James, 1978; Masur, 1978; Sachs and Devin, 1976; Shatz and Gelman, 1973). Overall, non-handicapped preschool age children seem to make adjustments that are appropriate in that (1) communicative effectiveness is increased (e.g., use of syntactically less complex utterances, but greater use of attentional devices and more redundancy when interacting with younger companions) and (2) social rules in relation to task demands are observed.

Are young handicapped children able to make these adjustments? Are these children sufficiently sensitive to situations and task demands as well as to the characteristics of their companions (e.g. chronological age, developmental level, linguistic abilities) to enable them to make appropriate modifications? Although research is limited, it does appear that adjustments generally similar to those of comparable groups of non-handicapped children do occur. For example, language-impaired children interacting with adults, same-age peers, and toddlers do adjust their use of imperatives, contingent queries, self-repetitions, and total number of questions in a manner similar to normally developing age-mates (Fey and Leonard, 1984). Mildly developmentally delayed young children also have demonstrated an ability to adjust their language to the characteristics of their companions. Recordings of the communicative exchanges of mildly delayed children during free-play with non-handicapped, other mildly delayed, as well as moderately and severely delayed companions revealed adjustments in syntactic complexity, semantic diversity, and pragmatic aspects of language highly similar in magnitude and direction to those of normally developing children (Guralnick and Paul-Brown, 1986). More recently, Guralnick and Paul-Brown (in press) confirmed that the communicative adjustments of a group of 4-year-old mildly delayed children were similar to those of a developmentally matched group of normally developing children, particularly in relation to pragmatic aspects of language. However, it is important to note that concerns exist about the ability of mildly delayed (Guralnick and Paul-Brown, 1986) and language-impaired children (Fey, Leonard, and Wilcox, 1981) to adjust their communicative interactions when the chronological ages or developmental differences of companions are less marked.

Moreover, despite these similarities, it is important to recognize that the conclusions on communicative adjustments noted above were based primarily on utterance-by-utterance analyses of data summed to obtain overall frequencies, or on proportions of utterances or utterance types as addressed to different listener groups. On some occasions, the immediate effects of a preceding utterance were analysed. However, as discussed in the next section, the utterance-by-utterance approach to assessing communicative adjustments has many limitations. More recently developed social/communicative process and sequential analysis measures may provide a different perspective on handicapped children's communicative skills.

**Process and sequential measures**

The measures of social participation, individual social behaviours, and the utterance-by-utterance communicative measures have been able to capture many important features of a most complex social process. However, such static measures do not allow an appreciation of the actual processes that young children employ as they solve social interaction problems, particularly as sequences of events unfold over time. In fact, an appreciation of the 'long-view' of social exchanges with a corresponding ability to adjust appropriately to a companion's feedback while persisting in accomplishing one's social goals, is an essential characteristic of peer-related social competence (Asher, 1983; Guralnick, 1981a).

In recent years, a number of methodological and conceptual advances have enabled behavioural scientists to obtain a better understanding of these processes. It has become well recognized that it is essential to provide a framework for interpreting the sequences of interactions that occur. Specific social tasks, such as children's efforts to obtain entry into group play or sequences in which children request certain goods or services from a companion, are common and important social episodes that can be identified for analysis (see Guralnick, 1986). As Dodge *et al.* (1986, p. 3) point out:

> The concept of the social task is crucial to an understanding of social competence, for it is only with reference to a specified task that a child's performance can be judged to be effective or ineffective and competent or incompetent. When a task is not specified, the judge must use an implicit (and idiosyncratic) reference point. The social task thus provides the context for understanding social behavior.

Social tasks are often arranged or contrived in order to maximize the opportunities for events of interest to occur and to permit a wide range of measures to be utilized. For example, research by Putallaz and Gottman (1981), Putallaz (1983), and Dodge, *et al.* (1986) have demonstrated how peer entry behaviours in analogue situations can provide important insights into the social behaviours that correspond to different levels of children's social competence as assessed by sociometric status measures. These analogue models have proved to be extremely valuable and have demonstrated they are valid representations of events that occur in more natural encounters among children.

Although there are many benefits to using a contrived setting, social tasks can also be studied within the context of more typical child–child interactions. In this approach, specific tasks or episodes characterizing situations or events are identified from the flow of behaviour and analysed accordingly. Social tasks that have been evaluated in this manner include children's dispute settlements (Brenneis and Lein, 1977), conflict resolution (Eisenberg and Garvey, 1981), the use of behaviour requests (Garvey, 1975, Guralnick and Paul-Brown, 1984; Levin and Rubin, 1983; Parkhurst and Gottman, 1986), and entry strategies (Corsaro, 1979). Analyses of episodes derived in this manner can also be used to characterize the social interaction strategies of different groups of children such as those who are socially integrated and those who are socially isolated (e.g. Rubin and Borwick, 1984).

One of the most conceptually productive outcomes of efforts to analyse interaction patterns as they extend across social episodes has been the integration that has occurred between the fields of social and communicative processes. The emergence of the fields of developmental pragmatics (Ochs and Schieffelin, 1979) and child sociolinguistics (Ervin-Tripp and Mitchell-Kernan, 1977) has provided a framework for assessment of the more subtle and complex aspects of children's social/communicative strategies. These rich analyses of children's peer interaction have recently been combined with rigorous statistical approaches that can segment the stream of behaviour while still maintaining an emphasis on dependence among interactions and the significance of specific social interaction patterns (Gottman, 1983; Sackett, 1978, 1987).

Unfortunately, applications of these new approaches to the study of handicapped children's peer relations have not yet been explored. As will be discussed later, although analyses of communicative sequences of non-handicapped children interacting with handicapped companions have been evaluated (e.g. Guralnick and Paul-Brown, 1984), virtually nothing is known about the entry skills, strategies used to obtain goods and services from peers, or the conflict resolution techniques employed by young handicapped children.

Current research by Guralnick, Paul-Brown, and Groom (in preparation) is attempting to address these important issues. Specifically, the sequences of communicative interactions of mildly developmentally delayed children involved in directive episodes during a series of playgroups are being evaluated. Videotaped records of mildly developmentally delayed 4-year-olds interacting in free play with 3- and 4-year-old non-handicapped children or with other 4-year-old delayed companions have been reviewed to identify directive episodes (100 minutes of videotape per child obtained over a four-week period). Each directive episode consists of an initial directive turn, defined as a request to initiate, change, or stop a companion's action or activity where verbal or behavioural compliance is expected. In addition, to be considered an episode, non-compliance in some form must have resulted on the part of the companion, with a subsequent communicative interaction by the speaker pursuing the initial directive. As such, each directive episode reflects more than a passing interest on the part of the mildly delayed speakers to obtain their interpersonal goals. Since this social task is such a prominent part of children's interactions (see Levin and Rubin, 1983), the social/communicative strategies utilized by delayed children should provide an important index of their peer-related social competence.

Each of these episodes has been tracked and coded for both speaker and companion turns until some resolution to the initial directive occurred. A number of general types of data were available. Two types of information assessed the general tone and character of the overall episode. First, it was important to determine whether the speaker softened the directive request through some form of mitigation, such as the use of polite speech forms or providing a reason for the directive within the initial directive turn, or whether the speaker simply uttered a command, typically in the imperative form. Second, the primary purpose of the episode was determined and provided a sense of the affective nature of the overall exchange. Stopping an action ('Don't do that!') or requesting assistance ('Can you help me with these scissors?') clearly provide differing frameworks within which children will organize their communicative strategies.

The outcome of each episode is of course important, as children will vary dramatically in terms of their success in gaining their interpersonal goals. Distinguishing between full and complete compliance and modified compliance (the latter usually resulting from some form of compromise) can be contrasted with episodes in which children simply switch topics or do the task themselves whenever possible.

However, the primary intent of the analysis of behaviour request episodes is the identification of interactive strategies that are employed as children pursue some resolution to their initial directives. A series of over thirty possible interactive strategies has been identified. The affective tone, willingness to negotiate, persistence, and reciprocal nature of the exchanges are dimensions that characterize these strategies. Specific examples include counter-compromise, mitigate or minimize, insist-positive, insist-negative, postpone, provide reason for prior directive, and information-seeking request. Utilizing both conventional and sequential analyses focusing on adjacent turns, indices of what appear to be important peer-related social processes (see Asher, 1983; Dodge *et al.*, 1986; Gottman, 1983) can be identified for individual children from analyses of these strategies. For example, justification of directives tends to be a successful strategy to resolve conflict (Eisenberg and Garvey, 1981; Parkhurst and Gottman, 1986). In addition, connectedness, as indexed by responding with an informative response to an information-seeking request, is an important measure of the quality of children's relationships. Establishing a negotiating position through interactions surrounding the acceptance or rejection of proposals and counter proposals or other compromises may also reflect important social processes that can be evaluated through sequential analyses of these directive episodes.

Although these data are still being analysed (Guralnick *et al.*, in preparation), peer-related social competence difficulties that mildly delayed children exhibit in this important social task are nevertheless emerging. In comparison to either non-handicapped 4-year-olds or to a developmentally matched group of non-handicapped 3-year-olds, mildly delayed children tend to utilize strategies and processes that are not nearly as adaptive, appropriate, or successful. Their purposes differ, there is evidence for a lack of connectedness and flexibility, and there is limited use of more sophisticated strategies to achieve their interpersonal goals. Firm conclusions, however, must await a complete analysis of the data.

## INTERACTIONS WITH NON-HANDICAPPED PEERS

Now that a number of the fundamental peer interaction difficulties which handicapped children experience have been identified, the nature and quality of social exchanges occurring between handicapped and non-handicapped children will be examined with the specific purpose of determining whether there are any 'developmental advantages' (Hartup and Sancilio, 1986) for handicapped children. Specifically, in this section, the degree to which handicapped children are socially integrated with non-handicapped children when placed in the same settings will be evaluated in terms of developmental opportunities for observational learning or involvement in more advanced forms of play. Following this analysis, the social/communicative environment provided by non-handicapped children will be examined in terms of its potential developmental impact on handicapped companions. Finally, the communicative adjustments by non-handicapped children to the developmental characteristics of handicapped children will be of special interest.

### Social integration

A surprisingly large number of studies have been directed toward analysing the extent to which young handicapped children are integrated with non-handicapped children in classroom settings (e.g. Arnold and Tremblay, 1979; Cavallaro and Porter, 1980; Guralnick, 1980; Guralnick and Groom, 1987a; Ispa, 1981). Diverse groups of children, varying in type and severity of disability, have been included in these studies. In addition, the chronological ages of the non-handicapped children as well as the type and quality of programmes have been equally diverse. Overall, and despite this variability, the findings are quite clear: handicapped children form a socially separate subgroup in preschool settings. In general, non-handicapped children tend to interact far less frequently with handicapped children than they do with other non-handicapped classmates. This statement holds irrespective of the measure used to evaluate the extent of integration (e.g. positive social exchanges, peer sociometric ratings, visual attention). Moreover, greater degrees of social separation are found for children with more severe disabilities (see Guralnick, 1981b).

A recent investigation by Guralnick and Groom (1987a) illustrates how the issue of evaluating social integration can be approached. In this study, a special effort was made to avoid many of the methodological problems that have plagued previous research in this area. Specifically, sampling bias that is usually associated with evaluations of social integration within existing, intact classroom groups (the standard practice of previous research for practical reasons) was minimized by systematically sampling from populations of delayed and non-handicapped children to form a series of specially created mainstreamed playgroups.

In addition, the study of intact classes does not permit investigators to vary systematically the characteristics of the non-handicapped children in the setting, particularly their chronological ages, or even attempt to match children on the basis of developmental level. As a consequence, it is difficult to evaluate the extent to which social integration in previous studies was affected by these factors. In fact, in a majority of the studies that were conducted, non-handicapped children were typically one year younger than their handicapped classmates making it difficult to separate out the effects of chronological age from developmental status.

Fortunately, the mainstreamed playgroup approach permitted the systematic selection of children to establish the appropriate chronological age and developmental level matches. Accordingly, in the Guralnick and Groom (1987a) study, playgroups were selected so that each was composed of three normally developing 3-year-olds, three normally developing 4-year-olds, and two mildly developmentally delayed 4-year-olds. The delayed children were selected so that a developmental match was achieved with the non-handicapped 3-year-olds and a chronological age match with the non-handicapped 4-year-olds. An important aspect of this study was that children were initially unacquainted with one another. Therefore, the social integration patterns that were obtained would be free of bias from previous reputations of the children and existing social status hierarchies. This was of special concern since in many of the previous studies children were brought together only during free play situations but were in separate classes for delayed and non-handicapped children.

Eight such playgroups were formed, each operating 2 hours per day for four weeks. During that time, children's social and communicative interactions were recorded using videotaped and audio records obtained through a one-way mirror in an observation room adjacent to the playgroup in conjunction with the use of radiotelemetry microphones and wireless transmitters worn by children in the playgroups. To evaluate the extent to which children representing each of the three groups interacted with children from their group or the other two groups, the frequency of positive social interactions was used to develop a preference score that took into consideration the availability of children in any particular playgroup session. Expected frequencies of interaction were calculated and compared with observed values.

When analysed in this manner, the non-handicapped older group (4-year-olds) revealed a marked preference for interacting with other non-handicapped older children. In contrast, there was a negative preference (lower than expected interaction levels) for children in both the non-handicapped younger and mildly delayed peer groups. However, non-handicapped younger children did not show a significant preference for either of the two non-handicapped peer groups, but did reveal a negative preference for the mildly delayed peer group similar to that which was observed for the 4-year-old non-handicapped children. Accordingly, both groups of non-handicapped children exhibited a negative preference for the mildly delayed group. Finally, the mildly delayed children themselves produced an especially interesting pattern. Specifically, the mildly delayed group preferred to interact more with their chronological agemates (4-year-old non-handicapped children) than with the 3-year-olds. They also interacted with other mildly delayed children to the extent to which they were available; i.e., no negative or positive preferences. These preference patterns were confirmed by peer sociometric measures as well. Taken together, the results present a clear picture of social separation in that both groups of non-handicapped children held a negative preference for mildly delayed children. Of equal importance was the fact that mildly delayed children were interacted with proportionately less frequently than even the developmentally matched group of non-handicapped 3-year-olds. Accordingly, preference is related to developmental status (i.e. existence of a developmental delay) rather than developmental level.

These findings are certainly not unexpected, as subgroups of young children form on the basis of numerous characteristics including sex, chronological age, socioeconomic status, and popularity (see Guralnick, 1986, for discussion). It is important to recall the earlier discussion in which it was concluded that developmentally delayed children show peer-related social competence deficits beyond those which would be expected on the basis of their developmental levels. Even the development of friendships between delayed and non-handicapped preschool children, based on mutual preference, is problematic (Guralnick and Groom, 1988a). Since children's social skills contribute significantly to the extent to which they are involved in constructive and elaborate child–child interactions, the patterns of social separation are to be expected. In fact, the pattern of social separation is continued into the later school years (Taylor, Asher, and Williams, 1987).

**Developmental opportunities**

The question remains as to whether this pattern of social separation is sufficient to prevent handicapped children from taking advantage of those developmental opportunities that may arise from interactions with non-handicapped children. Available evidence suggests that, in fact, many potential benefits do exist. For example, despite the pattern of social separation, interactions occur frequently between handicapped and non-handicapped children. Interestingly, as noted, mildly delayed children even prefer to interact with non-handicapped age-mates. Moreover, they are generally successful in gaining an appropriate response to their social initiations. Non-handicapped children are also highly responsive to the initiations of more severely disabled children (Strain, 1984a). Of particular note was the finding by Guralnick and Groom (1987a) that when mildly delayed children engaged in group play, consisting of elaborate forms of mutual interactions, their play partner was a non-handicapped child on approximately 60% of the occasions. In addition, when more passive measures such as proximity to peers were used as the index for establishing a preference measure, far less social separation was obtained (Guralnick, 1980; Guralnick and Groom, 1987a). As a consequence, considerable opportunities for observational learning appear to exist for handicapped children in mainstreamed settings.

An alternative way to address this issue is to examine more directly those social interactions occurring between handicapped and non-handicapped children when placed together systematically in dyads. This provides a perspective on what occurs when children do come into sustained contact with a particular companion as part of a larger group activity, and complements the information obtained from those free-play group situations. In a recent study of dyadic peer interactions involving mildly developmentally delayed children, Guralnick and Groom (1987b) did find that pairing mildly delayed children with non-handicapped age-mates produced more frequent involvement in more advanced levels of social play and more frequent social interactions in comparison to pairings with non-handicapped younger or other mildly delayed children. Apparently, the more active and interactive non-handicapped older group had sufficient social competence to be able to engage the delayed children more frequently in productive social interactions. Moreover, the extremely low level of peer interactions found in dyads composed only of mildly delayed children suggests further that more developmental opportunities can be found in settings that provide access to non-handicapped companions. However, it is important to note that not all disability groups will yield similar results. Specifically, children with sensory handicaps appear to pose special problems in their interactions with non-handicapped children (e.g. Vandell and George, 1981).

**Communicative adjustments to handicapped children**

Any assessment of potential developmental advantages to handicapped children that can result from involvement with non-handicapped peers must consider communicative interactions. The substantial discrepancies that often exist between a handicapped child's chronological age and developmental level pose important challenges to non-handicapped peers to adjust the linguistic and other features of their communicative exchanges to the levels of their companions. In the absence of such adjustments, it is difficult to see how any possible developmental advantages to handicapped children could exist.

As discussed in an earlier section of this chapter, the abilities of preschool age non-handicapped children to adjust communicatively have been demonstrated when interacting with chronologically younger non-handicapped children. In fact, many of the linguistic adjustments to younger children, such as reduced syntactic complexity, parallel adjustments made by parents to their developing children. In many respects, these adjustments by non-handicapped children have created a linguistic environment that appears to be adapted to the level of the companion in a manner that improves communicative clarity between speaker and companion and provides a linguistic environment that promotes communicative development (see Guralnick, 1981a; Lederberg, 1982 for discussion).

The expectations in terms of the communicative value of these adjustments should, however, be kept in perspective. Clearly, adjustments are needed, particularly in critical linguistic features such as syntactic complexity and semantic diversity. The adjustments by non-handicapped children to companions at different chronological ages do appear to be based both on initial perceptions of the situation and the capabilities of the listener, as well as moment-to-moment modifications that occur in accordance with feedback from the listener (Guralnick, 1981a). Yet, linguistic environments created by young children are certainly not exact replicas of those provided by parents, as many didactic functions tend to be absent in peer–peer speech (Martinez, 1987). Moreover, as discussed below, many adjustments by non-handicapped children are also likely to be governed by the quality of the interpersonal relationships existing between the participants, particularly in relation to social status. This interplay among cognitive and associated characteristics of the listener, environmental factors, and interpersonal relationships necessitates careful interpretation of any communicative adjustments that might result when a companion is a handicapped child.

Nevertheless, a series of research studies focusing on adjustments by non-handicapped preschool children when interacting with developmentally delayed companions has yielded some consistent findings (Guralnick and Paul-Brown, 1977, 1980, 1984, 1986, in press; Guralnick *et al.*, in preparation). Specifically, when addressing severely and moderately delayed children, it has been well established that non-handicapped preschool age children reduce syntactic complexity (e.g. mean length of utterance) and semantic diversity (e.g. type-token ratio) of their speech in comparison with speech directed to developmentally more advanced companions. In addition, the functional aspects of speech are altered as proportionally more directives but fewer informational statements or informational requests are addressed to less advanced companions. Moreover, certain discourse features of speech, such as an increased use of repetitions or gestures, are found more often when companions have significant developmental delays. Interestingly, when specific episodes which track children seeking to obtain compliance to their behaviour requests are analysed (Guralnick and Paul-Brown, 1984; Guralnick *et al.*, in preparation), non-handicapped children show high proportions of adaptive strategies responsive to the feedback of their delayed companions. Similarly, in comparison to exchanges with other non-handicapped children, more frequent combinations of adaptive strategies along with a greater reliance on non-verbal techniques, such as demonstration and exemplification, are found when interacting with companions with significant delays.

Although not every study yielded exactly the same pattern for each measure, the overall results suggested that an appropriate linguistic environment was being provided for children with severe and moderate developmental delays by non-handicapped children. The adjustments seemed to be responsive to the cognitive and linguistic abilities of their companions and, as a consequence, appeared to improve communicative clarity and provide a progressive linguistic environment for the delayed children. Directive utterances appeared to serve as strategies for probing the comprehension of companions with limited cognitive and language abilities. Correspondingly, the use of adaptive and flexible strategies by non-handicapped children to gain compliance with their requests were also techniques likely to result in increased comprehension by the delayed children. It is important to recognize, however, that these studies were concerned with adjustments to children with development delays—adjustments which might not occur to children with other disabilities (see Vandell and George, 1981).

It can be argued that, taken together, these communicative adjustments by non-handicapped children provide potential developmental advantages to children with significant developmental delays. Adaptive linguistic adjustments such as those described above certainly could not occur when companions have similar disabilities. A number of questions remain, however. It is uncertain as to how finely-tuned those adjustments are to the delayed children. In fact, distinctions between moderately and severely delayed children are rarely found in the adjustment patterns of non-handicapped children.

## Mildly delayed children

Of equal concern, however, is recent evidence suggesting that, for mildly developmentally delayed children, perceptions of their social status by non-handicapped children or difficulties in interpersonal relationships may compromise any potential developmental advantages. When delayed and non-handicapped children are similar in terms of developmental level, a feature of many studies involving mildly developmentally delayed children, it is reasonable to expect that any adjustments by non-handicapped children would be similar for both groups. This has been confirmed in a number of studies for syntactic and semantic measures (e.g. Guralnick and Paul-Brown, 1977, 1980, 1986). However, analyses of the speech style of non-handicapped children in relation to mildly delayed children have revealed some disconcerting patterns. For example, Guralnick and Paul-Brown (1984) noted that non-handicapped children rarely asked questions of mildly delayed companions and chose to justify or mitigate their requests almost exclusively to other non-handicapped children. Interpreted within a sociolinguistic framework (Ervin-Tripp and Mitchell-Kernan, 1977), there exists a concern about the quality of the interactions occurring between mildly delayed and non-handicapped children. In fact, these speech style patterns and other less 'peer-like' communicative exchanges to delayed children are consistent with their lack of social integration and lower ratings on peer sociometric measures discussed earlier.

A more recent study by Guralnick and Paul-Brown (in press) analysed the speech style directed to mildly delayed 4-year-old children by non-handicapped 3- and 4-year-olds. As noted earlier, the mildly delayed children were matched in terms of chronological age to the older non-handicapped children and in terms of developmental level to the non-handicapped 3-year-olds. Although a wide range of measures was used for this utterance-by-utterance analysis, most interest focused on the speech style and affective quality of interactions. Specifically, behaviour request categories of strong (inflexible, explicit requests), weak (use of mitigation or softening such as the use of politeness forms, tag questions, inferred directives, or offering justification), joint ('let's' or 'we' requests), and attentional (e.g. 'look') directives provided the focus for assessing speech style. Disagreement and agreement measures yielded information regarding the affective quality of exchanges.

The results of this study revealed that non-handicapped children addressed more strong but fewer joint directives to mildly delayed than to other non-handicapped children. This study also revealed that more directives, irrespective of type, and more attempts to clarify a message but less sharing of information, occurred when companions were mildly delayed than when they were non-handicapped children. A substantial proportion of disagreements involved mildly delayed children. Moreover, these patterns held for both 3- and 4-year-old non-handicapped children.

Interestingly, this pattern of outcomes is quite similar to the one observed for children with more severe developmental delays (Guralnick and Paul-Brown, 1980, 1986). The more frequent use of directives can be seen as an effort by non-handicapped children to establish and maintain involvement with children less capable than themselves. The absence of self-initiating, organizing type activities characteristic of many mildly delayed children (Guralnick and Groom, 1985, 1987a) suggests that the increased use of directives is an appropriate adjustment by both older and younger non-handicapped children. Similarly, the proportionally less information sharing that was observed may well reflect difficulties in establishing relationships, or perhaps indicates the more limited information processing and expressive language skills evident in their delayed companions. Difficulties in establishing and maintaining social contact may also be reflected in the greater proportion of message clarification requests that were directed to the mildly delayed group.

Despite these apparently reasonable explanations suggesting the appropriateness of this pattern, results of the analyses focusing on speech style and affective quality suggest that factors other than cognitive-communicative ones may be at least partially responsible for this interaction pattern. Specifically, the fact that proportionally more strong directives were directed to mildly delayed children than to the two non-delayed groups is of concern. This speech style difference may have reflected an adjustment to the cognitive limitations of the delayed children, since unmitigated directives are almost always issued in a more concise, specific, and more comprehensible form than mitigated directives. To evaluate if this was the case, a comparison was made of communicative interactions occurring to the younger non-handicapped group; the group matched in terms of developmental level to the mildly delayed children. If the use of strong directives reflected an effort to minimize cognitive demands on the listener, a similar speech style pattern should be evident when interacting with this developmentally matched non-handicapped group as well. However, this did not turn out to be the case, as directive types were distributed to younger non-handicapped children in a manner similar to those addressed to the older non-handicapped group, but not to the mildly delayed children. This result is consistent with the finding that other measures of cognitive demand, specifically mean length of utterance and proportion of complex utterances, did not vary when non-handicapped children addressed delayed or non-handicapped children.

An alternative to the cognitive demand hypothesis is that the speech style modifications in strong directives are governed by social status and interpersonal factors. In fact, the unusually high proportion of disagreements involving mildly delayed children combined with their less preferred social status in the mainstreamed playgroups (Guralnick and Groom, 1987a) suggests that these interpersonal perceptions and relationships may well be responsible for differences in speech style. An especially relevant finding is that this speech style pattern was also found for mildly delayed children interacting with other mildly delayed companions. As a consequence, although this pattern cannot be considered to be a developmentally productive one from the perspective of mildly delayed children, the problems are not limited to exchanges with non-handicapped companions.

In partial summary then, an extensive body of research has suggested that there may well be special developmental opportunities available to handicapped children as a consequence of their involvement with non-handicapped peers. Most of the research, however, has focused on young children with developmental delays. Settings which include non-handicapped peers appear to be highly socially interactive and responsive, allow for frequent opportunities for meaningful observational learning involving developmentally advanced peers, and provide a communicative environment in which appropriate adjustments are made in accordance with children's developmental levels. However, a number of negative factors have been observed as well. Specifically, tendencies toward social separation of handicapped children are apparent even though mildly delayed children, in particular, prefer to interact with companions who are non-handicapped. In part, the social separation reflects the social skills deficits of delayed children, evident even when matched developmentally to non-handicapped children, as well as to difficulties in interpersonal relationships. As a consequence, handicapped children are perceived as being of lower social status and are treated accordingly as reflected in speech style analyses. As noted, this latter pattern is also found when delayed children interact with other delayed children.

## COMPARISONS BETWEEN INTEGRATED AND SPECIALIZED ENVIRONMENTS

Assuming that the developmental opportunities associated with involvement with non-handicapped children are of greater significance than any negative features that may exist, it would be reasonable to expect that these potential benefits would eventually translate into developmental gains for handicapped children. The design of comparative studies to evaluate this hypothesis is, of course, an extremely complex problem and, like any experiment concerned with the efficacy of different conditions or treatments, is subject to many threats to its internal and external validity (see Guralnick, 1988). The practical problems encountered in establishing comparisons in which children are assigned in a random fashion to equivalent programmes differing only in terms of the availability of non-handicapped children have been considerable. In fact, even when opportunities present themselves to assign subjects randomly, they are usually so infrequent that it is impossible to carry out systematic research focusing on programmatic factors, such as the type of children's disabilities, curriculum model, or ratio of handicapped to non-handicapped children. Programmatic factors have been shown to be critical in governing the outcomes of integrated or mainstreamed programmes, particularly in relation to child–child social interactions (Guralnick, 1981c). Unfortunately, comparisons between established groups of children enrolled in integrated and specialized programmes, even when similar to one another on important demographic variables, nevertheless allow alternative interpretations of outcomes (e.g. Cooke *et al.*, 1981; Novak, Olley, and Kearney, 1980).

In view of these constraints, many researchers have adopted some variation of within-subjects experimental designs thereby avoiding the equivalence of subject problem. For example, in group designs, comparisons of peer interactions are made when handicapped and non-handicapped groups of children are playing with peers similar to themselves (e.g. specialized programmes) in contrast to occasions when the groups are brought together (i.e. integrated). Researchers systematically manipulate the occurrence of those integrated occasions and seek to ensure that no differences in settings or related factors that might influence child–child interactions can be identified other than the characteristics of one's peers.

In designs involving dyads rather than groups, the child's partner is systematically changed. In this way, many more comparisons can be made since, for example, it is highly feasible to arrange for a handicapped child to first be paired with another handicapped child, then with a non-handicapped child similar in chronological age, and finally with another non-handicapped child dissimilar in chronological age. By counterbalancing for order of the pairings, important experimental questions can be addressed.

Despite the ability to avoid many confounding factors, there are many limitations to these within-subjects designs. Of most concern is the fact that only the *immediate* effects of participation with children different in terms of developmental status can be achieved. Moreover, there are many factors that mitigate against the occurrence of social exchanges between initially separate groups of children brought together episodically with one another in integrated settings. Familiarity and reputational factors are most prominent in this regard (see discussion by Guralnick and Groom, 1987a) and should be considered when interpreting the results of these studies. As a consequence, this approach may minimize any potential benefits from the placement of heterogeneous groups of children in the same setting.

Investigations involving dyads create special issues since the artificial nature of the situation could yield results that have little validity beyond that unique situation. On the other hand, dyadic interactions are commonly occurring forms of social exchange between preschool children, and the setting itself often frees children from the direct influences of the group and even the teachers. In fact, many of the patterns found in dyadic exchanges are highly similar to those obtained in assessments of social interactions in larger group situations (Guralnick and Groom, 1987b). Hopefully, some consistency in the outcome patterns will emerge that will allow generalizations across these design-related but potentially influential factors.

Such consistency has, in fact, been obtained. Whether or not comparisons are based on between-subjects designs, using either pre-existing groups of children or random assignment, or within-subjects designs involving groups or dyads, the following two outcome patterns can be stated with confidence: (1) no adverse effects on children's peer-related social behaviours have been observed for either handicapped or non-handicapped children as a consequence of involvement with one another; and (2) a small but potentially beneficial effect for handicapped children from interaction with non-handicapped children has been obtained. Specifically, with regard to the latter point, more constructive levels of play have been found to occur as have increases primarily in the frequency of occurrence of peer-related social interactions (see initial reviews by Guralnick, 1981b, 1982; Peck and Cooke, 1983).

For example, Field *et al.* (1981), Beckman and Kohl (1987), Guralnick and Groom (1988b), and Strain (1984b) found increases in positive social interactions for handicapped children involved in integrated settings in comparison with when they participated only with other handicapped children. Similarly, Jenkins, Speltz, and Odom (1985) found more social 'peer entry' behaviour for handicapped children participating in an integrated programme. With regard to the cognitive aspects of play, Guralnick (1981d) found reduced levels of inappropriate play for severely delayed children when in integrated as opposed to specialized settings. In addition, a comparison of mainstreamed and specialized settings for mildly delayed children (Guralnick and Groom, 1988b) also indicated more frequent occurrences of constructive play and a tendency to play less functionally (stereotypic, repetitive play) when participating with normally developing children in the mainstreamed setting.

Comparisons involving dyadic pairings have yielded similar results. In a recent study (Guralnick and Groom, 1987b), mildly developmentally delayed children engaged in more positive interactions, more conversation, but less solitary play when paired with non-handicapped as opposed to other mildly delayed children. However, one notable exception to the pattern can be found in a study of dyadic interactions of hearing-impaired and normal hearing children (Vandell and George, 1981). In contrast to findings with other disability groups, in which interactions increased as a consequence of participation with non-handicapped children, both children in dyads composed of either hearing or hearing-impaired children (i.e. like dyads) interacted more effectively than did dyads composed of a hearing and hearing-impaired child (mixed dyads).

Even when considering the generally consistent positive findings, the issue remains whether these patterns are producing developmentally meaningful changes. One aspect of this problem revolves around increases in frequencies of positive exchanges as a consequence of involvement with non-handicapped companions. Although the frequency of positive interactions has face validity and is certainly a prerequisite to more complex forms of peer-related social interactions, evidence for the occurrence of more sophisticated social interaction patterns as a result of involvement with developmentally more advanced peers either has not been considered or not been found (e.g. Guralnick, 1981b). Reductions in less constructive forms of play that have been obtained do appear to have developmental significance, however, as appropriate object-oriented play is an important correlate of developmental progress and serves as the framework for more advanced forms of social exchange (Rubin, Fein, and Vandenberg, 1983).

Even in the Guralnick and Groom (1988b) study in which more substantial gains in peer-related social exchange were obtained than found in previous investigations, the fact remains that certain complex forms of peer-related social interactions, such as group play, were not altered simply through participation or even active involvement in play situations with more advanced peers. The availability of non-handicapped children of similar chronological ages in a setting in which non-handicapped children were the dominant peer group (i.e. being in a mainstreamed as opposed to an integrated environment) was probably responsible for the substantial increases in the frequency of peer interactions in the Guralnick and Groom (1988b) investigation. Nevertheless, even though many of the individual social behaviours that did increase in frequency were associated with higher levels of peer-related social competence, increases in more elaborate forms of social play were not observed.

## COMPREHENSIVE INTERVENTION: CONCLUSIONS AND IMPLICATIONS

Clearly, from the evidence reviewed, we cannot expect that the natural social forces involving heterogeneous groups of children will create learning opportunities sufficient to overcome the significant peer social interaction deficits of handicapped children. This is not to say that involvement with more advanced peers does not have beneficial effects. As has been presented, not only have positive outcomes been documented, but it is reasonable to suggest that the absence of the more active and responsive social environments provided by non-handicapped children will prevent meaningful peer-related social development from reaching optimal levels. This latter point has been made strikingly clear in research in which peers have been used as confederates of interventionists, being trained to promote the peer interactions of handicapped children (Strain and Odom, 1986). Although this procedure can be highly effective, gains in peer-related social behaviour are only maintained when handicapped children are placed in settings containing non-handicapped peers.

The success of modifying children's social interactions through changes in the developmental characteristics of their peers carried out in larger playgroups (e.g. Guralnick and Groom, 1988b), through specific pairings (e.g. Furman, Rahe, and Hartup, 1979; Guralnick and Groom, 1987b), or as a consequence of peer confederate training (e.g. Strain, 1984b), has probably been due largely to an externally imposed social pattern, i.e., prompts, direction by the more dominant peer group, in combination with sanctions for inappropriate play activities. Some permanent intrinsic changes in peer competence are certainly also likely to result as a consequence of these procedures, as existing social interaction skills are strengthened and new positive interaction patterns develop. However, as has been seen, for the vast majority of children with disabilities, this circumstance does not appear to be sufficient to yield the types of changes that result in more elaborate and perhaps more long-lasting forms of interactive play. Unfortunately, it is increases in these elaborated play patterns which provide the most meaningful index of improved social competence.

## CONCLUSION

What must occur, then, in order to produce developmentally significant and presumably long-term effects on young handicapped children's peer-related social competence? What appears to be needed is a comprehensive intervention programme focusing specifically on young children's peer-related social competence. A critical component of such an intervention programme would include an assessment instrument capable of capturing the critical elements, major influencing factors, and essential processes of peer interactions. To be of value, this instrument must be grounded firmly in a developmental framework. In turn, the information gathered would be used to generate a systematic *individualized* series of interventions. Although the involvement of non-handicapped or advanced peers is likely to have an important role in both the initial intervention and the maintenance (i.e. generalization) phases of any peer interaction programme, these initial intervention efforts would be centred on selected environmental and social competence issues.

In essence, it is the content, process, and general environmental influences of peer-related social competence that must guide our approaches to these problems. Recent advances in developmental psychology, revealing how children form acquaintances (e.g. Gottman, 1983) or process social information (e.g. Dodge, *et al.*, 1986), are essential features that must be incorporated into any comprehensive programme. Critical social tasks, such as entry into peer groups, conflict management, successfully gaining goods and services in directive episodes, or repair of conversations (Parkhurst and Gottman, 1986; Guralnick *et al.*, in preparation) have not yet found their way into the assessment of handicapped children's peer-related social competence or the design of intervention programmes. Similarly, the interference of even relatively minor behaviour problems with productive peer relations (see Guralnick and Groom, 1985), and the nature of children's preferences for play activities, must also be considered. Finally, environmental events and family factors that affect interactions with peers must receive attention. This includes the social perceptions held by companions or specific physical or social settings that seem to influence peer interactions as well as the substantial influences family members can have on both developing and maintaining the level of their child's peer-related social competence.

It may well be that we have reached the point of diminishing returns for those studies that seek to determine the impact of involvement with advanced peers on peer-related social competence. We have already pressed to developmentally meaningful limits what can be accomplished through the simple presence of non-handicapped children or even to the structuring of interactions with advanced peers. The participation of non-handicapped children can perhaps be most constructively viewed as a necessary but not sufficient condition for promoting the peer-related social competence of handicapped children. After nearly two decades of research in this area, we should be pleased with our accomplishments, but it appears wise now to direct our attention to more fundamental developmental processes, including environmental and family influences.

In many ways, this is a very natural return from an almost fractionated approach to child–child social interactions. Somewhere along the line the processes of cognitive, language, and social development became separated from the study of social competence. Moreover, the contributions of developmental and clinical child psychology, including the role of the family, became isolated from the analyses of group processes in classrooms, substituting structural and environmental factors for the more fundamental elements of social behaviours. Hopefully, future efforts will capitalize on the knowledge and methods associated with all of these important domains and create those programmes that will yield truly developmentally meaningful and permanent gains in the peer-related social competence of handicapped children.

## REFERENCES

Arnold, W., and Tremblay, A. (1979). Interaction of deaf and hearing preschool children, *Journal of Communication Disorders*, **12**, 245–251.

Asher, S. R. (1983). Social competence and peer status: recent advances and future directions, *Child Development*, **54**, 1427–1434.

Asher, S. R., Markell, R. A., and Hymel, S. (1981). Identifying children at risk in peer relations: a critique of the rate-of-interaction approach to assessment, *Child Development*, **52**, 1239–1245.

Bakeman, R., and Brownlee, J. R. (1980). The strategic use of parallel play: a sequential analysis, *Child Development*, **51**, 873–878.

Barnes, K. E. (1971). Preschool play norms: a replication, *Developmental Psychology*, **5**, 99–103.

Bates, E. (1975). Peer relations and the acquisition of language. In M. Lewis and L. A. Rosenblum (eds), *The Origins of Behavior: Vol. 4. Friendship and Peer Relations* (pp. 259–292). New York: John Wiley & Sons.

Beckman, P. J. (1983). Characteristics of handicapped infants: a study of the relationship between child characteristics and stress as reported by mothers, *American Journal of Mental Deficiency*, **88**, 150–156.

Beckman, P. J., and Kohl, F. L. (1987). Interactions of preschoolers with and without handicaps in integrated and segregated settings: a longitudinal study, *Mental Retardation*, **25**, 5–11.

Brenneis, D., and Lein, L. (1977). "Your fruithead": a sociolinguistic approach to children's dispute settlements. In S. Ervin-Tripp and C. Mitchell-Kernan (eds), *Child Discourse* (pp. 49–65). New York: Academic Press.

Bristol, M. M. (1987). The home care of children with developmental disabilities: empirical support for a model of successful family coping with stress. In S. Landesman and P. M. Vietze (eds), *Living Environments and Mental Retardation* (pp. 401–422). Washington, DC: American Association on Mental Retardation.

Cavallaro, S. A., and Porter, R. H. (1980). Peer preferences of at-risk and normally developing children in preschool mainstream classrooms, *American Journal of Mental Deficiency*, **84**, 357–366.

Connolly, J. A., and Doyle, A. (1981). Assessment of social competence in preschoolers: teachers versus peers, *Developmental Psychology*, **17**, 454–462.

Cooke, T. P., Ruskus, J. A., Apolloni, T., and Peck, C. A. (1981). Handicapped preschool children in the mainstream: background, outcomes, and clinical suggestions, *Topics in Early Childhood Special Education*, **1**(1), 73–83.

Corsaro, W. A. (1979). "We're friends, right?": children's use of access rituals in a nursery school, *Language in Society*, **8**, 315–336.

Crawley, S. B., and Chan, K. S. (1982). Developmental changes to the free play behavior of mildly and moderately retarded preschool-aged children, *Education and Training of the Mentally Retarded*, **17**, 234–239.

Crnic, K. A., Friedrich, W. N., and Greenberg, M. T. (1983). Adaptation of families with mentally retarded children: a model of stress, coping, and family ecology, *American Journal of Mental Deficiency*, **88**, 125–138.

Cunningham, C. E., Rueler, E., Blackwell, J., and Deck, J. (1981). Behavioral and linguistic developments in the interactions of normal and retarded children with their mothers, *Child Development*, **52**, 62–70.

Dodge, K. A., Pettit, G. S., McClaskey, C. L., and Brown, M. M. (1986). Social competence in children, *Monographs of the Society for Research in Child Development*, **51**(2, Serial No. 213).

Doyle, A., Connolly, J., and Rivest, L. (1980). The effect of playmate familiarity on the social interactions of young children, *Child Development*, **51**, 217–223.

Easterbrooks, M. A., and Lamb, M. E. (1979). The relationship between quality of infant–mother attachment and infant competence in initial encounters with peers, *Child Development*, **50**, 380–387.

Eisenberg, A. R., and Garvey, C. (1981). Children's use of verbal strategies in resolving conflicts, *Discourse Processes*, **4**, 149–170.

Ervin-Tripp, S., and Mitchell-Kernan, C. (eds) (1977). *Child Discourse*. New York: Academic Press.

Farber, B. (1975). Family adaptations to severely mentally retarded children. In M. J. Begab and S. A. Richardson (eds), *The Mentally Retarded and Society: A Social Science Perspective*. Baltimore: University Park Press.

Fey, M. E., and Leonard, L. B. (1984). Partner age as a variable in the conversational performance of specifically language-impaired and normal-language children, *Journal of Speech and Hearing Research*, **27**, 413–423.

Fey, M. E., Leonard, L. B., and Wilcox, K. A. (1981). Speech style modifications of language-impaired children, *Journal of Speech and Hearing Disorders*, **46**, 91–96.

Field, T., Roseman, S., DeStefano, L., and Koewler, J. H., III. (1981). Play behaviors of handicapped preschool children in the presence and absence of nonhandicapped peers, *Journal of Applied Developmental Psychology*, **2**, 49–58.

Furman, W., Rahe, D. F., and Hartup, W. W. (1979). Rehabilitation of socially-withdrawn preschool children through mixed-age and same-age socialization, *Child Development*, **50**, 915–922.

Garvey, C. (1975). Requests and responses in children's speech, *Journal of Child Language*, **2**, 41–63.

Garvey, C. (1986). Peer relations and the growth of communication. In E. C. Mueller and C. R. Cooper (eds), *Process and Outcome in Peer Relationships* (pp. 329–345). Orlando, Florida: Academic Press, Inc.

Gelman, R., and Shatz, M. (1977). Appropriate speech adjustments: the operation of conversational constraints on talk to two-year-olds. In M. Lewis and L. A. Rosenblum (eds), *The Origins of Behavior: Vol. 5. Interaction, Conversation, and the Development of Language* (pp. 27–61). New York: John Wiley & Sons.

Goffman, E. (1963). *Stigma*. Englewood Cliffs, NJ: Prentice-Hall.

Goldman, J. A. (1981). Social participation of preschool children in same- versus mixed-age groups, *Child Development*, **52**, 644–650.

Gottman, J. M. (1983). How children become friends, *Monographs of the Society for Research in Child Development*, **48**(3, Serial No. 201).

Gottman, J. M., and Katz, L. F. (1989). The effects of marital discord on young children's peer interactions with a best friend, *Developmental Psychology*, **25**, 373–381.

Guralnick, M. J. (1980). Social interactions among preschool children, *Exceptional Children*, **46**, 248–253.

Guralnick, M. J. (1981a). Peer influences on the development of communicative competence. In P. Strain (ed.), *The Utilization of Classroom Peers as Behavior Change Agents* (pp. 31–68). New York: Plenum.

Guralnick, M. J. (1981b). The efficacy of integrating handicapped children in early education settings: research implications, *Topics of Early Childhood Special Education*, **1**(1), 57–71.

Guralnick, M. J. (1981c). Programmatic factors affecting child–child social interactions in mainstreamed preschool programs, *Exceptional Education Quarterly*, **1**(4), 71–91.

Guralnick, M. J. (1981d). The social behavior of preschool children at different developmental levels: effects of group composition, *Journal of Experimental Child Psychology*, **31**, 115–130.

Guralnick, M. J. (1982). Mainstreaming young handicapped children: a public policy and ecological systems analysis. In B. Spodek (ed.), *Handbook of Research on Early Childhood Education* (pp. 456–500). New York: The Free Press/Macmillan.

Guralnick, M. J. (1986). The peer relations of young handicapped and nonhandicapped children. In P. S. Strain, M. J. Guralnick, and H. M. Walker (eds), *Children's Social Behavior: Development, Assessment, and Modification* (pp. 93–140). New York: Academic Press.

Guralnick, M. J. (1988). Efficacy research in early childhood intervention programs. In S. L. Odom and M. B. Karnes (eds), *Early Intervention for Infants and Children with Handicaps: An Empirical Base* (pp. 75–88). Baltimore: Brookes Publishing Co.

Guralnick, M. J. (1989). Social competence as a future direction for early intervention programs, *Journal of Mental Deficiency Research,* **33**, 275–281.

Guralnick, M. J., and Groom, J. M. (1985). Correlates of peer-related social competence of developmentally delayed preschool children, *American Journal of Mental Deficiency*, **90**, 140–150.

Guralnick, M. J., and Groom, J. M. (1987a). The peer relations of mildly delayed and nonhandicapped preschool children in mainstreamed playgroups, *Child Development*, **58**, 1556–1572.

Guralnick, M. J., and Groom, J. M. (1987b). Dyadic peer interactions of mildly delayed and nonhandicapped preschool children, *American Journal of Mental Deficiency*, **92**, 178–193.

Guralnick, M. J., and Groom, J. M. (1988a). Friendships of preschool children in mainstreamed playgroups, *Developmental Psychology*, **24**, 595–604.

Guralnick, M. J., and Groom, J. M. (1988b). Peer interactions in mainstreamed and specialized classrooms: a comparative analysis, *Exceptional Children*, **54**, 415–425.

Guralnick, M. J., and Paul-Brown, D. (1977). The nature of verbal interactions among handicapped and nonhandicapped preschool children, *Child Development*, **48**, 254–260.

Guralnick, M. J., and Paul-Brown, D. (1980). Functional and discourse analyses of nonhandicapped preschool children's speech to handicapped children, *American Journal of Mental Deficiency*, **84**, 444–454.

Guralnick, M. J., and Paul-Brown, D. (1984). Communicative adjustments during behavior-request episodes among children at different developmental levels, *Child Development*, **55**, 911–919.

Guralnick, M. J., and Paul-Brown, D. (1986). Communicative interactions of mildly delayed and normally developing preschool children: effects of listener's developmental level, *Journal of Speech and Hearing Research*, **29**, 2–10.

Guralnick, M. J., and Paul-Brown, D. (in press). Peer-related communicative competence of preschool children: developmental and adaptive characteristics, *Journal of Speech and Hearing Research.*

Guralnick, M. J., Paul-Brown, D., and Groom, J. M. (in preparation). *Sequential Analysis of Behavior Request Episodes in Young Children.*

Guralnick, M. J., and Weinhouse, E. M. (1984). Peer-related social interactions of developmentally delayed young children: development and characteristics, *Developmental Psychology*, **20**, 815–827.

Hartup, W. W. (1978). Peer interaction and the processes of socialization. In M. J. Guralnick (ed.), *Early Intervention and the Integration of Handicapped and Nonhandicapped Children* (pp. 27–51). Baltimore: University Park Press.

Hartup, W. W. (1983). Peer relations. In E. M. Hetherington (ed.), *Handbook of Child Psychology: Vol. 4. Socialization, Personality, and Social development* (pp. 103–196). New York: John Wiley & Sons.

Hartup, W. W., and Sancilio, M. F. (1986). Children's friendships. In E. Schopler and G. B. Mesibov (eds), *Current Issues in Autism: Social Behavior in Autism* (pp. 61–79). New York: Plenum.

Higgenbotham, J., and Baker, B. M. (1981). Social participation and cognitive play differences in hearing-impaired and normally hearing preschoolers, *The Volta Review*, **83**, 135–149.

Ispa, J. (1981). Social interactions among teachers, handicapped children, and nonhandicapped children in a mainstreamed preschool, *Journal of Applied Developmental Psychology*, **1**, 231–350.

James, S. L. (1978). Effect of listener age and situation on the politeness of children's directives, *Journal of Psycholinguistic Research*, **7**, 307–317.

Jenkins, J. R., Speltz, M. L., and Odom, S. L. (1985). Integrating normal and handicapped preschoolers: effects on child development and social interaction, *Exceptional Children*, **52**, 7–17.

Krakow, J. B., and Kopp, C. B. (1983). The effects of developmental delay on sustained attention in young children, *Child Development*, **54**, 1143–1155.

Ladd, G. W., and Golter, B. S. (1988). Parents' management of preschooler's peer relations: is it related to children's social competence? *Developmental Psychology*, **24**, 109–117.

Lederberg, A. R. (1982). A framework for research on preschool children's speech modifications. In S. Kuczaj, II (ed.), *Language Development: Vol. 2. Language, Thought, and Culture* (pp. 37–73). Hillsdale, NJ: Lawrence Erlbaum.

Levin, E. A., and Rubin, K. H. (1983). Getting others to do what you want them to do: the development of children's requestive strategies. In K. E. Nelson (ed.), *Children's Language* (Vol. 4, pp. 157–186). Hillsdale, NJ: Lawrence Erlbaum.

Lewis, M., Feiring, C., and Brooks-Gunn, J. (1987). The social networks of children with and without handicaps: a developmental perspective. In S. Landesman, P. Vietze, and M. Begab (eds), *Living Environments and Mental Retardation* (pp. 377–400). Washington, DC: American Association on Mental Retardation.

Lieberman, A. F. (1977). Preschoolers' competence with a peer: relations with attachment and peer experience, *Child Development*, **48**, 1277–1287.

MacDonald, K. (1987). Parent–child physical play with rejected, neglected, and popular boys, *Developmental Psychology*, **23**, 705–711.

MacDonald, K., and Parke, R. D. (1984). Bridging the gap: parent–child play interaction and peer interactive competence, *Child Development*, **55**, 1265–1277.

Martinez, M. A. (1987). Dialogues among children and between children and their mothers, *Child Development*, **58**, 1035–1043.

Masur, E. G. (1978). Preschool boys' speech modifications: the effect of listeners' linguistic levels and conversational responsiveness, *Child Development*, **49**, 924–927.

Novak, M. A., Olley, J. G., and Kearney, D. S. (1980). Social skills of children with special needs in integrated and separate preschools. In T. M. Field, S. Goldberg, D. Stern, and A. M. Sostek (eds), *High-risk Infants and Children: Adult and Peer Interactions* (pp. 327–346). New York: Academic Press.

Ochs, E., and Schieffelin, B. B. (eds). (1979). *Developmental pragmatics*. New York: Academic Press.

Parker, J. G., and Asher, S. R. (1987). Peer relations and later personal adjustment: are low-accepted children at risk? *Psychological Bulletin*, **102**, 357–389.

Parkhurst, J., and Gottman, J. (1986). How young children get what they want. In J. Gottman & J. Parker (eds), *Conversations of Friends: Speculations on Affective Development* (pp. 315–345). New York: Cambridge University Press.

Parten, M. B. (1932). Social participation among preschool children, *Journal of Abnormal Social Psychology*, **27**, 243–269.

Pastor, D. L. (1981). The quality of mother–infant attachment and its relationship to toddlers' initial sociability with peers, *Developmental Psychology*, **17**, 326–335.

Peck, C. A., and Cooke, T. P. (1983). Benefits of mainstreaming at the early childhood level: how much can we expect? *Analysis and Intervention in Developmental Disabilities*, **3**, 1–22.

Putallaz, M. (1983). Predicting children's sociometric status from their behavior, *Child Development*, **54**, 1417–1426.

Putallaz, M. (1987). Maternal behavior and children's sociometric status, *Child Development*, **58**, 324–340.

Putallaz, M., and Gottman, J. M. (1981). Social skills and group acceptance. In S. R. Asher and J. M. Gottman (eds), *The Development of Children's Friendships* (pp. 116–149). Cambridge: Cambridge University Press.

Roper, R., and Hinde, R. A. (1978). Social behavior in a play group: consistency and complexity, *Child Development*, **49**, 570–579.

Rubin, K. H., and Borwick, D. (1984). Communicative skills and sociability. In H. E. Sypher and J. L. Applegate (eds), *Communication by Children and Adults: Social Cognitive and Strategic Processes* (pp. 152–170). Beverly Hills: Sage Publications.

Rubin, K. H., and Krasnor, L. R. (1980). Changes in the play behaviours of preschoolers: a short-term longitudinal investigation, *Canadian Journal of Behavioural Science*, **12**, 278–282.

Rubin, K. H., and Lollis, S. P. (1988). Origins and consequences of social withdrawal. In J. Belsky and T. Nezworski (eds), *Clinical Implications of Attachment* (pp. 219–252). Hillsdale, NJ: Lawrence Erlbaum.

Rubin, K. H., Daniels-Bierness, T., and Hayvren, M. (1981). Social and social-cognitive correlates of sociometric status in preschool and kindergarten children, *Canadian Journal of Behavioural Science*, **14**, 338–349.

Rubin, K. H., Fein, G. G., and Vandenberg, B. (1983). Play. In E. M. Hetherington (ed.), P. H. Mussen (Series ed.), *Handbook of Child Psychology: Vol. 4. Socialization, Personality, and Social Development* (pp. 693–774). New York: Wiley & Sons.

Rubin, K. H., LeMare, L., and Lollis, S. P. (in press). Social withdrawal in childhood: developmental pathways to peer rejection. In S. R. Asher and J. D. Coie (eds), *Children's Status in the Peer Group*. New York: Cambridge University Press.

Rubin, K. H., Maioni, T. L., and Hornung, M. (1976). Free play behaviors in middle- and lower-class preschoolers: Parten and Piaget revisited, *Child Development*, **47**, 414–419.

Rubin, K. H., Watson, K. S., and Jambor, T. W. (1978). Free-play behaviors in preschool and kindergarten children, *Child Development*, **49**, 534–536.

Sachs, J., and Devin, J. (1976). Young children's use of age-appropriate speech styles, *Journal of Child Language*, **3**, 81–98.

Sackett, G. P. (1978). Measurement in observational research. In G. P. Sackett (ed.), *Observing Behavior: Data Collection and Analysis Methods* (Vol. 2). (pp. 25–43). Baltimore: University Park Press.

Sackett, G. P. (1987). Analysis of sequential social interaction: some issues, recent developments, and a causal inference model. In J. Osofsky (ed.), *Handbook of Child Development, 2nd edition* (pp. 855–878). New York: Wiley & Sons.

Shatz, M., and Gelman, R. (1973). The development of communication skills: modifications in the speech of young children as a function of listener, *Monographs of the Society for Research in Child Development*, **38**(5, Serial No. 152).

Smilansky, S. (1968). *The Effects of Sociodramatic Play on Disadvantaged Preschool Children*. New York: John Wiley & Sons.

Smith, P. K. (1978). A longitudinal study of social participation in preschool children: solitary and parallel play reexamined, *Developmental Psychology*, **14**, 517–523.

Stone, N. W., and Chesney, B. H. (1978). Attachment behaviors in handicapped infants, *Mental Retardation*, **16**, 8–12.

Strain, P. S. (1984a). Social interactions of handicapped preschoolers in developmentally integrated and segregated settings: a study of generalization effects. In T. Field, J. Roopnarine, and M. Segal (eds), *Friendships in Normal and Handicapped Children* (pp. 187–207). Norwood, NJ: Ablex.

Strain, P. A. (1984b). Social behavior patterns of nonhandicapped and nonhandicapped-developmentally disabled friend pairs in mainstream preschools, *Analysis and Intervention in Developmental Disabilities*, **4**, 15–28.

Train, P. S., and Odom, S. L. (1986). Peer social initiations: effective intervention for social skills development of exceptional children, *Exceptional Children*, **52**, 543–551.

Taylor, A. R., Asher, S. R., and Williams, G. A. (1987). The social adaptation of mainstreamed mildly retarded children, *Child Development*, **58**, 1321–1334.

Vandell, D. L., and George, L. B. (1981). Social interaction in hearing and deaf preschoolers: successes and failures in initiations, *Child Development*, **52**, 627–635.

Vandenberg, B. (1981). Environmental and cognitive factors in social play, *Journal of Experimental Child Psychology*, **31**, 169–175.

Waters, E., Wippman, J., and Sroufe, L. A. (1979). Attachment, positive affect, and competence in the peer group: two studies in construct validation, *Child Development*, **50**, 821–829.

White, B. N. (1980). Mainstreaming in grade school and preschool: how the child with special needs interacts with peers. In T. M. Field, S. Goldberg, D. Stern, and A. M. Sostek (eds), *High-risk Infants and Children: Adult and Peer Interactions* (pp. 347–371). New York: Academic Press.

White, B. L., and Watts, J. C. (1973). *Experience and Environment* (Vol. 1). Englewood Cliffs, NJ: Prentice-Hall.

Wright, M. J. (1980). Measuring the social competence of preschool children, *Canadian Journal of Behavioural Science*, **12**, 17–32.

CHAPTER 14

# Smoking Education and Peer Group Influence

MICHELLE J. MORGAN* and J. RICHARD EISER†

**School of Psychology, University of Wales College of Cardiff, PO Box 901, Cardiff CF1 3YG, UK*

*†Department of Psychology, Washington Singer Laboratories, University of Exeter, Exeter EX4 4QG, UK*

## INTRODUCTION

Health education is a field where several researchers have attempted to take concepts from social and developmental psychology and put them to practical use. Such 'practical use' is traditionally conceived of in terms of changing people's behaviour in the direction of the adoption of a more healthy life-style, or—particularly with children and adolescents—dissuading individuals from taking up habits that are injurious to their health. This whole enterprise depends critically on the existence of an agreed body of knowledge linking particular habits with particular health outcomes. Uncertain evidence about such a linkage seriously constrains both the forcefulness with which advice can be given and the likelihood that it will be accepted as credible. For this reason, the lion's share of health educational activity has been distributed over a rather narrow range of topics, with cigarette smoking, alcohol and drug abuse and, more recently, AIDS, top of the list. In this chapter, our specific focus will be on health education aimed at dissuading young people

Children Helping Children
Edited by H. C. Foot, M. J. Morgan and R. H. Shute

from taking up smoking, although some of our argument may also be applicable to other topics.

Whereas it was traditional within the fields of smoking education to view the peer group as a negative or 'bad' influence, we wish, in this chapter, to argue that the qualities and characteristics of the peer group may be harnessed as a force for good. Before describing a few of the more closely evaluated smoking education programmes, it is important to consider how the field has become limited, practically, theoretically, and to no small extent, ideologically, by a number of assumptions about the aims of health education on the one hand and relevant psychological processes on the other. In criticizing these assumptions and the limitations that they have imposed, we are not trying to dismiss previous contributions to the field, but rather to argue for a broader definition of the aims of health education and a broader sampling and use of psychological theory.

## HEALTH EDUCATION AND HEALTH PROMOTION

The aims of health education are often defined at a general level as promoting better health. Indeed, the terms 'health education' and 'health promotion' are sometimes used interchangeably, and to the obfuscation of both. More appropriately, the term 'health promotion' should be reserved for activities designed primarily to attract publicity to health issues and to increase the importance that is attached to such issues by both ordinary people and decision-makers. Activities such as 'fun runs', for instance, may convey implicit messages that exercise is both pleasurable and 'normal' for ordinary people. Mass media advertising campaigns may *remind* people of health issues at times and in places where they might otherwise be thinking of other things. However, it is difficult to make a strong case for such activities in terms of any *new* information they convey. For better or worse, such activities are a form of propaganda, the purpose of which is not specifically to inform, still less to educate, but rather to win public acceptance, in the name of 'better health', for changed standards of individual behaviour and (perhaps more rarely) for environmental interventions.

It is, of course, notoriously difficult to demonstrate that any single promotional campaign has been responsible for any particular public health or behavioural outcome. Nonetheless, there clearly have been massive shifts in societal views on issues such as smoking and the rights of non-smokers, against which the effectiveness of individually-oriented attempts at behavioural modification is puny by comparison (Leventhal and Clearly, 1980). The fear of AIDS may be promoting an even more rapid shift in attitudes to sexual behaviour within society as a whole. Whatever the role of any initial impetus given by health promoters, after a while, such shifts in societal attitudes appear to become self-sustaining, and perhaps self-limiting, in ways that are difficult to attribute to the activities of any single agency.

There are even more general difficulties in evaluating the effectiveness of health promotion. These arise from how 'better health' itself should be assessed and conceptualized. In some contexts, but by no means all, population mortality and morbidity statistics may provide appropriate measures, at least where the cause of death or illness is accepted. Reliance on such statistics alone, invites the objection that health is partly a subjective affair, culturally and socially defined, and not completely reducible to greater longevity or the absence of identifiable disease or injury. Such subjective aspects may not lead to great discrepancies from orthodox medical definitions of health and illness in the case of a patient dying from AIDS or lung cancer, but by no means all examples are so non-controversial. Consider notions of 'normal' body weight, for instance: millions of Western women regard themselves as 'overweight' with respect to a cultural 'ideal' even though their actual weight is less than average for their age and height and carries no specific risk to health. Furthermore, there are dangers in attempting to differentiate between the not-yet-ill in terms of degrees of 'healthiness'. Obviously, so-called risk factors can be measured and one can say, quite correctly, that an individual high on such risk factors will be more *likely* to become ill than someone low in these same factors, other things being equal.

For all the consideration that needs to be given to long-term and cumulative disease processes, however such likelihood is not *in itself* a state of ill-health, but a statistical abstraction. Of course, there is often no clear cut-off point, in terms of any physical indicators, that allows one to say that one person is definitely 'healthy' and another not. Indeed, the use of the 'healthy-ill' dichotomy may be frequently misleading. Nonetheless, the use of probabilistic indicators of health has led to the terms 'healthy' and 'unhealthy' being applied to the risk factors themselves rather than to the physical end-states which they may predict with varying degrees of accuracy. Thus we talk of 'unhealthy working conditions', 'healthy eating' and so forth.

Such usage is so widespread and convenient that it is vain to try and change or resist it. However, it is a form of short-hand or metaphor that sometimes can be dangerous. The danger lies in the elision from talking of certain behaviours as contributory causes of illness to talking of them as *illnesses in themselves*. Thus, smokers may be seen as needing to be 'cured' of their smoking habit. In some quarters, at least, a return to a view of homosexuality as an 'illness' or 'disorder' may similarly be not too far away. The risk is that the health promotion activist may come to see the change or even eradication of such behaviours as an end in itself and synonymous with 'better health', without regard to the uncertainty of any linkage of such behaviours with physical conditions, or of any resultant physical conditions with subjective feelings of well-being and happiness.

Defining the goal of health education as that of promoting 'better health', therefore, is fraught with difficulties, and can lead to the undertaking of many activities that can hardly be described as 'educational'. An alternative, which is not the tautology that it sounds, is to define the goal of health education as that of *educating people about health*. The term 'education' implies the imparting of knowledge and conceptual skills to enable people to ask and answer questions for themselves. With children at least it can also imply the imparting of social skills on which self-reliance will depend. Above all, it stresses the development of *understanding*, including the understanding of uncertainty. Whereas a health promotion perspective can run into problems whenever there is any 'fudging' of a one-to-one relationship between forms of behaviour and physical health outcomes, a more educational approach can lead to a more integrated view of how personal behaviour and other factors can contribute to greater risk or safety as far as ill-health or injury is concerned: it can help people deal with information, even where there is no single answer and much of the information is conflicting.

## PSYCHOLOGICAL ASSUMPTIONS CONCERNING INDIVIDUAL RATIONALITY

If we look at the kind of psychology that has been used as the basis for planning health educational or promotional interventions, what is striking is its emphasis on *individual* cognitive and affective processes. Such a bias is common in many fields of psychological research, but it is worrying if what one is looking for is some representation of health and behaviour as an interaction of social and environmental, as well as personal, factors. A good deal has been written concerning the ability of different theories of attitudes and decision-making to predict behaviour (see, e.g. Ajzen and Fishbein, 1980; Eiser and Van der Pligt, 1988). The results of such research can be summarized quite briefly:

(1) people tend to express stronger intentions to behave in ways that they expect will produce good rather than bad consequences;
(2) there is debate about the effects of communicating bad consequences in such a way as to arouse fear, but fear-arousal can nonetheless contribute directly to persuasion if certain conditions are fulfilled (Sutton, 1982);
(3) people tend to express stronger intentions to behave in ways that they expect will gain them the approval, rather than the disapproval, of others.

From this starting point, many programmes aimed at dissuading young people from smoking have provided information about longer and shorter term health consequences, in ways designed to arouse greater or lesser degrees of fear. Such programmes have also tried to convey the message that engaging in such 'unhealthy' behaviour will lose one friends rather than gain one any. At a straightforward level, such a persuasion strategy is quite reasonable. However, the focus is very much on the single individual as the recipient of such information. A question hardly raised is that of how such information is received and interpreted by young people in groups and as members of groups. Yet this question is of central importance to the present volume. Its neglect reflects a more general bias in the traditional conceptualization of the relationship between groups and individuals. Simply stated, the capacity for rational, thoughtful (and hence 'healthy') action is assumed to be a property of the individual, and is best nurtured by isolating and protecting the individual from the influence of 'the group', which, by contrast, is irrational, mindless and the source of 'unhealthy' influence. Social influence is not something that can be harnessed to good ends, through 'children helping children'. Rather, it is something that must be 'resisted'.

There are two interrelated notions here. The first is that of 'unhealthy behaviour as conformity', the second that of 'conformity as unhealthy'. The first notion appears empirical enough—until one looks at the evidence. Many large-scale surveys have demonstrated quite reliable associations between the health-related habits of young people and those of their family members and friends (e.g. Bynner, 1969; McKennell and Thomas, 1967). Young people who smoke, for instance, tend to name more smokers among their friends than those who do not smoke. From this it is often inferred that the 'peer group' is a source of influence that pushes young people in the direction of smoking.

In fact, such evidence is extremely ambiguous when it comes to drawing inferences about causality. What we have is a correlation. To interpret this correlation in causal terms we need a model, however crude, of the relevant processes. This does not present a problem for the interpretation of the correlation with *parental* smoking in causal terms. We can easily assume that parental smoking 'comes first', we know that parental example and reinforcement can influence many other types of behaviour, and we can define who someone's parents are independently of any criterion such as a match in attitudes and behaviour.

Interpreting 'peer group influence', or even finding it, is not so simple. We cannot assume that the 'peer group' is somehow already 'out there' (doubtless smoking, drinking and generally misbehaving) before our individual respondent enters the drama and receives its malign influence. The relationships that define the peer group are not independent of those that constitute the potential effects of social influence. More simply, the individual respondent defines—and to some extent chooses—the membership of his or her own 'peer group'. The question of how the peer group influences the individual thus can be recast in terms of how the individual defines his or her membership of different groups. It is quite as plausible, on the evidence, to suggest that young people define their peer groups in terms of shared attitudes and habits as to suggest that such shared attitudes and habits are a *product* of a common group membership. Moreover, similarity of economic and demographic circumstances, proximity of homes, common schooling and such like can contribute both to friendship choice and to a closer match in attitudes and behaviour (Eiser and Van der Pligt, 1984).

## Social identity and social influence

Social psychological research on the notion of 'social identity' (Tajfel, 1978; Turner, 1982) offers a more interactive view of processes of social influence. The essence of this approach is that people seek a positive self-definition based on perceptions of their own similarity and dissimilarity to other people. This leads to them regarding themselves as members of particular social groups and categories, differentiated from other groups and categories. Much research has considered factors that influence this 'self-categorization' process (Turner, 1985)—how different aspects of a person's identity (e.g. class or ethnicity) may acquire greater salience or subjective importance within some social contexts rather than others, and how engaging in group behaviour (e.g. political protest; see Reicher, 1984) can lead individuals to develop new definitions of their group membership.

Related research has looked at the consequences of self-categorization for social influence. According to Turner (1982), the likelihood that people will accept a norm as applicable to themselves depends critically on the behaviours prescribed by the norm being seen as *criterial attributes* of a social group or category to which they belong. Similarly, the likelihood that one person will accept another's behaviour (or opinion) as a suitable model for imitation will depend on their sharing of a common category membership, the ability of the other person to define what is normative for that category and the nature of the behaviour—whether it is criterial for group-membership or not (Abrams *et al.*, 1988; Hopkins, 1988).

In concrete terms, this means that the strength of any 'peer group influence' to take up smoking does not simply depend on the number of one's peers who smoke, but on the way in which the 'peer group' is defined and subdivided into categories of personal significance to their individual members, on the extent to which smoking or not smoking covaries with such category membership, and on the extent to which smoking is perceived as a criterial attribute of category membership (smoking helps define membership, and is not just incidentally correlated with it). These conditions *may* apply, but not always, and not for everyone. Indeed, the correlational evidence that young smokers have more smokers among their friends may be taken to imply a subdivision of the 'peer group' into smaller friendship groups. We do not know exactly how such friendship selections are made. Although we can infer that smoking/non-smoking is non-randomly associated with whatever criteria are used, we cannot say for sure that smoking is a criterial, rather than incidental, attribute of group-membership (Eiser and Van der Pligt, 1984). Under what circumstances will a group that *happens* to include a relatively large proportion of smokers (or non-smokers) come to treat smoking (or non-smoking) as normative for the group as a whole? Until we can answer this kind of question, we cannot claim to understand how group membership influences smoking or any other health-related behaviour.

This highlights a central irony within the 'unhealthy behaviour as conformity' notion—that many 'unhealthy' behaviours are in fact *minority* activities, at least if one takes a sufficiently wide view of the population to which any individual belongs. There is no more empirical reason to apply the label of 'conformist' to young smokers than to young non-smokers. So why has it happened? The answer seems to lie in a tradition of social theorizing that has sought to portray the isolated individual as the source of rationality and purity, but the wider social group as the source of mindless and destructive impulses. The classic expression of this was Le Bon's (1895) analysis of 'the crowd', which guided many right-wing regimes in their suppression of political protest (see Reicher and Potter, 1985). However, there are many less extreme versions of the 'conformity' notion that presuppose a similar distinction between the 'thinking' individual and the 'unthinking' crowd—between strong, healthy individuals and weak, unhealthy conformists.

But *which* crowd, *which* conformists? As we have seen, we cannot reproduce this distinction between 'individualists' and 'conformists' on numerical grounds alone. Some kinds of conformity are 'good' (but we do not use the term 'conformity' in such contexts) and likewise some kinds of non-conformity are 'bad' (but called deviance rather than individualism). To a worrying extent, there is an implicit discourse here that denigrates as 'irrational' such influence as emanates from 'crowds' or social groups *occupying positions of lower status within society*—traditionally (and, in many respects, still) the working class (who, of course, show more than their fair share of 'unhealthy' habits), but also the less educated (which amounts to much the same) and the young. Quite simply there is a subplot of implicit conflict between those allied to an established order (of which the medical profession is an important part) and those who are alienated to lesser or greater extents from that order. Much of the reason why there has been so much concern with the 'peer group' is the assumption (by adults) that young people's social relationships with those of the same (age) status as themselves may provide them with a kind of power base of solidarity to encourage and sustain a degree of alienation from, and rejection of, the authority of the established adult order of society. When approached in this way, health promotion is not a form of education, but a process of social control.

Some of the intervention programmes we are about to review tend, it must be acknowledged, to view 'peer group influence' as something that ought to be resisted. However, it does not need to be so. As the emphasis moves from persuasion to education, so there has been an increasing realization that the influence of peers can be as beneficial as it has sometimes been assumed to be damaging. Young people learn a great deal from other young people anyway. The challenge for health educators is to help shape such learning in ways that take account of real medical evidence on the one hand, and of young people's aspirations for autonomy on the other. The balance that has to be struck is one between a respect for such autonomy and the responsibility to communicate information and advice that could save lives. Such autonomy does not need to be marked by the taking up of habits that increase one's likelihood of an early death. Advice on how to stay healthy does not need to be construed as being ordered around by one's elders, and one way in which this can be avoided is by involving young people themselves as sources of advice and models for behavioural imitation. This strategy has its own dangers. The fact that someone is 'young' does not mean that he or she will be accepted as a valid role model by anyone else who is 'young'—there are other social categories than those based on age alone. However, if used successfully, it can lead to a consideration of broader issues that can be dealt with satisfactorily by adult-led information-based 'teaching'.

## A SELECTIVE REVIEW OF SMOKING EDUCATION PROGRAMMES

Up until the late 1970s, the majority of school health education programmes, particularly those focusing on smoking prevention, were based on informational fear-arousal models. Traditionally these programmes emphasized communicating knowledge of the long-term health risks of smoking including lectures, posters and films on the increased risk of lung cancer, emphysema and heart disease. While these programmes were successful in teaching children about the dangers of smoking and often resulted in stronger verbalized attitudes against smoking, they had very little or no effect on smoking behaviour (Thompson, 1978). The question was, therefore, what type of information in what type of social context would facilitate the desired behavioural change?

### Peer models

Evans (1976) argued that for intervention programmes to be effective they should be based on social-psychological communication models and social learning theories. More specifically, Evans proposed using an application of Bandura's (1971) social learning theory which emphasizes the role of social models and vicarious learning in the acquisition and maintenance of behaviours, together with a behavioural variation of McGuire's (1969, 1974) cognitive inoculation model. McGuire suggests that existing attitudes may be strengthened by 'inoculating' children against the social pressures—peer pressure, mass media and parental modelling—to smoke. Evans further suggested that traditional anti-smoking messages may fall into a 'time perspective' trap in that they focus almost entirely on the future dangers of smoking whereas McGuire's analysis of effective communication suggests that messages which are closely suited to the present values and attitudes of the target audience will be more effective than other types of message. Consequently, Evans argued that anti-smoking messages designed for adolescents should emphasize the immediate social and physiological effects of smoking.

Based on this persuasive communication model, Evans and his colleagues (Evans, Raines and Hanselka, 1981, 1984) developed and tested the first of the social influences programmes for smoking prevention. Although the Houston team did not have peer tutors as such they used non-smoking, same-age peers, rather than adult authority figures to narrate the films they produced. These films gave information on the immediate physiological effects of smoking, the difficulties of smoking cessation, the perception of smoking and smokers by non-smokers, and the three types of social pressures that influence adolescents to begin smoking (i.e. peer pressure, mass media and parental modelling). In a fourth film same-age peers acted out situations in which students are exposed to the pressures to smoke, together with model behaviour depicting ways to resist such pressures. In addition, posters developed from still shots from the films were produced for display in classrooms throughout the school year. Films were shown on consecutive days and followed by a discussion of resistance to persuasion.

The experimental evaluation of Evans's programme involved a total of 13 junior high schools assigned to one of three experimental or four control conditions. The three experimental groups received aspects of the programme (full treatment, full treatment except the Pressures to Smoke film, and immediate physiological effects information only) during grades 7, 8 and 9. Testing involved a 15-item computer-scored questionnaire on current smoking behaviour, future smoking intentions (including information items) and the nicotine-in-saliva test which was used to verify the reported smoking and to increase the honesty of these reports. The control schools included the repeated measurement condition (children in this group received all 12 testings including the nicotine-in-saliva measure), the pre-test/post-test control group, the repeated measurement control using only reported behaviour and the after-only control group in which a single measurement was carried out in four schools not previously involved in the study. Observations in the eighth and ninth grade suggested that groups receiving the programme exhibited less smoking behaviour and indicated less intention to smoke than did groups in the control conditions. Evans claimed significant programme effects on the basis of approximately 9.5% of treatment students versus 11 to 14% of control students reporting smoking two or more cigarettes per day by the end of grade 9. Furthermore, Evans argued that knowledge generated by the film was significantly related to smoking intention and behaviour. However, caution must be exercised in interpreting these results. Firstly, the schools involved were not randomly assigned to conditions. More importantly, owing to administrative difficulties, groups were combined during the study so that only three conditions remained by the ninth grade. Since subjects were not identified across time, successive cross-sectional rather than longitudinal analyses were undertaken, restricting the degree of causality which can therefore be inferred. Furthermore, interpretation of the cross-sectional analyses is hampered by the changing sample size over time. The authors themselves suggest that given the quasi-experimental nature of the study it might be regarded as 'an encouraging first approximation suggesting promise for such applications of social learning—persuasive communications theory' (Evans *et al.*, 1981 p. 413). It is worth adding that it could also be considered to be an encouraging first use of peer models rather than adult authority figures in smoking education.

Despite the methodological weaknesses of the Houston studies the theoretical derivations of the programme were sufficient to inspire other researchers to develop and test further this approach to smoking prevention.

## Cross-age peer tutors

The Harvard/Stanford project (McAlister *et al.*, 1980; Perry *et al.*, 1980) was based on the inoculation-communication model but introduced two major innovations. Firstly, the Stanford researchers argued that during adolescence the peer group becomes increasingly important while the influence of adults diminishes, particularly for adolescents who smoke. Evidence that adolescents who smoke show a greater tendency towards rebelliousness, unconventional behaviour and autonomy (Jessor and Jessor, 1977) led the team to explore peer teaching as a method of modelling and teaching the social skills necessary to resist pressures to smoke. The team argued that peers can be chosen as believable models who may be successful in terms of adolescent norms; that is, they should be attractive, popular and even apparently rebellious but remain non-smokers. Secondly, the team wanted to increase the likelihood of the techniques to resist social pressures being incorporated into the students' behavioural repertoire. Consequently the team introduced role playing into the programme whereby the students in class acted out situations requiring resistance to social influence. Project CLASP (Counselling Leadership Against Smoking Pressures) employed high school students as 'peer' teachers to conduct smoking prevention classes with children in the seventh grade. The programme consisted of three sessions on consecutive days with four booster sessions during the remainder of the school year. Sessions included small group discussions on social pressure, peer pressure, assertiveness training, social anxiety and stress; public commitments not to smoke; modelling of resistance-to-smoke skills by the peer leaders together with rehearsal of the skills by the seventh grade pupils. The programme was evaluated using three schools in California. The experimental school was selected on the basis of a previously identified high level of smoking among older students and was compared with two non-randomly selected control schools. At the end of the seventh, eighth and ninth grades, self reports of smoking (validated using a test of exhaled carbon monoxide) were significantly lower in the treatment school compared with one of the control schools (the other control school had been dropped from the analysis due to methodological difficulties). Similar results were also reported for alcohol consumption and marijuana use. However, due to the anonymity of the self-report questionnaires, individual subjects were not followed longitudinally and analyses were restricted to cross-sectional comparisons. Moreover, since the schools were not randomly selected the results could have been biased by existing differences between the two schools or to statistical regression owing to the selection of the treatment school based on a higher than average preprogramme smoking rate.

Applying the same theoretical model, the High School Smoking Prevention Program (Perry *et al.*, 1983) attempted to assess the relative effectiveness of social skills and health consequences programmes and to compare college students ('peer-teaching') with health educators as programme disseminators on the rate of smoking among high school students. This is one of the few projects to have concentrated on children in high school as opposed to junior high school. In a $2 \times 3$ factorial design five classes in each of four schools in North California were randomly assigned to one of three treatment conditions. One programme concentrated on the social consequences of smoking, one on the long-term health risks (fear arousal approach) and one on the immediate and long-term physiological effects. In two schools class teachers were trained to conduct the programme and in the other two schools college students acted as 'peer teachers' for the three one-hour sessions. Assessment consisted of self reports of smoking and other health behaviours plus a measure of exhaled carbon monoxide. Results suggested that all three programmes worked equally well. Of the 82 pupils who reported weekly smoking at the pre-test in February, 23% reported no smoking in the week prior to the post-test in May. No significant differences were found between treatment conditions, probably due to the small sample sizes, although there was a trend towards a treatment–instructor interaction. The data suggested that class teachers may be more effective with the traditional health consequences curriculum whereas college student teachers may be more effective in those classes concerned with social pressures. Perry *et al.* (1983) argued that since college-age peers are more proximal models for adolescents, it is not surprising that they are more effective at disseminating a social pressures curriculum. While this finding obviously requires substantiation by a larger scale study, it suggests that it may not be sufficient simply to consider either the message in terms of curriculum content, or the adult or peer model, in isolation but rather it may be essential to take into account the credibility of the model for the particular message involved. Peers may be excellent models for a social consequences programme whereas regular teachers may have low credibility in this field and the reverse may tend to be true for traditional long-term health risk messages.

## Same-age peer tutors

The Minnesota project followed in the same theoretical and conceptual mould but was the first study to test the value of same-age peer leaders. Moreover, the study attempted to identify the necessary or sufficient conditions for treatment effects by separating out aspects of the overall programme. Beginning in 1979, two studies were conducted to compare a short-term influences with a long-term influences curriculum (Arkin *et al.*, 1981; Murray *et al.*, 1984). In the first study all adult-led sessions were conducted by members of the research project staff, whereas in the second, to overcome any possible Hawthorne effect, regular classroom teachers were used. The long-term influences curriculum emphasized knowledge of the long-term health risks including the effects of cigarette smoking on the lungs, the heart, blood pressure, blood cholesterol levels, and on an unborn fetus. Students watched films, listened to lectures and participated in classroom activities for five one-hour sessions. Fear arousal techniques were not employed. The short-term influences curriculum emphasized the covert and overt social pressures to smoke and included skills training sessions to teach students to recognize the pressures to smoke and to resist them using a variety of techniques. During role play students were encouraged to develop and verbalize counter-arguments to persuasive communications. Particular emphasis was placed on correcting students' normative expectations for smoking since previous research had indicated that children of this age typically overestimate smoking rates among their peers. During the five sessions only immediate social and physiological effects of smoking were considered. Three videotapes on social pressures and how to resist them were developed by the project team to support the classroom activities. In addition to the main comparison, three delivery strategies for the short-term influences curriculum were compared. In one group all classroom activities were led by adults (project members in the first study and school teachers in the second). In a second group all classroom sessions were run by same-age peer opinion leaders. The students in this group were asked to name three people in their class whom they admired and respected. The three students most frequently nominated per class were selected as peer leaders and required to attend two half-day training seminars on group dynamics, leadership skills and the task of the programme sessions before programme commencement. In the final group peer leaders were again used but the videotapes were not included with the curriculum guide.

The entire seventh grade of eight suburban Twin Cities junior high schools participated in the studies. Schools were rank ordered on the basis of weekly smoking, assessed using self-reports and saliva thiocyanate measures, and then randomly allocated from the upper and lower halves of the smoking distribution to four treatment conditions: (i) long-term influences, (ii) adult led short-term influences with media, (iii) peer led short-term influences with media, (iv) peer led short-term influences without media. Two additional schools, not randomized, provided a non-equivalent control group for the second study. Using a composite smoking index (formed by averaging three self-report measures of smoking) and covarying for pre-test differences in parental, peer and sibling smoking patterns, Murray *et al.* (1984) did not find significant differences between the four treatment conditions in the short term regardless of whether project staff or school teachers were involved in the adult led condition. However, the second study data suggest that all four were effective in producing lower weekly smoking levels than the control groups. One year follow-up data from the first study indicate that among pre-test non-smokers both peer led groups had significantly lower average weekly smoking rates than the adult led group. Unfortunately no significant effects were found for pre-test experimental smokers. Data indicate that peer leaders are more effective in delivering short-term influences messages to non-smokers but there are difficulties with interpretation as pre-test baseline smoking was lower in the two peer led conditions (49.4% and 52.1%) compared with the other conditions (62.6% and 62.2%). Although the authors conclude that same-age peer leaders are a necessary condition for the successful use of their short-term influences curriculum a more conservative view would be that the data suggest increased efficacy of the peer led approach. It is also worth noting that peer leaders were simply required to adopt the teacher's traditional role and present programme material in the style and format prepared by the research team. There was no attempt to use peer leaders in a more active and creative way.

A five lesson curriculum (Smoking and Me) using group leaders and based on the Minnesota peer led social consequences curriculum has been produced by the Health Education Authority Smoking Education for Teenagers Project. To date, an evaluation of the effects of this curriculum on the prevention of smoking has not yet been undertaken.

**Lifeskills training**

In contrast with the specific nature of the social pressures approach, Botvin and Eng (1982), argued that the onset of cigarette smoking, like many other forms of behaviour, is likely to be the result of the interaction of several different factors. These factors, they suggested, include the traditional social influences: knowledge, attitudes and beliefs about health; and psychological factors such as an external locus of control, social anxiety, low self-esteem and low self-confidence. Nor did they see these factors as operating in any form of fixed effects model but rather saw the relative importance of each varying from individual to individual. Given a view of cigarette smoking as multi-determined, Botvin and Eng developed a broader and more comprehensive approach to smoking prevention. The Life Skills Training Program is a multi-factor health programme, the stated main objectives of which are to provide students with the necessary skills to resist direct social pressures to smoke; to decrease their susceptibility to indirect social pressures by increasing autonomy, self-esteem, self-mastery and self-confidence; to enable students to cope with anxiety, particularly social anxiety; to increase knowledge of the immediate consequences of smoking and to promote anti-smoking attitudes and beliefs. The twelve session curriculum covers a range of topics including smoking attitudes and beliefs, biofeedback, self-improvement, decision making, coping strategies for anxiety, communication and social skills, assertiveness training, peer and media pressure to smoke. As with previous interventions group discussion, modelling and behavioural rehearsal are the principal techniques used in this programme.

In their first evaluation of the efficacy of the Life Skills Training Programme, Botvin, Eng and Williams (1980) reported that following intervention with eighth, ninth and tenth grade children there were significantly fewer new 'experimental smokers' in the experimental group. However, given the lack of an objective measure of smoking status and the length of follow-up, firm conclusions could not be drawn.

In a subsequent evaluation, Botvin and Eng (1982) studied the effectiveness of the programme with a younger population when implemented by peer leaders. Two suburban New York schools were randomly assigned to experimental and control conditions. Students in the seventh grade were pre-tested for self-reported smoking status, smoking knowledge and psychological variables including locus of control, self-esteem and social anxiety together with a saliva thiocynanate test to increase validity. Peer leaders were recruited from the local high school. Twenty peer leaders who were non-smokers, popular, active in extracurricular activities, self-confident and assessed as having high credibility with potential smokers, were selected and required to attend a four-hour training workshop designed to familiarize them with the curriculum. Results indicated that only 8% of the treatment group began smoking in contrast with 19% of the control group, a difference which was statistically significant. Furthermore, smoking knowledge, psychological knowledge and advertising knowledge increased, whereas social anxiety and susceptibility to influence decreased. There were no significant effects on the rate of weekly smoking. One-year follow-up results indicated 56% fewer students in the experimental group reported weekly smoking compared with control group students. While these results were encouraging there was also evidence of erosion of the initial effects. At the time of the post-test there were 57% fewer new smokers in the experimental group than the control group, but by the one-year follow-up this gap had diminished to 25%. Thus the results demonstrate the effectiveness of a multicomponent programme when implemented by peer leaders but there is also evidence of a trend towards washout which suggests the need for 'booster' doses through adolescence rather than an emphasis on a once-and-for-all inoculation.

## Other issues

The Waterloo Smoking Prevention Program (Best *et al.*, 1984, Flay *et al.* 1985) was based on the social influences approach but added a decision-making component. The programme consisted of three major topics delivered in six one-hour weekly sessions delivered to sixth grade students. The first topic covered information including the negative consequences of smoking, population smoking rates, situations in which influences to smoke occur and methods of resisting such influences. The second topic covered skills development and used modelling and behavioural rehearsal to help children resist social pressures. The final topic covered decision making and commitment in which students were asked to list advantages as well as disadvantages of cigarette smoking, make a decision for themselves about smoking, and announce the decision to the class including the reasons behind it. Two maintenance sessions were delivered towards the end of grade 6 and three one-hour booster sessions were provided, two at the beginning of grade 7 and one at the beginning of grade 8 to maintain contact and review social influences. The programme included a media component in which the films originally developed by Evans were reproduced for the Canadian context using student actors, one or two years older than the target students, from the local theatre group. Peer leaders were not used in the classroom but programme sessions were delivered by college students rather than school teachers.

In the evaluation 22 schools in Ontario were assigned, not always randomly, to either an experimental or control condition. Treatment schools received the Waterloo Smoking Prevention Program whereas schools in the control condition received the smoking education normally available through their health education curricula. Self-reported smoking, saliva thiocyanate, knowledge, attitudes, beliefs and intentions were measured at pre-test, immediate post-test, the beginning and end of grade 7 and at the end of grade 8. The results of the study were complex. The programme appeared to have some effect on smoking prevention. By the end of grade 8 only 40% of programme students who were non-smokers at the pre-test had tried smoking compared with 53% of control students. The programme had an immediate effect on students classified as experimental smokers or quitters (that is they claimed to have tried smoking but given it up) which was still apparent at the end of grade 7 but which had dissipated by the end of the eighth grade. The longest effects were found with students who were at the greatest risk for smoking given the social influences on them. By the end of the eighth grade 67% of the high-risk students who were non-smokers at pre-test remained non-smokers whereas the same was true for only 22% of high-risk controls. However, given the use of college age health educators rather than peer leaders or school teachers there is a possibility of a Hawthorne effect. More importantly there was considerable variation between schools with some treatment schools showing a high incidence of smoking on which the programme had little or no effect. An interesting issue is whether the programme would have been more effectively implemented by peer leaders in these schools.

The Waterloo project has raised questions concerning the target population for prevention programmes, the context in which programmes work best and the conditions under which they are normally effective. Results from a survey of smoking prevalence among pupils from ten co-educational comprehensive schools in the Bristol conurbation suggest a clear relationship between smoking prevalence and the place of smoking education in the school curriculum (Eiser, Morgan and Gammage, 1988). Within the six schools where smoking education was undertaken predominantly within biology/science lessons as distinct from social education aspects of the curriculum, the overall percentage of self-reported daily smokers was 15 per cent compared with 10 per cent in the remaining schools with a lower science bias. This finding did not appear to be influenced by the social class catchment of the schools even though individual pupils' smoking was related to their own fathers' occupational status. It may well be, therefore, that the location within the curriculum and the overall context are important determinants in the effectiveness of health programmes.

The St. Thomas' Health District Community Health Council has used an entirely different setting for health education in the form of the Lambeth children's health club (Plamping, Thorne and Gelbier, 1980; Smith, 1981). Health education was offered as a weekly after-school event in which discussions focused on nutrition, smoking, the body, child development and the environment. One of the characteristics of the club was the responsibility given to children involved. Not only were the children allowed to suggest ideas, make decisions and organize activities, but they were also asked to act as peer tutors for other children outside the club. The largest scale peer tutoring project organized by the club, concerned dental health (50 children attended the club during the study and nearly one hundred were taught outside the club). The children decided where they would like to teach and chosen venues included hospitals, youth clubs and streets (perhaps significantly children did not choose their own school as an appropriate site). To make the lessons as exciting as possible the children used plaque-disclosing tablets, models and devised two games—dental snakes and ladders and dental bingo. Unfortunately no formal evaluation was undertaken.

Overall, it would appear that several factors influence the effectiveness of health programmes. Firstly, the content of the programme: those interventions which focus on immediate issues for the target population such as social influences, immediate physiological effects of health risk behaviours, life skills and decision making are more effective than traditional fear arousal, long-term health risk programmes. Secondly, the programme disseminators: despite the methodological problems, the research suggests that interventions are better implemented by peer leaders, either cross-age or same-age, than adults. Furthermore, there is evidence that peers are particularly effective models when a social influences curriculum is used. Finally, the context in which the programme is presented may affect its efficacy. The challenge for health education in the future to explore a more flexible approach to peer led programmes including cooperative learning strategies, active tutorials and group work (see chapters by Ashman and Elkins, Cowie and Ruddock, Greenwood, Carta and Kamps, in this volume for further discussion of these techniques).

## CONCLUSIONS

The question of how children can help children within the context of smoking education raises fundamental issues concerning not only the nature of social influence, but also of educational philosophy. If a sense of perspective is not retained, health education can cease to be educational at all, but instead take the form of an attempted process of social control that seeks to impose behavioural standards from above in the name of 'better health'. If this process of control is too transparent, it can all too easily alienate the very people that could benefit most from the advice that is being offered. 'Health for all' is an honourable goal to pursue, but it is neither necessarily an end in itself, nor the touchstone of every moral choice.

Education is about understanding, tolerance and the capacity for informed and reasoned decision-making. Professional educators should have these qualities, but they do not (fortunately) have a monopoly of them; nor are they the only people who can nurture such qualities in others. So much of what goes on in schools is premised on a distinction between the authority of the teacher and the naivety of the pupils, that it is difficult sometimes to recognize that there are important areas where teachers are not necessarily the 'experts', even though they may have valuable experience to share. The social relationships that children and adolescents form with one another are not a closed book to a sympathetic adult, but they are a book with which the young people themselves have a closer day-to-day familiarity. Health education, no less than 'personal, social and moral education', cannot ignore these social relationships nor the 'expertise' of the young people themselves.

'Peer group influence' can be an integral part of health education and not its adversary. But for this to happen, we need more than 'stooges' for the adult point of view. When it comes to the communication of medical 'facts', it may be better to rely on the poise of an experienced practitioner than on the ability of a fifteen-year-old to read long words off an autoprompter. Even the use of 'peer leaders' runs the risk of a reintroduction of an expert–novice distinction, in a way that can undermine the constructiveness of more democratically organized discussion groups.

The potential benefits of easier departures from more traditional forms of teaching and classroom organization should not be underestimated. As already mentioned, Eiser, Morgan and Gammage (1988) found lower rates of smoking in schools where pupils recalled being taught about smoking within the social education rather than the biology/science part of the curriculum. Discussion of varied opinions, values and personal relationships rather than merely a didactic inculcation of 'facts', can be helpful to a whole range of broader educational objectives.

Understanding peer relationships and their influence on health can and should be an important part of education, but fostering such understanding does not fit easily into the way education, or schooling, is thought of by many teachers and pupils. The small selection of programmes we have described represent attempts at innovation in curriculum development. It is still too early to predict how broadly such innovations will be adopted within schools generally, and across different topic areas. Ultimately, however, it is on such general changes in educational practice that much of the effectiveness of these and future programmes will depend.

## REFERENCES

Abrams, D., Wetherell, M., Cochrane, S., Hogg, M. A., and Turner, J. C. (1988). Knowing what to think by knowing who you are: self-categorization and the nature of norm formation, conformity and group polarization. Submitted for publication.

Ajzen, I., and Fishbein, M. (1980). *Understanding Attitudes and Predicting Social Behaviour*. Englewood Cliffs, NJ: Prentice-Hall.

Arkin, R. M., Roemhild, H. F., Johnson, C. A., Luepker, R. V., and Murray, D. M. (1981). The Minnesota smoking prevention program: a seventh-grade health curriculum supplement, *The Journal of School Health*, November, 611–616.

Bandura, A. (1971). *Social Learning Theory*. New York: General Learning Press.

Best, J. A., Flay, B. R., Towson, S. M. J., Ryan, K. B., Perry, C. L., Braun, K. S., Kersell, M. W., and d'Avernas, J. R. (1984). Smoking prevention and the concept of risk, *Journal of Applied Social Psychology*, **14**, 257–273.

Botvin, G. J., and Eng, A. (1982). The efficacy of a multicomponent approach to the prevention of cigarette smoking, *Preventive Medicine*, **11**, 199–211.

Botvin, G. J., Eng, A., and Williams, C. L. (1980). Preventing the onset of cigarette smoking through life skills training, *Preventive Medicine*, **9**, 135–143.

Bynner, J. M. (1969). *The Young Smoker*. Government Social Survey 55383, London, HMSO.

Eiser, J. R., and Van Der Pligt, J. (1984). Attitudinal and social factors in adolescent smoking: in search of peer group influence, *Journal of Applied Social Psychology*, **14**, 348–363.

Eiser, J. R., and Van Der Pligt, J. (1988). *Attitudes and Decisions*. London: Routledge.

Eiser, J. R., Morgan, M. J., and Gammage, P. (1988). Social education is good for health, *Educational Research*, **30**, 20–25.

Evans, R. I. (1976) Smoking in children: Developing a social psychological strategy of deterrence, *Journal of Preventive Medicine*, **5**, 122–127.

Evans, R. I., Rozelle, R. M., Maxwell, S. E., Raines, B. E., Dill, C. A., Guthrie, T. J., Henderson, A. H., and Hill, P. C. (1981). Social modeling films to deter smoking in adolescents: results of a three year field investigation, *Journal of Applied Psychology*, **66**, 399–414.

Evans, R. I., Raines, B. E., and Hanselka, L. (1984). Developing data-based communications in social psychological research: adolescent smoking prevention, *Journal of Applied Social Psychology*, **14**, 289–295.

Flay, B. R., Ryan, K. B., Best, J. A., Brown, R. S., Kersell, M. W., d'Avernas, J. R., and Zanna, M. P. (1985). Are social psychological smoking prevention programs effective? The Waterloo Study, *Journal of Behavioural Medicine*, **8**, 37–59.

Hopkins, N. (1988). Adolescent social groups and social influence. Unpublished Ph.D. Thesis, University of Exeter.

Jessor, R., and Jessor, S. (1977). *Problem Behavior and Psychosocial Development*. New York: Academic Press.

Le Bon, G. (1895) (translated 1947). *The Crowd: A Study of the Popular Mind*. London: Ernest Benn.

Leventhal, H., and Cleary, P. D. (1980). The smoking problem: a review of the research and theory in behavioral risk modification, *Psychological Bulletin*, **88**, 370–405.

McAlister, A. L., Perry, C., Killen, J., Slinkard, L. A., and Maccoby, N. (1980). Pilot study of smoking, alcohol and drug abuse prevention, *American Journal of Public Health*, **70**, 719–721.

McGuire, W. J. (1969). The nature of attitudes and attitude change. In G. Lindzey and E. Aronson (eds), *The Handbook of Social Psychology* (Vol. 3). Reading, Mass.: Addison-Wesley.

McGuire, W. J. (1974). Communication-persuasion models for drug education: experimental findings. In M. Goodstadt (ed.), *Research Methods and Programs of Drug Education*. Toronto: Addiction Research Foundation.

McKennell, A. C., and Thomas, R. K. (1967). *Adults' and Adolescents' Smoking Habits and Attitudes*. Government Social Survey, 55353/B. London: HMSO.

Murray, D. M., Luepker, R. V., Johnson, C. A., and Mittelmark, M. B. (1984). The prevention of cigarette smoking in children: a comparison of four strategies, *Journal of Applied Social Psychology*, **14**, 274–288.

Perry, C., Killen, J., Slinkard, L. A., and McAlister, A. L. (1980). Peer teaching and smoking prevention among junior high school students, *Adolescence*, **XV**, **(58)**, 277–281.

Perry, C. L., Telch, M. J., Killen, J., Burke, A., and Maccoby, N. (1983). High school smoking prevention: the relative efficacy of varied treatments and instructors, *Adolescence*, **XVII**, 561–566.

Plamping, D., Thorne, S., and Gelbier, S. (1980). Children as teachers of dental health education, *British Dental Journal*, **149**, 113–115.

Reicher, S. D. (1984). The St. Pauls' MOT; an explanation of the limits of crowd action in terms of a social identity model, *European Journal of Social Psychology*, **14**, 1–21.

Reicher, S., and Potter, J. (1985). Psychological theory as intergroup perspective. A Comparative analysis of 'scientific' and 'lay' accounts of crowd events, *Human Relations*, **38**, 167–189.

Smith, R. (1981). Health education by children for children, *British Medical Journal*, **283**, 782–783.

Sutton, S. R. (1982). Fear-arousing communications. A critical examination of theory and research. In J. R. Eiser (ed.), *Social Psychology and Behavioural Medicine*. Chichester: Wiley.

Tajfel, H. (ed.) (1978). *Differentiation between Social Groups: Studies in the Social Psychology of Intergroup Relations*. London: Academic Press.

Thompson, E. L. (1978). Smoking education programs, 1960–1976, *American Journal of Public Health*, **68**, 250–257.

Turner, J. C. (1982). Towards a cognitive redefinition of the social group. In H. Tajfel (ed.), *Social Identity and Intergroup Relations*. Cambridge: University Press.

Turner, J. C. (1985). Social categorization and the self-concept: a social cognitive theory of group behaviour. In E. J. Lawler (ed.), *Advances in Group Processes: Theory and Research*. Vol. 2. Greenwich, CT: JAI Press.

CHAPTER 15

# Childhood Illness—the Child as Helper

ROSALYN H. SHUTE* and DOUGLAS PATON†

**Department of Optometry, University of Wales College of Cardiff, PO Box 905, Cardiff CF1 3YJ, UK*

*†Department of Management, University of St Andrews, Kinessburn, Kennedy Gardens, St Andrews, Fife KY16 9DJ, UK*

## INTRODUCTION

Improvements in medical technology, medical treatments and health care practices have resulted in a situation where acute and infectious diseases have become more preventable and easier to treat. One consequence of this has been the focusing of clinical research and practice on the prevention and management of chronic, i.e. long-term, disorders (Varni, 1983). These developments also mean that children with chronic illness who previously had a low life expectancy are surviving into adulthood; for example, children with cystic fibrosis are surviving for longer with the help of antibiotics, dietary supplements, physiotherapy and, more recently, heart–lung transplants. However, such individuals will now have to face new problems, as the nature of chronic illnesses means that they are treatable but not curable. They must, therefore, be managed over a long time-period, with the patients taking over a progressively more substantial proportion of responsibility as they grow older, i.e., the emphasis is on the development of self-care. While much attention has been devoted

Children Helping Children
Edited by H. C. Foot, M. J. Morgan and R. H. Shute

to dealing with the physical aspects of chronic illness, only recently has consideration been given to the psychological and social problems underpinning adaptation to and coping with its long-term effects (Drotar, 1981).

About 10% of children suffer from chronic disorders (Pless and Douglas, 1971; Willis, Culbertson, and Mertens, 1984), the commonest being asthma, epilepsy, cardiac conditions, cerebral palsy, orthopaedic conditions and diabetes mellitus (Mattson, 1972). Although only 1% have difficulties severe enough to interfere with the ability to carry out ordinary age-appropriate tasks, the nature of these conditions results in their having a disproportionate impact on the child, the family and health care resources. While it is not inevitable that chronic illness will lead to serious difficulties, there is evidence that the chronically sick child is at greater risk than a healthy one of developing psychosocial problems (e.g. Cadman *et al.*, 1987; Keller, 1953; Roghmann and Haggerty, 1970). Because of its long-term nature, its promotion of dependency on others and its disruptive effects on others' relationships and behaviour, chronic illness should be framed within a dynamic social context. The chronic illness not only creates special problems for the child, it also affects the child's relationships with others, including parents, siblings and peers. The patient should be viewed within an environmental context which comprises these significant others and which is necessarily affected by the illness which, in turn, influences the patient's ability to cope and adjust (Johnson, 1985). Because of the complex interdependencies involved it seems appropriate to develop theory and practice within a systems framework. Adopting such an approach affords greater opportunity for understanding the impact of chronic illness in total on the child and on others important in his or her life.

The purpose of the present chapter is threefold: firstly, to outline a social-cognitive model of child development which acknowledges the role of peers; secondly, to examine how chronic illness affects development and to identify some potential problem areas; and thirdly, to suggest some ways in which other children might help to promote good adjustment to chronic childhood illness. While chronic illness is the primary focus, some of the issues considered are also applicable to children with other types of disability and some (such as the problems associated with educational disruption) may also have relevance in certain instances of acute illness. It is hoped that this bringing together of previously disparate literatures will stimulate new approaches to research and practice in the field of chronic childhood illness.

## A SOCIAL COGNITIVE FRAMEWORK

The child development literature of the last two decades reveals a growing interest in the interactions between social and cognitive development (Butterworth, 1982). There has been a parallel development of awareness of the relationship between social competence and other measures of adaptation (Michelson, Foster, and

Ritchay, 1980): children who manifest social deficits may display reduced cognitive performance and academic achievement, while the reverse is true for socially competent children. Experimentally, emphasis has been placed on investigating how social interactions relate to cognitive progress. For example, experiments have demonstrated how adult–child dyads interact to gradually transfer responsibility for problem-solving from expert (adult) to novice (child) (Wertsch *et al.*, 1980). There are also increasing numbers of studies which show how a child's cognitive development can be influenced by interaction with other children (e.g. Perret-Clermont, 1980).

It might also be hypothesized, taking a Piagetian perspective, that cognitive development will, in turn, affect social functioning, i.e., that the child's increasing sophistication in reasoning will be as applicable to the social as to the non-social world. Furthermore, the child's developing cognitive powers will be applied not just to objects and people 'out there', but to the child's own self and to his or her relationships with the outside world. This notion is akin to the concept of 'metacognition' (Flavell, 1979). This relates to an individual's knowledge and experiences pertaining to intellectual enterprises; it is thus reflexive in nature, 'cognition about cognition', although there is also implicit recognition of the relevance of social factors. In the present context, explicit consideration is given to the application of cognitive processes to both cognitive *and* social events; the wider term 'social-cognitive monitoring' will therefore be used to refer to cognitive processes which have a social content. Thus social-cognitive monitoring does not differ in nature from other cognitive processes, but is identified by its content. It is not simply concerned with making sense of incoming social information, but is involved in the production of the child's own social behaviour. An example pertinent to the sick child is provided by Allen's observation that a child's reaction to help will depend on his or her interpretation of the meaning of the help; this will in turn depend on the child's understanding of the norms applicable to the social context (Allen, 1983).

A philosophical problem should be noted here (although the present chapter is not the place to explore it in depth). It concerns the assumption that both social and non-social cognitive processes exist; Vygotsky argues that all knowledge is, ultimately, socially derived (Wertsch, 1985), in which case cognition would be indistinguishable from social-cognitive monitoring. The present view, retaining social-cognitive monitoring as a separate entity, draws attention to the importance of the interaction between social and cognitive processes, while also allowing for the possible existence of non-socially derived knowledge. (It could be argued, for example, that a sick child's understanding of the illness arises from both social and personal events—the asthmatic discovers that it is not always possible to perform the same activities as peers, and also that it is not always possible to perform the same activity as yesterday.)

The present authors have adopted Butterworth's (1982) suggestion that systems theory may provide a useful approach to integrating social and cognitive aspects of

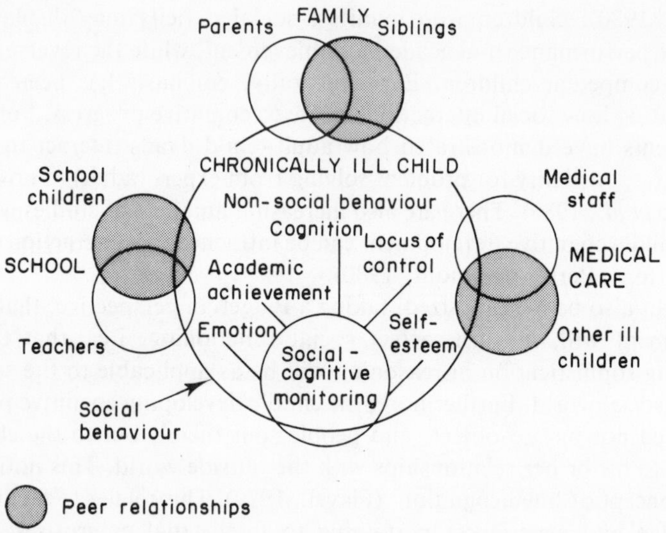


FIGURE 15.1. Aspects of development of the chronically ill child

development. We present here a preliminary outline of a new integrative approach to development. It is intended as a heuristic framework within which further developments in theory and practical disease management can occur. It is not possible, within the confines of the present chapter, to explore fully the complexity of the underlying concepts; however, it is intended to at least give an awareness of how the presence of chronic illness in the child impinges on various social systems, and how these in turn affect (and are affected by) the social, cognitive and emotional functioning of the child, as indicated in Figure 15.1.

The chronically ill child's social behaviour occurs within three main systems: the family, the school and medical care settings (e.g. hospital, GP's surgery). Within each system the child interacts with adults (parents, teachers, medical staff) and with other children (siblings, school associates and other ill children). An important feature of child–child relationships, as compared with adult–child relationships, is that they are characterized by equality rather than being based on authority differences. It should be noted that, while the child's own social interactions afford direct links with these three systems, secondary linkages may also affect the child as, for example, when parents consult with teachers and medical staff about the child's welfare.

Social-cognitive monitoring links the child's cognitive system and social interactions, and its integrative processes are seen as responsible for producing self-esteem and locus of control orientation (these concepts and their relevance to the sick child are elaborated below). Academic achievement is also viewed as a product of social-cognitive monitoring. Social-cognitive monitoring is also seen as a precursor of emotion—the affective component of the child's evaluation of its current social-cognitive state. The importance of this is that a frequent concern of those involved in the management of chronic illness is the reduction of the child's negative emotions although, as pointed out by Fielding (1984), this is often aimed primarily at improving compliance with treatment rather than at simply making the child feel happier.

Finally, the child's non-social behaviour is viewed as interacting with the child's cognitive processes (although whether this system should truly be present is related to the philosophical issue mentioned previously).

For the sake of clarity of presentation, the model as illustrated in Figure 15.1 is oversimplified. The most important omission is the dimension of time, which is difficult to represent in a diagram of this nature; it should be recognized that, while the basic relationships between the various systems apply throughout childhood, details will vary (e.g. academic achievement is not relevant for the infant). Another simplification is that the authority/equality distinction is represented as a dichotomy, whereas it might be more properly viewed as a continuum, with children older than the sick child occupying a mid-position. Furthermore, there are other systems which could be included, such as disease management, body image and a detailed breakdown of self-concept. Nevertheless, the model as presented helps to structure Johnson's (1985) observation that the sick child should be placed in a social context which influences and is influenced by, the child's ability to cope and adjust.

The advantage of the systems approach is that it recognizes the interactional nature of the processes involved. For example, the child's level of cognitive development will influence his or her understanding of the illness (Bibace and Walsh, 1980). This will, in turn (via social-cognitive monitoring) affect the child's interpretation of the behaviour of health-care staff. This interpretation will affect the child's behaviour towards those staff, whose responses will feed back (again via social-cognitive monitoring) to the child's cognitive system and, perhaps, change the understanding of the illness. A further example is afforded by the finding that a child's academic performance depends on both the teacher's perception of the child's ability and the child's own academic self-image (Davidson and Lange, 1970; Beane, 1983). A systems approach affords a wider perspective than much previous work which (as discussed by Eiser, 1985) was primarily concerned with the unidirectional effects of chronic illness on child and family. In terms of management of chronic illness, the systems approach emphasizes the need to consider how changes in one aspect of the child's life might have repercussions in other domains, as discussed by Marteau, Bloch and Baum (1987) in relation to diabetic children's metabolic control and psychological and family functioning. Such an approach also opens up the possibility of developing interventions in one system in order to promote positive effects in another. Later in the chapter some ways in which a child's peers might assist in the adjustment process will be considered. However, it is necessary first to establish what is meant by good adjustment, which will in turn be a function of the child's stage of development.

## Adjustment: a developmental perspective

Eiser (1985) has discussed previous models of adjustment to childhood illness, including Wright's (1960) social-psychological approach, based on self-concept, Mattson's (1972) coping approach and Pless and Pinkerton's (1975) integrated model, which emphasizes the fact that adjustment is not static. Eiser herself suggests that any single definition of coping or adjustment will be inappropriate, since developmental level is a critical factor, and she maintains that the child's understanding of health and illness is central.

The present model owes something to all these previous approaches, but incorporates them within a social-cognitive framework. The importance of level of development must be recognized: good adjustment in the infant will be quite different from good adjustment in the adolescent, and some of the considerations which are important at different stages will be brought out later in the chapter. In general terms, a chronically ill child's adjustment may be viewed as the degree to which he or she functions at age-appropriate levels in the social, cognitive and academic spheres, while maintaining good disease-management and high self-esteem. Clearly, it is unrealistic to expect any individual (sick or not) to perform maximally on all fronts simultaneously—most of us would be labelled maladjusted by such a criterion! The notion of compensation (as discussed below in relation to self-esteem) is therefore especially important for the chronically ill child, whose condition will introduce additional barriers into the developmental process, which is normally marked by increasing competence and independence. Since the sick child may display less competence in some areas, and a greater dependency than his or her healthy peers, the psychological concepts of self-esteem and locus of control are particularly helpful in this context.

## Self-esteem

Lawrence (1988) has discussed the notion of self-esteem as derived from the phenomenological approach of Carl Rogers (1951). He distinguishes between self-concept, self-image, ideal self and self-esteem. The self-concept is an awareness of one's own identity, and subsumes the self-image (the individual's awareness of his or her personal characteristics) and the ideal self (as the individual would like to be). Self-esteem is the individual's evaluation of the discrepancy between the self-image and the ideal self. The various facets of self-concept can be seen as a product of social-cognitive monitoring, i.e., they will be influenced by such factors as the evaluation of the child by others and the child's ability to make comparisons between the self and others.

Rogers (1961) has suggested that in Western culture the need to preserve self-esteem is central; thus self-esteem can be regarded as one measure of adjustment in the chronically sick child. The present view of self-esteem as a product of social-cognitive monitoring is incorporated into Figure 15.1.

An individual's self-esteem is unlikely to be high with regard to all aspects of his or her life, particularly if that person has special difficulties as a result of chronic illness. This will not necessarily be too damaging to overall self-esteem if there are compensatory areas of strength and the importance of weaker areas can be played down. If, however, a problem area is unavoidable, then global self-esteem will be at risk. Thus a chronically sick child who has, for example, fallen behind in schoolwork as a result of frequent absence will be repeatedly faced with academic failure. The result may either be low self-esteem, or a devaluation of the importance of academic achievement. The latter course, while maintaining high self-esteem in the short term, would lead to a reduction in motivation and a further downward spiralling of achievement, with serious consequences in the longer term (Lawrence, 1988). Kottke (1966) has described how immobility can lead to a similar circular, self-intensifying and self-destructive process. However, it is not necessarily the most severe conditions which lead to such an outcome; for example, a child confined to a wheelchair may downgrade the importance of sporting ability, whereas a child with a condition which imposes limitations more intermittently (e.g. asthma or diabetes) may be relatively more frustrated in attempts to compete with able-bodied peers. Several studies do support the contention that less severely afflicted children can be more maladjusted than those with greater disabilities; for example, this was found to be the case in children with varying degrees of juvenile arthritis (McAnarney *et al.*, 1974).

Low self-esteem has been reported for children with phenylketonuria (Moen, Wilcox, and Burns, 1977) and diabetes (e.g. Swift, Seidman, and Stein, 1967). Low self-esteem may exist within a constellation of other difficulties (Percell, Berwick, and Beigel, 1974). That this can occur in chronic illness was demonstrated by Sullivan (1979), who found poorer overall adjustment and more depression in diabetic girls with low self-esteem. Marteau, Bloch, and Baum (1987) demonstrated a significant relationship between a 'robust self-concept' and good metabolic control in diabetes. Such findings of relationships between a sick child's self-concept (especially self-esteem) and other areas of functioning demonstrate the value of a systems approach.

Finally, age of onset of illness is likely to have an important influence on self-esteem. As pointed out by Pless and Pinkerton (1975), the implications of chronic illness for self-concept may be quite different for a previously healthy child and a child sick from birth.

## Locus of control

Individuals are said to have an internal locus of control if they perceive their destiny to be controlled by their own inner resources of skill, competence and intellect; in contrast, externally-oriented people believe their destiny to be controlled by outside influences, such as chance and other people (e.g. Battle, 1968). As in the case of low self-esteem, there is evidence of an association between external locus of control beliefs in children and poor social adjustment (Nowicki and Strickland, 1973). The notion of a specific health locus of control has also been used (Parcel and Meyer, 1978). Perhaps an analysis similar to that used for self-esteem could be applied here, incorporating the notion of global locus of control derived from subsets relating to different areas (this, however, is something for future work to address). For present purposes, the main point is that locus of control, like self-esteem, is seen as a product of complex social-cognitive processes. It is also predicted to be linked with self-esteem in the following way: if a child believes his or her life to be in the hands of others, but sees the ideal self as being in control, then, if this is an important issue for the child, it will lead to a lowering of self-esteem. Evidence that self-esteem and locus of control are, in fact, linked, comes from the finding of Prawat *et al.* (1979) that high self-esteem is significantly related to a child's sense of control. This is to be expected in cultures which value independence.

It might be expected that children suffering from chronic illness, with its attendant increase in dependency, would have more external locus of control beliefs than their healthy peers (Eiser, 1985). While adult diabetics who are 'internals' have better metabolic control than 'externals' (e.g. Goldstein, 1980), the same may not be true for children: Evans and Hughes (1987) have reported that children with well-controlled diabetes may nevertheless be externally-oriented. This is presumably because their condition is being well-regulated by their parents rather than themselves and, while it has positive effects on their immediate health, it does not bode well for their future independence, social adjustment and good metabolic functioning.

Such findings indicate that the role of locus of control orientation in adjustment to chronic illness is complex. However, in view of the emphasis on the development of self-care in the management of chronic conditions, a move towards greater internality would seem desirable as the child matures. Thus interventions need to consider the likely effects on the child's locus of control orientation, while simultaneously taking account of effects on other systems. For example, increasing the child's self-management of the medical condition will only foster internality if the child is cognitively ready to cope, since failure will lead to poor disease management and perhaps a deepening of externality and lowering of self-esteem if parents are obliged to resume responsibility. This illustrates the fact that maintaining good overall adjustment is a fine balancing act between the various systems, and some may have to give way temporarily when others claim predominance—no one is likely to consider a child's peer relationships or school examination results to be of pressing importance when the child is admitted to hospital in a diabetic coma (although, once the child has recovered, it may be worth considering whether such aspects of the child's

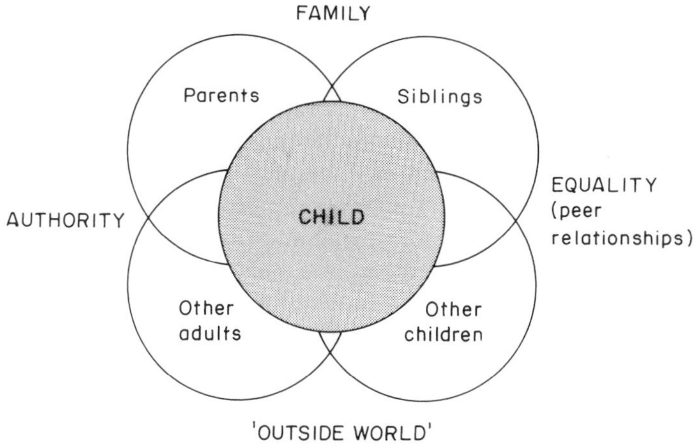


FIGURE 15.2. The child's 'social worlds'

life have contributed to poor metabolic control by interfering with disease management or causing stress-related hormonal changes).

## THE ROLE OF PEERS IN DEVELOPMENT

In 1951 Freud and Dann studied six children who had raised themselves as a group after losing their parents in World War Two; they had developed strong links with one another, and were not as emotionally disturbed as expected, given the all-encompassing role which adults, particularly mothers, were then believed to play in children's development. In recent years psychologists have increasingly recognized the important role that children play in one another's development. Hartup (1980) describes the child as inhabiting two social worlds, that of the family and that of child associates. Since sibling interaction usually precedes interaction with other children, he suggests that brothers and sisters can be seen as serving a bridging function between the family and the peer culture.

This analysis lends itself to the systems approach. While it would be possible to incorporate it into the model as shown in Figure 15.1, it is illustrated separately, for the sake of clarity, in Figure 15.2. This shows how the child's social interactions occur inside and outside the family and how, within both these settings, the child interacts with adults and with other children. Thus it can be seen how siblings form the bridge suggested by Hartup between the family and the world of children outside the home. The strength of coupling between the systems will change over the years, and the child's growing independence might be seen as a loosening of the coupling with parents and a strengthening of that with peers.

The model also characterizes the different quality of adult–child and child–child relationships as being based on authority differences. Adults have more power over children than children have over adults, by virtue of their greater physical and mental capacities, as well as the higher status afforded them by society (this is not, of course, to ignore the fact that children do have powerful means of influencing adults—ask any parent!). Child–child relationships, on the other hand, are essentially egalitarian in nature although, as noted earlier, older children may be seen as occupying an intermediate position.

It has become increasingly recognized that the special nature of peer relationships may give them a unique, as well as an important, role in a child's development. For example, Brittain (1963) found that while children use adults as a reference group with regard to future aspirations and achievement, other children serve this purpose in connection with status norms and identity issues, especially in adolescence. Hartup (1976) points out that poor peer relations in childhood are among the most powerful predictors of later social and emotional maladies; he cites evidence that, in the absence of the opportunity to encounter co-equals, children have problems in learning how to deal with aggression, in sexual socialization and in the development of moral values. Further support for the notion that peers may be independent, as well as important, contributors to social development, comes from peer-deprivation and observational studies in non-human primates (Suomi, 1979).

**Peer cooperation in education**

Thus far, the role of peers in development has been considered in terms of spontaneously-occurring interactions. However, there is also a large body of evidence which suggests that peers can be a valuable resource for encouraging cognitive development and academic achievement (e.g. Doise, this volume). The term 'peer cooperation' may be used to cover a wide variety of educational systems based on peer interactions. Two main types of peer cooperation can be identified: peer tutoring and peer collaboration (Foot, Morgan and Shute—Chapter 1). The value of both types is seen to lie at least partially in the egalitarian nature of child–child relationships.

In peer tutoring, the child is said to be at an advantage over an adult tutor in being closer to the pupil (tutee) in terms of developmental level, and therefore better able to take the perspective of the learner (Allen, 1976); there is evidence, for example, that children can be superior to adults at judging a child's non-verbal indicators of level of understanding (Allen and Feldman, 1976). In the case of tutoring, though, equality is not absolute, since the tutor is more knowledgeable than the tutee. The value of peer tutoring may be seen as lying in its combination of authority and equality—the tutor has sufficient status to function, but not so much as to make him or her 'remote' from the tutee. A gap of about two years is generally agreed to fulfil these requirements (Topping, 1988).

Tutoring is not simply a way of getting information across to a tutee, as the tutor also benefits academically, sometimes more so than the tutee; in fact, acting as a tutor to younger children can be a very beneficial form of remedial work for underachieving children (e.g. Ratti, 1980). Nor are the benefits of tutoring purely academic: it has frequently been reported to increase motivation and improve attitudes to the subjects under study. There are also many reports of increased self-esteem in participants; while the value of this for the normal population should not be over-estimated (Cohen, Kulik, and Kulik, 1982), peer tutoring is likely to be useful in this respect in the case of children at risk for low self-esteem (e.g. Ratti, 1980). Increased self-esteem is seen as depending on the status difference between tutor and tutee rather than their relative equality: in the case of the tutor, it results from the opportunity to act in an adult-like role, and in the case of the tutee, from the opportunity to associate with a higher-status child (Allen, 1976). There is the further suggestion that acting as a tutor can cause a shift towards an internal locus of control (see Imich, this volume).

While peer tutoring is based on an expert–novice paradigm, collaborative learning methods are much more dependent on the notion of equality. There is experimental evidence that children and young people who are co-equals can progress in terms of cognitive development through working together on problem-solving activities (e.g. Bearison, 1985). Such experiments have been devised in a Piagetian framework, and cognitive progress is seen as coming about through a process of resolving cognitive conflicts; the necessary discussion and argument are facilitated by the equality of the participants' status and cognitive powers. This is discussed further by Doise (this volume).

As the foregoing discussion makes clear (and in keeping with a systems perspective) peer cooperation has implications above and beyond the promotion of academic achievement. Its effectiveness depends crucially on the nature of the social context in which it occurs, and there are repercussions in terms of such measures of adjustment as self-esteem and locus of control.

## CHRONIC ILLNESS—PROBLEMS AND PEER HELPING

Thus far, a framework has been established for viewing development in a dynamic social-cognitive context, and the role of a child's peers in these processes has been noted. Attention will now be given to how the developmental process is affected by the presence of chronic illness, and to how peers might be a potential helping resource.

Despite the existence of much evidence that maladjustment is common, some researchers (e.g. Bedell *et al.*, 1977), have suggested that chronically ill children and their families are difficult to distinguish from the normal population in terms of psychosocial adjustment. Such findings have led Roberts (1986) to detect a move away from a deficit model towards a competence one.

Fielding (1984) is less prepared to accept that problems are not the norm, as the findings which suggest this are at variance with clinical experience. She suggests that this may be because researchers have sometimes regarded chronically sick children as a homogeneous group, which they certainly are not. In considering the effects of chronic illness, it is necessary to consider the basic social, cognitive and emotional needs of the child at each developmental stage, and to consider how these are affected by experience with the disease and its treatment. It is necessary to take account of a whole range of factors; these include type and severity of illness, age of onset, the course of the disease, its visibility, the degree of immobility imposed, the limitations caused by the necessity to adopt specific health-promoting behaviours, the scope for self-care, the degree of reliance on others and the child's ability to comprehend the nature of the condition and its treatment. Such factors will lead to fluctuations in adjustment patterns, causing problems in trying to draw conclusions about adjustment from a heterogeneous group sampled at a particular point in time, as well as having implications for the promotion of good adjustment in the individual case.

The systems framework adopted in the present chapter heightens awareness of how problems occurring in one area of functioning will have 'knock-on' effects influencing other areas. Equally, it suggests routes whereby problems arising in one system could be compensated for by interventions in another. The brief of this chapter is to examine in particular those ways in which other children might be helpful in the adjustment process. The remainder of the chapter focuses on problems which tend to arise in the contexts of the family, the school and medical care. It considers in particular problems which result from the disruption of normal peer relationships and those to which peer helping methods might be usefully applied. Problems for the siblings of sick children are also considered.

Taking the three social contexts as a basis for discussing these issues is somewhat arbitrary, given that the whole point of the systems approach is to give an awareness of the interrelationships between systems. However, approaching the issues in this way is perhaps appropriate since the family, the school and medical care settings are three fairly distinct contexts within which interventions could be applied, each involving largely different individuals in different geographical locations interacting with the child in different ways for different primary purposes. Nevertheless, it is important also to stress the linkages between the three systems, all of them ultimately having implications for the child's social, cognitive, academic and emotional functioning. Indeed, the present holistic approach suggests the value of strengthening links between the three systems, since good communications between home, school and medical care will ensure that all are pulling in the same direction to maximize the child's overall adjustment. This is not outside the bounds of possibility, as demonstrated by triadic interventions for behaviour problems (whereby the parent takes home management methods devised by the psychologist—Herbert, 1985) and companion reading (a method for tutoring reading designed to be applicable both for peer use in school and for parents and child at home—Pitchford and Story, 1988).

It is also vital to maintain a developmental perspective, which cuts across all three contexts. The type of cognitive and social functioning expected for the child's developmental stage needs to be taken into account in the interactions with the child. For example, peer relationships increase in importance as the child matures, and the child's level of cognitive development, which affects understanding of the illness, will obviously operate within all three social contexts.

The nature of the child's relationships with peers is essentially similar in all three contexts (although with a different 'flavour' in each), therefore some of the suggested interventions are similar within all three contexts.

### The family

The birth of an infant with a chronic condition requires considerable adjustment for the family. The presence of a sick infant leads to a concentration of parental attention on the needs of that individual at the expense of others, with an increased likelihood of conflict and discord within the family (e.g. Peck, 1979).

The evidence regarding the impact of childhood chronic illness on siblings is equivocal, since some studies report little evidence of psychological problems in siblings (e.g. Gayton *et al.*, 1977), while others report a variety of problems. This echoes the controversy over the amount of maladjustment found in chronically ill children themselves, and the confusion may be due to similar factors. Problems which have been reported include resentment towards the sick child because of the special care and attention he or she necessarily receives, and this may be exacerbated by feelings of shame associated with having a brother or sister who is different (Talbot and Howell, 1971). Siblings may face additional problems if parents extend or transfer protective attitudes and behaviours to them inappropriately (Talbot and Howell, 1971). There have also been reports of increased social isolation and feelings of isolation (Cairns *et al.*, 1979; Lavigne and Ryan, 1979), increased aggression (Breslau, Weitzman and Messenger, 1981) and increased behavioural and school problems (Peck, 1979). Kramer and Moore (1983) reported that the change in family relationships resulting from the presence of a sick child and recurring periods of separation of the healthy sibling from family members led to jealousy, resentment and guilt. Siblings have also been reported to have 'lower self concept' than those without a sick child in the family (Ferrari, 1987), and to worry about their sick brother or sister (Menke, 1987).

Children can suffer as a result of the loss of control that accompanies illness (Magrab, 1985). Matus, Kinsman, and Jones (1978) have reported the existence of external control beliefs in asthmatic youngsters. Parents often have to make the decision with regard to when responsibility for disease management passes from them to the child. This can be a difficult task, trying to balance the encouragement of independence and normal development, while still having to monitor and enforce restrictions resulting from disease management (Perrin and Gerrity, 1984). Parental reluctance to transfer responsibility may heighten feelings of disability by depressing the child's expectations regarding his or her potential and actual abilities and by preventing interaction with peers for fear of injury and poor disease management (Anderson, 1981). Problems relating to independence in the chronically sick child may be exacerbated during adolescence if the usual movement away from the family and towards the peer group is impeded; this may promote hostility towards parents and others in positions of authority (Rutter *et al.*, 1976).

The more the sick child is able to gain independence and take over managing his or her own condition, the more parental time will be freed up for other family members. Also, the better disease management that can be achieved, the fewer hospital visits that will be needed with their disruptive effect on the entire family, including siblings. Helping siblings to understand the nature of the disease may also help: Roberts (1986) has pointed out that non-disordered children's perceptions of a chronically ill child are affected by the degree to which they have been assisted in an understanding of the disorder. While professional help may be given in some cases where sibling problems become out of hand, the systems approach suggests that this would be best achieved through interventions involving the whole family, rather than simply treating the disordered sibling as 'the problem'. Family therapy may therefore be helpful. Liebman, Minuchin, and Baker (1974) have reported its use aimed at the prevention of children's asthma attacks, and Fielding (1984) has suggested its potential for helping the families of ill children to develop problem-solving strategies. Thus family therapy is of potential value both for improving disease management and coping with emotional issues (these may, of course, be closely related). The importance of including all family members is indicated by the finding of Menke (1987) that the worries which healthy siblings have about their sick brothers and sisters do not accord with their parents' beliefs about what those worries are.

In the literature on chronic illness in childhood, the role of siblings is ignored except in identifying them as a likely source of problems, such as those discussed above, while their potential as a helping resource has been neglected. In fact, as the present model makes clear, a sick child who misses a great deal of school, thereby losing out on peer contact in that context, may find at home the opportunity to develop along those dimensions which have been shown to be most influenced by contact with co-equals, such as social skills and morality.

Involving siblings in managing the disease might help to relieve pressure on parents and reduce any feelings of isolation and jealousy but, taken too far, could increase resentment if 'duties' encroached too much on the healthy siblings' activities. The authors are not aware of any studies on this, but there are anecdotal cases, such as that of the child with cystic fibrosis whose older siblings took over preparing and administering his medications when their mother became allergic to them.

A further promising area for exploration is in tutoring between siblings. That this is feasible has been shown in the case of mentally handicapped children, whose older siblings have been trained to tutor them in a variety of everyday skills; older sisters are particularly effective in this respect (e.g. Dodd, 1988). A chronically ill child who has missed a great deal of school could benefit from tutoring by an older brother or sister. This could also be done in reverse, the chronically sick child acting as a tutor for younger brothers and sisters. This would be possible even for a sick child who is behind in schoolwork since, as already noted, acting as a tutor is a good form of remedial learning in itself. Tutoring, as discussed earlier, may have beneficial effects on systems other than the purely academic: it may positively influence the child's self-esteem and locus of control orientation, since the child is being given a (possibly rare) opportunity to take on an adult-like role and act as the helper rather than the helped.

The potential of siblings to enhance their 'bridging role' between the family and the peer culture warrants further investigation. For example, siblings could help in the provision of explanations of the sick child's problems to other children, and serve as a social as well as an academic link with school during periods of absence.

### School

An important problem which often faces chronically sick children at school is difficulty with peer relationships. This has been reported for diabetics (Delbridge, 1975) and children with leukaemia (Eiser, 1980), and teachers have reported social problems for asthmatic youngsters who miss a great deal of school (Anderson *et al.*, 1983). Orr *et al.* (1984) found that chronically sick adolescents were less likely than their peers to be dating.

Peer problems may sometimes result from the necessity for the sick child to adopt ways of behaving that are out of step with those of peers, and this may become more pronounced as the child grows older and (under normal circumstances) moves closer to the peer group. For example, the adolescent with cystic fibrosis will have to refrain from smoking, and renal patients should avoid 'junk' food. There may be physical barriers interfering with integration into peer-group activities. For example, children with cystic fibrosis may display growth failure in adolescence, increasing the likelihood of behavioural and emotional problems (Boyle *et al.*, 1976; Landon, 1980). Similar problems will face the child with muscular dystrophy, who may by now be confined to a wheelchair. The child with leukaemia, besides facing a painful and frightening illness, may be distressed by hair loss accompanying treatment. As discussed by Millstein, Adler, and Irwin (1981) young people with chronic illness may be more concerned with the immediate social effects of illness than with medical consequences. They are perhaps justified in their worries, since many sick children do experience rejection by peers (e.g. Perlman and Routh, 1980).

Roberts (1986) discusses how several factors appear to influence other children's perceptions of their chronically ill peers, including the observability of the condition, the level of cognitive development of peers, familiarity with or direct experience of another person with the disorder, and the degree to which they have been assisted in acquiring an understanding of the disorder. Roberts suggests that a useful strategy would be to influence the understanding of the disease by school associates which could in turn have a significant impact on the child's own self-acceptance (via social-cognitive monitoring, on the model put forward here).

One approach is to arm the sick child with explanations and answers for school associates' likely questions. Another approach would be to put the explanations on a more formal basis, with the child tutoring the class about the condition; however, this would require careful organization, as the authors have anecdotal evidence of the disastrous consequences of a teacher asking a child to do this without warning or preparation; this could even be counterproductive and stigmatize the child further. A useful and sensitive approach would be for the entire class to carry out projects on health issues and present them to classmates. Children with other, more minor problems, such as the necessity to wear spectacles, or with experience of broken limbs could also base their work on their own cases. The ill child, rather than simply being different, would then be the expert on his or her own condition. In addition, the child would be involved in researching the condition, thus increasing his or her own knowledge, which could have spin-off benefits in terms of good disease management. That children can successfully learn about health matters in this way has been demonstrated by the children's health club in Lambeth, London, where just such methods have been utilized by children to learn with enjoyment about various health matters such as dental care and nutrition (Levane *et al.*, 1980—see also Morgan and Eiser, this volume).

On the basis of studies of the mentally handicapped (e.g. Fenrick and Petersen, 1984), it might also be expected that a sick child's relationships with peers would be improved by mutual involvement in cooperative schemes *per se*, whatever the nature of the subject-matter, since appropriate interaction can help to break down prejudice.

While the chronically ill child may face problems with peers while at school, there may also be problems of social isolation which result from frequent absence. If there are siblings they will help to offset this, and there may be opportunities for mixing with other children in the context of medical care, such as in hospital or at diabetic camps. Such contacts will be especially important if there are no siblings.

Chronically ill children may also face problems at school relating to intellectual impairment. This is frequently seen as an inherent aspect of the illness, but is more properly viewed as a result of interaction between the illness and the environment. There may, indeed, be instances in which the child's medical condition does impinge directly on intellectual functioning, e.g., infection in spina bifida may cause intellectual and perceptual difficulties, anti-histamines can induce drowsiness or excitability, steroid treatment may affect memory (Mearig, 1985; Suess and Chai, 1981) and allergies may impair hearing and reading abilities (Freudenberg, 1980). However, the importance of other factors must also be recognized. Kottke (1966) reported a progressive dulling of the intellect resulting from immobility: the imposed confinement and reduction of sensory stimulation can lead to impaired sensory receptivity and reduced sensory processing efficiency. Decreased school attendance may further contribute to intellectual problems. Illness may lead to disruption of schooling because of repeated hospitalization or having to stay at home during periods of exacerbation; missing school has been cited as an important factor undermining academic achievement for asthma (Freudenberg, 1980), cystic fibrosis (Lawler, Nakielny, and Wright, 1966) and haemophilia (Travis, 1976), and a progressive cycle of missed school and loss of motivation may ensue (Freudenberg, 1980). Decreased academic achievement is, at least in part, socially determined. While some conditions, such as diabetes, haemophilia and asthma do not appear to directly cause intellectual impairment, this may result indirectly from both poor school attendance and differential treatment by significant others (Creer and Yoches, 1977). Teachers may assume that chronic illness and handicap automatically imply intellectual impairment, and this may be compounded by the child's own poor academic self-image. This has been discussed in the case of spina bifida by Hunt and Holmes (1975) and Tew and Laurence (1975). Further evidence for the existence of such processes comes from a study by Cayler, Lynn, and Stein (1973) which demonstrated reduced intellectual functioning in children who had been misdiagnosed as having heart disease. Orr *et al.* (1984) found that chronically ill adolescents were more likely to have left school than their healthy counterparts, and those still in the educational system had less clearly formulated plans for the future.

Home-tutoring provision for chronically ill children (and for convalescent acutely ill children) appears to be extremely sparse. When a child misses school through illness, catching-up missed work seems to generally take the form of simply copying-up notes from classmates' books, especially in the case of older children. There is clearly potential here for the use of peer cooperative learning methods to be applied, both for tutoring (mainly useful for learning facts and skills, such as reading) and for collaborative learning, to promote conceptual development. School associates (as well as siblings) could be involved in this, visiting the sick child at home (thus also helping to bridge periods of absence) or during school time (either during lesson time or breaks). As discussed in the case of siblings, the sick child could act as tutor as well as tutee, for both academic and social gains; this could also give the child the opportunity to go over material intended for a younger age-level without loss of self-esteem, as the child would then be preparing it as a teacher instead of learning it as a backward pupil. The potential role of cooperative learning in chronic illness has been demonstrated by CHIP, the Chronic Health Impairment Project in Baltimore, USA, which runs a peer tutoring scheme as part of its programme of activities (Baird and Ashcroft, 1985).

**Medical care settings**

The potential for sick children to act as a helping resource for one another was recognized in the Planck Report on hospitalized British children as long ago as 1964: within the hospital school they could 'co-operate with one another and forget their illnesses' (Planck, 1964). As elaborated later in this section, the present view is that sick children can help one another in ways which are more wide-ranging and positive than simply 'taking their minds off their illnesses' (although this might sometimes be valuable).

An important aspect of medical care is the child's own understanding of the condition and its treatment, and a developmental perspective is essential here. During early childhood, children often conceptualize illness as resulting from some misdeed on their part, or from some magical cause (Brewster, 1982). Similarly, the child's comprehension of medical procedures is in terms of their immediate consequences for him or her, and are often seen as a punishment for being bad. In the later childhood years children have a better understanding of the nature of their illness and its treatment, but this is still phrased in concrete terms, i.e., illness is caused by inhaling or swallowing bugs or germs; children's greater understanding of empathy permits the inference that medical treatments are intended to help them get better, but this empathic understanding is still essentially concrete, the child believing that health care staff only know the child is in pain if she or he screams or cries. The adolescent is capable of understanding in fairly sophisticated terms the causes of his or her condition and its treatment: the young person can now acknowledge that illness can have multiple causes, and can result from an interaction between internal and external factors.

Compliance with medical treatments will clearly be better if communication between the child and medical care staff is improved. Even if staff are aware of the above described general pattern of development, there is wide individual variation, so it is important for staff to have an idea of the kinds of beliefs an individual child has about his or her condition (Fielding, 1984). One way of approaching this might be through group work. In an educational context, discussions between groups of children about scentific matters can help teachers to tap misunderstandings which children have (Bell and Freyberg, 1985), so perhaps a similar approach could be used with groups of sick children, organized by nursing staff, the hospital teacher or paediatric psychologist. It has been suggested that misperceptions could be corrected by staff either by offering alternative explanations at the same level as the child's current explanation, but phrased more positively, or for an explanation to be offered at the next stage of development. Such discussions might also help to advance children's conceptual understanding, through the processes described earlier in the case of collaborative learning.

The use of children to promote other children's understanding of medical procedures has been tried in the past, for example, with peer modelling films aimed at preparing children for hospital admission and demonstrating self-administration of insulin injections to newly-diagnosed diabetic children (e.g. Gross *et al.*, 1985). The authors are not aware of any systematic use of 'live' children in this way, but there may be scope for the development of schemes both within a hospital setting and in other settings such as diabetic camp. The social and academic advantages to tutors and tutees would accrue as already discussed with, perhaps, an additional advantage: Mattson (1972) has noted that the opportunity to identify with a well-functioning individual with the same condition fosters good adjustment in the chronically-ill child. An anecdotal example which has come to the attention of the authors is of a girl who, on her own initiative, went to give explanations to children admitted to hospital for an orthopaedic procedure which she herself had undergone. Another ten-year-old British girl with cancer has recently written a book to help other children suffering from the same condition (Gillespie, 1989). The difficulty she had in understanding explanations provided by adults was partly what motivated her to write the book. Another example is provided by the use of peer reinforcement with haemophiliac boys undergoing physiotherapy (Varni *et al.*, 1983). Thus peer-based techniques can be useful both for reducing the impact of stressful procedures and for the straightforward giving of information.

Another aspect of hospital life is the extent to which educational opportunities are provided. The National Association for the Welfare of Children in Hospitals survey (1982) found that no statistics are available on educational provision in British hospitals. Provision appears to be variable in both quantity and quality, adolescents faring particularly badly. A study by McNab (1987) indicated that the main complaints of hospitalized adolescents are boredom and the presence of younger children on the wards. The hospital teacher (where one exists) has a very difficult task in trying to meet the educational (and, often, emotional) needs of a changing population of children varying in age and ability. This situation bears some similarity to the vertical grouping of village schools, where tutoring was once widely employed. Thus the hospital situation would seem ideal for utilizing tutoring methods, so that the children are usefully occupied (rather than simply being kept quiet with endless jigsaws), the older children being paired up with the younger ones. Older children who make frequent or prolonged visits could be trained in methods like paired reading in order to give younger children who are learning to read the benefits of individual tuition. Again, this would give the older children an opportunity to adopt adult-like, competent roles, thus fostering internality and high self-esteem. A knowledge of the various cooperative learning methods which have been developed would thus be a very useful tool for the hospital teacher.

Finally, there is the possibility of self-help groups for children being organized. Although research on self-help groups for the chronically ill and their families has been described as 'embryonic' (Borman, 1985), it is thought that benefits accrue through cohesiveness, universality, altruism and sharing common values and beliefs, as well as information-sharing.

By and large, chronic-illness self-help groups appear to be aimed more at the parents than the child (although, of course, the systems perspective suggests that the child may ultimately derive benefit too). An exception is the Candlelighters organization in the United States, for the families of children with life-threatening diseases, which has arrangements for children to speak to each other by telephone (Borman, 1985). The authors have also been told of a self-help group in Liverpool, England, for children with cystic fibrosis, set up by the children themselves. Group therapy (already in use for children with behaviour problems—see the chapter by Shute and Pates, this volume) might also have a part to play, perhaps organized by paediatric psychologists where these exist. Such settings may give children the opportunity to share problems, and perhaps discuss issues which they are reluctant to broach with their parents, possibly because of a fear of worrying them. As mentioned earlier, this would also give hospital staff the opportunity to gain insight into children's worries and misunderstandings. It might also be worth considering the possibility of implementing 'buddy' systems, whereby each child is paired up with a special, supportive friend; this has a long history of use in the non-medical context of US schools and, more recently, has been utilized by adult AIDS sufferers. Thus it might be worthwhile developing peer-helping methods aimed at dealing with the emotional aspects of chronic childhood illness as well as its medical and educational repercussions.

## CONCLUSIONS

The purpose of this chapter has been to identify the part which a chronically sick child's peers can play in promoting good adjustment. This has been done within a social-cognitive developmental framework. Consideration has been given to potential problems and to peer-based interventions within the contexts of the family, the school and medical care, with a systems perspective drawing attention to the links that exist between different spheres of functioning. Fostering good adjustment during childhood will maximize sick children's later chances of integrating into society and finding employment, as well as feeling good about themselves.

Much of what has been suggested is untried (within the context of chronic illness) but it is hoped that it will give an impetus to future research in the area and draw attention to the potential of peer-based methods to those seeking ways of helping chronically sick children. In no way are peer helping methods seen as some kind of panacea, but they could form part of the armoury of those concerned with promoting good adjustment in the chronically sick youngster.

Given that adults are in authority over children within the social contexts of the family, the school and medical care, peer-helping methods cannot succeed without the support and encouragement of parents, teachers and medical staff. It has to be recognized that it will be no easy matter to foster the acceptance of the suggested interventions as adults (and children themselves) may doubt their ability to act in such capacities, because of existing attitudes towards the roles of adults and children within society (see Cowie and Rudduck's chapter, this volume). Children also have to overcome the barrier of being 'non-professionals'; the value of even non-professional adults in therapeutic contexts is far from being universally recognized (e.g. Shute and Curtis, 1989).

However, the interventions suggested need not be reserved for 'therapeutic' and 'remedial' situations, but could be applied with foresight in a preventive way to promote the all-round adjustment of the child. Roberts' (1986) view that there is a move away from a deficit model of chronic illness towards a competence model is relevant here.

Stress has also been laid on giving the child the opportunity to act as helper rather than helped, to manage his or her own disease as far as developmental level permits, in order that the child attains maximum potential, a process aided by others' seeing the child as capable. Under such conditions, the child's self-esteem will be maximized, and it may be that performing well in one field of endeavour will compensate for areas in which the child has insurmountable deficits; Burton (1975) has described some children with cystic fibrosis who compensated for their inability to compete with peers on a physical level by concentrating on academic excellence. Award-winning Irish writer Christy Nolan has been confined to a wheelchair since birth with cerebral palsy, and is unable to communicate verbally. He has recorded the vital role which his sister and school-friends played in his adjustment. Not everyone can hope to write as brilliantly as he does, but he demonstrates how a young person can cope with even the severest chronic disability within a supportive family and 'with a little help from his friends'.

## REFERENCES

Allen, V. L. (1976). Children helping children: psychological processes in tutoring. In J. R. Levin and V. L. Allen (eds), *Cognitive Learning in Children: Theories and Strategies*. New York: Academic Press.

Allen, V. L. (1983). Reactions to help in peer tutoring: roles and social identities. In J. D. Fisher, A. Nadler and B. M. DePaulo (eds), *New Directions in Helping*, Vol. 3. New York: Academic Press.

Allen, V. L., and Feldman, R. S. (1976). Studies on the role of tutor. In V. L. Allen (ed.), *Children as Teachers: Theory and Research on Tutoring*. New York: Academic Press.

Anderson, J. M. (1981). The social construction of illness experience: families with a chronically ill child, *Journal of Advanced Nursing*, **6**, 427–434.

Anderson, H. R., Bailey, P. A., Cooper, J. S., Palmer, J. S., and West, S. (1983). Morbidity and school absence caused by asthma and wheezing illness, *Archives of Disease in Childhood*, **58**, 777–784.

Baird, S. M., and Ashcroft, S. C. (1985). Need-based educational policy for chronically-ill children. In N. Hobbs and J. M. Perrin (eds), *Issues in the Care of Children with Chronic Illness*. San Francisco: Jossey-Bass.

Battle, N. (1968). Locus of control and achievement in middle class and lower class children. Unpublished doctoral dissertation, Indiana University.

Bearison, D. J. (1985). Transactional cognition. Paper presented to International Society for the Study of Behavioural Development, Tours, France.

Beane, J. A. (1983). Self-concept and self-esteem in the middle school, *N.A.S.S.P. Bulletin*, May 1983, 63–67.

Bedell, J. R., Giordani, B., Amour, J. L., Tavormina, J., and Boll, T. (1977). Life stress and the psychological and medical adjustments of chronically ill children, *Journal of Psychosomatic Research*, **21**, 237–242.

Bell, B., and Freyberg, P. (1985). Language in the science classroom. In R. Osborne and P. Freyberg (eds), *Learning in Science*. Auckland: Heinemann.

Bibace, R., and Walsh, N. E. (1980). Development of children's concepts of illness, *Pediatrics*, **66**, 912–917.

Borman, L. D. (1985). Self-help and mutual aid groups. In Hobbs, M. and Perrin, J. M., *Issues in the Care of Children with Chronic Illness*. San Francisco: Jossey-Bass.

Boyle, I. R., di Sant'Agnese, P., Sack, S., Millican, F., and Kukzycki, L. L. (1976). Emotional adjustment of adolescents and young adults with cystic fibrosis, *Journal of Pediatrics*, **88**, 318–326.

Breslau, N., Weitzman, M. and Messenger, K. (1981). Psychological functioning of siblings of disabled children, *Pediatrics*, **67**, 344–353.

Brewster, A. B. (1982). Chronically ill hospitalized children's concepts of their illness, *Pediatrics*, **69**, 355–362.

Brittain, C. V. (1963). Adolescent choices and parent-peer cross-pressure, *American Sociological Review*, **28**, 385–391.

Burton, L. (1975). *The Family Life of Sick Children*. London: Routledge & Kegan Paul.

Butterworth, G. (1982). A brief account of the conflict between the individual and the social in models of cognitive growth. In G. Butterworth and P. Light (eds), *Social Cognition: Studies of the Development of Understanding*. Sussex: Harvester.

Cadman, D., Boyle, M., Szatmari, P., and Offord, D. (1987). Chronic illness, disability, and mental and social well-being: findings of the Ontario Child Health Study, *Pediatrics*, **79**, 805–812.

Cairns, N., Clark, G., Smith, S., and Lansky, S. (1979). Adaptation of siblings to childhood malignancy, *Journal of Pediatrics*, **95**, 484–487.

Cayler, G. C., Lynn, D. B., and Stein, E. M. (1973). Effects of cardiac 'nondisease' on intellectual and perceptual-motor development, *British Heart Journal*, **35**, 543–547.

Cohen, P. A., Kulik, J. A., and Kulik, C. C. (1982). Educational outcomes of tutoring: a meta-analysis of findings, *American Educational Research Journal*, Summer 1982, **19**(2), 237–248.

Creer, T., and Yoches, C. (1977). The modification of an inappropriate behaviour pattern in asthmatic children, *Journal of Chronic Diseases*, **24**, 507–513.

Davidson, M., and Lange, G. (1970). Children's perceptions of their teachers' feelings towards them related to self-perception, school achievement, and behaviour, *Journal of Experimental Education*, **29**, 107–118.
Delbridge, L. (1975). Educational and psychological factors in the management of diabetes in childhood, *Medical Journal of Australia*, **2**, 737–739.
Dodd, K. (1988). Older siblings as teachers of their mentally-handicapped brothers and sisters. Paper presented to Annual Conference of the B.P.S., Leeds, April.
Drotar, D. (1981). Psychological perspectives of chronic childhood illness, *Journal of Pediatric Psychology*, **6**(3), 211–228.
Eiser, C. (1980). How leukaemia affects a child's schooling, *British Journal of Social and Clinical Psychology*, **19**, 365–368.
Eiser, C. (1985). *The Psychology of Childhood Illness*. New York: Springer-Verlag.
Evans, C. L., and Hughes, I. A. (1987). The relationship between diabetic control and individual and family characteristics, *Journal of Psychosomatic Research*, **31**, 3, 367–374.
Fenrick, N. J., and Petersen, T. K. (1984). Developing positive changes in attitudes towards moderately/severely handicapped students through a peer tutoring programme, *Education and Training of the Mentally Retarded*, April 1984, 83–90.
Ferrari, M. (1987). The diabetic child and well sibling: risks to the well child's self-concept, *Children's Health Care*, **15**(3), 141–148.
Fielding, D. (1984). Chronic illness in children. In F. Watts (ed.), *New Developments in Clinical Psychology*. Chichester: BPS and Wiley.
Flavell, J. H. (1979). Metacognition and cognitive monitoring: a new area of cognitive-developmental enquiry, *American Psychologist*, **34**(10), Oct 1979, 906–911.
Freud, A., and Dann, S. (1951). An experiment in group upbringing, *Psychoanalytic Study of the Child*, **6**, 127–168.
Freudenberg, N. (1980). The impact of bronchial asthma on school attendance and performance, *Journal of School Health*, **50**, 522–526.
Gayton, W., Friedman, S., Tavormina, J., and Tucker, F. (1977). Children with cystic fibrosis: psychological test findings of patients, siblings and parents, *Pediatrics*, **59**, 888–894.
Gillespie, J. (1989). *Brave Heart*. Century Hutchinson.
Goldstein, L. (1980). Relationship of health locus of control and individual diabetic management. Unpublished master's thesis, Pace University, New York.
Gross, A. M., Delcher, H. K., Anderson, J. E., and Stiger, M. (1985). Video teacher: peer instruction, *The Diabetes Educator*, Winter, 1985, p. 30.
Hartup, W. W. (1976). Peers, play and pathology: a new look at the sociobiology of human development. Paper to National Advisory Council in Child Health and Human Development, Bethesda, Sept. 1976.
Hartup, W. W. (1980). Peer relations and family relations: two social worlds. In M. Rutter (ed.), *Scientific Foundations of Developmental Psychiatry*. London: Heinemann.
Herbert, M. (1985). Triadic work with children. In F. Watts (ed.), *New Developments in Clinical Psychology*. Chichester: BPS and Wiley.
Hunt, G. M., and Holmes, A. E. (1975). Some factors relating to intelligence in children with treated spina bifida cystica, *Developmental Medicine and Child Neurology*. **17**, 65–70.
Johnson, S. B. (1985). The Family and the child with chronic illness. In D. C. Turk and R. D. Kerns (eds), *Health, Illness and Families*. New York: Wiley.
Keller, M. (1953). Progress in school of children in a sample of families in the eastern health district of Baltimore, Maryland, *Milbank Memorial Fund Quarterly*, **31**, 391–410.

Kottke, F. J. (1966). The effects of limitation of activity upon the human body, *Journal of the American Medical Association*, **196**, 825.

Kramer, R. F., and Moore, I. M. (1983). Childhood cancer: the special needs of healthy siblings, *Cancer Nursing*, **6**, 213–217.

Landon, C. (1980). Self-image of the adolescent with cystic fibrosis, *Journal of Youth and Adolescence*, **9**, 521–528.

Lavigne, T., and Ryan, M. (1979). Psychological adjustment of siblings of children with chronic illness, *Pediatrics*, **63**, 616–627.

Lawler, R., Nakielny, W., and Wright, N. (1966). Psychological implications of cystic fibrosis, *Canadian Medical Association Journal*, **94**, 1043–1046.

Lawrence, D. (1988). *Enhancing Self-Esteem in the Classroom*. London: Chapman.

Levane, L., Beattie, A., Plamping, D., and Thorne, S. (1980). Children's Health Club, St. Thomas' Health Council: A Report. Unpublished report.

Liebman, R., Minuchin, S., and Baker, L. (1974). The use of structural family therapy in the treatment of intractable asthma, *American Journal of Psychiatry*, **131**, 535–540.

Magrab, P. R. (1985). Psychosocial development of chronically ill children. In Hobbs, N. and Perrin, J. M., *Issues in the Care of Children with Chronic Illness*. San Francisco: Jossey-Bass.

Marteau, T. M., Bloch, S., and Baum, J. D. (1987). Family life and diabetic control, *Journal of Child Psychology and Psychiatry* **28**(6), 823–833.

Mattson, A. (1972). Long-term physical illness in childhood: a challenge to psychosocial adaptation, *Pediatrics*, **50**, 801–811.

Matus, I., Kinsman, R. A., and Jones, N. F. (1978). Pediatric patient attitudes towards chronic asthma and hospitalization, *Journal of Chronic Diseases*, **31**, 611–618.

McAnarney, E., Pless, I. B., Satterwhite, B., and Friedman, S. (1974). Psychological problems of children with chronic juvenile arthritis, *Pediatrics*, **53**, 523–528.

McNab, S. (1987). Adolescents' reactions to hospitalisation and to the hospital teacher: an exploratory pilot study. Unpublished project in part requirement for the degree of BSc, University of Wales.

Mearig, J. S. (1985). Cognitive development of chronically ill children. In Hobbs, N. and Perrin, J. M. (eds), *Issues in the Care of Children with Chronic Illness*. San Francisco: Jossey-Bass.

Menke, E. M. (1987). The impact of a child's chronic illness on school-aged siblings, *Children's Health Care*, **15**(3), 132–140.

Michelson, L., Foster, S. L., and Ritchay, W. L. (1980). Social skills assessment of children. In B. B. Lahey and A. E. Kazdin (eds), *Advances in Clinical Child Psychology*. New York: Plenum.

Millstein, F. G., Adler, N. E., and Irwin, C. E. (1981). Conceptions of illness in young adolescents, *Pediatrics*, **68**, 834–839.

Moen, J. L., Wilcox, R. D., and Burns, J. K. (1977). PKU as a factor in the development of self-esteem, *Behavioral Pediatrics*, **90**, 1027–1029.

Nowicki, S., and Strickland, B. R. (1973). A locus of control scale for children, *Journal of Consulting and Clinical Psychology*, **40**, 148–154.

Orr, D. P., Weller, S. C., Satterwhite, B., and Pless, I. P. (1984). Psychosocial implications of chronic illness in adolescence, *Journal of Pediatrics*, **104**, 152–157.

Parcel, G. S., and Meyer, M. P. (1978). Development of an instrument to measure children's health locus of control, *Health Education Monographs*, **6**, 149–159.

Peck, B. (1979). Effects of childhood cancer on long-term survivors and their families, *British Medical Journal*, **1**, 1327–1329.

Percell, C. P., Berwick, P. T., and Beigel, A. (1974). The effects of assertive training on self-concept and anxiety, *Archives of General Psychiatry*, 502–504.

Perlman, J. L., and Routh, D. K. (1980). Stigmatizing effects of a child's wheelchair in successive and simultaneous interactions, *Journal of Pediatric Psychology*, **5**, 43–55.
Perret-Clermont, A. N. (1980). *Social Interactions and Cognitive Development in Children*. London: Academic Press.
Perrin, E. C., and Gerrity, P. S. (1984). Development of children with a chronic illness, *Pediatric Clinics of North America*, **31**, 19–31.
Pitchford, M., and Story, R. (1988). Companion reading: group instruction peer tutoring and in-service for teachers. In R. Burden (ed.), *Effective Learning. Part 2: Educational and Child Psychology*, **5**(4), 29–34.
Planck, E. (1964). *Working with Children in Hospitals*. London: Tavistock.
Pless, I. B., and Douglas, J. W. (1971). Chronic illness in childhood. 1. Epidemiological and clinical observations, *Pediatrics*, **47**, 405–414.
Pless, I. B., and Pinkerton, P. (1975). *Chronic Childhood Disorder: Promoting Patterns of Adjustment*. London: Henry Kimpton.
Prawat, R. S., Grisson, S., and Parish T. (1979). Affective development in children, Grades 3 through to 12, *Journal of Genetic Psychology*, **135**, 37–49.
Ratti, M. C. (1980). Comrades in distress, *Links*, **5**(2), 19–22.
Roberts, M. C. (1986). *Pediatric Psychology*. Oxford: Pergamon.
Roghmann, K. J., and Haggerty, R. J. (1970). Rochester child health surveys. 1. Objectives, organization and methods. *Medical Care*, **6**, 47–54.
Rogers, C. R. (1951). *Client-centred Therapy*. Boston: Houghton Mifflin.
Rogers, C. R. (1961). *On Becoming a Person*. Boston: Houghton Mifflin.
Rutter, M., Graham, P., Chadwick, O. F. D., and Yule, W. (1976). Adolescent turmoil: fact or fiction, *Journal of Child Psychology and Psychiatry*, **17**, 35–56.
Shute, R., and Curtis, K. (1989). Dysphasia therapy: a respectable occupation? In J. R. Crawford and D. M. Parker (eds), *Developments in Clinical and Experimental Neuropsychology*. New York: Plenum.
Suess, W. and Chai, H. (1981). Neuropsychological correlates of asthma: brain damage or drug effects, *Journal of Consulting and Clinical Psychology*, **49**, 135–136
Sullivan, B. J. (1979). Adjustment in diabetic adolescent girls, *Psychosomatic Medicine*, **41**, 119–138.
Suomi, S. J. (1979). Peers, play and primary prevention in primates. In M. W. Kent and J. E. Rolf (eds), *The Primary Prevention of Psychopathology: Promoting Social Competence and Coping in Children*. Hanover, NH: University Press of New England.
Swift, C. R., Seidman, F., and Stein, H. (1967). Adjustment problems in juvenile diabetes, *Psychosomatic Medicine*, **29**, 555–571.
Talbot, N. B., and Howell, M. C. (1971). Social and behavioral causes and consequences of disease among children. In N. B. Talbot, J. Kagan and L. Eisenberg (eds), *Behavioral Science in Pediatric Medicine*. Philadelphia: Saunders.
Tew, B., and Laurence, K. (1975). The effects of hydrocephalus on intelligence, visual perception and school attainment, *Developmental Medicine and Child Neurology*, **17**, 129–134.
Topping, K. (1988). *The Peer Tutoring Handbook*. London: Croom Helm.
Travis, G. (1976). *Chronic Illness in Childhood: Its Impact on the Child and Family*. Stanford, CA: Stanford U.P.
Varni, J. W. (1983). *Clinical Behaviour Paediatrics*. New York: Pergamon Press.
Varni, J. W., Masek, B., and Katz, E. R. (1983). Behavioral pediatrics: biobehavioral assessment and management strategies. Workshop presented to the World Congress of Behavior Therapy, Washington.

Wertsch, J. V., McNamee, G. D., McLane, J. B., and Budwig, N. A. (1980). The adult-child dyad as a problem-solving system, *Child Development*, **51**, 1215–1221.

Wertsch, J. V. (1985). *Culture, Communication and Cognition: Vygotskian Perspectives*. Cambridge: CUP.

Willis, D. J., Culbertson, J. L., and Mertens, R. A. (1984). Considerations in physical and health related disorders. In S. J. Weaver (ed.), *Testing Children* 185–196. Kansas City, MO: Test Corporation of America.

Wright, B. (1960). *Physical Disability: A Psychological Approach*. New York: Harper & Row.

CHAPTER 16

# Group Therapy with Children and Adolescents


ROSALYN H. SHUTE* and RICHARD PATES†

**Department of Optometry, School of Psychology, University of Wales College of Cardiff, PO Box 905, Cardiff CF1 3YJ, UK*

*†Community Drug Team, South Glamorgan Health Authority, 46 Cowbridge Road East, Canton, Cardiff CF1 9DU, UK*


## INTRODUCTION

Children present for therapy for a variety of reasons. There may be concern over the child's behaviour or emotional state, perhaps following some traumatic happening. It has been estimated that such problems occur in 10% of children, with 2% to 3% being seriously disturbed (Abramowitz, 1976). Experience suggests that, while the type of therapy received may sometimes be determined by the knowledge-based decision of a significant adult or referring agent, it is frequently decided in ignorance of the type of therapy available locally or at the particular whim of the referring agent. The choice of therapies available may in any case be limited, especially outside large metropolitan areas.

In practice, therefore, choice of therapist may be quite arbitrary, style of treatment then being dictated largely by the theoretical model preferred by the particular therapist. Thus one child may receive individual therapy, while another with essentially similar problems is treated within a group setting. The aim of this chapter is to examine the development of theory and practice in group


Children Helping Children
Edited by H. C. Foot, M. J. Morgan and R. H. Shute

therapy with children and adolescents, although theoretical literature in the area appears to be distinctly lacking. 'Group therapy' as used here indicates at least two children working together with an adult therapist or therapists, although it may occasionally be the case that not all the children are in need of therapy themselves, but are there to assist those who are. Group therapy may be distinguished from individual approaches, from family therapy and from self-help groups; brief consideration will be given to each of these before moving on to examine the varieties of group therapy which have been developed and to discuss the theoretical considerations which are relevant for facilitating an appropriate match between problem and therapy.

### Individual approaches

A child presenting with a problem that is diagnosed as being the result of faulty learning or maladaptive response behaviour may be treated by behavioural methods. The aim is to change, through operant or classical conditioning, behaviour that has been reinforced inappropriately, and understanding by the child is not necessary. The use of behaviour therapy with children is now widespread and is appropriately used with many childhood disorders. Many pre-school behaviour problems, such as temper tantrums, habit disorders, toileting and sleep problems are successfully treated by such methods (e.g. Wright and Walker, 1977).

For children able to gain insight into their behaviour or predicament, the use of psychotherapy may be appropriate. Individual work between therapist and child will aim at resolution of the underlying problem, perhaps aided by such techniques as play therapy and bibliotherapy (Roberts, 1986).

### Family therapy

Family therapy is based on the principle that the child is one element of a homeostatically-operating system, which need not be a nuclear family, but could be an extended or one-parent family. A problem relating to the child's behaviour may be maintained by the system, therefore the aim of therapy is to change the whole system appropriately to deal with the problem, by seeing the family together as a unit. Thus the focus is not on the individual, but on the individual as a function of his or her psychosocial context (Walrond-Skinner, 1976).

### Self-help groups

Self-help/mutual aid groups are small-scale voluntary organizations consisting of individuals who face similar problems. As will be discussed later, their therapeutic value may lie in mechanisms which differ from those described by professional therapists (Borman, 1985), but insights gained from studying them may eventually be beneficial for improving professionally guided group therapy. However, much research remains to be done in this area as far as adults are concerned, and although there are occasional anecdotal reports of self-help groups set up by young people, research in the area appears to be non-existent.

## THE BEGINNINGS OF GROUP THERAPY WITH CHILDREN AND ADOLESCENTS

Group therapy with young people appears to have its roots early in the twentieth century, and its origins have been documented by Rachman and Raubolt (1984), on whose work the following account is based. They cite J. L. Moreno as the first clinician to work with adolescents in a group setting, in Vienna in 1911. He developed a 'theatre of spontaneity' where children could interact with one another and, he believed, give outlet to their creative self-expression while simultaneously getting rid of hostility. He took this notion of psychodrama to the United States in 1925. It was aimed at children between the ages of four and sixteen who were, apparently, not emotionally disturbed. Moreno originated the peer nomination method of sociometric analysis, still in use today as a means of identifying children with social skills deficits (Moreno, 1934).

Immediately following the First World War, Adler established child guidance clinics throughout Vienna and Munich in order to prevent and treat the delinquency expected to result from the traumas of war (Adler, 1930). A group-treatment approach was utilized, but this mainly took the form of the guidance work occurring before an adult audience, who reacted with self-disclosure, advice, etc., and there was no interaction between age-peers on personal difficulties.

The first true user of adolescent group therapy was Aichorn, again working in Vienna in line with Freudian principles (Aichorn, 1935). As noted by Rachman and Raubolt, the use of group work was prompted by pragmatic considerations: it was used with children whose problems were deemed severe enough to warrant institutionalization, and staffing was insufficient for individual treatment (an interesting parallel may be drawn here with the use of peer tutors to overcome staff shortages in education—see Wagner, this volume). Working with Aichorn, Lager made the first systematic attempt at grouping the adolescents for best psychotherapeutic effect, and he developed six categories for group composition: intellectual deficits; easily-remediated social difficulties influenced by environmental factors; deeply-rooted social difficulties requiring active retraining; characterological failures; disturbances in mental equilibrium with 'motivated aggressiveness'; and so-called 'unmotivated aggressiveness'. The groups were reported to be therapeutically as well as economically advantageous, since the counsellors could devise different methods suitable for use with each homogeneous group. Rachman and Raubolt also noted the important shift away from the administration of corporal punishment to such children towards humane rehabilitation.

While Moreno was setting up his theatre of spontaneity in Vienna, Slavson began organizing children's clubs in Brooklyn, based on democratic principles of self-discovery (Slavson, 1937). When he joined the Jewish Board of Guardians in 1934 he was approached to work with adolescent girls who seemed to be afraid of adults. The hope was that they might be better able to respond to one another. Borrowing ideas from progressive education, creative activities and trips were organized for the girls, and this work was the origin of activity-based group therapy. Slavson believed that creativity was the key to treatment, referring to it as 'the-drive-to-be-the-cause', which he believed would give them improved self-identities and greater self-confidence; this sounds very like modern-day notions of locus-of-control (see Imich, this volume). He believed that one of the most valuable contributions of group work was the amount of spontaneous praise received from peers. Slavson saw his work as a synthesis of psychoanalysis, progressive education and social group work in neighbourhood centres, and it earned him the title of 'Father of Group Therapy'. However, Slavson's contribution to adolescent group therapy was largely theoretical, based in part on observations of the work of Gabriel (discussed below).

Rachman and Raubolt noted that in the early days no distinction was made between children and adolescents as far as group therapy was concerned but that this came later when theorists began to see adolescence as a separate developmental stage in the life cycle. Redl (1945) worked with delinquent adolescents, and emphasized the importance of interactional patterns between group members and between group leaders and youngsters; he was concerned that group therapy could actually be counterproductive if such processes were ill-considered, and developmental level was seen as crucial in this. Lowrey (1942) rejected the use of activity approaches with adolescents, arguing that materials might interfere with a therapeutic process which should be aimed at greater self-understanding.

Gabriel (1943, 1944) was probably the first therapist to organize an all-adolescent interview therapy group, and she combined activity and discussion approaches, within a psychoanalytic framework. Raubolt and Rachman (1979) regarded her as one of the foremost, yet unrecognized, clinicians in the history of adolescent group therapy.

Wollan and Gardner (1938) used athletics as well as other activity work and discussion with boys on probation in Boston, and were apparently the first workers to apply the term 'group therapy' to their work with adolescents. Wollan emphasized the adolescents' need for self-determination, even encouraging their own suggestions on how therapy should proceed.

Rachman and Raubolt concluded that right from its beginnings, adolescent group therapy has emphasized 'educational activities, crafts and play in an atmosphere that fosters social awareness, development of potentialities, and a respect for democratic principles'.

## SOME LATER EXPERIMENTS WITH GROUP THERAPY

More recent writers, such as Schaefer, Johnson, and Wherry (1982), have continued to express a belief in the value of peer therapy. In 1985 the second author was involved in running a pilot project in Cardiff on group therapy with nine- to eleven-year-olds with peer relationship and behavioural problems. Individual therapy with these children had been tried but had not been totally successful so, as in some of the early work described above, the impetus for the project was partly pragmatic in nature. A review of the relevant literature at that time revealed relatively little of substance. However, a few reports were found which proved useful in providing background information in setting up the project, and these are outlined below before giving a description of the Cardiff project.

Several writers expressed views on the relative values of activity and discussion work. Epstein and Altman (1972) converted a conventional activity group for impulsive nine- to eleven-year-olds into a discussion group and found that more could then be achieved; they pointed out that verbal discussions are not beyond the scope of the young child and that verbal interchange group therapy was preferable to a loosely-structured activity group. Egan (1975) felt a combination of activity and discussion to be especially appropriate for 'latency' children (i.e. taking a Freudian view, those aged about six up to puberty), the group techniques providing a setting approximating real life and thus enhancing generalization of the therapeutic effects; Egan maintained that in the early stage of the group experience the children should be allowed complete freedom short of injury or destruction of property to enable them to act out fantasies while realizing that extreme behaviour is not permitted. (It is interesting to note here that, working with highly aggressive children back in the 1930s, Aichorn took such a strong view that the children should not be subject to adult influence that they completely demolished their quarters!) Lovasdal (1976) used a combination of play and group therapy with four boys aged nine to thirteen referred for peer relationship problems, and reported that the group provided a positive experience for the children, providing therapeutic peer influences towards more positive social interactions. Clifford and Cross (1980) reported the use of group work with institutionalized disturbed latency boys to help improve peer and staff relationships; during play sessions peers pointed out to one another why inappropriate behaviours produced negative feelings towards the offender.

As far as group size was concerned, Yalom (1975) cited seven as an ideal number for adult groups with an accepted range of five to ten, but attrition after the commencement of the group must be allowed for.

There were also reports of the value of running simultaneous groups for parents. Hock (1977) reported the value of parallel psychotherapy groups for parents and children with psychological problems related to asthma; the parents met at the same time as the child group met for relaxation and assertiveness training, and the parent group was especially useful in maintaining gains made by the children. Hoffman *et al.* (1981) also reported the use of parallel groups, the children participating in an activity group while the parents gained an opportunity for support in dealing with their children and exploring personal problems as they related to the problematic behaviour of their sons.

### The Cardiff project

The project centred on a group of children who had peer relationship and behavioural problems: they were all bullying or being bullied by other children, they displayed behavioural problems at home (where there were often marital difficulties) and one had attempted suicide. In line with previous work, referrals were only accepted of children with this fairly homogeneous set of problems, and within a limited age range of nine to eleven; it was decided to eliminate from the study children who had already moved up to secondary education, as it was anticipated that they would have rather different problems to face, related not just to their greater maturity but to the need to settle into new, much larger, schools. A closed group of about ten children with approximately equal numbers of boys and girls was planned, but this proved impossible in practice: dropouts and new admissions occurred during the first four of the ten weekly sessions, leaving a core group of five boys and one girl.

Next, a decision had to be made about the role of the adult therapists. The intention was to minimize their role, and to this end a system of rotating therapists was adopted, to prevent any individual adult from becoming the all-controlling figurehead for the group. There were two male and two female therapists, one of each sex being present each week, and with one therapist attending on two consecutive weeks for the sake of continuity. Two of the therapists were social workers, one a senior registrar in psychiatry and one a clinical psychologist. The intention was for the group to be run as democratically as possible but, again, this did not work out as intended, since the children had great difficulty in deciding what activities to undertake, and the therapists had to step in to avoid frustration and boredom among the children. This is in accord with Epstein and Altman's (1972) report that a greater degree of directiveness from the adults achieved the best results. This is likely to be so because of the very nature of the children's presenting problems: they probably lacked the social skills needed for the interpersonal negotiation of activities, and this will be a focus for later discussion.

The groups were intended to be run as a mixture of activity and discussion, with an increase in the latter as the weeks passed. This occurred quite naturally, the final two sessions consisting entirely of talk; discussion moved from non-threatening topics to threatening ones, such as the presence (or absence) of fathers in the home, types of punishment used and friendships. The games used depended on co-operation rather than competition, for example, co-operative drawing and games of trust involving blindfolds.

In view of the earlier reports on the value of parallel parent groups, such a group was run for the mothers, most of whom were single parents.

Although there was no formal evaluation, the mothers were asked to fill in seven-point rating scales about their children's behaviour and emotional state at the start of the project, at the end, and at three-month follow-up. The mother's perceptions of their children showed a positive trend between the start and end of therapy, but insufficient forms were returned at three months to enable analysis of the longer-term effects to be carried out. The therapists felt that two of the children changed markedly over therapy, becoming increasingly happy and integrated into the activities of the group, and their mothers' comments were in accord with this observation. In fact, all the mothers reported that their children had benefited from the group, and they themselves felt less isolated because they identified with other mothers facing similar problems and felt better able to handle their children. There were suggestions that the parent group might continue after formal therapy ended. Comments from the mothers included, 'The group was very helpful to D and we both enjoyed it'; 'It did help me very much to come to terms with the problems G and I had, and to be able to talk to people who sometimes could understand what we were going through and seeing that other people's problems were even greater than ours'.

Although qualitative impressions were that the group had been successful, this project provided little concrete evidence on the effectiveness of activity and discussion group work with children with peer relationship difficulties, and in this it is typical. Abramowitz (1976) reviewed over forty papers looking at the efficacy of group psychotherapy with children, and concluded that findings were equivocal. The question of efficacy will be given further consideration later, but the experience of the Cardiff project does suggest that practical difficulties relating to group numbers are likely to create problems for evaluation attempts, over and above the well-known difficulties of evaluating psychotherapy in general.

## DEVELOPING CHILDREN'S SOCIAL SKILLS

The importance of children's peer relationships is amply documented in the various chapters of this book. Children who manifest social deficits are more likely to suffer from a whole range of other problems, such as poor academic achievement (Hartup, 1970), low self-esteem (Percell, Berwick, and Beigel, 1974) and later mental health problems (Kohn and Rosman, 1972). While a simple causal relationship must not be assumed, helping children with peer relationship problems to develop social skills will be of benefit whatever definition of social competence is adopted. For example, Trower (1979) sees social skill as a route to achieving personal goals, so the child who lacks such skill will frequently face negative outcomes.

For children who have problems with peer relationships, actually involving them with peers and giving them the opportunity to develop social skills is an obvious way of approaching the problem (although not the only way—for example, Jones, 1987, has proposed how peer problems can be tackled via the family). However, simply placing the children together will not suffice, and examples have already been given in which peer therapy was found ineffective when involvement of the adult therapist was minimal: some kind of intervention is needed, in determining group composition, activities, laying down safety rules, or whatever.

Nevertheless, simply placing children together is useful for assessment purposes as it gives the therapist the opportunity to observe the children's interactions. In the Cardiff experiment, children developed individual roles within the group as the weeks passed, such as the clown, the scapegoat and the hero; although these were purely subjective impressions gained by the therapists, this does illustrate how group work can be of value in offering the opportunity for *in vivo* behavioural observation of children's interactional styles, as well as the chance to gain insights into their difficulties through group discussion.

Peers can also play an assessment role not just in therapy itself, but in helping to identify children with peer problems. For example, sociograms can be used either to identify children who are rejected or neglected by peers, or to rate children on particular characteristics. Such measures have been found to correlate with maladaptive social behaviour (e.g. Ladd, 1983), and Michelson, Foster, and Ritchey (1981) concluded that such methods have a part to play in screening for socially rejected or ignored children, and for socially validating behaviour change.

Several workers have reported attempts to improve the social skills of rejected and neglected children by involving them with peers in various ways. For example, Furman, Rahe, and Hartup (1979) found that the level of interaction of isolated four- and five-year-olds increased following special play sessions with another child, especially if that child was younger. Others have used modelling (based on social learning theory—e.g. Bandura, Ross and Ross, 1961). O'Connor (1972) reported increased levels of social interaction following the showing of a film depicting a withdrawn child engaging in gradually more complex peer interactions, but Gottman (1977) failed to reproduce this finding. Keller and Carlson (1974) found such symbolic modelling to be effective for increasing the performance of behaviours already in the child's repertoire, but not for establishing new skills. Oden and Asher (1977) and Ladd (1981) showed that specific coaching in social skills, practised with a peer, improved the sociometric status of isolated children in comparison with straightforward play sessions, and the effect persisted at retest a year later; such reports of long-term benefits of social skills training have, however, rarely been demonstrated (Spence, 1983). Particularly interesting is the finding of Coie and Krehbiel (1984) that the status of children improved even more after academic skill training than after social skill training; this finding acts as a warning against making simplistic, unidirectional assumptions about cause and effect in child development, and emphasizes the need to look at interactions between aspects of a child's life which are often treated separately, both theoretically and therapeutically (Shute and Paton, this volume).

**Peer pair therapy**

In the mid-1970s, reports began to appear in the literature of the use of peer pair therapy, or duo-therapy, with children experiencing peer problems (e.g. Bender, 1976). It is based on Sullivan's (1953) premise that social growth is facilitated by direct experience of interpersonal interaction and conflict resolution. Through such experiences, the child learns that differing perspectives can be brought to bear on the same situation, and that interpersonal negotiation is necessary for co-ordination to occur.

Selman and colleagues (e.g. Lyman and Selman, 1985) have developed this notion in their clinical work with troubled children. Selman's interpersonal negotiation strategy model is based on Werner's (1948, 1957) orthogenetic principle whereby development proceeds in hierarchical fashion from a relatively global to a differentiated state. Social perspective co-ordination is defined as the child's capacity to differentiate and integrate the self's and other's point of view through an understanding of the relation between a peer's and the self's thoughts, feelings and wishes (Selman, 1980). He elaborates three stages, preceded by the 'undifferentiated egocentric' stage, between the ages of about three and six, when a child sees a friend as a momentary physical playmate, and interpersonal strategies are physically mediated fight or flight reactions. In stage 1 of co-ordination (ages five to nine), the 'subjective differentiated' stage, interpersonal understanding is based on one-way assistance and negotiations take the form of commands and obeyance. In stage 2 ('reciprocal self-reflective', ages seven to twelve) understanding of friendship is based on fair-weather co-operation, and reciprocity occurs. In stage 3 ('mutual third person', ages ten to fifteen) friendship is understood in terms of mutual sharing, and true interpersonal collaboration occurs.

This model provides a basis for rating children's understanding of interpersonal relationships and their actual behaviour in negotiations with a peer, and thus enables treatment goals to be set and changes to be monitored and quantified. Selman is particularly interested in how children's level of behaviour accords with their intellectual understanding of the issues. He has developed ways of measuring both: cognitive understanding can be tapped by such interview measures as 'The Friend's Dilemma' (Selman, 1980), while behaviour is observed and rated during peer–peer interaction sessions during which the children negotiate how to spend their time and share food, toys and attention.

The therapist's role is one of stage-setting, structuring and facilitating reflection, and the latter may be aided by videotaped feedback and another therapist acting in an observational capacity. The goal is for the therapist's structuring role to become less necessary as the sessions continue.

Clinical work using this technique has led Lyman and Selman (1985) to suggest that troubled children may bring three types of maladaptive behaviour into the peer therapy situation. The first type of child is one who scores at a low level both on understanding and behaviour, therefore therapy needs to be aimed at developing that understanding. A second type may have a high level of understanding of interpersonal issues, but regress in practice, under stress; therapy is then aimed at helping the child to identify and deal with those particular situations. With the third type of child, Lyman and Selman are less confident about the value of peer therapy to help: this is the child who has difficulty integrating affective aspects of the self with socio-behavioural aspects (as in the case of the child who said, 'I feel sad—shall I cry?').

This work represents a great step forward in therapy for peer relationship problems, as it has an explicit theoretical basis and the concepts are clearly operationalized and quantifiable.

**Developmental delay**

Wallander and Hubert (1987) have also made a valuable contribution to the field of peer social dysfunction by their consideration of the peer interaction difficulties frequently faced by children with a variety of developmental disabilities, including mental handicap, learning disability, attention deficit disorder (hyperactivity) and physical disability. A consideration of the problems of such children has led them to produce a sequential model of social skill development (although it might be appropriately regarded as a hierarchical model like Selman's). Aspects of social behaviour related to the individual are considered separately from those related to the environment, and within each of these two categories several components are identified, the assumption being that each in the sequence presupposes the existence of the previous one.

The first component related to the individual is *knowledge of the skilful behaviour*, requiring adequate intellectual functioning, the attention necessary for learning, vicarious learning experiences and retention of information. The second component is *performance readiness*, requiring acceptable physical appearance, the requisite motor ability, and an appropriate emotional state. Thirdly comes *performance of behaviour under normal circumstances*, necessitating the ability to assess situation demands and make judgements about appropriate behaviour, to inhibit inappropriate behaviour and the development of a readily accessible response repertoire. The fourth component of the individual is *behaviour performance under high stress*, requiring the modification of existing skills and perspective-taking ability.

The first environment-related component is the *opportunity to learn* skills, which needs exposure to appropriate models, expectations appropriate to developmental level, differential reinforcement or feedback, and practice. Second is the *opportunity to display* skills, requiring the appropriate physical and social structures. Finally, *support for generalization and maintenance* of skills requires the presence of skilled adults and skilled peers.

Wallander and Hubert drew implications for assessment and practice from this model, some of which are outside the scope of the present discussion. However, the model does suggest ways in which peer therapy (and other therapies) should be used. Problem components within the individual should be targeted through modelling, behavioural instruction and interpersonal problem-solving strategies, whereas environment-related components should be tackled through management of physical and social structure, manipulation of consequences, and peer initiation strategies. Thus, for example, vicarious learning could occur through the use of modelling, perhaps using videotape as discussed earlier in the case of non-handicapped, socially-withdrawn children. Modelling has, in fact, been used with delayed children, together with adult reinforcement to successfully increase the verbal interaction level of developmentally delayed children (e.g. Cooke, Cooke, and Apolloni, 1978). Wallander and Hubert also mention the possibility of extending the use of coaching to handicapped children, to be used in conjunction with modelling, role-play practice and reinforcement. In practice, developmentally delayed children are likely to have deficits in a number of respects, so that multiple interventions may be the most effective.

There is also the question of generalization: will a child who has learned behaviours within an artificial setting transfer them to his or her natural world? Wallander and Hubert have discussed this, and have suggested the use of such methods as having the children's parents present during training to take the lessons learned outside—the parent can thus be viewed as a discriminative stimulus for the emission of the behaviour, and as a reinforcer to maintain the behaviour outside the immediate therapeutic setting. For a further discussion of techniques for improving the communicative competence of young mentally handicapped children, see the chapter by Guralnick (this volume).

Before leaving this section on the use of peers to help develop social skill in children who lack it, it is worth noting the comment of Michelson, Foster, and Ritchey (1981) that no a priori definition of social skill exists. They argue that a more thorough understanding of the social mores existing across differing age ranges would provide greater clinical and research data with which to plan and implement salient social and treatment goals. The approaches of Selman and of Wallander and Hubert represent important moves in the right direction by offering models of how social skills develop.

## GROUP THERAPY BASED AROUND LIFE-EVENTS

Discussion so far has centred on children who have been identified as having peer relationship problems. Group therapy is also in use with children who have experienced some traumatic life event, such as parental divorce (Kaminsky, 1986), parental substance abuse (Le Pantois, 1986) or sexual abuse. As an example of such a group, the work of Peake (1987) with sexually abused adolescents will be discussed.

Peake has offered several reasons for the choice of this type of therapy with such children. Firstly, group work offers the children a unique opportunity to know that they are not alone, which contrasts sharply with their previous experience of feeling alone and isolated. Secondly, the group offers an opportunity for sharing experiences in a setting of confidentiality which does not mirror the earlier secrecy surrounding the abuse. Thirdly, group work offers the opportunity to develop appropriate contact skills, which are often lacking in such children. Fourthly, the group offers contact with others who could form the basis of a later social support network after termination of formal therapy, including self-help groups (Peake, 1986).

Peake does not suggest that group work should form the exclusive basis for therapy, and believes that a family perspective should be maintained throughout. She took a developmental perspective, and found it better to group children in terms of social and emotional maturity rather than chronological age. Yet again, the experience of the therapists was that they needed to exert a fair degree of control, or else the children would behave in a highly disruptive manner to avoid discussing painful topics such as sex education.

As Peake noted, few workers in the field of sexual abuse have set out to evaluate their chosen mode of therapy. She attempted to do so, but found little statistical support for the value of the group work. This is discussed further below.

It is not always at all clear what the therapeutic mechanisms within groups of this nature are supposed to be. There often seems to be an underlying psychoanalytic notion of catharsis inherent in disclosure, together with the idea that adolescents experiencing emotional problems may be prevented in some way from forming the greater attachment to the peer group typical at this age.

Groups of this kind, based as they are on the experience of similar life events, have much in common with self-help groups, and Peake noted that self-help groups are sometimes a spin-off of professional therapy. The mothers of the 'problem children' in the Cardiff experiment also expressed a wish to continue meeting at the termination of formal therapy. It may be, then, that group therapy for such problems has benefits in common with self-help groups. Borman (1985) has noted the paucity of research on these groups, as they do not exist on professional turf. Such findings that do exist, though, suggest that their therapeutic mechanisms differ from those identified by professional therapists.

While the latter emphasize insight, feedback, self-disclosure and expression of affect, self-help groups offer above all universality—a sense of belonging with others who have experienced and understand similar difficulties. Self-help groups also foster communication, provide participants with social support and respond to their many cognitive and emotional needs. They involve the development of ideologies and belief systems, which appear to be important in sustaining those who experience life crises, acting as 'cognitive antidotes' in the face of further difficulties (Antze, 1979). A deeper understanding of such mechanisms may be of great value in the future development of group therapy for both adults and adolescents.

A further useful perspective may be provided by work on 'coping', although there does not seem to be any previous literature specifically drawing together concepts of coping and group therapy with children nor, indeed, any truly developmental model of coping during childhood and adolescence (Eiser, 1989). Lazarus and Folkman (1984) define coping as '. . . constantly changing cognitive and behavioural efforts to manage specific external and/or internal demands that are appraised as taxing or exceeding the resources of the person' (p. 141). Coping may be problem-focused or emotion-focused, and a number of subcategories of coping responses have been described, such as seeking social support and information, redefining the situation and problem-solving. Eiser (1989) has discussed how such notions could be valuable in helping chronically ill children to cope with the various stressful features of their lives. In the present context, a valuable approach would be to identify how interpersonal processes within group therapy might promote intrapersonal changes relevant to the development of good coping strategies.

## EVALUATING THE EFFECTIVENESS OF GROUP THERAPY

In general, it seems to be the case that relatively few clinicians have been concerned with attempting to evaluate group treatment. In 1976, Abramowitz reviewed over forty reports of group therapy with children with emotional and behavioural problems, and reported that she could come to no firm conclusion about effectiveness because of a variety of drawbacks. Many of the papers reviewed had inadequately described methodology and poor empirical verification of differences in treatment modalities. She also commented that many papers reported using novice therapists or brief treatments, and felt that it was naive to expect improved psychological functioning under such circumstances. She did conclude, though, that group psychotherapy based on behavioural techniques was on a firmer footing than that based on group play and verbal approaches, and argued for multiple-treatment approaches.

Hardwick, Pounds, and Brown (1985) also discussed the problems of evaluating group work for developing social skills, and noted similar methodological problems. The assessment techniques mentioned by them were parent and teacher checklists, self-reports, sociometry and observation in both real and simulated social situations. They argued that a combination of techniques is likely to prove most valid and reliable, but acknowledged that this is very time-consuming. In their own work in a school for maladjusted children they used a teacher rating scale on 'social behaviour at school', and found at ten weeks' follow-up that the children in the experimental group had improved significantly. However, the control children also improved, although at a lower level of statistical significance. Their study draws attention to further problems which arise when attempting to evaluate group work in an institutional setting: a double-blind design proved too difficult to implement, so that the teachers' judgements may have been influenced by their knowledge of which groups the children were in; in addition, a Hawthorne effect may have resulted, perhaps fuelled by the need to keep the teachers informed about and committed to the project. In the opinion of those workers, however, imperfect evaluation is preferable to none.

Despite such difficulties, it is nevertheless in the field of social skills training that the clearest evidence exists for the value of peer therapy. As discussed earlier, a number of studies suggest that the use of peers in evaluating and training social skills in rejected and ignored children can be effective (at least in the short term), particularly when used in conjunction with other techniques, such as coaching. The work of Selman and his colleagues and of Wallander and Hubert is pointing the way to a new sophistication in this area, with the development of models which enable the quantification of social behaviour within a developmental context, and thus facilitate measurement of the effectiveness of treatment.

Peake (1987) attempted to measure the efficacy of group work for improving the emotional status of sexually-abused adolescents, by means of several pre- and post-therapy measures, including an interview, the Bene Anthony Family Relations Test, and a questionnaire on feelings about abuse and the group work. Overall, few significant changes occurred taking the groups as a whole. Peake pointed out that, even if there had been, a causal relationship between therapy and change could not necessarily be inferred. Likewise, the lack of significant change could mean that therapy was ineffective, perhaps too short, or that the measures were not valid indices of improvement, or that extraneous variables confounded the results. She mentioned the practical and ethical problems in setting up control groups to overcome such problems. This is a matter of general interest in the case of therapies of all kinds, and the ethical objections can be met by timing the start of therapy differently for different groups, or by comparing different treatments (such as individual versus group therapy) rather than using untreated controls. However, practical problems may still remain, such as problems with subject numbers. It may also be the case that so-called homogeneous groups of subjects will in fact differ in their individual responses to treatment, which did seem to be the case in Peake's study; despite the lack of overall significance levels, the therapists found individual responses to be helpful in guiding further treatment. Single case experimental designs, in which each subject acts as his or her own control, may well offer a way forward: they are in increasing use within clinical contexts (Barlow and Hersen, 1984).

The other major source of difficulty in evaluating treatment for emotional problems is the clear definition and operationalization of the aims of treatment, and new approaches are needed here. Peake noted the value of the Bene Anthony Test in indicating the high percentage of abused children who felt that their greatest involvement was with Mr Nobody, and this may afford a measure of abused children's often-reported feelings of isolation. Repertory grid techniques (Kelly, 1955) may also offer a way of measuring the emotional responses of adolescents.

Finally, Peake argued for the value of qualitative indices of improvement, which seem to be close to universally positive in the area of group therapy with children. She pointed out that a comment, anecdote or drawing by a child may be just as telling as a standardized test. Having said that, though, she ended by arguing for the necessity for good evaluative studies in the field.

## CONCLUSION

This chapter has examined the development of group therapy for children and adolescents during the course of the twentieth century. Much of the early work was motivated by psychoanalytic principles, and this influence is still evident today. Rachman and Raubolt (1985) have noted that theory has not kept pace with practice. They are referring, presumably, simply to the fact that the usage of group therapy has continued, since the present examination of the literature suggests that there has been remarkably little development in practice over the last sixty years, with each new generation of practitioners seeming to rediscover similar principles.

However, we are now moving, if only slowly, away from the days when children from four to 16 were treated alike, and the latest ideas on children's social and cognitive development and their interrelationship are beginning to inform practice; for example, models of children's understanding of friendship are being used to guide peer pair therapy for peer relationship problems. The strongest evidence for the efficacy of peer work lies in the area of social skills training, particularly when it is used in conjunction with other methods, although its long-term effectiveness is still in doubt. Suggested ways forward for group work aimed at alleviating emotional problems have also been put forward, such as the idea that it would be beneficial to examine how group work might promote the development of coping skills. Much work remains to be done in this area, but hopefully there will be better evaluative studies in future.

Despite the questions hanging over the effectiveness of peer therapy for children and adolescents, some empirically-derived points of consensus among practitioners have emerged. Few seem to regard peer therapy as 'the answer' to children's emotional and behavioural problems, and a number have advocated multiple approaches. It has been suggested, for example, that a child who has been sexually abused within the family may benefit from both peer group work and family therapy. Also, it has been shown that a child with peer relationship difficulties may gain more from coaching in social skills in addition to peer work than from peer work alone. Multiple, integrated approaches may therefore prove to be the most effective in the long run. It must be recalled that a child's identified problem rarely occurs in isolation. The children in the Cardiff experiment, for example, all presented with peer relationship problems, but most also came from homes where there were marital problems, and separate group work with the parents was considered valuable as an adjunct to the peer group work. Another example is provided by the finding that children with social skills difficulties can benefit more from academic skills training than from direct training in social skills. Again, this emphasizes that the 'whole child' should be the object of therapy, and one possible explanation for the failure of therapy to achieve or to maintain improvements is that the interventions are too limited in scope and counteracted by other forces operative in the child's world. A systems approach may be useful in this regard, as is discussed elsewhere in this volume (Shute and Paton).

Another point of concern to many group therapists working with children is an ethical one. A democratic value system seems to lie at the heart of much peer work (as becomes evident at many points throughout this book). However, with the possible exception of Aichorn, group therapists seem to have found a particular difficulty in carrying through their ideals, finding themselves obliged to be more directive than they would like to be, since therapy becomes ineffective otherwise. Maybe such workers would find it helpful to take the following view: children presenting for therapy are already facing some life situation where they have little control, whether it be through parental abuse, the inability to form peer relationships, or whatever; it may be inevitable that the adult therapist must first take control in order to help those children to develop abilities which will enable them to eventually exert more control on their own lives.

Finally, it is noteworthy that qualitative evaluations of group work by therapists, and by children and parents, are in general very positive. Such work is clearly fulfilling a need, and it must be recalled that troubled children cannot wait until proven and perfect methods of helping them have been developed. For those professionals seeking practical guidance on group work with children, whether to deal with emotional problems concerning loss, sexual abuse, parental divorce, hospitalization, handicap or simply to set up parent and toddler groups, Silveira, Trafford, and Musgrove's (1988) book *Children Need Groups* will be very useful; although in no way an academic book, the authors' underlying grasp of many relevant issues shines through.

## REFERENCES

Abramowitz, C. V. (1976). The effectiveness of group psychotherapy with children, *Archives of General Psychiatry*, **33**, 320–326.

Adler, A. (1930). *Guiding the Child*. New York: Greenberg Publishing.

Aichorn, A. (1935). *Wayward Youth*. New York: Viking Press.

Antze, P. (1979). Role of ideologies in peer psychotherapy groups. In M. Lieberman and L. Borman (eds), *Self-Help Groups for Coping with Crisis*. San Francisco: Jossey-Bass.

Bandura, A., Ross, D., and Ross, S. (1961). Transmission of aggression through imitation of aggressive models, *Journal of Abnormal and Social Psychology*, **63**, 575–582.

Barlow, D. H., and Hersen, M. (1984). *Single Case Experimental Designs*. (2nd edn). New York: Pergamon.

Bender, B. (1976). Duo-therapy: a method of casework treatment of children, *Child Welfare*, **55**, 95–108.

Borman, L. D. (1985). Self-help and mutual aid groups. In M. Hobbs and J. M. Perrin, *Issues in the Care of Children without Chronic Illnesses*. San Francisco: Jossey-Bass.

Clifford, M., and Cross, T. (1980). Group therapy for seriously disturbed boys in residential treatment, *Child Welfare*, **59**, 560–565.

Coie, J. D., and Krehbiel, G. (1984). Effects of academic tutoring on the social status of low-achieving, socially rejected children, *Child Development*, **55**, 1465–1478.

Cooke, S. R., Cooke, T. P., and Apolloni, T. (1978). Developing nonretarded toddlers as verbal models for retarded classmates, *Child Study Journal*, **8**, 1–8.

Egan, M. H. (1975). Dynamisms in activity discussion group therapy (ADGT), *International Journal of Group Psychotherapy*, **25**, 199–218.

Eiser, C. (1989). Coping with chronic childhood disease: implications for counselling children and adolescents. In Shute, R. H. and Penny, G., *Health Psychology: Perspectives on Theory, Research and Practice*. Counselling Psychology Quarterly (Special Edition), vol. 2, part 3.

Epstein, N., and Altman, S. (1972). Experiences in converting an activity group into verbal group therapy and latency-age boys, *International Journal of Group Psychotherapy*, **22**, 93–100.

Furman, W., Rahe, D. F., and Hartup, W. W. (1979). Rehabilitation of socially-withdrawn preschool children through mixed-aged and same-age socialisation, *Child Development*, **50**, 915–922.

Gabriel, B. (1943). Group treatment for six adolescent girls, *Newsletter, American Association of Psychiatric Social Workers*, **13**, 65–72.

Gabriel, G. (1944). Group treatment for adolescent girls, *American Journal of Orthopsychiatry*, **14**, 593–602.

Gottman, J. (1977). The effects of a modeling film on social isolation in preschool children: A methodological investigation, *Journal of Abnormal Child Psychology*, **5**, 69–78.

Hardwick, P. J., Pounds, A. B., and Brown, M. (1985). Preventative adolescent psychiatry? Practical problems in running social skills groups for the younger adolescent, *Journal of Adolescence*, **8**, 357–367.

Hartup, W. W. (1970). Peer interaction and social organization. In P. H. Mussen (ed.), *Carmichael's Manual of Child Psychology*, Vol. 2. New York: John Wiley & Sons.

Hock, R. A. (1977) A model for conjoint group therapy for asthmatic children and their parents, *Group Therapy, Psychodrama and Sociometry*, **30**, 108–113.

Hoffman, T. E., Byrne, K. M., Belnap, K. L., and Steward, M. S. (1981). Simultaneous semipermeable groups for mothers and their early latency-age boys, *International Journal of Group Psychotherapy*, **31**(1), 92–98.

Jones, M. (1987). Making friends and influencing people: family approaches to peer problems in childhood and adolescence, *Australia and New Zealand Journal of Family Therapy*, **8**(3), 131–136.

Kaminsky, H. (1986). The divorce adjustment education and support group for children, *Conciliation Courts Review*, June, **24**, 145–149.

Keller, M. F., and Carlson, P. M. (1974). The use of symbolic modelling to promote social skills in pre-school children with low levels of social responsiveness, *Child Development*, **45**, 912–919.

Kelly, G. (1955). *A Theory of Personality: The Psychology of Personal Constructs*. New York: Norton.

Kohn, M., and Rosman, B. L. (1972). Relationship of preschool social-emotional functioning to later intellectual achievement, *Developmental Psychology*, **6**, 445–452.

Ladd, G. W. (1981). Effectiveness of a social learning method for enhancing children's social interaction and peer acceptance, *Child Development*, **52**, 171–178.

Ladd, G. W. (1983). Social networks of popular, average and rejected children in school settings, *Merrill-Palmer Quarterly*, **29**, 283–307.

Lazarus, R. S., and Folkman, S. (1984). *Stress, Appraisal and Coping*. New York: Springer.

Le Pantois, J. (1986). Group therapy for children of substance abusers, *Social Work with Groups*, **9**(1), 39–51.

Lovasdal, S. (1976). A multiple therapy approach in work with children, *International Journal of Group Psychotherapy*, **26**, 475–486.

Lowrey, L. G. (1942). Group therapy: a survey of practices at the Jewish Board of Guardians 1935–1941, *Jewish Board of Guardians Report*.

Lyman, D. R., and Selman, R. L. (1985). Peer conflict in pair therapy: clinical and developmental analyses. In M. W. Berkowitz (ed.), *Peer Conflict and Psychological Growth. New Directions for Child Development* 29, September. San Francisco: Jossey Bass.

Michelson, L., Foster, S., and Ritchey, W. (1981). Social skills assessment of children. In B. B. Lahey and A. E. Kazdin (eds), *Advances in Clinical Child Psychology*. New York: Plenum.

Moreno, J. L. (1934). *Who Shall Survive? A New Approach to the Problem of Human Interrelations*. Washington DC: Nervous and Mental Disease Publishing.

O'Connor, R. D. (1972). Relative efficacy of modeling, shaping and the combined procedures for modification of social withdrawal, *Journal of Abnormal Psychology*, **79**, 327–334.

Oden, S., and Asher, S. R. (1977). Coaching children in social skills for friendship making, *Child Development*, **48**, 495–506.

Peake, A. (1986). Intra-familial child sexual abuse: group work with adolescent victims. Unpublished M. Phil. thesis, University of Manchester.

Peake, A. (1987). An evaluation of group work for sexually abused adolescent girls and boys, *Educational and Child Psychology*, **4** (3–4), 189–203.

Percell, C. P., Berwick, P. T., and Beigel, A. (1974). The effects of assertive training on self-concept and anxiety, *Archives of General Psychiatry*, 502–504.

Rachman, A., and Raubolt, R. (1984). The pioneers of adolescent group psychotherapy, *International Journal of Group Psychotherapy*, **34**(3), 387–413.

Raubolt, R. R., and Rachman, A. W. (1979). Betty Gabriel: the forgotten pioneer of adolescent group psychotherapy. Unpublished manuscript.

Redl, F. (1945). The psychology of gang formation and the treatment of juvenile delinquents, *The Psychoanalytic Study of the Child*, vol. 1, New York: International Universities Press.

Roberts, M. C. (1986). *Pediatric Psychology: Psychological Interventions and Strategies for Pediatric Problems*. New York: Pergamon Press.
Schaefer, C. E., Johnson, L., and Wherry, J. M. (1982). *Group Therapies for Children and Youth*. New York: Jossey Bass.
Selman, R. L. (1980). *The Growth of Interpersonal Understanding*. New York: Academic Press.
Silveira, W. R., Trafford, G., and Musgrove, R. (1988). *Children Need Groups. A Practical Manual for Group Work with Young Children*. Aberdeen: The University Press.
Slavson, S. R. (1937). Personality qualifications for workers in group therapy, *Proceedings National Conference of Jewish Social Work*, 1937, 154–159.
Spence, S. H. (1983). Teaching social skills to children, *Journal of Child Psychology and Psychiatry*, **24**, 621–627.
Sullivan, H. S. (1953). *The Interpersonal Theory of Psychiatry*. New York: Norton.
Trower, P. M. (1979). Fundamentals of interpersonal behavior: a social-psychological perspective. In A. S. Bellack and M. Hersen (eds), *Research and Practice in Social Skills Training*. New York: Plenum Press.
Wallander, J. L., and Hubert, N. C. (1987). Peer social dysfunction in children with developmental disabilities: empirical basis and a conceptual model. *Clinical Psychology Review*, **7**, 205–221.
Walrond-Skinner, S. (1976). *Family Therapy. The Treatment of Natural Systems*. London: Routledge & Kegan Paul.
Werner, H. (1948). *Comparative Psychology of Mental Development*. Chicago: Follet.
Werner, H. (1957). The concept of development from a comparative and organismic point of view. In D. Harris (ed.), *The Concept of Development*. Minneapolis: University of Minnesota Press.
Wollan, K. I., and Gardner, G. (1938). A group-clinic approach to delinquency, *Mental Hygiene*, **22**, 567–584.
Wright, L., and Walker, C. E. (1977). Treating the encopretic child. *Clinical Pediatrics*, **16**, 1042–1045.
Yalom, I. (1975). *The Theory and Practice of Group Psychotherapy* (2nd edn). New York: Basic Books.

# A Concluding Perspective

CHAPTER 17

# Where Do We Go From Here? A Personal View by an Educationalist

DAVID FONTANA

*Department of Education, University of Wales College of Cardiff, PO Box 901, Cardiff CF1 3YG*

## INTRODUCTION

Suppose I take a group of educationalists, or politicians, or parents or men or women in the street into a classroom in any school in the land during a typical school day. And suppose I ask them to survey the scene in front of them and tell me how many teachers they can see. What would their answer be? Ninety-nine times out of a hundred, for educationalists as well as for our men and women in the street, the answer would be 'one'. And of course they would be right, if by teacher they mean the number of adults standing up in front of the class and organizing the pupils' learning experiences.

They would be right because they are looking at the class in terms of one particular way of seeing. They would be looking at it in terms of their own particular myth, that in a classroom there is only one person who is doing the teaching and all the rest are doing the learning. But suppose I decided to explore this myth with them. Suppose I asked the teacher standing up in front of the class 'what have *you learnt* during this lesson?' He or she would probably answer something like this: 'I've learnt that Philip doesn't understand some of the basic concepts he needs if he's to succeed in work of this kind. I've learnt that Sonia knows the answers to every question I've put to the class. I've learnt that

Children Helping Children
Edited by H. C. Foot, M. J. Morgan and R. H. Shute

Mary works much better if I move her away from Jane. I've learnt that the boys in my class are generally more interested in this work than the girls. I've learnt that I *can* keep my temper with Brian. I've learnt that there are some gaps in my own knowledge that I need to fill. I've learnt from Michael a more creative way of handling some of the ideas I've been using . . .'. And so on and on.

Now suppose I ask one of the children 'what have *you taught* during the lesson?'. Once he escapes from his own version of the myth (namely 'me as learner') he might answer along the lines of: 'I taught the teacher I work better if she praises me instead of nagging me. I showed my friend how to do one of the problems he was stuck on. I whispered the answer to the girl in front when the teacher asked her a question, I taught the boy behind that if he kicks me under the desk I kick him back . . .' and so on.

What do these two sets of answers mean? They mean that because of our myth of the class as composed of one teacher and thirty or so learners, we miss the fact that in reality it is an intricate network of mutual teaching and learning experiences. In reality, instead of one teacher and 30 learners, we have 31 teachers and 31 learners. Failure to grasp this point means that we ensure that the great majority of these experiences are haphazard and ineffective. We miss the opportunity to make the class a much richer learning environment. Indeed, we often actively hinder things by our propensity to punish children for giving each other unauthorized help. 'Work on your *own*' we tell them. 'Stop discussing it and get on with it'. 'Ask *me* if you want any help'.

In our pursuit of the myth, we also miss the vital point that sometimes pupils are *better at helping each other than we are.* They appreciate each other's difficulties more clearly. They can choose a more comprehensible language in which to talk to each other, and a more appropriate set of analogies. They come fresh from their own difficulties, instead of insulated from them by long years of successful experience. They also appreciate more clearly each other's emotional problems, the way it actually *feels* to be struggling over one's work, to see other pupils forging ahead, to face the humiliation of being dependent always upon adult teacher help, to do badly in tests and examinations.

No one who has read this book has any excuse for remaining fixed in this myth. Together the authors have demonstrated that in a wide range of situations, children can help children effectively and happily. In the educational context, evidence has been put forward to show that not only does the pupil-as-learner benefit from these helping experiences, so too does the pupil-as-tutor. Which is hardly surprising. Teaching a subject to someone else is one of the best ways of formalizing our own thinking about it. It makes the subject more coherent, more memorable. It improves our confidence, and often helps us to see new and exciting possibilities. At the personal and social level, it increases our self-esteem and our sense of social usefulness. It is hard *not* to see yourself as socially valuable when others so obviously benefit from your social contribution.

Similarly in the therapeutic context and in the family context, the authors have shown the breadth and the depth of the ways in which children can and do help each other. No parent, watching the way in which siblings relate and play with each other, can doubt that much of a child's social skill learning, much of his learning on how to get on with others, on how to assert himself, on how to compromise, on how to lead and on how to follow, on how to initiate and how to acquiesce, comes from other children rather than from adults. Children take each other as role models. They use each other as resources. They imitate amd mimic each other, they exercise power over each other, they participate with each other in group behaviours, they experience the strength of their own emotions in relation to each other. And particularly in adolescence, when the search for identity becomes particularly acute, they find or fail to find much of themselves through the peer group and through its collective judgements and practices.

What has not emerged so strongly from the book is the extent to which the adult can benefit from the process of encouraging and abetting children helping children. If we look, for example, at the educational context, there can be no doubt of the advantages to the teacher of a good peer tutoring system, and herein lies a fruitful area for more extended research. By tapping the tutor-potential of a class of children, the teacher not only takes some of the burden of work from her own shoulders, she potentially increases the social cohesion and sense of responsibility of her pupils. A child with learning difficulties becomes 'our' problem instead of just the teacher's problem. Equally important, the teacher is given the opportunity to learn more about her craft from observing the way in which pupils best help each other. Through their first-hand knowledge of the scope and limitations of a child's thinking, children can give teachers valuable clues on how teaching strategies and materials can most effectively be structured and presented.

## WHY THE NEGLECT OF PUPIL TUTORING?

In view of the manifold benefits of pupil tutoring, why isn't it more widely used? Wagner (Chapter 2) traces the honourable history of this kind of tutoring, culminating in its sad decline in an atmosphere of confusion and uncertainty. There were, of course, some valid reasons for this decline (more about these shortly), but for an underlying cause we have to look beyond matters of detail and into the educational philosophy of the last century or so. It would take a whole book to tease out the intricacies of this philosophy, but an important aspect for our purposes is that many of the values and models of the burgeoning state education system, in England and Wales at least, were inherited from those of the long-established public schools sector. The grammar school is the best example of the results of this inherited tradition, but the influence of the public school system (through which many of the politicians entrusted with decisions about state education have themselves come) has outlived the demise of selective secondary education and still lives on in even the humblest village school.

The cornerstone of this system was competition. Not only competition in academic matters, where the idea of the 'form order' was firmly entrenched, but in social matters too. One only has to read the autobiographies of those who underwent a public school education in the earlier part of this century (for example, Robert Graves, 1929; Osbert Sitwell, 1946) to realize that the system often deliberately set pupil against pupil, in the odd belief that such insanity 'built character'. Later biographies chronicle scant improvement (e.g. Richard Church, 1955, John Betjeman, 1960). Within the state system, the infamous practice of moving children up a class not by age but by meeting set 'standards' of achievement added further fuel to the notion that children were in school to shine in comparison with their peers, and devil take the hindmost.

Under a competitive as opposed to a cooperative system, self-esteem comes from one's position in the pecking order rather than from one's ability to help others. 'Helping', in fact, is often seen as actively counter-productive, since it strengthens the possibility of someone lower in the hierarchy leapfrogging over one's head. What you have you guard zealously from others, instead of offering to share. Indeed, offering to share can be interpreted by one's peers as a sign of incurable naivety, of an inability to read the rules of the system and recognize what it takes to make a success of life—even of a culpable (albeit perhaps unintentional) attempt to undermine the system, and make life harder for everyone else vulnerable to leapfrogging from below.

Though there is little recent research in the United Kingdom into the social relationships in secondary school of the calibre of that carried out by Hargreaves (1967) and by Lacey (1970) some two decades ago, it seems probable that comprehensive education for the 11+ age group has improved the atmosphere for cooperation in secondary schools, though there is scant evidence that it has greatly improved its incidence. Whether the impending introduction of statutory testing at set ages throughout the years of compulsory schooling will help or hinder matters remains very much to be seen.

## THE ROLE OF THE TEACHER IN THIS NEGLECT

Teachers are, of course, inseparable from the educational philosophy just outlined. They may or may not believe in it or have been responsible for its introduction, but as part of the system built upon it they have played and continue to play a major part in sustaining it. But their role extends beyond merely upholding the competitive ethos. Like most professional groups, teachers as a body zealously guard their professional status. Teaching, they imply, is something that must be left to the teaching profession. We see this in the way in which teachers have resisted the idea of enrolling parents, even informally, as partners in the educational process, and we can identify it more subtly in their reluctance to enrol the children either. Beyond professional status, there is no hard research to help us isolate the reasons for reluctance in the latter case, but my own experience of the profession, coupled with my work with teachers on in-service courses, suggests strongly that there is a belief it is 'outdated' or 'unprofessional' to use children to tutor each other. Teachers who do so are either lazy ('getting the children to do their work for them') or unskilled ('unable to grasp just how difficult it is to teach properly').

Before peer-tutoring or other forms of peer-based learning can become accepted as a valuable part of the academic and social life of educational institutions, the resistance of teachers to the ideas involved must be overcome. As made clear by Cowie and Rudduck (in Chapter 11), we need a far-reaching change in our value systems. Not an easy thing to achieve, though the research findings summarized in the preceding chapters should go a long way towards convincing at least the more receptive members of the teaching profession. I spoke earlier of the myth of one teacher and 30 learners in the typical class. For the myth to be dispelled, teachers need help in seeing that it is the *good* teacher who is able to recognize the educational potential of having 31 tutors in the class instead of just one, and who is able to organize both classroom mechanics and teaching strategies to realize this potential.

## OBJECTIONS TO PEER-TUTORING

However, before we give unqualified approval to a system of peer tutoring, there are a number of questions that remain to be answered. Not all aspects of such a system will be automatically positive, and there are risks involved if we allow our approach to it to become too uncritical. The worst of these risks is that, once they have been persuaded to accept it, some teachers may see the system as an easy option, a substitute for properly organized teacher activity. To operate such a system, teachers will need careful training in a range of specialist skills, each of which will have to be identified and reified.

At this point, it is salutary to ask ourselves why the systems of Bell and of Lancaster foundered. If pupils teaching pupils has so much to commend it, why did it not become an established part of educational practice? Doubtless political factors played some part, as is evident from Wagner's historical chapter (Chapter 2). But there were educational reasons too. As Chapter 2 indicates, a far-sighted educationalist like James Kay-Shuttleworth was opposed to it, perhaps because he recognized the 'shallowness of the education provided by it'. We deny the power of the educational process if we put it too readily in the hands of those untrained in its use.

The Bell and Lancaster systems were only as good as the pupils who did the tutoring, and as the public began to demand more from education and as the knowledge to be transmitted increased in complexity and the resources available for education expanded, the systems were replaced by something conceived to be superior.

This is not of course to go back on myself and start to deny the value of pupils teaching pupils, merely to insist that to reach its proper potential the system needs to be correctly applied. Which brings me to the specific considerations that have to be borne in mind if such correct application is to be made. The best way to look at these considerations is to pose a range of questions, arising from the material in this book, to which the advocates of peer tutoring will be required to provide satisfactory answers. Unless and until they can (and in my view the task is not a specially daunting one), we must be cautious in the claims we make for pupils teaching pupils and in the urgency with which we advocate the introduction of the system.

1. We rightly emphasize the positive psychological *advantages* that accrue to the successful pupil-tutor (e.g. Chapters 5 and 10). But there are also potential *disadvantages*. In addition to those touched on in Chapter 9, we need to know how we can guard against the pupil-tutor developing an inflated sense of his/her importance and abilities, and how we can prevent them from becoming too assertive, too wedded to the sense of superiority (even power) over a fellow pupil. Even experienced teachers have to be alert to the temptations towards self-aggrandisement offered by the profession. How can a similar alertness be developed in children?

2. Tutoring involves a relish for the task and a willingness to work with others. Many children have these qualities in equal measure to adults, but do they have the other personal qualities essential in a good tutor? Patience, for example; and a readiness to understand that the learner would learn if he or she could. A good teacher knows that few pupils are intentionally obtuse. However slow-witted the pupils may seem, they are usually doing the best they can. Exasperation and impatience on the part of the tutor only make learning more difficult. Can we expect such understanding from pupil-tutors, especially if they feel that time which could usefully be spent upon their own work is having to be devoted to that of their fellows?

3. What criteria should be used in deciding who pupil-tutors whom? Should the pupils themselves, both tutors and learners, be given a say, or should the decisions be taken by the teacher? Although good democratic classroom practice demands the former, what happens when tutor and learner choice do not match? And in particular what happens if there is a slow learning pupil whom nobody wants to tutor? The class teacher can of course take responsibility for them, but what covert lessons would *ipso facto* be transmitted to the class as a consequence?

4. What would be the reactions of parents and how would they be best won over to the system? In an educational framework which hitherto has relied, as I indicated earlier in the chapter, upon competition rather than upon cooperation, many parents of able pupils will look askance at their child being called upon to give time to slower learning fellow pupils.

5. What implications would pupils teaching pupils have for school or college organization (including the simple logistics of how best to arrange class and lecture rooms, and to contain noise levels within acceptable limits)? How in particular would it fit in with the requirements imposed by external examinations or, in the case of England and Wales, with statutory assessment at set intervals from age seven onwards?

6. Are all subjects equally suitable for peer tutoring? Are, for example, creative subjects such as art or music or drama as suitable as more factual subjects such as mathematics and grammar? And, as stressed by Greenwood (Chapter 9), how are we to ensure quality control and adequate lesson content coverage?

7. What constraints would be imposed by age/sex differences? For example, at what age do pupils become suitable for pupil tutoring? And should boys tutor girls and vice versa, or should the sexes be segregated? How will boys react to being tutored by girls and girls to being tutored by boys? Will boys resent female tutors? Will girls suppress their performance when working with boys? Will some pupils deliberately hold back the standard of their work in order to be tutored by each other? Should there always be an age gap between learner and tutor, so that the former can readily 'give permission' to the latter to be cleverer than him or herself? Guralnick (Chapter 13) touches on the extent to which changing a child's tutor-partner can influence results, and there are a range of variables here which will need to be carefully examined by situation-specific research.

8. Can pupil-tutors be dissuaded from discussing the work of their learners with peers? Is it desirable that they should be so dissuaded? What would such discussion, particularly if it is deprecatory, do for the self-esteem of the learners?

9. How can pupils best be instructed in the art of tutoring? Some aspects of this art, such as the 'Pause, Prompt, Praise' method of teaching reading (Chapter 6) are relatively easy to learn. Others, such as helping the learner see *why* he or she has made a particular mistake in mathematics, are much less so. Should pupil-tutors be restricted therefore to only the simplest of tasks, which in a sense denies the power of many of the arguments in favour of the introduction of the system.

10. Finally, and perhaps most importantly of all, *is* it possible for one pupil to tutor another when the former is not yet an 'expert' in the subject being taught? Cognitive learning theorists, taking their cue from the pioneering work of Bruner (e.g. Bruner, 1960), stress that good teaching is only likely where the teacher knows the deep structure of his or her subject. A tutor who knows only a little more about a subject than the learner cannot initiate the latter effectively into this deep structure, or respond effectively to questions on meaning and causality.

In a short concluding chapter it is possible to pose these questions but not possible fully to answer them. Nevertheless, a few preliminary guidelines can be offered. I offer these guidelines in terms of what we would need to do if we were considering introducing a pupil tutoring system into the average school, primary or secondary. For convenience, I will group the guidelines under the respective headings *The Pupil*, *Tuition*, and *Subject Matter*.

## The pupil

Many of the queries posed in the questions offered above can be answered if we have more knowledge on how pupils themselves best conceive of a peer tutoring system. Sociometric research shows that it is possible to draw up very precise 'maps' of the attitudes towards each other of a group of pupils. Pupils can be very explicit indeed over who they would and would not like to work with. Applying the principles of sociometry to our present concerns, it would be possible to map out pupils' expressed preferences for each other as tutors and as learners.

If we were introducing a peer tutoring system into a school, a map of this kind would be an essential preliminary. If we are to ask pupils to tutor pupils, this suggests we believe in their sense of personal responsibility and judgement. This belief must be demonstrated from the outset if we are adequately to call upon these factors. Imposing a system upon pupils, and then expecting them suddenly to produce the qualities necessary to make it function adequately, shows a basic misunderstanding both of child psychology and of child education.

Further, the map would need to be constructed for each school and perhaps for each class within each school. As pointed out by Ashman and Elkins (Chapter 10), the dynamics in each classroom differ. Thus extracting generalities from any one piece of research and attempting to apply them in all schools will lead inevitably to failure. In this of all areas, research must be situation specific. The task of the researcher here is not to provide teachers with generalizable results but to offer them research techniques with which they can generate results of their own.

Sociometric evidence produced within each school or each class will show clearly children's proclivities for working with each other. What it will fail to show of course is what you do with those pupils who do not fit readily into the system. What is required here is a re-orientation of values. Reference is made in Chapter 10 and earlier in the present chapter to the competitive as opposed to the cooperative nature of our educational philosophy, and a great deal of work needs to be done if this nature is to be changed. A first step in this work, in accordance with a behavioural approach to human performance, is to ensure that pupils are reinforced for helping each other. Much of this reinforcement, as indicated by Ashman and Elkins (Chapter 10) and earlier in the present chapter, is intrinsic. Pupils gain in self-esteem from the knowledge that they are of value to each other, while the very act of helping their fellows aids them in formalizing their own thinking about the material which they are endeavouring to convey.

But extrinsic reinforcement is also required, at least in the initial stages. Schools reward their pupils for a variety of skills and undertakings, and the need now is to expand this reward system until it covers the giving of aid and support one to another. Each school knows best its own pupils, and it is, therefore, the task of each school to decide how best this system shall operate. But the more stimulating and the more public it becomes, the better its chances of success. No school that lays reasonable claim to efficiency of organization and to a sensitivity towards its pupils can excuse failure to operate such a system with a fair chance of success.

Of course, this begs the question of how to prepare pupils for operating a peer tutoring system. In spite of the impressive research that has been carried out so far in this area we do not yet have sufficient idea on how pupils *themselves* think that the system should operate. There will be strong individual differences from one school to another, and to modify George Kelly's famous first principle ('If you want to know what's wrong with the patient why don't you ask him; he might just know!'—Kelly 1955), if you want to know how pupils can best help pupils, why don't you ask them, they might just know. To have most chance of success, a school must understand how the pupil tutor sees his or her task, and how the learner best conceptualizes the kind of help which he or she most needs.

It is remarkable how seldom (at a practical as opposed to a research-based level) we actually ask pupils how *they* feel the learning environment can best be structured. The key questions here are 'what do you feel you need to know in order to cope with what you're doing?', and 'how can you best be helped to know it?'. Even young children can answer these questions in a constructive way if the questions are put to them in a spirit of enquiry rather than of interrogation.

The answers to the second of these questions will give us valuable information on how to structure a peer tutoring environment. As a follow-up, we can then ask questions designed to provide answers to others of the ten queries I listed in the last section. For example 'Would you like to be helped by a member of your own or of the opposite sex?' 'By someone your own age or someone older?' 'Do you want your learning experiences to be a secret between you and your tutor, or does it matter if other children know about them?'.

### Tuition

Knowing the kind of help that children feel they need will give us valuable insights into how to structure a peer-based learning system. But it will not, of course, answer all our questions about methodology. We shall derive further help from asking the question 'How do you think you can most usefully help other pupils to learn?'. To this we can add our own basic understanding of the processes of learning and helping. In particular the role respectively of insight, of coding, of schedules of reinforcement, and of course of memory optimization. Through the use of this understanding we can achieve the systematic and planned approach to information presentation and acquisition emphasized in Chapter 9.

Vital to this stage, however, is the recognition of what a peer-based learning system *cannot* achieve. Doise (Chapter 3) tells us that 'through co-ordinating their actions with others, children are led to construct new co-ordinations they are not capable of individually', and this ties in with my earlier point that certain kinds of learning may be managed more effectively with peer tutors than with adult teachers. But there are limits. In my question number 10 above I asked about *meaning* and *causality*. Can children satisfactorily help each other in these more difficult areas of understanding? If this book had been written a few years back, there would inevitably have been a chapter by a Piagetian looking at the limits placed upon peer tutors by the tutor's own levels of cognitive development. If, for example, you are yourself still at the stage of concrete operations, what will this mean for your ability to aid the understanding of others?

Once more, answers to this question may need to be situation specific. They may apply for this tutor and for this learner and for this teaching subject, but not for that tutor and that learner and that teaching subject. But limits there are on the scope of peer teaching, and we need to know what these are before we can make proper use of the system within any individual school. And once we know these limits, we then have to be very careful that the peer tutor is not used as a second-class citizen, entrusted only with the hack work and not with anything exciting or creative. Foot, Shute, Morgan and Barron (Chapter 4) alert us to this danger when they quote research which suggests peer tutoring is most successful when applied to tasks which are essentially rule governed, and when focused upon the exchange of information and skills. If we're not careful, we have here only what Bruner (1960) calls the *middle language* of a subject, that is the results of other people's exploration and discovery, rather than those of the learner him or herself.

This would mean that the learner within the peer tutoring dyad would have few opportunities to—again to use Bruner's terminology—go beyond the information given. Instead of acting as a springboard, the teaching and learning act would merely be stereotypical. A restraint and a constraint instead of a stimulus to move forward into new territory.

Working at this stereotypical level is a handicap for the tutor as well as for the learner, and raises again the issue of how parents will react to their children being used in this way. Parental support for peer tutoring will not be particularly easy to obtain, and will depend very much upon the recognition by parents that their children are gaining positive benefit from their tutor roles. And, parents being parents, these benefits will need to be rather more tangible than the social and affective variables that stem from enhanced social awareness and enhanced self-esteem. Vital as these benefits are, they are recognized much more readily by psychologists and by enlightened educationalists than they are by the majority of parents.

Shute and Paton (Chapter 15) and Morgan and Eiser (Chapter 14) indicate the effectiveness of peer cooperation in specialist areas outside the school curriculum. But in these areas parental anxieties may be of a different kind, and more readily allayed, than they are where mainstream education is concerned. And if peer tutoring is to become more than a peripheral activity, it is in this mainstream area that maximum impact must be effected. In practical terms, what this means is that our attention must be focused not just upon attempts to demonstrate the efficacy of peer tutoring, but upon attempts to place this tutoring within the total context of what we understand child education to be. Again, through Chapters 4 and 10, for example, this book provides pointers in the right direction. But we cannot pretend yet to have travelled very far. The future is promising, but by no means assured.

**Subject matter**

There are three major variables within any educational act: the learner (the pupil), the teaching/learning methodology (tuition), and the material to be learnt (subject matter). Each of these places constraints upon the learning act, and each must be properly understood if the effectiveness of this act is to be maximized. I have looked briefly at the pupil and at tuition, and it now remains to look at the subject matter. Philosophers of education (e.g. Peters, 1960) stress the concept of *forms of knowledge*. Each subject in the curriculum is identified—and rendered distinct from other subjects—by its own particular *form*. This form is evident in the methodology adopted by the subject for generating new knowledge and for demonstrating existing paradigms, and by the nature of the factual information produced by this methodology.

The question we need to ask is whether all forms of knowledge lend themselves to peer tutoring, or whether certain of them lie beyond its scope. Bruner, in one of the most influential statements made about education in modern times, insists that any subject can be taught to any pupil in some intellectually honest way (Bruner, 1966). But can we extend this and say that 'any subject can be taught *by any competent peer tutor*' in this way? Can we, to return to my earlier example, teach creative subjects such as music or poetry or dance or painting in this way? Can we teach the skills of writing? Can we teach reasoning? Much of course will depend upon the age and the ability levels of the learner and the tutor, but do these subjects demand a degree of expertise in the teacher that is beyond anyone other than the acknowledged expert?

I also referred earlier to Bruner's insistence that the teacher know the deep structure of a subject if he or she is effectively to teach it. Keeping, as it were, one page ahead of the learner in the textbook is not good enough. Should a peer tutor only be allowed to tutor if he or she can demonstrate they know enough of the deep structure to satisfy Bruner's criterion? Clearly, much thought needs to be given to issues of this kind before peer tutoring can be given a universal seal of approval.

My own view is that a team approach by subject (form of knowledge) specialist, educational psychologist and teacher is needed in each subject area if forms of knowledge (together with specific content areas within each of these forms) suitable for peer tutoring are to be identified. And here of course taxonomies such as those of Bloom (Bloom *et al.*, 1956) and Krathwohl (Krathwohl *et al.*, 1964) are likely to prove invaluable. It may be, for example, that this team will recognize peer tutoring as effective at certain age and ability levels at the (to take Bloom's taxonomy) *knowledge*, *comprehension* and *application* levels of a given teaching subject, but not at the *analysis*, *synthesis* and *evaluation* levels. Decisions would then need to be taken on how peer tutoring and teacher tutoring could be linked together, with teacher tutoring taking over at the top three levels of the taxonomy.

Further work would then be needed to determine how the peer tutor should recognize and code learning failure at the three initial levels, and at what point this failure should be referred to the teacher for more specialist help.

## CHILDREN HELPING CHILDREN IN OTHER CONTEXTS

The emphasis upon education and the classroom in the last sections must not suggest that there are no issues to be addressed when it comes to children helping children within therapy and within the family. Shute and Pates (Chapter 16) and Cooper and St John (Chapter 12) respectively deal with these two contexts, and indicate to us the extent to which, even more than in the case of the classroom, both have suffered from relative neglect. If we take therapy first, experience with adults shows that desirable psycho-social change may take place more readily in group than in individual therapy (e.g. Jennings, 1986). Groups carry with them a particular dynamic which allows people to test out personal change as it occurs, particularly in the area of social assertion and social skills.

There is no reason to suppose that a different dynamic operates with children (particularly adolescent children, where group norms assume a particular power over individual behaviour). Two immediate problems suggest themselves, however, in work of this kind. The first is the extent to which such group work can be client driven. With adults, successful group work involves the therapist as initiator and facilitator, but once the appropriate dynamic emerges, he or she takes on a much more passive role. Is such an approach appropriate with children? Or must the group (or the dyad), whatever our declared non-interventional intention, remain ultimately adult directed?

This may seem a plea for mayhem, but realistically, if children have something to offer as therapists which is denied—by virtue of their more mature years—to adults, then the therapeutic initiative must in some areas be ceded to children themselves. We assume that children are disqualified from an initiatory role by virtue of their restricted life experience, yet in certain cases children are much more able than adults to see why their peers are failing socially and personally, and to identify the most appropriate strategies for helping them. In the context of children helping children, how can the therapist best provide the broad scaffolding within which children can empower each other socially and personally, yet without obtruding his or her role? Shute and Pates (Chapter 16) talk of a system of rotating therapists, and there are various other possibilities such as prior consensus between children and therapist on the restrictions within which the latter will operate, but broadly the question remains for us to answer.

The second problem that presents itself is one of assessment. In all therapeutic areas assessment remains a major difficulty, but with children the difficulty is magnified by the inability of many children to define for themselves the exact nature of a more positive life experience. This inevitably limits the value of their self-reports. On the other hand, child behaviours are not necessarily a reliable guide to inner experience, which casts doubt on adult monitoring and on some of the rating scales upon which such monitoring relies. Is there a way in which we can validly assess the results of child–child therapeutic interactions? Those of us who believe in children helping children must answer yes, but it remains for us to prove our point.

Turning to children helping children within the family, rather different problems occur. Cooper and St John (Chapter 12) show clearly the impact that sibling help has upon child progress, but we are left with the thorny question of how we can influence within-family behaviours. The family therapist may help in a limited number of individual cases, where deficits of one sort or another have already been identified, but for the mass of the population, the machinery by which we can operate leverage upon domestic relational behaviours remains unclear. This is not of course an argument against the force of the data advanced by Cooper and St John. Simply a query as to how one moves from pure to applied endeavour in this particular field.

## CONCLUSION

If this book demonstrates anything, it demonstrates the potential richness of children helping children. If the aim of the editors and of the individual authors is to be realized, it will open up this area for further debate and research, and will bring home to educationalists, therapists, parents and other interested adults the opportunities we are spurning through our virtual neglect of it. As I have tried to show in this final chapter, there are many and varied questions that remain to be answered before 'children helping children' can be enabled (or allowed) to take its proper place within the educational and therapeutic systems. But once its benefits are properly acknowledged, these questions can be tackled with every prospect of success.

It is often said that professional people like teachers and therapists are a conservative bunch. If the accusation is true, there must be reasons for this conservatism. Perhaps teachers and others working with children realize that, dealing as they are with impressionable young minds and emotions, there must be a degree of caution before we embrace the new and discard the old. In a sense, in sensitive areas such as working with children, the onus of proof rests with the advocates of any new method rather than with the defenders of the status quo. The advocates of children helping children have many challenges still to meet before they are able satisfactorily to discharge this onus of proof. But an effective start has been made, and it is right to hope that this book will give increased stimulus and direction to the next phase of the adventure.

## REFERENCES

Betjeman, J. (1960). *Summoned by Bells*. London: John Murray.

Bloom, B. S. *et al.* (1956). *Taxonomy of Educational Objectives. Handbook I: The Cognitive Domain*. London: Longmans Green.

Bruner, J. S. (1960). *The Process of Education*. New York: Norton.

Bruner, J. S. (1966). *Towards a Theory of Instruction*. New York: Norton.

Church, R. (1955). *Over the Bridge*. London: Heinemann.

Graves, R. (1929). *Goodbye to All That*. London: Cassell.

Hargreaves, D. (1967). *Social Relationships in a Secondary School*. London: Routledge & Kegan Paul.

Jennings, S. (1986). *Dramatherapy Theory and Practice: A Source Book for Clinicians*. London: Croom Helm.

Kelly, G. A. (1955). *The Psychology of Personal Constructs*. (2 vols.) New York: Norton.

Krathwohl, D. L. *et al.* (1964). *Taxonomy of Educational Objectives. Handbook II: The Affective Domain*. New York: David McKay.

Lacey, C. (1970). *Hightown Grammar*. Manchester: Manchester University Press.

Peters, R. S. (1960). *The Concept of Motivation*. London: Routledge & Kegan Paul.

Sitwell, O. (1946). *The Scarlet Tree*. London: Macmillan.

# Index